GO»
AHEAD
REALSCHULE BAYERN

9

Cornelsen

GO»
AHEAD
REALSCHULE BAYERN

Go Ahead · Band 9

Im Auftrag des Verlages konzipiert und erarbeitet von	Rebecca Robb Benne, Kopenhagen, Dänemark; Ursula Fleischhauer, Hannover (Language file); Petra Ullrich, Bessenbach (Skills file)
unter Mitarbeit und beratender Mitwirkung von	Annette Baader, Nürnberg; Klaus Berold, Kulmbach; Gerlinde Eberhardt, Surberg; Christina Forstner, Lenggries; Martin Fritze, Bad Abbach; Oliver Kosina, Regensburg; Carmen Lux-Younts, Lauf a. d. Pegnitz; Petra Ullrich, Bessenbach
in Zusammenarbeit mit der Englischredaktion	Klaus Unger (Projektleitung); Jutta Seuren (koordinierende Redakteurin); Michael Dunkel, Franziska Gräbe, Mara Leibowitz, Paulina Schäffer, Kathrin Spiegelberg, Friederike von Bülow, Olivia Wintgens
Vokabelanhänge	Ingrid Raspe, Düsseldorf
Lizenzmanagement	Britta Bensmann, Rebekka Gerlach und Anna Mozer
Illustrationen	Bildbad, Jutta Melsheimer & Kai Hofmann, Berlin
Layoutkonzept	finedesign, Büro für Text & Gestaltung, Berlin; designcollective, Team für Mediengestaltung, Berlin
Technische Umsetzung	designcollective, Team für Mediengestaltung, Berlin
Umschlaggestaltung	Cornelsen Verlag Design unter Verwendung der Entwürfe von hawemannundmosch, Berlin

www.cornelsen.de

Dieses Werk berücksichtigt die Regeln der reformierten Rechtschreibung und Zeichensetzung. Ausnahmen bilden Originaltexte, bei denen lizenzrechtliche Gründe einer Änderung entgegenstehen.

1. Auflage, 1. Druck 2021

Alle Drucke dieser Auflage sind inhaltlich unverändert und können im Unterricht nebeneinander verwendet werden.

Druck: Firmengruppe APPL, aprinta Druck, Wemding

ISBN 978-3-464-31120-2 (Schülerbuch)
ISBN 978-3-060-33915-0 (E-Book)

PEFC
PEFC/04-32-0928

PEFC zertifiziert
Dieses Produkt stammt aus nachhaltig bewirtschafteten Wäldern und kontrollierten Quellen.

www.pefc.de

Dein Englischbuch enthält folgende Teile:

Unit 1 bis 4	Die vier Kapitel des Buches
Revision	Üben und Vertiefen
Partner pages	Aufgaben für Partnerarbeit
More ideas	Weitere Redemittel für einige Übungen
Fast finishers	Weitere Aufgaben
Wordbank	Zusätzliche Wörter zu bestimmten Themen
Text file / TF	Interessante Texte, passend zu den Units 1 bis 4
Language file / LF	Zusammenfassung wichtiger Sprachregeln
Skills file / SF	Beschreibung wichtiger Lern- und Arbeitstechniken
Vocabulary	Wörterverzeichnis zum Lernen der neuen Wörter
Dictionary	Alphabetisches Wörterverzeichnis zum Nachschlagen *(English-German)*

Die Units bestehen aus diesen Teilen:

W & P Words and pictures	Einstieg in die neue Unit
Text 1 / Text 2	Neue Texte und Themen mit vielen Aktivitäten und Übungen
Introduction	Texte und Aufgaben zum Entdecken von Regeln und Üben wichtiger Strukturen
Skills training	Listening – Reading – Speaking – Writing – Mediation – Viewing
Study skills	Lern- und Arbeitsmethoden
YOUR CHECK	Lernfortschritt feststellen
YOUR TASK	Gelerntes kreativ anwenden
ACROSS CULTURES	Informationen zu kulturellen Gemeinsamkeiten und Unterschieden

In den Units findest du diese Symbole:

(Symbol: zwei Personen)	Partnerarbeit
(Symbol: Gruppe)	Gruppenarbeit
(Symbol: Kopfhörer)	Text auf CD und MP3
VIEWING	Filmclip auf DVD
More ideas → p. 81	Zu dieser Übung findest du unterstützende Redemittel im Anhang.
(Symbol: Kopiervorlage)	Frage deinen Lehrer / deine Lehrerin nach einer Kopiervorlage.
Fast finishers 2 → p. 87	Nachdem diese Übung erarbeitet wurde, gibt es eine zusätzliche Übung im Anhang.
WB 1-2, p. 8	Auf dieser Seite im Workbook findest du passgenaue Übungen zur Schülerbuchseite.

Verweise in den Units:
LF = Language file
SF = Skills file
TF = Text file
WB = Workbook

Für deine Arbeit mit den Units ist außerdem wichtig:

- Am Anfang jeder Unit findest du auf der rechten Seite eine Liste mit Lernzielen. So weißt du, was du nach dieser Unit auf Englisch kannst.
- Unten auf den Unit-Seiten findest du Sätze mit einem grünen Häkchen. Sie zeigen dir, was du nach der Erarbeitung dieser Seite kannst.

Unit 1 – Life in Australia

Unit 2 – My world of work

Unit 3 – The digital age

Unit 4 – Indian images

ANHÄNGE

*fakultativ

Unit 1 Life in Australia

In this unit you will

- discover the geography and wildlife of Australia.
- learn about the history of Australia and the culture of the first Australians.
- explore the feelings and attitudes of characters in a story and a film.
- explain the rules of a sport.

➜ At the end of the unit you'll make webpages about Australia.

1 A country and a continent

Look at the pictures and the map on p. 8. What do they tell you about Australia? What else do you know about the country? Tell your partner.

2 VIEWING Australian road trip

a **Watch the video. Then make a list of the activities, animals and places that you remember.**

activities	animals	places
swimming	...	...

b **Watch the video again. What adjectives describe your impressions of Australia best? Give reasons. If you've been to Australia, tell your partner about your experiences.** More ideas → p. 81

3 A family travel programme

1.1

Listen to a tour guide and look at p. 8. Complete the family travel programme.

Stop 1	Sydney	See the ..., learn about ... and visit the Convict Museum, do a Harbour Bridge ..., hang out at the famous ..., try ...
Stop 2	the outback	... Alice Springs (... hours), visit Uluru, the sacred ... of the indigenous Australians, explore the outback on ...
Stop 3	...	Go scuba-... or snorkelling on the Great Barrier Reef, see ..., fish and coral. Visit the Daintree Rainforest: see ..., ... and other birds and animals.

4 Safety tips

1.2

Listen carefully to the tour guide's tips. Then take turns to explain one of the safety posters A–C.

When you're in the sun / in the outback / at the beach, remember to ...

You should ... / You shouldn't ...

Be careful of ... TF 1-2 → pp. 97f.

➜ I can talk about my first impressions of Australia. ✔

First Australians

Thinking about the aim of a text, its design and how it is written helps you to identify the type of text.

1 The history of the first Australians

a Skim the five texts and match each one to the correct text type.

- a an advert
- b a review
- c an infographic
- d information from a website
- e an open letter
- f a personal letter
- g a speech
- h a testimony

b Explain what helped you to decide.

1

www.example.com/FirstAustralians

The first Australians were the indigenous Aboriginal peoples and the Torres Strait Islanders who probably came to Australia from Asia about 45,000–50,000 years ago.
They believe that in the Dreaming their ancestor spirits came to the earth and created its animals, plants, caves, rivers, mountains and people. Then the spirits changed themselves into trees and stars and rocks. These things and places are therefore sacred to indigenous Australians. They believe the spirits of the ancestors are passed on to their descendants. For them, the Dreaming is all around them in the living world and part of the past, present and future.

2

Dear fellow Australians,

After British explorer James Cook landed on the shore of Australia in 1770, indigenous Australians were killed by Europeans and died of diseases brought by them: by 1900, 90% had died. The others had to integrate into white communities. From 1910 to the 1970s, 100,000 indigenous children were taken from their parents and their land, and they were brought up as white children in children's homes – our stolen generations. The government finally apologized in 2008.

But what has changed? Yes, our culture is now seen to be important and tourists are not allowed to climb Uluru any more. But 35% of children in out-of-home care are indigenous and the government continues to cut money for indigenous organizations. We need more than an apology.

Jenny Marika, Yirrkala, Northern Territory

3

For the pain, suffering and hurt of these stolen generations, their descendants and for their families left behind, we say sorry. To the mothers and the fathers, the brothers and the sisters, for the breaking up of communities, we say sorry. And for the indignity [...] this inflicted on a proud people and a proud culture, we say sorry. ◇

(Prime Minister Kevin Rudd, 2008)

4

"My name is Valerie Linnow. […] I was two when I was taken from my parents. My brother said that he was looking after us, the whole nine of us, and he said that mum went down to the shop and the next minute that the welfare just came and grabbed the whole lot of us … and separated us. Three sisters went to Cootamundra, three sisters to Bomaderry, three brothers went to [another home]. I often tried to go into the nursery to see the two young sisters. And I got caught from one of the sisters [children's nurses] and I got thrown into one of these big dark rooms with all the blankets, calling out to my mum, I was crying in the dark room. And she came in, one of the sisters came in, she said, 'You haven't got a mummy, you haven't got a daddy, cut that talk out.' So I learned to cut the … didn't mention their names. … The only mum I had was in my dreams." ◇

5

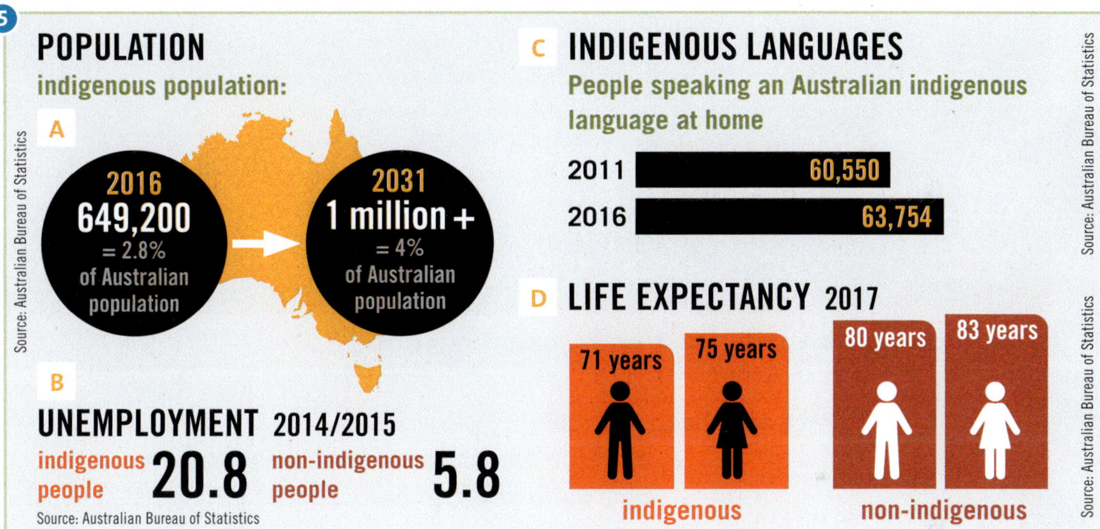

2 A history of injustice

Read the texts carefully and complete the mind map.

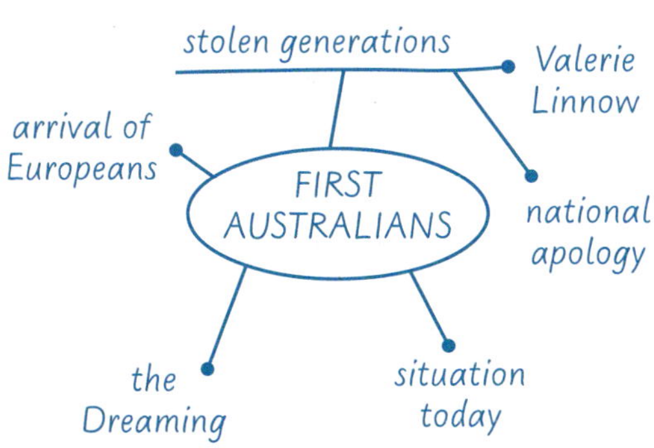

More ideas → p. 81

Fast finishers 1 → p. 87

3 Then and now

Discuss the questions.

1 Is it important that the prime minister made a public apology? Why?

2 How does Valerie Linnow's story make you feel? Why? Explain what you think she missed as a child and what effect this might have had on her later life.

3 Think about what you learned last year about native people in the USA and Canada. What is similar and what is different in Australia?

More ideas → p. 81

4 What positive aspects for the future can you find in the texts?

TF 3 → p. 100

I can recognize different types of texts and understand their aim. ✔ WB 1-3, pp. 4-5

Indigenous Australian art: past and present

1 From rocks to canvas

Read about Aboriginal art. Explain why some artists paint with dots.

Thousands of years ago the first Australians painted on rocks and on tree bark. There were over 250 indigenous languages, but they had no written form. So back then and still today indigenous Australians often pass on their culture and history through art. They usually draw sacred designs in the sand when they are telling these important stories. In the 1970s an Australian teacher noticed these designs while he was teaching near Alice Springs and watching the storytellers. The elders talked to the teacher because he had asked children to paint things from their culture. Men, and later women, began to paint on canvas after the teacher had encouraged them to make permanent pictures.

Artists can only paint parts of their Dreaming which ancestors pass down through their family. Some artists began to paint with dots, so that other people couldn't understand their sacred stories. The artists used natural materials for the colours. Today younger artists are interpreting their stories in different ways and painting in brighter colours – like the artist who is painting the picture on the left.

LOOK AT LANGUAGE: present and past tenses (revision)

a Match the tenses with the correct use.

1 simple present	a for an action in progress in the past
2 present progressive	b for an action that happened before another action in the past
3 simple past	c for regular actions and states in the present
4 past progressive	d for actions in progress in the present
5 past perfect	e for completed actions at a specific time in the past

b Find two examples for each tense in 1.

c What signal words are used with each tense? Make a list from the text and add other time phrases.

LF 1 → p. 114

2 Body painting for dancers

Complete the information with the correct present and past tenses.

Today body painting also (1 help) ... indigenous dancers to tell a story. This tradition (2 start) ... thousands of years ago and body art at that time (3 show) ... indigenous Australians' connection to the land. While they (4 dance) ..., the dancers also (5 wear) ... jewellery from animal teeth, stones and feathers. After Europeans (6 take) ... much of the indigenous Australians' land, these traditions (7 become) ... especially important. Today, while they (8 dance) ..., dancers often (9 become) ... the spirit ancestor that they (10 present) ... in their story.

3 Coming of age

a Indigenous people use body paint for ceremonies when they become adults. What coming of age ceremonies do you know about or have taken part in? You can also talk about other important ceremonies when you were younger. More ideas → p. 81

I was confirmed last year. For my confirmation I wore ...

I wasn't confirmed because I'm Jewish / a Muslim. But ...

b Read the information. How is the coming of age ceremony of the Yolngu people different today from the past?

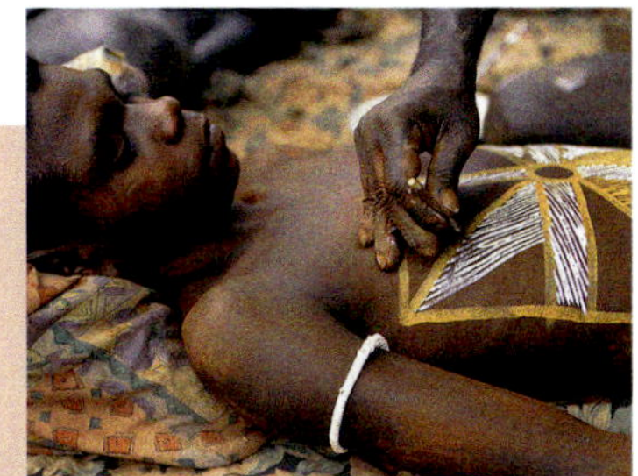

In Arnhem Land, Northern Territory, Yolngu boys become adults between ten and sixteen years of age. The ceremony teaches boys discipline. There didn't use to be discipline problems, but now the situation has changed. Elders paint the boy's body for the ceremonies. In the past elders also used to make a permanent mark on the child's body: they used to put a ring in the boy's ears or nose, or make scars. Elders also used to put marks on their own bodies to celebrate the event.

LOOK AT LANGUAGE: *used to*

a Look at the examples of *used to* in 3b. What verb form comes after *used to*?
What is the negative form?

b When do we use *used to*? Choose A, B or C.
A for actions that didn't happen very often in the past
B for actions that started in the past and finished in the present
C for actions that often happened in the past, but not in the present

LF 2 → p. 115

4 NOW YOU

Think about hobbies or activities that you used to do as a child. Tell your partner one thing you used to do, and one thing you didn't use to do in the past, but do now.

I used to go to the park with my dad every weekend. Back then we didn't use to watch as much TV as we do now.

More ideas → p. 82

5 Q & A about boomerangs

Complete the Q & A with the correct present or past tense.

Q: In the past, what (1 indigenous people / make) ... boomerangs from?
A: They (2 make) ... them from branches and tree roots.
Q: What (3 they / use) ... them for?
A: They (4 used to / kill) ... animals like kangaroos with them while they (5 hunt) ... These boomerangs (6 be) ... longer and straighter than returning boomerangs and they (7 not come back) ... after the hunters (8 throw) ... them.
Q: Today indigenous Australians (9 not use) ... boomerangs as weapons, do they?
A: No, indigenous people only (10 use) ... returning boomerangs as sport and in competitions.
Q: Why (11 the guy in the picture / hold) ... boomerangs? (12 he / take part) ... in a competition?
A: He (13 not / do) ... that, he (14 dance) ... in a show.

→ I can talk about activities in the past and present. ✔

WB 2-3, p. 7

Venomous creatures

1 Venomous creatures
You're looking at a webpage about venomous animals. Your little sister sees the pictures and has some questions. Answer them in German.

1 Wo findet man diese Spinne?
2 Ich weiß, dass Quallengift gefährlich ist. Was kann man dagegen tun?
3 Warum hat der Oktopus diese Farben?
4 Ist das eine Zecke unten rechts? Wieso ist sie gefährlich?
5 Welches Tier ist am gefährlichsten? Warum?

Sydney funnel-web spider

These spiders eat other insects and snails. They're found in New South Wales, especially in forest areas. However, they are also often found in backyards and swimming pools and sometimes in houses. Funnel-web bites are very dangerous because the venom can attack a person's nervous system and lead to death. However, if victims are given antivenom soon after, there is no danger.

Blue-ringed octopus

This octopus lives in coral reefs and hides on rocks. To frighten its enemies away, its skin becomes bright yellow and its blue rings flash brightly. Their venom is very strong: one octopus has enough to kill ten adults. The venom causes people to stop breathing, so anybody who is bitten by a blue-ringed octopus should get help immediately. There is no antivenom for a bite by this octopus, but if you get help with breathing, you may survive.

Box jellyfish

This big jellyfish lives in the warm waters of Western Australia, the Northern Territory and Queensland. In summer they can be found in bays and rivers. This jellyfish is the most venomous creature on earth. The only way to calm the stinging is to put vinegar on the area. When jellyfish venom enters the blood, it can cause the heart to stop and victims can die in minutes, so they need attention immediately.

Australian paralysis tick

These ticks are found on Eastern Australia's coasts. They feed on animals and birds including farm animals and pets. They are very small and have an oval body. Usually it is the female that bites people: they go under the skin and get bigger as they suck blood. Ticks can cause allergic face paralysis and strong allergic reactions. Take out the tick with tweezers or put insect repellent on it.

SF 6 → p. 131 TF 4 → p. 101

I can explain important information in German. ✔

Having a conversation

1 Talk like an Aussie

1.3 **a** Listen to a conversation between two Australians. What are they talking about?

b WORDS Look at these words and phrases. How would you say them in British English?

1. **G'day, mate.**
2. **How ya going?**
3. We're having a **barbie** tomorrow **arvo**.
4. The **oldies** will be there too.
5. **Cheers**, mate.

ACROSS CULTURES

Australians are known for their friendliness and their relaxed and informal attitude to life.
They're also known for their informal language and love of shortening words like Australian (= Aussie), and names like David (= Davo).
How is this the same or different in Germany?

c What are the words short for? What sounds do they end in?

1. Ow, the **mozzies** are biting me!
2. I had cereal for **brekkie**.
3. I always have a **bikkie** with my tea.
4. **Avo** on toast is my favourite lunch.
5. I'm going to Spain, but I don't speak the **lingo**.

2 SOUNDS & STRESS Australian English

1.4 **a** Listen and say which sentence (a or b) is an Australian speaking? In which sentence is a British person speaking?

1.5 **b** Listen again to the Australian sentences and repeat. Discuss what sounds are different to British English in each sentence.

3 A conversation at a barbecue

1.6 Listen to a conversation between Archie and Emir. Complete the questions that they ask.

1. What part of Australia ...?
2. That's ..., right?
3. Have you ever been ...?
4. What does your mum ...?
5. Do you play ...?
6. What's your ...?
7. What else do you do ...?
8. Have you got any ...?

4 NOW YOU

You meet somebody new at a party or a sports event. Ask and answer questions to get to know each other. You can use the questions in 3 and other questions. Fast finishers 2 → p. 87

- Start the conversation: say hello, introduce yourself
- Show interest, ask general questions and then follow-up questions.
- Keep the conversation going: Use *Well ..., So ..., What I mean is ..., Erm ...*
- Ask if you don't understand: *What do you mean? Can you say that again, please?*

SF 7 → p. 132

→ I can have a successful conversation. ✔

Coast to Coast

(by David Fermer)

1 Secrets

a Look at the picture on the book cover and read the description. What could the conflict about right or wrong be about? What do you think Cooper does after he finds the boy Bashir?

b Read the first part of the story (until line 94). Describe what Cooper and his friend Kate do.

ACROSS CULTURES

Immigrants who arrive on boats and have no documents are taken to detention centres for health and security checks. These centres are often criticized for their bad, prison-like conditions.

Darwin, Northern Territory, Australia. When 17-year-old Cooper Jackson discovers a half-drowned Afghan boy, Bashir, on the beach one night, he is drawn into a conflict about right or wrong, and takes a journey into the darkest corners of Australia's 'stop the boats' policy.

1.7

'What are we going to do?' Kate asked on the way home that evening, and the 'we' in her question made me love her that little bit more.

I shrugged my shoulders. Whatever we did, it would be wrong.

'He can't stay illegal forever, but to go to the cops now …' Kate said. She looked up at the evening sky. 'It doesn't feel right.'

I agreed. The thought of Bashir being sent to a detention centre made me feel ill. He hadn't come all this way to be locked up.

'We should teach him English,' Kate suggested as we crossed the bridge to Rapid Creek. 'Make sure he can face the difficulties of daily life in Australia.'

'We could get into trouble,' I told her.

'It's too late for that.'

We didn't have a plan. The only thing we did have was time. As long as Bashir was with us, we could give him the best start to his new life in Australia. We didn't want to lose that chance.

Over the next few days, we started to get organized. We brought pots and pans to the beach hut, bottles of drinking water. We gave Bashir a bowl to wash his dishes, towels to dry them. We made holes in the wall of the hut so that Bashir could look out before leaving. It didn't matter if people saw him on the beach or in the woods, but we didn't want anybody seeing him going to and from the hut.

Kate and I became experts in secret operations. I took Bashir's clothes home regularly and washed them. Kate encouraged her dad to tidy his wardrobe and get rid of all his old clothes. We gave Bashir a CD player and headphones and some batteries for it. Kate had a lot of audiobooks like 'Harry Potter' and 'Lord of the Rings'. Bashir listened to them around the clock. Kate borrowed a textbook on English grammar from the local library and photocopied the whole thing. Bashir did exercises during the day, and after school we went to the hut to check his work.

We told him everything he needed to know about Australia: about the cities and the land, about our history and current affairs. It was a crash course in becoming Australian, and Kate and I were the best possible teachers. It made us realize how much we loved our home. I even took my laptop and showed Bashir some rugby matches. I explained Australian Rules football to him. I didn't need to explain cricket. Bashir had already learned the rules of the game in Pakistan.

At the same time Kate and I contacted a couple of organizations we thought could help: the Refugee Council of Australia and another organization to help children who had come without their parents. We wrote them emails under a false name. We thought it was better to be on the safe side. If they knew who we were, they could find Bashir. If they didn't, he was safe.

The answers that came all said the same: 'Being illegal in Australia is not a long-term solution. We recommend that you go to your local authorities and find out what support they can offer.' What else could they say? No one was going to encourage us to help an illegal immigrant.

For some reason Kate and I still didn't do what they suggested. We thought that we could help Bashir better than anyone else, even if he had to live in a hut for a while. At least he had his own place and two friends who cared for him. He kept the hut clean and tidy. He cooked and studied and went fishing every day. He soaked up everything we told him. It wasn't the best of lives, but there were worse.

[***]

1.8

Life could have gone on like that forever if something hadn't happened a short time later. I was at the hut on a Friday afternoon, helping Bashir with some English grammar, when suddenly the door opened and my dad was standing there. I don't know if he was squinting because it was dark inside or because he was surprised to see me, but it took him a while to speak.

'Coop?'

'Dad?'

Dad hadn't been to the hut for at least a year. His private life had stopped when his campaign to become Lord Mayor of Darwin started.

'Who is this?' he asked, looking at Bashir.

'Oh yeah ...,' I said. Bashir and I exchanged a look. I could see the fear in his eyes. 'This is a mate of mine.'

Dad came into the hut, squinting at Bashir.

'Why is he wearing your clothes?'

I didn't have a good answer to that. Bashir was wearing my old Australian cricket shirt, the one with my name on it, so it didn't make much sense to deny it.

'What are you guys doing here?' Dad asked, his eyes scanning the books in front of us.

'We've got tests soon,' I explained.

'You didn't tell me you still came down here.'

'Nor did you.'

Usually that would have been enough to start an argument, but instead Dad chose to ignore it. He looked at Bashir, trying to decide who he was.

'What's your name?'

Bashir looked at me nervously. I gave him a nod.

'My name is Bashir,' he said. Even his accent was starting to sound Australian.

'Bashir?' Dad repeated as if trying to solve

a riddle. 'Do you go to school with Cooper?'

Again Bashir looked at me like a drowning swimmer. There was no way we were going to get out of this.

'No, Dad', I said. 'He's from Afghanistan. He came here on a boat. I found him on the beach.'

It was pretty direct, I know, but there was no easy way to tell him.

What followed was a silence like I've never heard before. It was deeper than the night, stiller than the plains of the outback.

The fact that it was most probably going to end in one huge explosion made it all the harder to bear. But the explosion didn't come, Dad didn't shout. He just looked at me, perfectly calm, and said, 'We have to talk. Outside.'

2 Cooper's dad finds out

a Now read the rest of the story. Explain how Cooper's dad found out about Bashir and how his dad reacted.

b What do you think Cooper's dad says to him? Exchange ideas.
More ideas → p. 82

3 What do the sentences mean?

Match the sentences in the story with the correct meaning. There are two extra meanings.

1 Kate and I became experts in secret operations. (line 35f.)
2 Bashir listened to them around the clock. (line 43)
3 We thought it was better to be on the safe side. (line 73f.)
4 He soaked up everything we told him. (line 91f.)
5 It didn't make much sense to deny it. (line 118f.)
6 Bashir looked at me like a drowning swimmer. (line 142f.)

A We couldn't say it wasn't true.
B We didn't know it was dangerous.
C He looked at me helplessly.
D We didn't want to do something dangerous.
E We got better and better at hiding things.
F He found it hard to study.
G He learned very quickly.
H He did it all the time.

4 USE OF ENGLISH Word families

Use the word given in capitals to form a word of the same word family.

Kate is a good friend to Cooper and she is very (1) … . She has lots of good (2) … . She (3) … brings Bashir her dad's old clothes and she brings him a grammar book to learn English. Cooper gives Bashir (4) … about Australian sports. Bashir is in Australia (5) … and that's dangerous.

HELP
SUGGEST, SECRET
EXPLAIN
ILLEGAL

5 Bashir's point of view

a How do you think Bashir felt …
before he left Afghanistan • when he got to Australia • when Cooper found him on the beach • while he was living in the hut

b You are Bashir. Write a diary entry about how you felt when Cooper's father appeared. Write what you dream of doing in the future. More ideas → p. 82

→ I can understand a story from different points of view. ✔

Bruce Lee played badminton too

Bruce Lee played badminton too is a short film by Taiwanese-Australian director Corrie Chen. Her films explore the topics of identity and belonging.

1 The film title

a Look at the title. Who was Bruce Lee?

b Look at the photo of Nic at the bus stop. Describe him and the group.

2 VIEWING Nic's dream

a Read the questions. Then watch the film and think about them.

1 What is Nic's dream? How does he prepare for it?
2 What does his dad think about his son's dream?
3 What about his mother? How does she react?
4 What do his parents think about their new neighbours from Taiwan?
5 What does Nic think about Jenny?
6 What happens in the tournament? What does Jenny say to Nic before she gets in the car?

b Discuss the questions with the class. Then say if you liked the film and why (not).

3 VIEWING The final match

a Watch the tournament scenes again. Pay attention to:

- the music when Nic goes into the gym
- how the first Chinese guy feels and why
- the music when Nic plays against the guys
- the camera shots when Jenny and Nic play
- the music when Nic plays Jenny
- how Nic feels at the end of the tournament

b Which effects do the director's choices have on the viewer? Fast finishers 3 → p. 87 SF 2 → p. 126

4 After the match

Role-play a conversation between Nic and his dad after the match.
Partner B: You're Nic. Look at page 76. Partner A: You're Nic's dad. You start.

- Say congratulations to Nic on the match.
- Say you're proud of Nic anyway.
- Say Nic was a good loser.
- Ask what Jenny said to him at the end.
- Ask why she said this.
- Say what you think about that. Then suggest you and Nic do an activity together.

I can understand the feelings of characters in a film. ✔

Increasing your vocabulary

1 Find collocations: sport verbs

a Words which go together are called collocations. Find the correct verbs which go with these sports: *do, go* or *play*. Use an online dictionary or a collocations dictionary for help.

athletics • boxing • cricket • judo • scuba-diving • snorkelling

b What sports do you do? Tell a partner.

2 Find collocations: words that go with *sport* and *sports*

a Find words that go before 'sport'. Think of words you know and use an online collocations dictionary to find more.

amateur sport
ball sport
...

b Two of these word pairs aren't real collocations. Which ones? Check in a dictionary.

sports centre • sports channel • sports club • sports competition • sports equipment • sports event • sports facilities • sports fan • sports food • sports injury • sports place • sports venue

3 Learn and use synonyms and antonyms

a You know a synonym (=) and an antonym (≠) for these words. What are they? SF 13 → p. 136

1 The competition was hard.
2 The match started late.
3 The score was correct.
4 The fans were sad when their team lost.
5 The game was fantastic.
6 The runners were very fast.

b You have three minutes. Make a list of as many pairs of synonyms and antonyms as you can.

4 Learn idioms

a Idioms are phrases that have a special meaning. For example:
The ball is in your court. means *It's your turn to do something.*

Decide what these idioms could mean. Then check in a dictionary.

1 You're skating on thin ice.
2 Let's get the ball rolling.
3 Keep your eye on the ball!

b Find two more idioms which come from the field of sport.

Step by step: increasing your vocabulary

- Use online dictionaries to find and learn collocations.
- Learn and use synonyms and antonyms.
- Check the meaning of idioms and learn them.

SF 15 → p. 137

→ I can increase my vocabulary using online dictionaries. ✔

Describing sports

ACROSS CULTURES

The three most popular sports in Australia are Australian Rules football (Aussie Rules), rugby and cricket. What are the three most popular sports in Germany?

1 Aussie Rules

Look at the pictures and read this description of Aussie Rules. Choose a heading for each section. There are two extra headings.

a Famous teams and players
b Rules and scores
c Where the sport is played
d Practice and training
e A short explanation of the sport
f Clothes and equipment

1 ...
Australian Rules football is a special Australian ball sport which is played between two teams of 18 players. Both men and women play the sport, and spectators at matches are usually half men and half women.

2 ...
Aussie Rules is played outdoors with an oval ball on an oval field. There are two tall goalposts at each end of the field and two short posts (called 'behind posts') next to each goalpost. The line between the goalposts is the goal line and the line from the goal posts to each behind post is called the behind line.

3 ...
Players wear T-shirts, shorts and football boots. They usually wear mouthguards and some players wear headguards.

4 ...
The game has four parts of twenty minutes. When a player kicks the ball through the goalposts and scores a goal, he or she scores six points. When the ball crosses the behind line, it scores one point.
Players can run with the ball, they can kick the ball and they can hit it with their fist. Players aren't allowed to throw the ball, but they can try and catch it from a kick. The team that scores the most points wins the game.

2 Sports places and equipment

a Answer the questions.

1 Where do you play Aussie Rules and what equipment do you need at that place?
2 What equipment and clothes do players need to play this sport?

b Find collocations in paragraph 4 for what players do.

1 verb + ball (five collocations)
2 score + noun (two collocations)
3 win + noun (one collocation)

3 A description of a fantasy sport

a Create a fantasy sport. Use your headings in 1a and make notes.
Wordbank 1 → p. 91

b Write a short description of your sport. Use the headings and your notes in 3a. SF 22 → p. 144

c CHECK Read your description again and check your grammar and spelling.

d Put your descriptions on the walls and desks. Read them and decide who has the most exciting fantasy sport.

→ I can describe a sport. ✔

WB 1, p. 12

1 YOUR CHECK

Do the tasks and then check your answers on page 226 at the back of the book. Did you get most of the answers right? Well done! Can you do better? Then look at the unit and at the **Vocabulary** and the **Language file** again.

1 Check your vocabulary

a Complete the names of the animals.

1 k _ ng _ r _ _
2 c _ m _ l
3 j _ llyf _ sh
4 T _ sm _ n _ _ n d _ v _ l
5 cr _ c _ d _ l _
6 _ ct _ p _ s
7 d _ ng _
8 p _ rr _ t

b What would a British person say?

1 Tomorrow **arvo** we're going out.
2 **Cheers**!
3 Would you like to come to a **barbie**?
4 Do you speak the **lingo**?
5 There are a lot of **mozzies** here!
6 I'm here with my **oldies**.

c Match these collocations.

1 kick	a of your team
2 congratulate	b snorkelling
3 be proud	c a ball
4 be a spectator	d a player
5 play in a	e at a match
6 go	f tournament

2 Check your language

a Complete the information with the correct past and present tenses.

Indigenous people (1 live) ... in Australia when the Europeans (2 arrive) ... . Many of them (3 die) ... because white people (4 bring) ... diseases with them. Today indigenous Australians (5 fight) ... to save their culture. They (6 present) ... their ancestors' stories in art and dance.

b Complete the sentences.

When I was a child ...

1 I used to eat ...
2 I used to play ...
3 I used to like ...
4 I used to ...
5 I didn't use to ...

3 Check your speaking

Two conversations have got mixed up. Put them in the right order and practise them together. Start the conversations with the sentences in red and blue.

You: I'll wash it out with vinegar.
Child: Help!
You: Yes, I can. I have some tweezers.
Child: Do I need to go to hospital?
You: Yes, it is.
Child: Is it out now?
You: I don't know. Let's ask the lifeguard.

Child: Can you take it out?
You: What's happened?
Child: Can you help me? I've been bitten by a tick.
You: Yes, I can see it, it's sucking your blood.
Child: I've been stung by a jellyfish. The sting hurts!

4 Check your writing

Write to an Australian friend about the stolen generations. Say what you think about what happened and about the apology. Use these words: take away, bring up, land, terrible, suffer.

Hi Lou, At school I've just learned about ...

Plan a trip to Australia

GET READY

You're going to plan a 14-day trip to Australia.
In your group, brainstorm ideas:

- cities you would like to visit
- other places you want to explore
- animals you would like to see
- activities you would like to do

I'd like to visit Tasmania and see Tasmanian devils. But it would also be fun to go to Melbourne and see an Aussie Rules match.

GO AHEAD

Each student chooses an idea, finds out more information and makes notes for your trip. You can also find pictures to show other students.
Exchange ideas.

- Decide how you are going to travel and what your travel plan looks like (you can draw it on a map).
- Make a list of tips to remember when you are there.
- Decide what you need to organize and do before you go.
- Decide what you need to take.

FINISH

- Tell your class about your trip. Explain where you want to go and what you want to do. Show your map with your journey and pictures. Explain what things you need to organize, what advice is important and what you want to take.

Our journey starts in ...
It's here on the map.
There we're going to ...
Then we're going to ...

Before we leave, we have to ...
We're going to take ...
In Australia, it's important to be careful of the sun, so ...

- Listen to the other groups. Ask questions to check details or ask for more information.
- Decide which trip presented by the other groups you would like to go on and why.

Unit 2 My world of work

Jack

Brady

Teresa

SCHOOL FILMS presents

HIGH SCHOOL JOBS

Hannah

Liz

Aisling

Marcos

Sara

In the USA, lots of high school students have part-time jobs or do volunteer work in their free time. In this documentary, eight American high school students talk about their jobs and what they do with the money they earn.

In this unit you will

- discuss part-time and volunteer jobs at home and abroad.
- read job adverts, write your CV and write a cover letter.
- make formal phone calls.
- discuss the automation of jobs.
- learn new techniques to improve your presentations.

➔ At the end of the unit you'll give a presentation about your work experience or about a possible future job.

ACROSS CULTURES

Part-time jobs in the USA and the UK:
You can work when you are 14. But when you are under 16, you can't work in school hours or for more than three hours on a school day.
When can you have a job in Germany? How long can you work on a school day?
College fees USA:
$10,000 – $35,000 a year (usually including room and food on campus)
College fees UK:
about £6,000 a year
Students in the USA often save money in a college fund for their fees and living expenses (room on campus and food). In both countries it is also possible to take out student loans.
When you go to college or do a training course in Germany, do you have to pay fees and also pay for your living expenses?

1 VIEWING 1 Part-time jobs

a **Five students on p. 24 have the part-time jobs in the box. What do you think they have to do in their jobs? Make a network with your partner for each job.**

babysitter • cashier • dog walker • shop assistant • waitress

b **Now watch the video and match the students with the jobs in a. Who doesn't have a job and why?**

c **Watch again. Take notes on how much the students are paid and what they do with the money.**

2 VIEWING 2 Brady's job

Watch Brady talk more about her job. Explain why she likes it and what she spends her money on. What is hard about the job?

3 VIEWING 3 Two volunteers

Marcos and Sara are volunteers at a neighbourhood house. Describe what they do and how many hours they spend there. Why do they volunteer?

4 Your job

a Do you have a part-time job or a volunteer job?

- If you have a job, tell your partner:
  What do you do? What do you get paid?
  What do you do with your money?
- If you don't have a job:
  Explain why not. Tell your partner which job from 1 or 3 you would prefer to do and why. Or explain what your dream part-time or volunteer job would be. Wordbank 2 → p. 92

b Do a quick survey in your class. How many students have jobs and what kind of jobs? TF 5 → p. 102

➔ I can describe and discuss part-time and volunteer jobs. ✔ WB 1-2, p. 17

Work and study abroad

1 A new experience

Imagine you can study or work abroad: Where would you like to go and what would you like to do? Tell the class. The ideas in the box can help you.

I'd like to / I'd love to ...

- spend a year in an English secondary school / an American high school.
- volunteer: be part of a childcare / health care / education / wildlife conservation project abroad.
- do an internship in an international English-speaking company (paid or unpaid).
- travel around the world / to the USA / to Asia / ...
- do an apprenticeship with a person or company abroad.

1.9 2 Two reports

Work in pairs. Partner A: Read Marina's report. Partner B: Read Artem's report.
Then tell your partner about:

- where this person went and why
- how the person and family prepared for the trip
- what it was like in the beginning
- what positive effects the experience had on him or her

LANGUAGE & LIFE EXCHANGES

Marina (16, Ingolstadt)

My grandparents offered to pay for me to study abroad for a year and I jumped at the chance. I wanted to improve my English and try living in a different country. My parents helped me set it up through a cultural organization which organized travel and my accommodation with a host family. I went to Brighton which is a really pretty town on the south coast of England. Before I went, I met several students who had just come back from their study abroad. It was really useful to get tips from them.

I was a bit nervous about staying with my host family. I'd talked to them online and got along with them fine, but it was hard to get used to living with a new family. I thought of giving up sometimes. I used to go in the shower so the family couldn't hear me when I cried! But after a while, I got used to being a part of the family and I've kept in contact with them since I left. They were a fantastic host family!

School was also hard at first. I used to help the teacher in German class and I could follow most lessons, but I had some problems with learning science in English.

My English got a lot better of course, and I learned a lot about school in England. But the best thing was making new friends and having so many fantastic experiences – like eating fish and chips on the beach!

watchtheplanet

Artem (18, Erlangen)

I've always dreamed of visiting Costa Rica. One day I found a sloth conservation project online – sloths are in danger because of the deforestation of the rainforest where they live. I convinced my parents to let me go for six months. Even though you're a volunteer, you have to pay for food and accommodation and travel insurance, so I saved money from my part-time job in a supermarket. I also had to get lots of vaccinations!

I was both excited and scared before I set off. I'm used to travelling, but my parents were worried. They had checked out the programme, but they were afraid it could be a scam. But it was all fine and I got a great welcome from the team.

The accommodation was very simple and I was a bit homesick for the first week, but I carried on with the programme and soon I didn't want to come home! The volunteers were from lots of different countries and we spoke English with each other. We watched the sloths and collected data three times a day. Occasionally we found a sloth which was injured and took it to the conservation centre to get well. The working conditions were good: between watching the sloths and also on Sundays we were free to go surfing at the beach, ride horses, play football and explore the rainforest (with a team member). I became much more independent and confident and I would totally recommend this programme.

3 Tips for going abroad

Read both reports and collect tips for going abroad to work or study in a list. Add other useful tips.

More ideas → p. 83

We use ***be used to* + *-ing form*** when we often do something and it is easy.
I'm used to travelling.

We use ***get used to* + *-ing form*** to say something was difficult, but it is getting easier.
It's important to get used to travelling alone. LF 3 → p. 115

4 USE OF ENGLISH Useful phrases

a Find phrasal verbs in the reports which mean the same as each of the words below.

Example: make a fast decision *jump at*

1 organize *(report 1, paragraph 1)*
2 have a friendly relationship *(1, para. 2)*
3 stop doing something *(1, para. 2)*
4 start a trip *(report 2, para. 2)*
5 find out more information *(2, para. 2)*
6 continue *(2, para. 3)*

b Replace the phrase in bold with a phrase containing the words in capitals so that the meaning is the same. Don't use more than five words. The reports can help you.

1 After a while, Marina **didn't find it difficult to be** with her new family. — GOT
2 Marina has **written and spoken to** her host family. — KEPT
3 He **got his parents' permission** to let him travel. — CONVINCED
4 **For Artem, travelling isn't new.** — USED TO

5 Two jobs abroad

Partner A: Look at page 76. Partner B: Look at page 78.

→ I can discuss study programmes and volunteer jobs abroad. ✔

Expats in Germany

1 Surprise!

Read what British expats in Bavaria wrote about German habits on a website. What do you think of their impressions?

ACROSS CULTURES

Germany has the strongest economy in the European Union and one of the strongest economies in the world. This means it attracts many 'expats' – people from abroad who live in Germany for a certain time. (Spain and France are also popular with expats.)
English is used as an international language all over the world and also in some German companies as their business language.

I moved to Germany a few weeks ago. I've already learned not to say 'How are you?' because you get a very long, honest answer! (Ellen, Rothenburg ob der Tauber)

Have you ever noticed that Germans are very direct? People have told me that my clothes don't look good or that I'm having a bad hair day. If you're English, it sounds very rude! (Ivan, Augsburg)

People are very punctual in Germany. I invited some friends to my flat last week and they were ten minutes early – not ten or fifteen minutes late like at home. (Victoria, Bamberg)

In the beginning I was surprised that most shops are closed on Sundays. I haven't got used to doing all my shopping on Saturdays yet, but I like having a day to do other things, like sport. (Glen, Murnau)

When I moved to Germany, I crossed the road on a red light if there was no traffic – like I do at home. People shouted at me! I've recently started waiting to cross even if there are no cars. (Mila, Würzburg)

German tea is very different to English tea. I ordered tea in a cafe last month and it was strange to get a teabag in a glass cup with no milk! However, I've just started drinking coffee and it's usually very good. (Harvey, Passau)

2 Habits

What habits have you noticed that other people have? What surprised you? What did you like? Tell your group.

More ideas → p. 83

When I was in ..., I noticed that ...
I've recently been to ... and ...
I've never been abroad, but a friend told me that ...

LOOK AT LANGUAGE: present perfect and simple past (revision)

a Look at 1 and find examples of the simple past (e.g. *I moved.*).

b Look at 1 again. Now find examples of the present perfect (e.g. *I've learned.*).

c Match these signal words with the correct tense:

ago • already • ever • just • last month • last week • not ... yet • recently

d Explain when we use the simple past and the present perfect.

LF 4 → p. 116

3 Another comment about Germany

a Complete what Carissa says about German bread.

I (1 eat) ... soft white bread all my life, so when I (2 move) ... to Germany last year, I (3 be) ... shocked when my German boyfriend (4 buy) ... hard dark bread. I (5 not like) ... it in the beginning, but I (6 already / get used) ... to it. I (7 not eat) ... white bread since I (8 come) ... here.

Fast finishers 4 → p. 88

b Explain why you chose simple past or present perfect in a.

4 An expat in Munich

1.10 a A German reporter is interviewing a young British photographer for the local English online paper. Listen and complete the reporter's notes.

Name: Dashiell Porter
Moved to Germany when & why? ...
Visited Germany before? / Speaks German? ...
Job and working conditions? ...
Best things about living in Germany? ...

b Help the reporter and write the report about Dashiell.

Dashiell Porter moved to Germany ...

5 Dashiell's future

Read the rest of the interview.

R: What about the future? **Are you going to stay** in Germany?
D: Yes, **I'll** probably **stay** in Munich. I like it here.
R: What about your job? Any plans there?
D: Well, I dream of having my own photography company, but that **isn't going to happen** until I have more experience.
R: Well, **I'll cross** my fingers for you. Good luck!

LOOK AT LANGUAGE: the future (revision)

Match the future forms in bold with the correct use.

a when we can see or know something is going to happen
b predictions about the future
c future plans
d spontaneous decisions and promises LF 5 → p. 117

6 DOUBLE CIRCLE Hopes for the future

Think about your hopes and dreams for the future. Make two circles and tell different students about what you'd like to do.

More ideas → p. 83
TF 6 → p. 103

I've always lived in Bavaria, but I'd like to live in ...
In the future I think I'll ...
I'm going to ...
I dream of ...

→ I can talk about the past and the future. ✔

Your curriculum vitae in English

1 Molly's CV

a Look at Molly Lehmann's CV. Put the headings a–h in the correct place in the CV (1–8).

a Digital skills
b Education and training
c Organizational skills
d Skills for specific jobs
e Personal statement
f Languages
g Work experience
h Communication skills

b Molly forgot to add these details to her CV. Put them under the correct headings.

a picture editing
b beginner Spanish
c good decision-making skills
d garden work for a neighbour
e online photo editing tools
f ability to look after children

CURRICULUM VITAE

Molly Lehmann
Weberkoppel 12, 80008 München
Mobile: 0162/2089465, Email: mollymlehmann@beispiel.de

(1) ...
I am a friendly and confident school student who enjoys meeting new people. I am good at working in a team, but also enjoy working independently and solving problems. I'm interested in working in a service job.

(2) ...

2019 – present	Saturday shop assistant in Young Fashion
2018 – present	Babysitter for two small children
2016 – present	Volunteer 'host sister' (My family is a volunteer host family for refugees.)

(3) ...

2015 – present	Michelle Obama Realschule, München
2011 – 2015	Grundschule an der Berliner Straße, München
2019	First-aid training

Personal skills

(4) ...: First language: German; Foreign languages: English, French

(5) ...: Good communication skills from my experience as a shop assistant and as a volunteer for a refugee organization

(6) ...: Good teamwork skills, good time management and general organization

(7) ...: Ability to deal with customers politely and helpfully

(8) ...: Microsoft Office skills, website design

2 Your strengths

a You're going to write a personal statement for your CV. Make a list of your strengths and special skills.
fit and healthy, good at sports, ...

b Write your personal statement. Look at Molly's statement for help.
I enjoy doing ...
I really like meeting ...
I'm good at making ...
I'm interested in working in / for ...

3 Your CV

a Now write the rest of your CV. Use Molly's CV and the headings in 1a to help you.
SF 4 → p. 129

b CHECK Swap your CVs and give your partner feedback: Is the structure right? Has your partner listed his or her strengths in the personal statement? Has your partner forgotten anything?
SF 17 → p. 138

 WB 1, p. 21

→ I can write my CV in English. ✔

Cover letters

1 Molly's cover letter

a Read the job advert. Would you like to apply for this job? What do you think are the good and bad aspects of this job?

b Look at Molly's cover letter. Explain how well her letter matches the advert.

N Nelson International Hotels

Part-time receptionists

For the busy month of August in our Munich hotel, we are looking for part-time receptionists who speak English and German to join our international team. You are friendly and enjoy chatting with guests, and can work flexible hours.

Reception activities include taking reservations, checking guests in and out and answering guest questions. You might also help out in the breakfast room when necessary.

✶ Please contact Andrew Smith (international staff manager) by using the online form and uploading your CV and cover letter in English.

Weberkoppel 12
80008 München

1 Nelson International Hotels
Attn: Andrew Smith

27th February 20...

2 Dear Mr Smith

3 I would like to apply for the job of part-time receptionist at Nelson International Hotels which I saw on the yournewjob website on 25th February.

4 I have experience of working with people in a clothes shop and always enjoy helping and talking to customers. I also work as a babysitter which requires a lot of patience and responsibility. I am used to being flexible and working flexible hours. I therefore think I have the skills that are required to be a receptionist.

5 I have school holidays in August and I can work at any time. I am attaching my CV and can provide references if you require them.

6 I look forward to hearing from you.

7 Yours sincerely

Molly Lehmann

Molly Lehmann

a In the **main paragraph** say why you are the right person for this job and refer to the advert. Use long forms *(I am)*.

b As a **closing greeting**, use 'Yours sincerely' (or 'Yours faithfully' for *Dear Sir or Madam*). Add your **signature**. (You can print your letter out, sign it and then upload a scan if you are making a digital application.)

c If you have a contact person, write to them directly. If not, use *Dear Sir or Madam* without a comma.

d Put your **address** on the right and the address of the employer on the left. Use 'Attn' (= for the attention of) for the contact person. Don't forget the date!

e Use a formal **closing sentence**.

f In your **introductory sentence(s)** write clearly which job you are applying for and where you saw the advert.

g Write when you are available to work and refer to your CV.

2 Tips for a good cover letter

Read the tips a–g on the right and match them with the correct place in Molly's letter (1–7). SF 5 → p. 130

3 Your cover letter

Partner A: Look at the job advert on p. 77.
Partner B: Look at the job advert on p. 78.
Fast finishers 5 → p. 88

→ I can write a cover letter. ✔

Formal phone calls

Notes about interview
On ... At ... At ... Room ...
Approximately ... minutes
Talk about me, do ... tasks
Discuss pay and ...
Be ...! Tell them if I can't come.
Make a list of ...

1 On the phone

When do you usually make phone calls? Who do you call and why do you use the phone instead of messaging?

2 Arranging a job interview

1.11

a Molly phones the international staff manager to arrange an interview. Listen and complete her notes.

b Listen again and check.

3 Business English

Read the sentences 1–8 and replace the informal words in blue with the formal words in the box.

approximately • attend • available • contact • ensure • inform • punctual • receive • require • suitable

1 I got an email from you.
2 You asked me to call you.
3 Are you free on that day?
4 It will take about ... minutes.
5 ... to see if you're right for the job.
6 Please make sure that you are on time.
7 Please tell us if you aren't able to come.
8 If you need more information, ...

4 Your phone call

Look at the useful phrases you can use in your phone call.

a Partner A: Look at p. 77.
Partner B: Phone about an interview with a local dog-walking company which is run by a British expat. Remember to use formal language. Your partner starts.

- You can work after school from 2.30 pm.
- You want to know how long a walk is and what the pay is.
- You can come for an interview on Saturday afternoon.

b Now swap roles. You are the Swedish owner of a local cafe and prefer to speak English.

- You want somebody to work on Saturdays as a waiter or waitress for five hours.
- No experience is required.
- You're interviewing on Sunday between 9 and 12 o'clock.

Start the call like this: Hello, The Swedish Cafe. [Your name] speaking. How can I help you?

If you can't hear properly:
The line is very bad.
I'm afraid I can't hear you.
Sorry, I didn't catch that.
Could you speak more loudly please?

If you don't understand:
I'm sorry, I don't understand. / I didn't understand that.
What do you mean?
Could you repeat that, please?

SF 9 → p. 133

→ I can make a formal phone call. ✓

The fun they had

(by Isaac Asimov)

Isaac Asimov (1920–1992)

was a Russian-born American writer and a professor of biochemistry. He wrote stories and books on many different subjects including science. This story was written in 1951.

1 School

a In your opinion, what are the best things about school? What don't you like about school? Tell your partner.

b Read the story. What year is it? What does Margie think of school and why?

Margie even wrote it that night in her diary. On the page for May 17, 2155, she wrote, 'Today Tommy found a real book!'

It was a very old book. Margie's grandfather once said that when he was a little boy his grandfather told him there was a time when all stories were printed on paper.

They turned the pages, which were yellow and crinkly, and it was very funny to read words that stood still instead of moving the way they were supposed to – on a screen, you know.

'What a waste,' said Tommy. 'When you're through with the book, you just throw it away, I guess. Our television screen must have had a million books on it and it's good for lots more. I wouldn't throw it away.'

'Same with mine,' said Margie. She was younger and hadn't seen as many telebooks as Tommy had.

She said, 'Where did you find it?'

'In my house.' He pointed without looking because he was busy reading. 'In the attic.'

'What's it about?'

'School.'

'School? What's there to write about school? I hate school.' Margie always hated school, but now she hated it more than ever. The mechanical teacher had been giving her test after test in geography and she had been doing worse and worse until her mother had sent for the inspector.

He was a round little man with a red face and a whole box of tools. He smiled at her and took the teacher apart. Margie had hoped he wouldn't know how to put it together again, but he knew how all right and, after an hour or so, there it was again, large and black and ugly, with a big screen on which all the lessons were shown and the questions were asked. That wasn't so bad. The part she hated most was the slot where

she had to put homework and test papers. She always had to write them out in a punch code they made her learn when she was six years old, and the mechanical teacher calculated the mark very fast.

The inspector said to her mother, 'It's not the girl's fault, Mrs Jones. I think the geography sector was a little too quick. Those things happen sometimes. I've slowed it down. Actually, her progress is quite satisfactory.'

Margie was disappointed. She had been hoping they would take the teacher away altogether.

So she said to Tommy, 'Why would anyone write about school?'

Tommy looked at her with very superior eyes. 'Because it's not our kind of school, stupid. This is the old kind of school that they had hundreds and hundreds of years ago.'

Margie was hurt. 'Well, I don't know what kind of school they had all that time ago.' She read the book over his shoulder for a while, then said, 'Anyway, they had a teacher.'

'Sure they had a teacher, but it wasn't a regular teacher. It was a man.'
'A man? How could a man be a teacher?'
'Well, he just told the boys and girls things and gave them homework and asked them questions.'

'A man isn't smart enough.'

'Sure he is. My father knows as much as my teacher.'

'He can't. A man can't know as much as a teacher.'

'He knows nearly as much.'

Margie said, 'I wouldn't want a strange man in my house to teach me.'

Tommy laughed. 'You don't know much, Margie. The teachers didn't live in the house. They had a special building and all the kids went there.'

'And all the kids learned the same thing?'

'Sure if they were the same age.'

'But my mother says a teacher has to be adjusted to fit the mind of each boy and girl it teaches and each kid has to be taught differently.'

'Just the same, they didn't do it that way then. If you don't like it, you don't have to read the book.'

'I didn't say I didn't like it,' Margie said quickly. She wanted to read about those funny schools.

They weren't even half finished when Margie's mother called, 'Margie! School!'

Margie looked up. 'Not yet, Mamma,'

'Now!', said Mrs Jones. 'And it's probably time for Tommy too.'

Margie said to Tommy, 'Can I read the book some more with you after school?'

'Maybe,' he said.

Margie went into the schoolroom. It was right next to her bedroom, and the mechanical teacher was on and waiting for her.

The screen was lit up and it said: 'Today's lesson is on

fractions. Please put yesterday's homework in the proper slot.'

Margie did so with a sigh. She was thinking about the old schools they had when her grandfather's grandfather was a little boy. All the kids from the whole neighborhood came, laughing and shouting in the schoolyard, sitting together in the schoolroom, going home together. They learned the same things, so they could help each other on the homework and talk about it.

And the teachers were people ...

The mechanical teacher was flashing on the screen: 'When we add the fractions ½ and ¼ ...'

Margie was thinking about how the kids must have loved it in the old days. She was thinking about the fun they had. ◈

2 In the story

Read the story again. True, false or not in the text?

1. Margie and Tommy thought it was strange that the words in the book didn't move.
2. They read books on a computer.
3. The inspector had to repair Margie's teacher because its teaching programme was too fast.
4. The mechanical teacher looks like a person.
5. Margie thinks men aren't smart enough to be teachers.
6. Margie didn't know that many years ago kids had lessons together in special buildings.

3 Teachers and teaching

a **Read what Tommy and Margie say about teachers. Is it true? Discuss.**

'Well, he just told the boys and girls things and gave them homework and asked them questions.'

'A teacher has to be adjusted to fit the mind of each boy and girl it teaches and each kid has to be taught differently.'

b **Look at the last part of the story (from line 115) and what Margie thinks about school in the old days (now). What do you think school will be like in 2155?**

TF 7 → p. 104

4 Smart machines

Discuss the questions with a partner.

1. Do you think machines can replace humans? What are the advantages and disadvantages of automation?
2. What jobs can smart machines or robots do now?
3. What jobs do you think could be replaced by smart machines or robots in the future? Why?

Fast finishers 6 → p. 88

Talk about work

Remember: You don't have to translate every word, just explain the meaning. But if you don't know an important word in English, you can paraphrase it. You can also use phrases to get time to think.
Oh, what's the word?
Just a minute ... SF 6 → p. 131

1 About jobs

Your friend Wesley from the USA is staying with you. He doesn't speak much German. Your grandad is visiting and he's not very confident about his English. Interpret for them.

My sister has started working from home. She couldn't get a full-time job with a company, so now she's self-employed.

Cool! Seine Schwester ...

Mein Glückwunsch an sie! Was macht sie denn beruflich?

Grandad says ...

Oh, she's a graphic designer. She designs the pages for different magazines.

Sie ...

Das ist ja toll. Ich sehe oft junge Leute im Café, die an ihrem Laptop arbeiten. Es muss als Freiberufler schwer sein, die nötige Disziplin aufzubringen.

...

Yes, that's true. But when you don't have a regular job, but you still have to pay rent and other expenses, I think that motivates you.

Wesley sagt ...

Ja, das verstehe ich. Aber man hat zumindest keinen Chef oder keine Chefin und etwas mehr Freiheit.

...

Yes, but I think it's a bit lonely too. I'd prefer to work with people in a team.

...

→ I can interpret in a discussion about working conditions. ✔

Improve your presentations

You already know how to give a good presentation! You can ...
- structure your talk.
- introduce different parts of your presentation.
- support your ideas with examples.
- refer to pictures and sources.
- keep talking when you forget something.

1 Getting attention

a You have learned a lot about giving presentations in English. But how do you get the attention of your audience right from the start?

Match each technique with the correct example for a presentation on dream jobs.

1 Ask the audience a *yes/no* question about themselves. *f*
2 Say a shocking fact or statistic.
3 Show an interesting, shocking or unusual picture.
4 Ask a rhetorical question (when you don't expect an answer).
5 Tell a story.
6 Use a quote.

a I want to start by asking you to look at this photo.
b When I was small, I didn't want to have an exciting job like a pilot or a superhero. I wanted to be a ... supermarket cashier.
c "Dream. Believe. Create. Succeed." (Anonymous)
d So what is the best job in the world?
e 85% of people hate their jobs.
f Do any of you have a dream job? Put up your hands.

b In *Your task* on p. 39, you're going to give a presentation on work experience (if you have done it) or a job you would like to do. Find a good example for each starting technique in 1a. Then compare.

2 Keeping attention

To keep attention, it's good to build changes into your presentation. Look at the tips. Can you add more?

1 Show a small number of interesting slides.
2 Switch off the screen and talk so the focus is on you.
3 Show a video that presents your ideas.
4 Move around.
5 Use an exciting visual prop.
6 Keep your presentation quite short.

3 Finishing

Make sure you ask if your audience has any questions.

Thank you for listening.
Do you have any questions?

Step by step: improve your presentations
- Get attention with an interesting start.
- Keep attention with changes of technique.
- Ask for questions. SF 11 → p. 134

I can get and keep attention in a presentation. ✔

You can find the answers for these tasks on page 227.

1 Check your vocabulary

a Rewrite a report by an exchange student using the phrasal verbs in the box.

carry on • check out • get along • give up • set off • set up

1 It's easy to organize study abroad.
2 You can find more information about study programmes online.
3 When I started my trip, I was nervous.
4 I had a good relationship with my family.
5 Don't stop when it gets hard!
6 Continue with your year abroad!

b Replace words 1–6 with a more formal word.

I hope you (1) **got** my letter. Just (2) **write or phone** me if you (3) **need** more details.

Yes, I'm (4) **free** at 10.30.

Good! Please be (5) **on time**! The interview will take (6) **about** an hour.

c Match these words with the correct definitions. There are two extra definitions.

	a when you don't have a job
1 apprenticeship	b a programme which offers work experience
2 automation	c when you work for yourself
3 expat	d using machines and robots instead of people
4 internship	e a person who designs buildings
5 self-employed	f a person who lives in another country for a certain time
	g time you spend learning a job, like a builder

2 Check your language

Complete the comment with the correct form of the verb.

Over the years, scientists (1 make) ... lots of human robots. In 2002 scientists (2 begin) ... to develop robots which look exactly like humans. Today we (3 be used to / see) ... these robots, but we still find them interesting because they look like us. Robots (4 take) ... over a lot of jobs. Maybe in the future robots (5 replace) ... us completely.

3 Check your speaking

Put the phone call in the right order and write who is speaking. Start with c. Then practise the call.

a Yes, hello Alex. Are you available on Monday at five o'clock?
b Thank you, goodbye.
c The Park Cafe, Alison speaking.
d Thank you for your time. I look forward to meeting you next week.
e Good, please come to the cafe.
f Yes, that's fine.
g This is Alex Schumann. I'm contacting you to arrange an interview.

4 Check your writing

Write a job advert for an interesting job. Use an idea below or your own idea. Look at the adverts on the partner pages for help.

- app designer
- dance teacher
- park ranger
- personal shopper
- private detective

Give a presentation

GET READY

You're going to give a presentation on your work experience (if you have done it) or a future job you would like to do. Work in a group of students with the same topic. Think of points that you should include.

For example: work experience

- name of job / where / job description
- working conditions: number of hours, breaks, ...
- colleagues
- company sustainability / social responsibility
- best experience / worst experience

For example: possible future job

- name of job and job description
- where it is possible to do this job
- why you are interested in this job
- what are the challenges of this job
- how you can get this job

> In the company where I did my work experience, sustainability was very important – the products were all made of sustainable materials and in the canteen you couldn't buy drinks in plastic bottles.

GO AHEAD

- Work alone. Explain or describe the points that you discussed above.
- Structure your presentation.
- Think of a good start to your presentation. Use your notes from p. 37.
- You can also include a short video similar to the ones on pp. 24–25.

FINISH

- Give your presentation. Use the tips on p. 37 to keep your audience's attention.
- Ask for questions.

> What is the worst possible thing that can happen when you do work experience? Well, I'm going to tell you about ...

> Thanks for listening. Does anybody have any questions?

> You said something about ... I didn't quite understand that.

- Get feedback and use it to improve your next presentation. SF 17 → p. 138

> I liked your opening. It was really clever.

> It was a good presentation, but I think you showed too many slides, I found it hard to concentrate. I think you could move around more, so that the audience look at you more, not just at the screen.

1 LISTENING On the phone

1.12

You are going to hear five people making phone calls. Choose the correct call (A–H) for each person. Write the correct letters next to the numbers 1–5 in your exercise book. There are three extra letters.

1 *call to ...*

A ask for information about a job
B arrange a job interview
C talk about sports results
D ask about opening hours
E chat about free time
F get medical advice
G report an emergency
H get tickets for a match

2 SPEAKING Asking for information

a **Partner B: Turn the book around.**
Partner A: You want to know more about a job advert for a supermarket assistant. Ask Partner B about the job. Ask:

- what type of person they are looking for
- what you have to do in the job
- what the working hours are
- what the pay is if you are under 18
- if there is any other useful information
- who you need to call to ask about the job

Ask questions to check if you don't understand.

b **Partner A: Read the information about a tourist event and answer Partner B's questions.**

The Aboriginal Experience

Attend the amazing Aboriginal Dance Show. Go on a Dreamtime walk with an indigenous guide and learn about hunting. Try throwing a boomerang. Enjoy listening to the powerful sounds of the didgeridoo. Learn about Aboriginal culture and your guide's family history. Do all this and more at the Aboriginal Experience!

In addition, you can visit our Picture Gallery with beautiful pictures produced by Aboriginal artists, some of which are for sale.

Our facilities include a cafe and restaurant and a shop where you can buy presents such as jewellery, bags and even football boots with dot designs.

Our team looks forward to welcoming you and sharing our culture with you.

a **Partner B: Read the job advert for a supermarket assistant and answer Partner A's questions.**

SuperSavers

Weekend supermarket assistant

We are looking for a reliable and friendly shop assistant to work weekends at our supermarket on Northern Road, Edmonton. You must be a team player and good at organizing your time. You will fill the shelves and keep the supermarket clean and tidy. If you are over 18, you may be asked to do jobs with more responsibility (training given).

You will work either from 7 am–12 or from 12–7 pm on Saturdays and Sundays.

Pay is £7.50 per hour for under 18s and £9.70 per hour for over 18s. Uniforms are provided.

Please call Jane Thompson on 03069 990123 for more information.

b **You want to know more about an event. Ask Partner B about *The Aboriginal Experience*. Ask:**

- what entertainment with dance there is
- what music entertainment you can do
- what other activities you can do
- if it is possible to buy pictures by Aboriginal artists
- if you can buy food there
- what presents you can buy

Ask questions to check if you don't understand.

3 USE OF ENGLISH Wildfires

Copy and complete the second sentence so it has a similar meaning to the first. Use 2–5 words including the word in brackets.

Example:

Temperatures in Australia continue to climb to over 40 degrees Celsius. (CARRY)
Temperatures in Australia *carry on climbing* to over 40 degrees Celsius.

1 Every summer, dry, hot weather causes wildfires. (BY)
Every summer wildfires ... dry, hot weather.
2 Firefighters often have to put out wildfires. (USED)
Firefighters ... wildfires.
3 Over the last few years, the fires have been harder to get under control. (WORSE)
Over the last few years, the fires ...
4 Thousands of animals have died in the fires. (OF)
The fires have led to the ... thousands of animals.
5 Experts say climate change is making the weather more extreme. (BECAUSE)
According to experts, the weather is becoming more extreme ...

4 VOCABULARY Job interviews: formal and informal English

Make a table in your exercise book. Put the words in the box into pairs. Decide which word is informal and which word is formal.

~~about~~ • ~~approximately~~ • attend • available • call • come to • contact • ensure • free • get • inform • make sure • need • on time • punctual • receive • require • right • suitable • tell

informal	formal
about	*approximately*

5 WRITING A cover letter

You want to apply for the supermarket job on p. 40. Write a cover letter for the job (130–150 words). Include:

- opening and closing greetings
- what job you are applying for
- why you are the right person for this job (personal strengths and skills)
- your work experience
- when you are available for a job interview

If you need more help, look at the cover letter on p. 31.

Unit 3 The digital age

In this unit you will

- discuss the positive and negative aspects of the internet and other digital media use.
- report what somebody says.
- critically evaluate adverts.
- explain instructions for a digital device.
- prepare and do a job interview.

➔ At the end of the unit you'll do a survey of media use in your class.

1 Digital media use

a Discuss the pictures on pp. 42 and 43. What aspects of media use and the internet do they show?

More ideas → p. 84

b Choose the picture that is most interesting to your group. Prepare a short group presentation: What aspects of media use does the picture deal with? Is it positive or negative? Say why you chose the picture.

2 VIEWING iRony

a The pictures on p. 42 are from a video about the internet and media use. Watch the video which is a type of poem. You don't need to understand everything. Focus on the voice, the music and the pictures. Then complete these sentences.

The message of this film is ...
I like / don't like this film because ...

b Watch the video again and complete these sentences.

This film ...

- *is important for teenagers because ...*
- *was made for ... because ...*
- *addresses an important social issue because ...*

c Discuss your ideas and reactions and then share your ideas with the class.

3 Positive ideas

a Write down more positive aspects of digital media use.

More ideas → p. 84

b Share your ideas with the class.

c How do you think digital media use has changed since this video was made? How might it change in the future?

TF 8 → p. 106f.

➔ I can discuss positive and negative aspects of digital media use. ✔

Logging off

1 ZIPPER Social media

Make a zipper. Ask and answer the following questions with the student opposite you. Then the student at the front of one line moves to the end.

Are you a social media user?

YES: When did you open your first account?

How many hours do you spend online and how do you use social media?

What platforms do you use and how often?

NO: Why not? Have you tried using social media?

ACROSS CULTURES

In the UK ...

- 95% of 15-year-olds use social media before or after school.

- One in three 15-year-olds spends at least six hours a day online.
- One in three children (34%) has had a negative experience when using social media.

- 63% of UK school students wouldn't miss social media if it didn't exist.

Do you think the situation in Germany is similar?

2 Offline

a **What do you think a digital detox is?**

b **Read the article and find out why Zendaya and Griffin did a digital detox.**

Digital detox

Are you tired of trying to present a better version of yourself online? Fed up with trying to get likes or with ads always popping up? That's what happened to Zendaya Bryant (15) and Griffin Harrison (16) from Plymouth.

'It was making me depressed,' says Zendaya. 'I used to post a lot of photos of myself online. No bikini photos or anything like that – we learn in school about online privacy and not posting inappropriate photos or sharing personal information, so I was always careful online. I just uploaded photos of me with my dog or with friends. My friends always liked my photos, but I was always checking for even more likes. **1** ■■■ The first thing I did when I woke up and the last thing I did before I went to sleep was check my phone. When I scrolled down through other people's pictures, it seemed everybody else had a way more interesting life than me.'

Zendaya's mum noticed she was unhappy and had a talk with her. She asked Zendaya to do a digital detox and log off from social media for a few weeks.

'At first I was really worried that I'd lose touch with my friends,' says Zendaya.

'But then I started meeting them more instead and people sent me texts when something was going on. My parents bought me a membership to the gym and now I go with a couple of friends twice a week. **2** ■■■'

Zendaya decided to give up social media completely. She says she doesn't miss it. 'The funny thing is,' she laughs, 'my mum is a real social media addict. I never noticed it before because I was always on my phone too. **3** ■■■'

Griffin Harrison also tried a digital detox. 'I'd built up a really big social media following,' says Griffin. 'But it was taking too much time, I uploaded new photos and blog pieces every day and they had to be perfect. I had this fake online me who always looked great, had an amazing girlfriend and always did cool stuff. But I was actually really tired all the time. 4 ■■■'

It took an attack on Griffin's account to change his lifestyle. 'A boy at school hacked into my account and posted all sorts of nasty things about me – that I was ugly, I just wanted attention, was totally fake, … . We found out who it was, it was somebody at school who was jealous of me. 5 ■■■ I decided to shut down my account and speak out about the dangers of social media.'

Despite this, Griffin couldn't stay off social media for long. 'I've set up a new account, but I just use it to keep up with what's going on. And the person online is now the real me.'

3 Missing sentences

1.13

Put sentences a–g in the correct gaps 1–5. There are two extra sentences. Then you can listen and check.

- a But the situation with this guy made me ask myself if I really wanted to carry on with my blog any more.
- b I hated her.
- c I also hang out more with friends at home.
- d I don't like sport.
- e Now it's me that tells her to switch off!
- f I was trying to prepare for my exams and I was only sleeping four or five hours a night.
- g When I didn't get a lot of likes, I felt hurt.

Fast finishers 7 → p. 89

4 WORDS Phrasal verbs

Find the phrasal verbs in the article for these definitions.

1. appear suddenly (lines 4–5)
2. move down (lines 24–25)
3. sign out (line 34)
4. get into (line 71)
5. close (lines 79–80)
6. say what you think (line 81)

5 Your digital media use

a Think: Which of these digital activities (or others) have you done recently?

checking social media • creating playlists • downloading music • gaming • messaging with friends • posting photos • reading online news • watching films or series • writing a blog or article • writing a status

Wordbank 3 → p. 93

b WALK AROUND Tell different partners about your media activities.

c Can you imagine doing a digital detox? What would you miss most? What effect do you think it would have?

TF 9 → p. 108f.

6 Your digital media diary

At the end of this unit, you're going to do a survey about digital media use. From today, keep a media diary about …

- what type of media you use, what you do and who with
- when you use media and for how long
- if you use German/English/…

Also keep a sleep diary.

I can discuss social media use. ✔

Online issues

1 What did they say?

a Scan Ava's conversation with her dad. What does he want to know?

Dad: Ava ...
Ava: Sorry, Dad, I'm (1) ... meet Milo!
Dad: OK, I just (2) ... to know what an influencer is.
Ava: Er ... OK. Well, it (3) ... somebody who (4) ... attracted lots of followers on social media because they have something to say about fitness or lifestyle or a hobby. Why do you want to know?
Dad: I (5) ... about them. They sell and advertise things, right?
Ava: Well, I (6) ... following Isla Lopez, she's a fitness blogger. She (7) ... actually sell things, but she sometimes has links to training clothes. ... Sorry, I (8) ... to go now. I (9) ... be back soon.

Ava: Hi Milo, sorry, I'm late. I was just talking to my dad and told him that I was going to meet you. He said that he just wanted to know what an influencer was.
Milo: OK. What did you say?
Ava: I said it was somebody who had attracted lots of followers on social media.
Milo: But why did he ask?
Ava: He said that he had read about them. You know he worries about online stuff. Anyway, I told him I was following Isla Lopez and that she didn't really sell things.
Milo: And then what?
Ava: I told him I had to go then and that I would be back soon.

1.14 **b** Listen to Ava's conversation with her dad and complete it. Then listen again and check.

LOOK AT LANGUAGE: reported statements

When we talk to each other, we use 'direct speech'. When we report what somebody said, we use reported (or indirect) speech. We introduce this with 'said' or 'told somebody'.

- Look at Ava's conversation with Milo and complete the sentences below.
- What word sometimes comes after 'said' or 'told somebody' in reported speech?
- How are the pronouns and verbs different in reported speech?

direct speech	reported speech
I'**m going to** meet Milo.	I told him that I ... meet Milo.
I **want** to know what an influencer **is**.	He said that he ... to know what an influencer ...
It'**s** somebody who **has attracted** lots of followers.	I said it ... somebody who ... attracted lots of followers.
I **read** about them.	He said that he ... about them.
I'**m following** Isla Lopez.	I told him I ... Isla Lopez.
She **doesn't** actually sell things.	I told him she ... actually sell things.
I'**ll** be back soon.	I said that I ... be back soon.

LF 6 → p. 118f.

2 Influencers

a Milo told Ava about two influencers, and Ava tells her friend Hanita. Finish her sentences.

1 I'm following a gamer called Tex.
2 Tex posts lots of great gaming videos.
3 I followed another gamer, but then this gamer started promoting lots of stuff.
4 I don't like 'in your face' advertising like that.
5 I've stopped following him.
6 I'll show you one of Tex's videos.

He told me that ...
He said ...
He said ...
He told me ...
He said ...
He said ...

b Do you follow any influencers? If you do, who are they and what sort of ideas or products do they promote? If not, why not? More ideas → p. 84

3 More changes

a Look at these sentences from the conversations in 1. What else changes apart from the verb?

> Sorry, I have to go now.
> I told him I had to go then.

b Another friend is reporting what Ava said the week before. Complete the sentences with the correct words.

> the day before • the following week • that week • the next day • then • there

1 **Ava:** I'm going to meet Hanita tomorrow.
Ava said she was going to meet Hanita ...
2 **Ava:** I went to see Milo yesterday.
Ava told Hanita she had gone to see Milo ...
3 **Ava:** I'm getting a new phone next week.
Ava said she was getting a new phone ...
4 **Ava:** I'll meet you here.
Ava said she would meet me ...
5 **Ava:** I want to finish my project this week.
Ava said she wanted to finish her project ...
6 **Ava:** I don't want to go online now.
Ava said she didn't want to go online ...

4 What Milo said

1.15

a Milo has left messages on your voicemail. Listen.
Partner A: Note down the 1st and 3rd message.
Partner B: Note down the 2nd and 4th message.

b Listen again and check. Then tell your partner what Milo said.

5 GAME Whispered messages

a Each person in your group should write a message on a piece of paper. It shouldn't be too short and it can be silly!

b Make a line. The first person whispers their message to the next person in line. The last person says the message. Is it correct?
Now the person at the end of the line goes to the front and whispers their message.

6 Questions

Ava's dad asks her questions about her media use. She tells Milo about the conversation. How long was she on her phone? Did she switch off her phone an hour before she went to bed?

Dad: How long were you on your phone yesterday evening?
Did you remember to switch off your phone an hour before you went to bed?

Ava: My dad asked me how long I had been on my phone yesterday evening. I told him I had only been on it for three hours! And he wanted to know whether I had remembered to switch off my phone an hour before I went to bed. Of course I hadn't! I was listening to music.

LOOK AT LANGUAGE: reported questions

Look at the questions Ava's dad asked and what Ava reported to Milo. How does she start her sentences?
What words does she add to the reported question without a question word?

LF 6c → p. 119f.

7 More questions

a Ava's dad asks her lots of questions about online safety. What does she tell Hanita?

1 Do you have a strong password?
2 How often do you change your password?
3 Do you always log off sites?
4 Are you careful about personal information?
5 Where is your phone now?

My dad worries too much! First he asked me if I had ... Then ...

b Ask and answer the questions in a.

8 Requests, orders and advice

Ava's dad talks to her about what to do and not to do. Which speech bubble contains an order, which one contains a polite request and which one advice?

Please look at me and listen.

You should be careful online!

Don't download music from illegal sites!

Ava: Dad asked me to look at him and listen. He advised me to be careful online. And he told me not to download music from illegal sites.

LOOK AT LANGUAGE: reported requests, orders and advice

Look at what Ava reported to Milo. What structures can we use to report requests, orders and advice?

LF 6d → p. 120

9 Dad has more to say

a What else does Ava report?

Dad **asked/told/advised** me (not) to ...

1 Please be sensible!
2 Don't listen to those social media influencers.
3 You shouldn't buy stuff that they promote.
4 Ask me about fitness!
5 Take this seriously please!

b What advice have other people given you about online use? Tell the class.

→ I can report what people said. ✔

Announcements

1 Tech on the go

When you're travelling to school or on longer trips, what do you use your phone for?

2 Four announcements

1.16

You will hear four announcements. Where is each announcement made? Write the correct number 1–4 for situations A–F. There are two extra situations.

A At school
B In a department store
C At a train station
D On the radio
E On a plane
F On a train

The general situation (including background noise) and keywords can help you. You don't need to understand everything. SF 1 → p. 125

3 What exactly do they say?

1.16

a **Listen to the announcements from 2 again. Choose the correct ending for each sentence.**

1 All electronic devices must be switched off or set to airplane mode ...
A for take-off and landing only.
B until passengers are in the airport building.
C until the plane arrives at the airport.
D until there is another announcement.

2 Today there is ...
A 20% off everything in the electronics department.
B a sale on headphones.
C a special offer on electronic devices.
D an online sale.

3 In quiet coaches, customers can't ...
A use mobile phones.
B use all mobile devices.
C talk to each other.
D eat loudly.

4 Jon Dawson will be looking at ...
A different aspects of home assistants.
B the best home assistant on the market.
C the tech behind home assistants.
D how to control smart devices in your home.

Read choices A–D for each question and listen carefully for details.

b **Compare your answers and listen again to check if necessary.**

The boy who harnessed the wind

(by William Kamkwamba and Bryan Mealer)

- official language: English
- 16 other languages including Chichewa

1 William's invention

a Read the information about William and answer the questions.

In our digital world, we often forget there are still areas where there is no Wi-Fi and even no electricity. Until recently, Wimbe in Malawi where William Kamkwamba lives, was one of these places. The economy of Malawi is based on farming. During a terrible famine, when William was 14 and his family only had enough food for one small meal a day, William had to drop out of school – his family couldn't pay his 80 dollar annual school fee. To help his family, William decided to build a windmill to produce electricity for his home and pump water for the fields. He used a book from the library, old materials from the scrapyard and his dad's bicycle.

1 What didn't exist in William's village?
2 What was the problem for William's family?
3 Why couldn't William go to school?
4 How did William want to help his family?

b Imagine you had no electricity and no Wi-Fi. What would you miss the most? Why?

Wordbank 3 → p. 93

2 The film

Watch the trailer for the film on the internet. What do you find out about the story?

William's windmills on the Kamkwamba farm in Wimbe

3 The story

Read the story and complete the sentences.

1 Before they saw the windmill make light, people thought this ...
2 They thought William was ...

Making the windmill

Gilbert and Geoffrey arrived around seven the next morning.

The windmill's frame weighed about ninety pounds and I knew the only way we would get it to the top was to use a pulley. I used my mother's thick clothes-line wire and tied it to the windmill's handle.

Taking the other end, I climbed the tower and put the wire over the top rung of the ladder, then dropped it down to Gilbert. Geoffrey stood on the middle rungs to guide the machine as it went up.

'Okay, Gilbert,' I shouted. 'Bring it up!'

Carefully he began pulling the wire. The frame rose into the air.

The three of us pulled at the wire with all our strength.

'Come on, guys,' I shouted.

'I'm pulling as hard as I can!' Gilbert said. 'Don't let it slip, Geoffrey!'

'You do your job and I'll do mine,' he replied.

Little by little, the windmill made its way up the tower. With each pull, it swung and hit its huge blades against the tower.

'Don't let the blades break!'

After half an hour, we finally had it close to the top. I grabbed the handle and screamed down to Gilbert, 'Tie it down!'

Gilbert put the wire around the pole and the windmill held. Then Geoffrey joined me at the top to secure it in place.

The day before, we'd made two holes in the wooden poles. We'd also taken the bicycle to Godsten's shop and he'd made two holes in the frame.

As Geoffrey pulled the bolts and nuts from his pocket, I held the windmill. I could feel the machine pulling in my hands.

'Make it fast, this thing is heavy!' I said.

Geoffrey put in the bolts and tightened them. Then we looked at each other and smiled. I could hardly wait to watch the blades spin.

While Geoffrey made his way down the tower, I stayed at the top. To the north, I could see the roofs of the trading centre and the brown huts behind the market. Then something strange began to happen. A line of people began walking in my direction. They'd seen the tower from the distance. Within a few minutes, there were a dozen people at the base. I recognized a few of them. One was named Kalino.

'What is this thing?' he asked.

Since there's no word in Chichewa for windmill, I used the phrase *magesti a mphepo*.

'Electric wind,' I answered.

'What does it do?'

'Makes electricity from the wind.'

'That's impossible,' Kalino said, laughing.

'Well,' I said, 'just stand back and watch.'

I climbed down from the tower and ran to my room to get the final piece. That morning I'd found a thick reed and cut a piece to hold the dynamo's small light bulb. I then put a long copper wire around the base of the bulb and put it through the reed, so that one end hung out the side. This was my socket.

Holding the socket and bulb, I climbed the tower again and connected their wires to the ones from the dynamo. As I worked, more and more people arrived.

'What do you think he's doing now?' asked a farmer named Banda.

'This is the *misala* from the scrapyard my children were talking about,' another man answered. 'His poor mother!'

Looking out, I saw my parents and sisters at the back of the crowd, eyes wide and waiting. Their mouths hung open, as if there were seconds left on the clock and I had the ball.

In addition to my family, there were about thirty adults, and just as many children. They pointed at me.

'Let's see how crazy this boy really is.'

Wind whistled through the rungs of the tower. The bicycle spoke was in the wheel to hold it in place, but now the machine moved, as if begging me to free it.

Here it goes, I thought.

I pulled the bicycle spoke out and the blades

began to spin. The tyre turned slowly. I needed it to go faster, immediately.

'Come on,' I begged.

Slowly, the blades moved faster.

Come on, I thought. *Come on*.

Just then the wind pushed against my body and inches above my head the blades began to spin like a set of angry propellers.

I held the bulb before me, waiting for my miracle. It flickered once. Just a flash at first, then an amazing bright light. My heart nearly burst.

'Look,' someone shouted. 'He's made light!'

It was beautiful light, and it was mine!

I threw my hands in the air and screamed with happiness, laughing so hard that I became dizzy.

I looked down at the eyes below ... now wide in disbelief.

'Electric wind!' I shouted.

One by one, the crowd began to cheer. They raised their hands in the air, clapping and shouting, '*Wachitabwina!* Well done!'

'You did it, William!'

'We doubted you, but look at you now!'

'That's right', I said. 'And I'm going bigger now. Just wait and see!' ◈

4 The windmill

a WORDS Read the text again and match the pictures with the correct words.

bicycle frame • bolt • dynamo • nut • pole • pulley • reed • spoke • wire

SF 14 → p. 136

b Explain how William and his friends made his windmill. Put the sentences in the right order.

1f, 2 ...

- a After that, William connected the wires.
- b In the morning, William cut a reed to hold the dynamo's bulb.
- c Finally, William took the bicycle spoke out of the wheel.
- d After tying the wire, Geoffrey put the bolts in the holes and tightened the nuts.
- e Then they tied the wire around the pole.
- f The day before, William, Gilbert and Geoffrey had made holes in the poles and the frame.
- g They pulled the windmill up to the top of the poles using the wire from Gilbert's mum's washing line.

Fast finishers 8 → p. 89

5 Reactions

Complete the sentences.

1. Before the demonstration, William felt ...
2. When the windmill produced light, William ...
3. When the crowd saw the light, ...
4. Then the crowd ...
5. In the end William said ...

→ I can understand and react to a true story. ✔

An ad for a home assistant

1 Home assistants
Do you or other students in the class have a home voice assistant? What can it do and how does it make life easier? What are the possible disadvantages of these devices?

2 You need an assistant!
Read the advert. Then try and convince your parents to buy this home assistant. Tell them in German what it can do.

3 Questions

a Your parents are interested, but have some questions and concerns. Answer their questions in German.

> Was kostet eigentlich der Spaß?
> Und wie lange läuft die Garantie?

> Das klingt wirklich gut, aber ich habe gelesen, dass diese Geräte die Privatsphäre beeinträchtigen können. Andere können eventuell hören, was man sagt.

b Read the set-up instructions. Your little brother wants to help you set up the assistant. Explain how to do that in German.

> Kann ich dir helfen, dieses Gerät einzurichten? Was muss man da machen?

Stevie

Play music. Turn on the lights or the TV. Find out the temperature. Listen to the news. Get information. Play games.
Home assistant Stevie can do all this and much, much more!
Stevie is a voice-controlled smart speaker designed to make your life easier, so you have time for the good things in life. Stevie is always ready to help!
At home you can use your voice to control smart devices like the TV, lights and door locks. Need food? No problem, just set up a shopping list and order what you want.
Are you a music lover? You can stream music from lots of different streaming services. If you want stereo sound, just use two devices.
Forget about problems with privacy. Just press a button to switch off the microphone. You can also delete your voice recordings at any time.
See our website for models and prices. Each device has a one-year warranty which does not affect your consumer rights.

Simple to set up and use!

Just follow the steps.
Step 1: Download the app from the app store.
With the app, you can set up and manage your assistant. To change the language from English, use the settings menu.
Step 2: Switch on your home assistant.
Plug the power adapter into the device and then into a power socket. The light ring turns on and Stevie says hello.
Step 3: Connect your assistant to your Wi-Fi network.
Follow the instructions on the app. If your assistant doesn't connect to your Wi-Fi network, unplug it, then plug it in again. If this still doesn't work, reset your assistant.
Step 4: Ask for help!
Say Stevie's name – this is the 'wake word' that wakes up the device. Then ask for help.

I can explain an English advert and instructions in German. ✔

WB 1, p. 37

Evaluating adverts

1 Advertising everywhere

a Take turns to describe the picture. SF 10 → p. 133

b Discuss where else you see adverts and what places you think are most effective. Think about *banner ads, billboards, pop-up ads, product placement, influencers, ...*

c How do you think you are influenced by adverts?

2 Two adverts

1.17

a Look at the two adverts. Listen to two students, Nadeem and Evie, who are talking about the ads, and complete some of their ideas.

A1 **It aims to promote** an ... lifestyle.
A2 **I think the target audience is** probably ...
A3 I like **the design** of the ... . The lemon suggests ...
A4 **It will appeal** to people who like ...
A5 The ad **tries to grab attention** through its ... colours.
A6 The name is simple, but **it** ... **well**.
A7 The advert **lacks** a ...

B1 The clothes have a simple, clean ...
B2 Both the adverts **contain this eye-catching** ... colour.
B3 This advert **is effective** because it contains the word ...
B4 It **addresses concerns** that the workers are ... properly.
B5 The ad **sends the reader the** ... that these clothes are made from environment-friendly materials.
B6 The two ads both **have that in** ...
B7 The first ad ... luxury, **whereas** the clothes advert focuses on being basic or simple.

A

B

b Do you agree with Evie and Nadeem's ideas? Why (not)? Can you add any other ideas? Explain why you would buy these products or not.

3 More adverts

Partner A: Look at p. 79. Partner B: Look at p. 80.

Wordbank 4 → p. 94

I can describe and critically evaluate adverts. ✓

An interview

1 Preparing for an interview

Mike Clark has an interview to work part-time in an electronics shop. Discuss these questions.

1 How do you think he should prepare for this interview?
2 What sort of clothes do you think he should wear?
3 What other tips do you have?

WALKER'S *electronics*

Part-time shop assistant
for family firm required.
You are an independent, organized young person with a good knowledge of digital and electronic devices. You must be a good team player.

2 VIEWING The interview

a Watch the interview. Decide if you think Mike will get the job, giving reasons for your answer.

b Compare your decisions. Did Mike follow your tips and ideas from 1?

3 VIEWING Good and bad points

a Watch the interview again. Make two lists: the good points and the bad points of the interview.

good points	bad points
– *answers the first question confidently*	– *is late for the interview*

b Explain what Mike could have done better.

4 Your interview

a You have an interview for the same job as Mike. Prepare the answers to these questions.

1 Can you tell me something about yourself?
2 What are your strengths and weaknesses?
3 Are you a good team player?
4 What are your interests?
5 Why do you want a job with us?
6 Do you have any questions about the job?

More ideas → p. 85
Fast finishers 9 → p. 89

b Role-play (and film) the interview using the questions from 4a. Remember your tips from 1 and what you learned from Mike's interview. SF 8 → p. 132
Then swap roles.

I can analyze the good and bad points of a job interview. ✔

3 YOUR CHECK

You can find the answers for these tasks on page 228.

1 Check your vocabulary

a Complete the words. Then answer the questions.

1 Do you have a social media a…?
2 Do you have a big social media f…?
3 Do you ever g… f… up with social media?
4 Do you ever feel j… of people you saw on social media?
5 Do you use a TV or music s… service?

b Replace the word(s) in blue with a phrasal verb. There are two extra verbs.

carry on • hack into • log off • pop up • shut down • scroll down • speak out • switch off

1 When you stop using an app, always remember to sign out.
2 It's annoying when ads suddenly appear.
3 Close your computer when you've finished using it.
4 You should say what you think about online bullying.
5 I spend a lot of time moving down the screen on my phone.
6 Somebody got into my social media account yesterday.

2 Check your language

Scott is telling a friend what a girl said about him to her friend Poppy. Finish his sentences.

1 I really like Scott.
2 He's very kind.
3 He cares about other people.
4 Does he have a girlfriend?
5 What is his phone number?
6 Please find out if he likes me.
7 Call him tomorrow!
8 Don't say I want to know!

1 She said (that) she …
2 She said I …
3 She told Poppy …
4 She asked …
5 She asked …
6 She asked Poppy …
7 She told Poppy to …
8 She told Poppy …

3 Check your speaking

Tell a partner about your favourite advert at the moment. Say what it is for and why you like it. Describe one detail of the advert and give one idea for making the ad even better.

4 Check your writing

Write a text message to your friend. Tell him or her about your new mobile phone or a games console. Say something about the brand, the size, the price, special features, …

Do a survey of media use

GET READY

You're going to do a group survey about your media use.

- Look at your media diary and tell your group about some of your media activities.
- Look at your sleep diary and tell your group how long you usually slept each night.
- Are there big differences in your group?

I played online games with my friend Elias for about two hours a day after school. I also watched a series on a streaming service at the weekend for two hours in the evening. I used social media on my phone for about an hour a day, at different times. And I read the news for half an hour every day.

GO AHEAD

Make a shared document online with the tables from the media and sleep diaries. Each group should put their results into the document.

- Make different charts for the results. You can use pie charts and bar charts.
- Each group should prepare at least one diagram. Decide which group will make a chart or diagram about:
  - social media
  - watching series or films
  - gaming
  - listening to the radio or music
  - messaging or talking online
  - reading news websites

SF 19 → p. 141

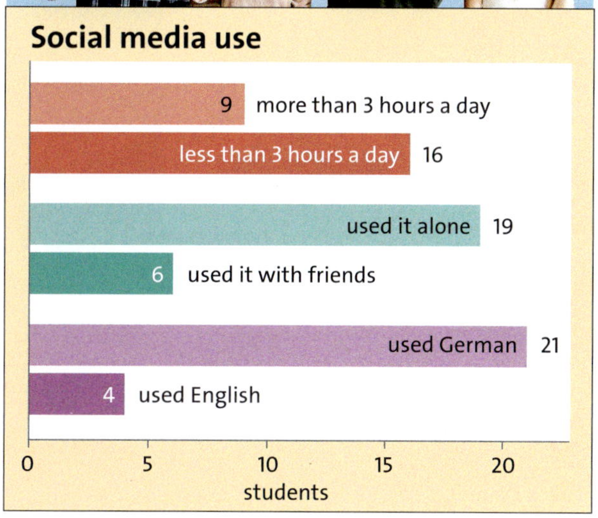

FINISH

Each group should present their chart or diagram to the class. Discuss the results and give your reactions.

- Do you think your class spends too much time on media?
- Do students in your class sleep enough?

Watching series or films is the activity that most students do at weekends.

I was surprised how many students spend two or three hours on social media every day. A lot of students listen to music a lot when they are doing their homework and I do that too.

Most students don't get enough sleep. Some students only sleep six hours per night.

Unit 4

Indian images

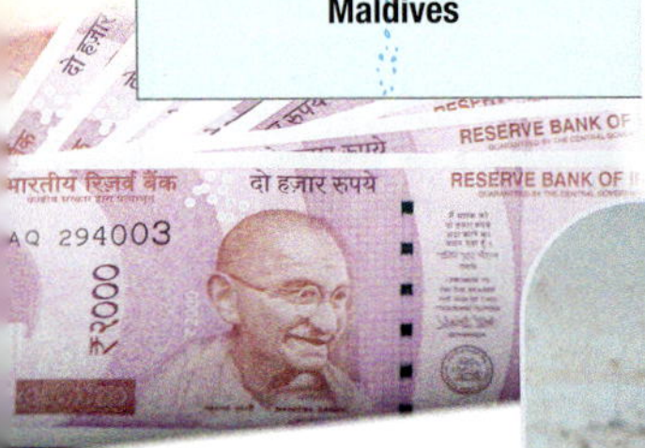

In this unit you will

- explain and discuss social issues in India.
- discuss how Indian films are made.
- give your opinion in a discussion and in an email.
- recognize facts and opinions in texts.

➔ At the end of the unit you'll make a podcast about an aspect of India.

1 A country of contrasts

1.18

a Look at the pictures and listen to a podcast about India. Put the pictures in the right order: *A, ...* Then compare.

b Read the fact file together and complete any information that you can. Then listen again. Partner A listens for the information for the purple numbers, Partner B for the blue numbers. Compare.

Capital: New Delhi with (1) ... million people
Currency: the Indian rupee
Population: (2) ... billion – second biggest after China. More than half the population is under (3) ... years old.
Main religions: Hinduism (Hindus) and (4) ... (Muslims). You will see cows nearly everywhere as they are sacred to Hindus.
Under British rule for nearly (5) ... years.
Independence: in (6) ...; the first (7) ... was Jawaharlal Nehru.
Equality: a lot of (8) ... and inequality between the regions, but (9) ... million people lifted out of poverty in the last ten years.
Increase in middle class: people who can spend (10) ... dollars a day.
Languages: official languages are Hindi and (11) ..., twenty-two recognized regional languages and (12) ... other languages.
Literacy: 82% of men, (13) ...% of women (regional differences)
Festivals: The most famous Hindu festivals are Diwali, the festival of (14) ... and Holi, the festival of (15) .... Eid al-Fitr is the most important Muslim festival, celebrating the end of Ramadan.
The most popular sport: (16) ...

2 Experience India

a Choose one photo and put yourself in that picture.

1. Who/What are you? Where are you?
2. What can you see/hear/smell around you?
3. What are you doing? How are you feeling?

More ideas → p. 85

b Tell your partner who listens and asks questions.

3 VIEWING Transport in New Delhi

a Watch a video clip about two forms of transport in New Delhi. Take notes on what you find interesting.

b Swap information and decide on the one thing you found most interesting.

➔ I can understand basic information about India. ✓

WB 1, p. 43

Four profiles

1 Four people

a Look at the four photos. What can you say about each person? Exchange ideas.

b Work in groups of four. Each student should scan one of the profiles to find this information:

1 what their background is (family, caste, religion)
2 what their job is
3 what problems or support they have had

c Exchange information about the four people in your group.

ACROSS CULTURES

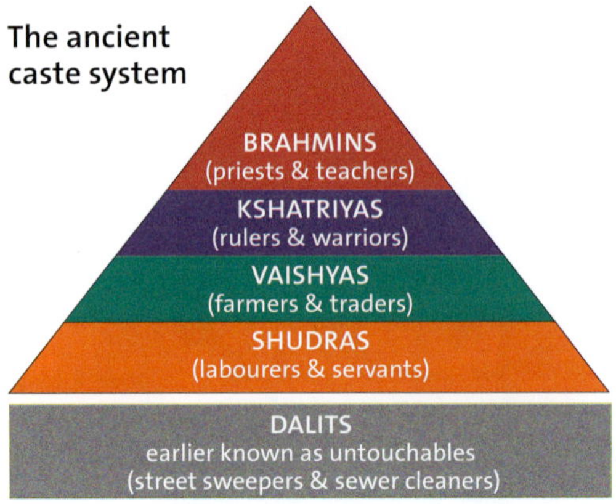

Discrimination because of caste is banned in the Indian constitution (1950), but there is still injustice and violence towards lower castes.
Would you say there is inequality and discrimination in Germany – for example, in the education system or in working life? Who experiences this and why do people experience this?

1.19

A *The street cleaner*

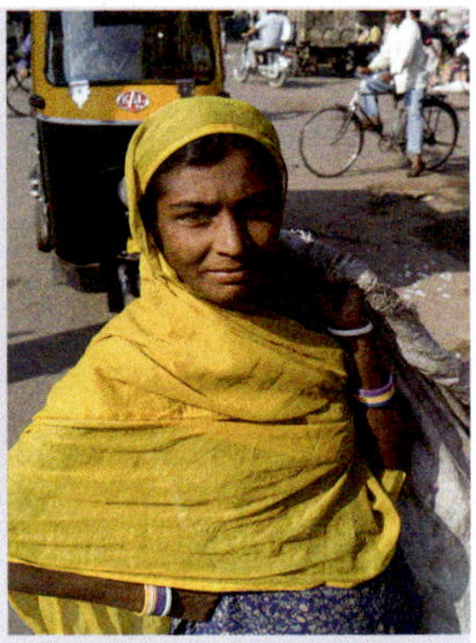

Kiruba Bhatt comes from a family of Dalits. She can write her name and recognize a few words of Hindi, but she is basically illiterate. Six days a week, she sweeps the streets and picks up rubbish. It is a hard and dirty job. In the past, caste was decided by birth and it was difficult to move from one caste to another. Caste had an effect on nearly all aspects of life and marriages between castes were not allowed. Outside the system were the 'untouchables', the Dalits, who did jobs connected to waste and animals. These jobs were usually given from one generation to the next. Dalits were avoided by other castes: they were not allowed to enter temples or to take water from the village well. In some villages this has not changed.
After independence, the government used quotas to increase the number of people from lower castes in government jobs to about 50% today. Kiruba earns a good salary of 150 rupees an hour (about 4 euros).

1.20

B *The scientist*

Ashok Kumar is a biochemist with an Indian pharmaceutical company in Hyderabad in the south of India. Hyderabad is a centre for pharmaceuticals and biotechnology and home to many Indian multinational companies. Ashok comes from a poor family in what was in the past a low caste. He got into a top college because of a government programme. Without positive discrimination programmes, it's very difficult for poor students to get into college. Ashok is lucky – only 3% of the working population has professional training and there is high unemployment among young people. Ashok says he has never experienced discrimination, and in cities caste is not usually an issue. Working with people from different backgrounds means that friendships with people from different castes are the norm.

1.21

C

The technology CEO

Parvati Gupta is the CEO of a small software company. She comes from a middle-class family. Parvati began as a programmer and worked her way up to the top position. Parvati is not alone as CEO of a technology company: almost all the technology multinationals in India have female bosses and many Indian companies too. In India, women employees are in the majority in the technology industry – more than in Silicon Valley.
The technology industry in India offers excellent IT services and many well-trained Indians who went to work in the US technology industry are now coming back. American software developers are also coming to work in India because there are often more chances to get ahead, especially for women.

1.22

D

The trader

Haarun Ali is a trader in the Muslim bazaar of Old Delhi. He has a small stall which he took over from his father where he sells jewellery. He enjoys talking to customers. When he isn't busy, he is able to drink chai and chat with the other Muslim stallholders.
In India there is no state religion, but Hindus are in the majority. Last year one of Haarun's fellow Muslim traders was attacked and beaten with sticks by a group of young Hindu men while others watched and filmed the attack on their phones. It shocked Haarun who has many Hindu friends and friends from other religions too. Although religion can be a sensitive issue, religious conflict and hate crimes like this do not happen very often.

2 Education and jobs

Skim the profiles and match them with statements 1–7. Write the correct letter of the profile (A–D). Each profile can be chosen more than once. The first one has been done for you.

What we learn from these four profiles of Indian young people is that ...

1 a government education programme has helped many low caste young people. *B*
2 occasionally there is violence between religious groups.
3 there are not enough jobs for young people in India.
4 half of government jobs go to people from lower castes.
5 more women than men work in IT in India.
6 caste is not important among friends.
7 American employees find India offers better job opportunities.

3 WORDS Literacy, work and marriage

Form a word from the same word family using the word in capitals.

1	Like many lower caste Indian villagers, Kiruba Bhatt is ...	LITERACY
2	But there is a big ... in literacy rates between states.	DIFFERENT
3	Dalits were ... avoided by other castes.	COMPLETE
4	Positive discrimination is ... for students from poor families.	HELP
5	The ... rate for Indian women in paid jobs is 31.2%.	EMPLOY
6	Hate crimes may be because of ... differences.	RELIGION
7	These crimes only happen ...	OCCASION

➔ I can understand and discuss social issues in India. ✔

WB 1, p. 44

Indian cinema

ACROSS CULTURES

The city of Mumbai is home to the popular Hindi-language film industry. The industry is often called 'Bollywood', which is a blend of 'Hollywood' and 'Bombay' (the official name of the city until 1995). Mumbai is India's largest city with a population of about twenty million.

1 Bollywood facts

Read the facts. If you've watched a Bollywood film, explain what it was like.

* Bollywood films are filled with colourful song and dance performances and there is usually a happy ending.
* The songs aren't sung by the dancers: they're recorded by professional singers and lip-synced by the dancers.
* A break is included because films are at least three hours long.
* The first Indian film was made over 100 years ago.
* In the first films women's roles weren't played by women, they were played by male actors.
* About a thousand films are made every year (more than in Hollywood) and in ten different languages.
* Bollywood films are watched by almost 14 million people in India every day – and by many more in other countries.
* Traditional films were usually based on family and romantic dramas. A trend for action films was started in the 1970s.

LOOK AT LANGUAGE: passives 1 (revision: simple present and simple past)

Remember: We use the passive when what happens is important and not who does the action. Complete the explanations.

For the simple present passive, we use am/are/ ... + past participle.
For the simple past passive, we use ... / ... + past participle.
If we want to say who did the action, we use the word ... LF 7 → p. 121

2 A popular Hindi film

a Complete the description. Use the passive (simple present or simple past).

The film *Lagaan* is an Indian film which (1 make) ... in 2001. The film (2 set) ... in an Indian village when India was under British rule. It (3 film) ... in a village in Gujarat on the west coast of India. Aamir Khan and Gracy Singh (4 choose) ... as the main characters.
In the film, the people in the village (5 make) ... to pay high taxes by the British. A British officer says if his team (6 beat) ... in a match of cricket by the villagers, the villagers needn't pay taxes for three years.

Gracy Singh

b Write a short description of your favourite film for a page on the school website. Answer as many questions as you can.

When was it made? Where and when is the film set? Where was it filmed? Which actors were chosen as the main characters? What main events are shown in the film?

Fast finishers 10 → p. 90

3 Why will it be remembered?

Read about why *Lagaan* will be remembered. Why will your favourite film from 2b be remembered?

Lagaan **can be seen** as an excellent example of Hindi cinema. It **has been watched** by millions of people in India and abroad, and the film and the actors **have been given** fantastic reviews. The actors were extremely happy when they found out that the film **had been nominated** for the Academy Award for best foreign language film, although it didn't win. *Lagaan* was number fourteen on a list of fifty films that **must be watched** before you die. The film **shouldn't be forgotten**. In the future, it **will be remembered** for its wonderful story and its popular soundtrack.

LOOK AT LANGUAGE: passives 2 (present perfect, past perfect, *will*-future, modals)

Look at the forms in bold in 3 and complete the explanations for other tenses and modals in the passive.

Present perfect passive:
… / … + *been* + past participle
Past perfect passive:
… + *been* + past participle
Future passive with *will*:
will + … + past participle
Passive with modals:
can / must / should + …
+ past participle LF 7 → p. 121

4 Aamir Khan

Complete the profile of Aamir Khan with the correct form of the passive.

Aamir Khan (1 can / see) … in many popular Hindi films. He became a child actor because he (2 offer) … a role in a film by his uncle who was a director. Since he started acting, his films (3 very much / appreciate) … by cinema fans. He is also a director and producer: *Lagaan* and the film *Dangal* (4 produce) … by him. He (5 very much / respect) … now for his work to reduce poverty. Khan (6 will / see) … in several films in the near future.

5 Behind the scenes

As in Hollywood, Indian actors have a lot of help to look good for their films. Match the sentences with the correct past participles.

1	Actors have their hair	a	put on.
2	They have special costumes	b	massaged.
3	They have their makeup	c	made.
4	They have their nails	d	styled.
5	They have their backs	e	manicured.
6	They have their pets	f	walked.

When we don't do something ourselves, but somebody else does it for us, we say we ***have something done.***

For example: *I have my hair cut (by the hairdresser) every two months.*

Compare: *I cut my hair.* (= I do it myself.)

6 NOW YOU

a **Partner B: Look at p. 80. Partner A: Make questions with *Have you … recently?***

1 hair / cut?
Have you had your hair cut recently?
2 nails / do?
3 teeth / look at?
4 eyes / check?

b **Ask Partner B your questions. Then answer his or her questions.**

Yes, I have. I had … last week / two weeks ago. / No, I haven't. I haven't had … recently.

Ask and answer two more questions.

Wordbank 5 → p. 95 TF 10 → p. 110f.

→ I can talk about Indian films. ✔

Taking part in a discussion

1 A holy river

a Read the information about the Ganges. Discuss ideas about what could be done.

For Hindus, the Ganges is a holy river. The waters are said to wash away sins. Pilgrims come from near and far to bathe in it. The problem is that the river is so polluted that it is dangerous. Many industries along the river produce different goods, such as leather, cloth, cars, paper and more. Dangerous chemicals from factories, farms, plus sewage from cities are pumped into the river. Bodies are cremated on the steps at the river's edge and thrown into the river because in the Hindu religion, this is very important.

b 1.23 Listen to a discussion by a group of students. What is their conclusion? Write one sentence. More ideas → p. 86

2 Discussion phrases

1.23 a Listen again and complete the phrases from the discussion.

1 The Ganges is ... to be the sixth most polluted river in the world.
2 In my ..., the worst problem is the sewage.
3 Sorry to ... you, but (...)
4 The ... is that (...)
5 Can I just ... what I was going to say?
6 I strongly ...
7 By the ..., this goes for (...)
8 I ... think (...) – So ... I.
9 I totally ... with you.
10 Yes, you're ...
11 Just let me ... one more thing.
12 In my ...
13 I ... think that's a good idea. – Neither ... I.
14 That's ...

We use *So do I* to say we also do something that somebody else does.
I like her arguments. – So do I.
We use *Neither do I / Nor do I* to say we also don't do something that somebody else doesn't do.
I don't agree with him. – Neither do I.
Nor is more formal than *neither*. LF 8 → p. 122

b Put the phrases from 2a in the table. Then compare. Add other phrases if you can.

1 describe an issue	2 give your opinion	3 agree	4 disagree	5 interrupt	6 keep talking
...	...	...	...	...	...

c Talk about the issues in the discussion. Say if you agree or disagree with the students. Which of your ideas from 1 did they mention? SF 12 → p. 135

3 In the hot seat

a Think about a polluted place in your area. It can be a place with water pollution, air pollution or problems with rubbish. Prepare arguments about the issue and what can be done.
More ideas → p. 86

b Take turns to sit in the hot seat. Describe your issue and give your opinion. Other students agree and disagree and politely interrupt. If they interrupt, say you would like to keep talking. Use the phrases in 2b. Fast finishers 11 → p. 90

→ I can take part in a discussion. ✔

An email with personal opinions

1 An email to you

Read the email from an Indian friend. According to Sandhya, why are arranged marriages successful? Find four reasons.

2 Opinions

When you write an informal email, you can use the same phrases to give opinions, agree and disagree as when you speak (see p. 64). Find the six phrases that Sandhya uses to do this.

3 WORDS False friends

a Sandhya uses some words that may be confusing for Germans. They look like German words but have a different meaning.
Choose the correct meanings for 1–4.

1 actually (line 7): *in fact / currently*
2 college (line 18): *a colleague / university*
3 eventually (line 27): *possibly / finally*
4 sensible (line 29): *logical / sensitive*

b Copy and complete the table with the correct meanings.

English	German	false friend	English
actually	....	*aktuell*	...
college	...	*Kollege*	...
eventually	...	*eventuell*	...
sensible	...	*sensibel*	...

c Add more false friends to your table in b.

4 Your email

Write a reply to Sandhya. Use the same phrases as Sandhya to start and finish your email. Say whether you agree or disagree with her. Give your opinion (use phrases from 2) and support it with two facts or ideas.

SF 12 → p. 135

ACROSS CULTURES

Arranged marriages are organized by parents or other family members and sometimes by professional matchmakers. They are not forced marriages and they are not marriages at a very young age. 74% of people in India say they prefer arranged marriages.

new message ×

Hi!
How are things? I hope you're OK.
Thank you for your email. You said you thought arranged marriages in India sound really old-fashioned. I agree that it might sound like that, but I don't think it's true.
Actually, a lot of young people are happy to have their marriage arranged. It means you don't have to worry about dating! In my opinion, the most important thing is that you have something in common with the person you marry. In India, if we find somebody we like, we can have an arranged marriage with that person. If not, our parents find somebody who suits us. They look for a good family, make sure the horoscopes match (the position of the stars at the time and place of your birth) and also look at personality and education (whether you went to college or not). Computers do a lot of the matching now.
The bride and groom meet each other with their families and then alone, and decide if they like each other. They can say no. It's also important that the two families like each other. I believe it's a good system.
Do you know that in India the divorce rate is under 2%? Neither did I, but I looked it up. In Germany it's about 35%. Eventually, a lot of love matches don't last. In my view, that means that arranged marriages are more sensible than love marriages!
Do you agree?
Write soon and let me know what you think!
Best wishes
Sandhya

➔ I can explain my opinions in an email. ✔

Lion

Saroo Brierley who was adopted by an Australian family at the age of 5, was born in India. As a small child he lived with his mother, his two big brothers Guddu and Kallu and his baby sister Shekila in a room in a poor neighbourhood ('Ginestlay') of the town of Khandwa. Saroo remembers feeling hungry most of the time and stealing or begging for food. His mother worked on building sites carrying rocks on her head six days a week, from morning until evening. The children were looked after by neighbours or looked after each other. Saroo stayed at home with Shekila or played in the streets. In his book Saroo writes that 'Harsh as all this sounds, I think we were reasonably happy.'

1 An Indian family

Read about Saroo Brierley's life as a small child in India. What do you remember of your life when you were five or younger? What does Saroo remember?

2 Lost

Read about how Saroo got lost. How did he end up a long way from his home town?

Saroo Brierley near his home in Hobart, Australia, May 2012

Guddu and Kallu were about fourteen and twelve, and spending very little time at home. I didn't see them more than two or three times a week. They were mostly searching the streets for whatever they could find to live on and sleeping nights in railway stations, where they sometimes earned food or money for sweeping. Most of the time they stayed at another town a few stops down the train line, about an hour away. They told me Ginestlay was no good, so they went to a place called something like 'Berampur' – I couldn't quite remember its name – where it was easier to find money and food. And they had started making friends there, all of them getting around by jumping on and off trains.

When I was about four or five, occasionally my brothers took me with them. If a conductor ever asked for a ticket, we got off and then got on the next train. We used to pass through a couple of very small stations – just platforms in the middle of nowhere – before arriving at the Berampur station on the edge of town. My brothers only let me go to the station as I might get lost. So I used to hang around the platforms while they worked. Instead of food we had a lot of freedom, and we liked it.

One night, when I was five years old, I was at home. I was tired from a day playing out in the streets, but excited that tonight almost the whole family was together for dinner. My mother was home from work and Guddu had come back to see us. Kallu was the only one missing.

That evening, Guddu stayed for about an hour, as the four of us ate together. He hadn't been home for some time and I missed hanging out with him and Kallu as a gang. I'd begun to feel I wasn't a little boy any more, to be left at home while they were out in the world.

When our mother went out, perhaps to see if she could get us some more food, Guddu said that he was leaving – going back to Berampur. The thought of being left behind, as always, was too much. I jumped up and said, 'I'm coming with you!' It was early evening – if I went with him, he was unlikely to get me back home that night. We'd have to stay together. He thought about it for a moment and then agreed – I was thrilled. We left Shekila sitting on the floor and were gone before my mother returned. She probably wouldn't have been too worried, with me in my brother's care.

Soon I was laughing as we sped through the night, Guddu carrying me on a bike he had hired through the quiet streets to the train station. What could be better? I was going off with Guddu without a plan for when we were coming home or where we might sleep. I didn't know how long he would let me stay with him, but I didn't care.

I still clearly remember the ride. I sat on the bar just behind the bike's handlebars with my feet resting on each side of the front wheel. It was a bumpy trip, but I didn't mind at all. [...]

Then Guddu said we'd walk the rest of the way, so I jumped off and he pushed the bike along the main street to the station, past the busy chai sellers.

When we were near the station entrance, Guddu hid the bike behind some thick bushes and we went to wait for the next train.

By the time the train arrived and we had jumped on, I was already becoming sleepy. We got as comfortable as we could on the hard wooden seats. I rested my head on Guddu's shoulder. It was getting late, and we'd be on the train for about an hour. [...]

By the time we got off at Berampur, I was so exhausted I lay down on a wooden bench on the platform. Guddu said there were a few things he needed to do. 'Just don't move. I'll come back in a little while and we can find somewhere to sleep the night.' He was probably going to try and find some food, or hunt for coins. I lay down, shut my eyes and must have fallen asleep straightaway.

When I woke up, the station was empty. I looked around for Guddu, but couldn't see him anywhere. There was a train at the platform where we'd got off, with its carriage door open, but I didn't know if it was the same one, or how long I'd been asleep.

I've often wondered exactly what I thought right then. I was still half-asleep and nervous at finding myself alone at night. Guddu said he wasn't going far – maybe he'd got back on the train? I climbed the stairs to have a look. I remember seeing some people asleep, and going back down in case they woke up and called a conductor. Guddu had said I should stay where I was, but he was probably in a different carriage, working, sweeping under the seats. What if I fell asleep on the dark platform again and the train left and I was alone?

I looked into a different carriage and found no one, but the empty wooden seats were more comfortable and felt safer than the quiet station. In a few moments, I was sleeping peacefully again.

When I woke up, it was daylight and the full sun was shining into my eyes. And the train was moving.

I jumped up. There was still no one in my carriage, and the landscape outside the windows was going past quickly. My brother was nowhere to be seen.

The low-class carriages weren't connected to each other with doors. Travellers boarded and left their carriage from doors at each end. I tried the doors at one end – they were both locked. I ran down the other end – the doors there were locked too.

I can still feel the panic that hit me when I realized I was trapped. I don't remember what I did in that moment – screamed, hit the windows, cried, cursed. I couldn't read any of the signs in the carriage, which might have told me where I was travelling.

I looked under all the benches, in case someone else was asleep somewhere. There was only me. But I kept running up and down, shouting out my brother's name, begging him to come and get me. I called for my mother, and my brother Kallu too. But no one answered and the train didn't stop. ◇

3 Who did what in the story?

Which person or people in the story ...

1 ate together on the night of Saroo's journey?
2 left home after the meal to get more food?
3 went to the local station on a bike?
4 was left alone at home?
5 got on a train to 'Berampur'?
6 felt really sleepy before getting on the first train?
7 went to find money or food at 'Berampur'?
8 lay down on a bench at 'Berampur' and fell asleep?
9 had disappeared from the station?
10 got on another train?
11 did Saroo call for when he was lost on the train?

Fast finishers 12 → p. 90

4 The long journey

a Saroo's journey ended in Kolkata. Look at the map. How far did he travel?

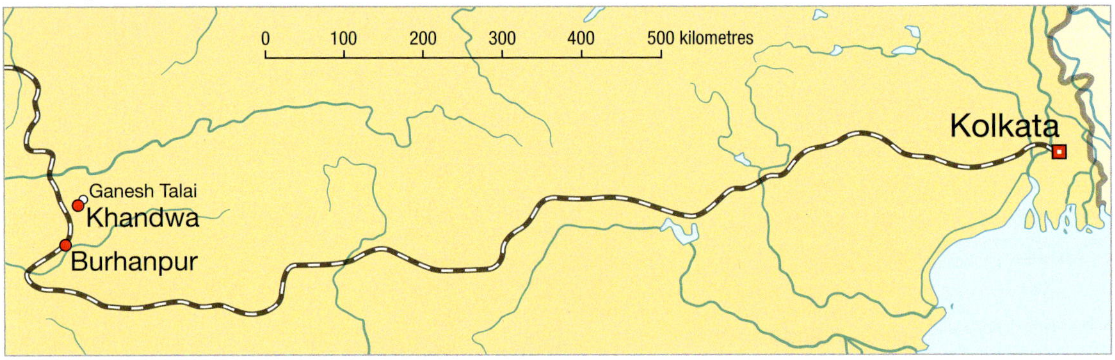

b Saroo lived on the streets of Kolkata before he was put in an orphanage. He told the staff there about his journey and that his family lived in 'Ginestlay'. Look at the map and paragraph 1 of the story. Why couldn't the staff find where Saroo came from?

c Discuss the questions.

1 Can you imagine doing a journey like this alone? How would you feel?
2 What is the longest journey you have been on? Where did you travel and how?
3 Where would you like to travel if you could travel anywhere? Why?

5 WORDS Word webs

a Copy the three word webs and put these words from the story in the correct web. SF 13 → p. 136

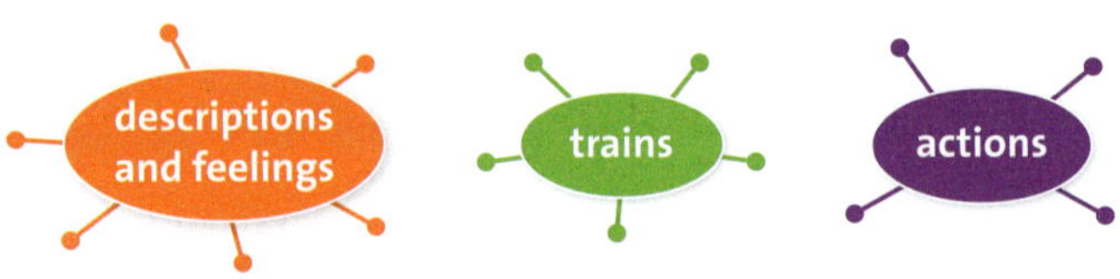

(to) board • bumpy • carriage • conductor • (to) curse • exhausted • harsh • (to) keep on • railway • reasonable • (to) rest • sleepy • stairs • thrilled • (to) wonder

b Take turns to explain what the words mean.

6 Going back home

Read how Saroo found his way back home from Australia and what happened. TF 11 → p. 112f.

I can understand and discuss a story. ✔

A day in Amar's life

Amar is 14 and loves cricket. He's a clever student and top of his class. But he has to earn money to help feed his family. He works two jobs six and a half days a week and goes to school in the afternoon.

1 Amar's jobs

Read the information about Amar and look at the video stills. What do you think his two jobs are?

2 VIEWING The first part of the morning

a Watch the first part of the video until Amar goes home for breakfast (until 3.06). What do you hear (music, conversations, voice-over, ...)? Take notes.

b Use your notes to talk about how sound is used in the film. What effect did this have on you? Discuss with the class. SF 2 → p. 126

3 The next part of the morning

a Sit back to back so Partner B can't see the screen.
Partner A: Tell your partner what happens when Amar comes home and when he goes to his next job (3.06–5.04): *Amar comes into his house. Then he ...*
Partner B: Listen.

b Watch this part of the film together.
Partner B: Did your partner describe this part well?

4 The afternoon

a Sit back to back so Partner A can't see the screen.
Partner B: Tell your partner what happens when Amar comes home at lunchtime and when he goes to school (5.04–8.00): *Amar comes home. First he ...*
Partner A: Listen.

b Watch this part of the film together.
Partner A: Did your partner describe this part well?

5 The end of Amar's day

a Watch the last part and answer the questions.

1 What time does Amar get home from work?
2 What does Amar do when he gets home?
3 What time do you think he goes to sleep?

b Discuss with your partner.

1 Describe Amar's family and his family life.
2 Describe your impressions of Amar.
3 Compare your daily life with Amar's.
4 Imagine your life was like Amar's. How would you feel? Give details and explain why.

Fast finishers 13 → p. 90

I can describe what happens in a film. ✔

The Golden Triangle

1 A trip to India

Your grandparents would like to go on a trip to India. Sandhya's family has sent you some information about a guided tour and also about the monsoon season. Read the information and then answer your grandparents' questions.

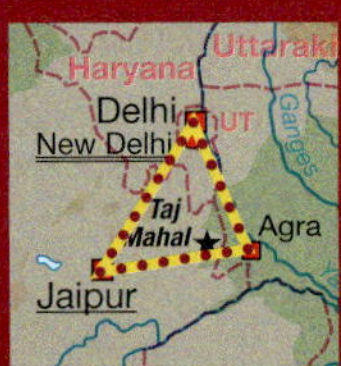

Welcome to India. This 7-day Golden Triangle tour is perfect for first-time visitors. Experience the amazing architecture and the rich culture of the beautiful cities of Delhi, Agra and Jaipur.

DAY 1 Our tour starts in the wonderful city of **Delhi** where you will be met on arrival and taken to your hotel. Later enjoy a fabulous Indian meal at a local restaurant.

DAY 2 Your tour guide will show you the highlights of Delhi such as the landmark Qutb Minar minaret from the twelfth century.

DAY 3 Travel by car to **Jaipur**. Visit the beautiful Hawa Mahal (the Palace of the Winds) and see the luxurious rooms of the City Palace.

DAY 4 Take a hot air balloon over Jaipur at sunrise and see the Pink City from the air – all its buildings were painted pink to impress Prince Albert who visited the city in 1876.

DAY 5 Travel to **Agra** and visit the beautiful Taj Mahal, the world-famous white monument which was built by Shah Jahan in the 1640s as a memorial to his wife Mumtaz who died after giving birth to their fourteenth child. She is buried there and so is he.

DAY 6 Travel back to Delhi. Take a rickshaw ride through the old town and visit the Chandni Chowk market where you can buy souvenirs such as colourful decorations.

DAY 7 Enjoy free time before you are taken to the airport in a private car. Relax by the hotel pool or do some last-minute shopping.

1 Was heißt eigentlich ‚landmark'?
2 Man kann also Jaipur von einem Heißluftballon aus sehen, richtig? Warum steht da etwas mit ‚pink'?
3 Den Tadsch Mahal kennen wir natürlich. Was steht denn darüber in der Broschüre?
4 Findet auf diesem Bild mit den bunten Dekorationen ein Fest statt?
5 Welche Aktivitäten sind für den letzten Tag vorgesehen?
6 Was steht in dieser Infografik über den Monsun? Ist er gefährlich?
7 Worauf beziehen sich die 75%?
8 Wann sollten wir diese Reise am besten unternehmen?

 WB 1, p. 51

➔ I can answer questions in German about a tour. ✔

Evaluating sources

You are doing some research about tea and have found texts 1–4. Read the texts and complete the table.

text	heading	text type	language examples	neutral or not?
1				
2				
3				
4				

- When you do research on the internet, choose reliable sites like well-known media sites, government sites (.gov) and organizations (.org).
- Check for fake sites: check site reviews on the internet.
- Check for fake news or wrong information: use different sites and check the facts. SF 21 → p. 143

1 Headings

Choose a heading for each text (two are extra).

a Is tea good for you?
b The negative effects of tea
c Helping to protect human rights on tea plantations
d The terrible lives of Indian tea workers
e What is the price of tea?
f Tea production and drinking habits

2 Text types

Match each text to a text type (a–g). There are three extra types.

a an advert
b an encyclopedia entry
c a news item
d information on a medical website
e instructions
f a private blog entry
g a report

1

Half of the workers on tea plantations live below the poverty line. A majority have no decent health care and are usually not able to get an education for their children. Women often do the hardest jobs.
Our research shows that the price of tea is too low and that plantation workers do not receive a fair share of the sale price. So that workers can be paid a decent wage, the price of tea must be raised.

2

More tea is produced in India than in any other country except China. India is the biggest tea-drinking country in the world with 90% of all Indian households drinking tea. The most popular way to drink tea is with spices, milk and sugar (masala tea). Darjeeling tea is drunk without sugar or milk. Butter tea, made with yak butter, is popular in areas of north-east India.

3

Tea has many health benefits. Lower in caffeine than coffee, it has been shown to be good for the heart and it is also said to help against cancer. Many people claim herbal teas such as mint help them to relax or reduce blood pressure, but there have been few significant studies in this area.

4

A recent strike in Assam has highlighted the disgusting conditions for tea workers. Tea plantation workers earn a miserable $2 a day. In addition, they often have no access to toilets and are forced to use dangerous chemicals without basic safety equipment. In my view, this is shocking. Child labour is also an issue on many plantations.
Please join me to protest about this!

3 Neutral language?

a Do the texts give a neutral picture of the topic? Or do they use language which gives an opinion? Find examples.

b Compare your ideas. Then decide if the language is neutral or not.

→ I can recognize facts and opinions in texts. ✔

4 YOUR CHECK

You can find the answers for these tasks on page 229.

1 Check your vocabulary

a Complete the sentences about India.

1 In India the money used is r... .
2 Most people are H... and speak H... .
3 C... are sacred animals for the people in 2.
4 The most popular sport is c... .
5 The c... system is still important.
6 Some people are i...: they can neither read nor write.
7 There are not enough jobs and there is a lot of u... among young people.
8 The government introduced p... d... to help people from poor backgrounds.

b Complete the word families.

verb	noun (person)	noun (thing)	adjective
employ	...	...	
		gold	...
marry		...	
...		pollution	
produce	...	...	
		religion	...
share		...	

c What can you have done at these places? *You can have ...*

1 a hairdresser's
2 a car wash
3 a dentist's
4 a sushi takeaway
5 a photography studio
6 mobile phone shop

2 Check your language

Complete the speeches with a passive form of the verbs in the box.

choose • describe • film • give • learn • sing • tell • write

The director:
As you know, the script (1) ... by writer Sanjay Chopra and the movie will (2) ... in Mumbai. Some information about the film has already (3) ... to the media. Your lines must (4) ... by next week.

The actor:
I've (5) ... as the main actor. I (6) ... about the film last year. The songs need to (7) ... by me. The film (8) ... as a winner.

3 Check your speaking

Take it in turns to give an opinion about these topics. Your partner agrees or disagrees and gives a reason.

I think ... is/are better than ...
I prefer ... to ...

1 musicals or action films?
2 festivals or sports?
3 meat or vegetables?
4 Indian food or German food?
5 train or plane journeys?
6 tea or coffee?

So do I / Neither do I because ...

4 Check your writing

You're on a Golden Triangle tour in India with your family. Write a message to a friend and tell him or her about your first impressions, the people, your favourite place and why you liked it.

Make a group podcast on an aspect of India

GET READY

You are going to make a group podcast about an aspect of India. In your group, choose one of these topics or another topic you are interested in.

- air pollution
- Indian food
- music
- slums and palaces
- tourism
- wildlife conservation
- women's rights
- yoga
- ...

I think we should do something on Indian food. I'd like to know what dishes are eaten for different meals and in different areas. How many Hindus are vegetarians? I know Hindus don't eat beef, but do they eat other meat? I don't know.

Neither do I, but I think it's a great topic.

- Each person in the group should look for information on your group's topic. Make sure that your information is from a reliable source. (see p. 71). SF 21 → p. 143

GO AHEAD

Share your information with the rest of the group.

- Decide who is going to:
  ... write a good introduction for the podcast which presents the topic.
  ... write the parts of the podcast which present information, advantages and disadvantages or different aspects of the topic.
  ... write the ending of the podcast.
- Decide if you want to add music and if you do, what kind.
  SF 20 → p. 142

FINISH

Each group should record their podcast.

- Check your language and pronunciation and that you speak in an interesting way.
- Present your podcast to the class. Other groups listen and think of questions.
- Give positive feedback first and then add what they can do better. SF 17 → p. 138

I've tried Indian food before in Germany, but I didn't really know much about it. I thought this podcast was good because I learned something new and it has inspired me to try and cook Indian food.

I was totally shocked by the women's rights podcast and the terrible violence that some women in India experience. I think this podcast was presented in a very clear way.

1 LISTENING India's tech industry

1.24

Listen to the interview and take notes in your exercise book to complete the sentences.

1 In the past India used to provide ...
2 Now Indian technology companies develop ...
3 This has been possible because of the increase ...
4 Many young people are leaving their homes ...
5 Bengaluru has ...
6 Two things which the tech industry in India needs are ...

2 SPEAKING Two photos

a Partner A: Describe photo 1 to Partner B. Partner B: Describe photo 2 to Partner A.

b Partner A and Partner B: Talk together about your photos. Compare and contrast the situations. First, compare the general situation. Then focus on the details that show differences or similar points.

In the background/foreground of the picture ...
On the right/left ...
The people in the picture look/seem ...
Perhaps/Maybe ...
This photo suggests that ...
In both pictures ...
In contrast with ...

c Now talk together about free time. Discuss what you and your friends do and what other people in your class or your family do.

I usually/often ...
I'm used to ...
I used to ..., but now ...

d Say what you think is important about free time and give reasons.

I think it's important that ...
This is because ...
In my opinion/view, ...

3 USE OF ENGLISH **Media use**

Complete the sentences. Use the word in capitals at the end of each line to form a word from the same family.

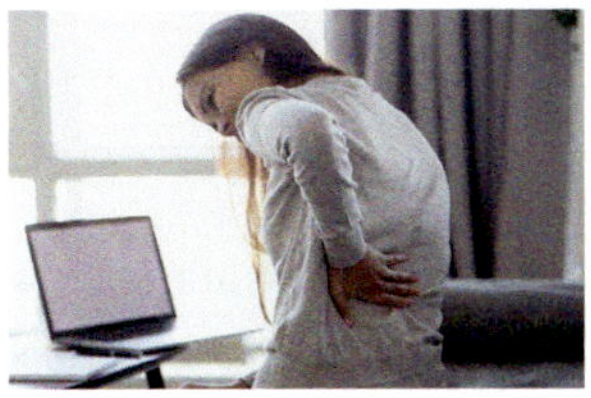

The pressure to build up an online (1) ... can cause teenagers great stress.	FOLLOW
But the use of media is also (2) ... for the body.	HEALTH
Using a computer or phone too long can (3) ... to problems with the back.	LEADER
Studies have also shown that teenager's eye problems have increased (4) ...	HUGE
I'd like to make everybody aware of the (5) ... of these problems.	EXIST
I would (6) ... everybody to spend less time on their screens.	ADVICE

4 VOCABULARY **Phrasal verbs**

a **Match the verbs in the first box with the correct words in the second box to make phrasal verbs. You need to use some words in the second box more than once. For three verbs, more than one combination is possible.**

check • give • hack • log • pop • scroll • set • shut • speak • switch

down • into • off • out • up

b **An English friend is explaining to her grandad how to order food online. Complete the conversation with the correct phrasal verbs from a. For sentence 7, there are two possible answers – write both.**

1 First you need to ... an account.
2 Then ... your new account.
3 Don't worry when adverts ...
4 You can ... the list of food here.
5 To see more things, ... here.
6 Put things in your basket and pay, and then remember to ...
7 Don't forget to ... your computer.

And that's it!

5 MEDIATION **An Indian recipe**

Look at the ingredients and the instructions. Your friend wants to make the recipe, but his English isn't very good. Tell him what he needs to make the recipe and how to make it.

Red lentil dal

Ingredients
vegetable oil
1 onion

2 cloves of garlic

1–2 green chillies
400g red lentils
3 tomatoes

Spices
2 teaspoons cumin[1]
1 teaspoon coriander
1 teaspoon garam masala (typical Indian curry powder)
2 teaspoons turmeric[2]

Instructions:
1 Put the red lentils in a pan with 700 ml water.
2 When the water has boiled, turn it down. Cover the pan and let the lentils cook for 20 minutes.
3 Add the turmeric to the lentils.
4 Chop the onion, garlic, chillies and tomatoes. Fry them in the oil in a frying pan.
5 Add the cumin, coriander and garam masala to the frying pan.
6 Mix everything from the frying pan with the lentils.
7 Taste and add salt and black pepper.
8 You can eat the dal with rice or with Indian bread.

[1]**cumin** [ˈkjuːmɪn] *Kreuzkümmel* [2]**turmeric** [ˈtɜːmərɪk] *Kurkuma*

Unit 1

4 After the match Unit 1 | p. 19 Ex. 4

Role-play a conversation between Nic and his dad after the match.
Partner B: You're Nic. Partner A is your dad – he starts the conversation.

- Say your dad doesn't need to say congratulations – you lost the match.
- Ask why.
- React to what your father says.
- Answer the question.
- Explain what happened at the fence in your garden.
- React to your dad's suggestion.

Unit 2

5 Two jobs abroad Unit 2 | p. 27 Ex. 5

Partner A:

a **Read this job advert. Then tell Partner B about the job – answer his or her questions.**
Start like this:
I've seen a really cool job in the UK.

b **Now ask Partner B about a volunteer job he or she has found.**
Find out:
- what the job is
- where it is
- what you have to do
- what the working conditions are like
- if your partner would like to do this job and why or why not

The Donkey Charity
Wharfedale, West Yorkshire

Donkey shelter volunteer

We are looking for a young person (16 – 18) to join our team for the summer and help with all aspects of looking after the donkeys.

You are very interested in saving animals from suffering and have experience of working with ponies, horses or donkeys.

This is a part-time volunteer job for 20 hours a week. Food and accommodation included.

Please contact Eleanor Knight using the online form.

3 Your cover letter Unit 2 | p.31 Ex.3

Partner A:

a You're looking for a job in your town where you can speak English. Look at the job advert and write a cover letter in English for the job. Use the tips and Molly's letter on page 31 to help you.

b CHECK Swap letters with your partner and give your partner feedback: Say if it is a good letter for the job – if not, make suggestions. SF 17 → p. 138
Make any language corrections that are necessary.

SpicyBurger

Part-time service worker

Our international team requires a young service worker (16/17) who can stay calm under pressure and who is patient and friendly with customers. You will work at the counter taking orders and also in the kitchen making food.

15 hours a week
€8 an hour

Please send your CV and a cover letter explaining why you would be a great addition to our team to:

Jan Schulz (manager)
jschulz@example.de

4 Your phone call Unit 2 | p.32 Ex.4

Partner A:

a You are the British owner of a local dog-walking company.

- You are looking for a dog walker to take three dogs for a walk two days a week at 3 pm.
- The walk should be about an hour.
- You pay €8 an hour.
- You are interviewing on Saturday all day.

Start the call like this:
Hello, Doggie Walkies, [Your name] speaking.

If you can't hear properly:
The line is very bad.
I'm afraid I can't hear you.
Sorry, I didn't catch that.
Could you speak more loudly please?

If you don't understand:
I'm sorry, I don't understand./
I didn't understand that.
What do you mean?
Could you repeat that, please?

b You're a student who has seen an advert for a job in a cafe. Call the Swedish owner in English and arrange an interview. Your partner starts.

- You can work all day Saturday.
- You speak English and German and for example Arabic/...
- You have no experience working in a cafe, but you have worked in a supermarket.
- You have to go to a family event on Sunday at 11.30 am, but you are available for an interview before then.

5 Two jobs abroad Unit 2 | p. 27 Ex. 5

Partner B:

a Ask Partner A about a volunteer job he or she has found. Find out:

- what the job is
- where it is
- what you have to do
- what the working conditions are like
- if your partner would like to do this job and why or why not

b Read this job advert. Then tell Partner A about the job – answer his or her questions.
Start like this:
I've found a great volunteer job in the USA.

Volunteer performer and community helper

We are a volunteer drama group. We travel around putting on shows and use our profits to help the local community we are staying in.

It helps if you can sing and dance, but if you can't – no problem, everybody is welcome and there are lots of ways to help. You decide how much of your time you can give, but there is a one-month minimum.

Travel and accommodation is included, but you will need to pay for your own food and other expenses.

Contact Edwin Johnson with your CV and cover letter.

The traveling
DRAMA GROUP USA

3 Your cover letter Unit 2 | p. 31 Ex. 3

Partner B:

a You're looking for a job in your town where you can speak English. Look at the job advert and write a cover letter for the job. Use the tips and Molly's letter on page 31 to help you.

b CHECK Swap letters with your partner and give your partner feedback: Say if it is a good letter for the job – if not, make suggestions. SF 17 → p. 138
Make any language corrections that are necessary.

Sorwin Hotel

Part-time lifeguard

We require a lifeguard for our outdoor pool in August when we have many English-speaking guests.

You must be fit and healthy, a good swimmer and have a life-saving certificate.
No experience necessary, but you must speak English.

You will work four hours per day.

We pay 15 euros per hour.

Please send a written application with your CV to Ellen Müller.

3 More adverts Unit 3 | p. 54 Ex. 3

Partner A:

a Look at this advert. Then describe it to Partner B without showing him or her the photo.

b Now listen to Partner B and try and see the advert in your mind. What product do you think the advert is for?

c Show each other your adverts and compare and contrast them. Talk about how effective you think they are and why.

SF 10 → p. 133

Wordbank 4 → p. 94

3 More adverts Unit 3 | p. 54 Ex. 3

Partner B:

a Listen to Partner A and try and see the advert in your mind. What product do you think the advert is for?

b Look at this advert. Then describe it to Partner A without showing him or her the photo.

c Show each other your adverts and compare and contrast them. Talk about how effective you think they are and why.

SF 10 → p. 133

Wordbank 4 → p. 94

Unit 4

6 NOW YOU Unit 4 | p. 63 Ex. 6

Partner B:

a Make questions with Have you ... recently?

1 bedroom / paint?

1 Have you had your bedroom painted recently?

2 takeaway food / deliver?

3 photo / taken?

4 something / repair?

b Answer Partner A's questions.
Then ask Partner A your questions.

Yes, I have. I had ... last week / two weeks ago.
No, I haven't. I haven't had ... recently.

Ask and answer two more questions.

Wordbank 5 → p. 95

Unit 1

2 VIEWING Australian road trip Unit 1 | p. 9 Ex. 2b

b **Watch the video again. Which adjectives go best with your impressions of Australia? Give reasons.**

Australia looks	awesome / beautiful / cool	because	the country is so big / the weather changes a lot / there are long distances to travel / ...
	dangerous		**you can** do a great road trip / go to the beach / go horse riding / go swimming / go surfing / ...
	exciting / inspiring		**there are** fantastic views / lots of different landscapes / not many cars on the road / sharks / skyscrapers / unusual animals / ...
	different / strange		**you can see** colourful fish / the desert / amazing forests / great waterfalls / ...

2 A history of injustice Unit 1 | p. 11 Ex. 2

Read the texts on pages 10–11 carefully.
Complete the mind map about the first Australians using the following questions to help you.

stolen generations: When? Who was taken? Where were they taken? Why?
arrival of Europeans: When? What did they do?
the Dreaming: What is it? What did the ancestor spirits create? What is sacred?
situation today: Population? Indigenous languages? Life expectancy?
national apology: Who apologized? What for? When?
Valerie Linnow: How old? Who took them? How many brothers and sisters? What were they told about their parents?

3 Then and now Unit 1 | p. 11 Ex. 3

3 Think about what you learned last year about native people in the USA and Canada. What is similar and what is different in Australia?
Think about:
The past: what happened when the Europeans arrived / native land / indigenous culture / treatment of native children
Today: indigenous culture and traditions (way of life, food, art, languages) / social problems

> Native Americans also ...
> Like first Australians, ...
> In Australia, Canada and the USA, indigenous people ...

3 Coming of age Unit 1 | p. 13 Ex. 3

a **Indigenous people use body paint for ceremonies when they become adults. What coming of age ceremonies do you know about or have taken part in? You can also talk about other important ceremonies when you were younger.**

I was confirmed.	The ceremony was in a church / ...
I had a bar / bat mitzvah.	I celebrated with ...
I didn't have a ceremony because ...	I had a party. / I wore ...
When I started school ...	During / After the ceremony ...
When I was younger / ... years old, ...	I got sweets / ...

4 NOW YOU Unit 1 | p. 13 Ex. 4

Think about hobbies or activities that you used to do as a child. Tell your partner one thing you used to do, and one thing you didn't use to do in the past, but do now.

When I was a small child, When I was ... years old, Before I started school,	I used to I didn't use to	ride my bike / go swimming / ... go to the park / the zoo / ... go on holiday to ... have violin lessons / dance lessons / ... play with action figures / soldiers/... bake cakes/cook/... eat pizza/takeaway/...	with my mum/dad/ parents with my grand-parents with my best friend	every week. on Saturdays. at weekends. once a month.

2 Cooper's dad finds out Unit 1 | p. 18 Ex. 2b

b What do you think Cooper's dad says to him? Exchange ideas. Choose from these sentences.

Are you crazy?
What were you thinking?
He's here illegally.
We can get into trouble with the police.
We can't help him.
We have to report him.
The poor guy!
Let's decide how we can help him.
He needs our help.
If we call the police, they'll send him to a detention centre.
We have to be careful.
I'm proud of you.
You're good kids.
Have you taught him English?

5 Bashir's point of view Unit 1 | p. 18 Ex. 5b

b You are Bashir. Write a diary entry about how you felt when Cooper's father appeared. Write what you dream of doing in the future.

When Cooper's dad appeared, I ...
... felt afraid/angry/disappointed/happy/ helpless/worried.
... had a feeling of excitement/hope/relief.
... didn't know what to think or feel.

My dream is to ...
live in Australia / make a new life for myself / stay with Cooper's family / finish my education / find a job / ...

Unit 2

3 Tips for going abroad
Unit 2 | p. 27 Ex. 3

Match the phrases to make useful tips.

1 Don't take	A of everything!
2 Make sure	B to every experience!
3 Visit interesting sights	C make friends with other Germans.
4 Take photos	D passport and other important documents.
5 Scan your	E as often as you can.
6 Don't just	F too much luggage (you have to carry it!).
7 Say yes	G you have more than one bank card.

2 Habits abroad
Unit 2 | p. 28 Ex. 2

What habits have you noticed in other countries?
What surprised you? What did you like? Tell your group.

I noticed that people ...
eat / drink ...
drive ...
(don't) enjoy ...
(don't) laugh at ...
like playing ...
listen to ...
speak ...
stand ...
wear ...

6 DOUBLE CIRCLE Hopes for the future
Unit 2 | p. 29 Ex. 6

Think about your hopes and dreams for the future.
Make two circles and tell different students about what you'd like to do.

I've always lived in Bavaria, ...
- but I'd like to live in France / Spain / the USA / ...
- and I'd like to stay here.

I'm going to ...
- be a nurse / ...
- help people.
- be happy.

In the future I think I'll ...
- follow my dreams.
- have a family.
- enjoy life.

I dream of ...
- being a famous artist.
- working for an international company.
- travelling around the world.

Unit 3

1 Digital media use Unit 3 | p. 43 Ex. 1a

a Discuss the pictures on pp. 42 and 43. What aspects of media use and the internet do they show?

Match these ideas.

1	baby plugged in	A	you're often on several devices
2	too much time on social media	B	is a waste of time
3	followers	C	you share experiences and support
4	product placement	D	you're addicted to likes and having followers
5	multitasking	E	your phone is like a prison
6	not free	F	you can talk to friends anywhere
7	digital social networks	G	you listen to music from all over the world
8	music	H	you're online from birth
9	digital communication	I	adverts are everywhere

3 Positive ideas Unit 3 | p. 43 Ex. 3a

a Write down more positive aspects of digital media use.

Think about:

- information and new ideas about the world
- world news
- communication skills
- social skills (problem-solving, decision making, etc.)
- role models and inspiring ideas
- creative activities and self-expression (sharing online slideshows, stories, collages, blogs, etc.)
- social and political activities (for example an environmental chat group)

2 Influencers Unit 3 | p. 47 Ex. 2b

b Do you follow any influencers? If you do, who are they and what sort of ideas or products do they promote? If not, why not?

lifestyle and hobbies
animal-friendly lifestyle
cooking
fitness
gaming
healthy lifestyle
political/social activities
sports

products
clothes and fashion
electronic devices
jewellery
hair and beauty products
pet food and toys
restaurants
sports equipment

4 Your interview Unit 3 | p. 55 Ex. 4a

a You have an interview for the same job as Mike. Prepare the answers to these questions.

1 Can you tell me something about yourself?
I'm in year ... at school and my favourite subjects are ...

2 What are your strengths and weaknesses?
For my strengths, I'd say I'm organized / good at talking to people / ...
For my weaknesses, I'm not very good at maths / ..., but I'm trying to improve that skill.

3 Are you a good team player?
Yes, I am. I'm in a football / handball team ...
I'm always good at doing group projects at school. I enjoy working with other people.

4 What are your interests?
I'm really interested in protecting the environment / making model cars / doing sport / ...

5 Why do you want a job with us?
I've looked at your company online and I think you care about the people that work for you / have exciting ideas / have an environment-friendly attitude / ...

6 Do you have any questions about the job?
What hours would I have to work?
Can I work at weekends?

Unit 4

2 Experience India Unit 4 | p. 59 Ex. 2a

Choose one photo and put yourself in that picture. Think about these questions.

1 **Who/What are you?**
I'm a fruit seller / an Indian boy / an Englishman / Gandhi / ...

2 **Where are you? What can you see / hear / smell around you?**
I'm in the street / at work / in a shopping mall / at a festival / ...
I can **see** people in the street / cars / cows / people having fun / the cricket ball / ...
I can **hear** customers talking / traffic / my mother talking / people laughing / ...
I can **smell** bananas / oranges / cars / cows / sweat / my feet / ...

3 **What are you doing? How are you feeling?**
I'm talking to my friend / customers / another politician about ...
I'm waiting for customers / the ball / ...
I'm working / shopping / ...
I'm putting coloured powder on my friend's face.
I feel tired / excited / bored / happy / hungry / ...

1 A holy river Unit 4 | p. 64 Ex. 1b

Listen to a discussion by a group of students.
What is their conclusion? Choose the best answer.

A The problem of human sewage is the most important.
B Human and animal sewage must be prevented from going into the Ganges.
C The problems of sewage and of soap and shampoo need to be addressed immediately.
D All the problems of pollution in the Ganges (human and animal sewage, the use of soap and shampoo, cremations) need to be solved immediately.

3 In the hot seat Unit 4 | p. 64 Ex. 3a

a **Think about a polluted place in your area. It can be a place with water pollution, air pollution or problems with rubbish. Prepare arguments about the issue and what can be done.**

Describe the issue
The problem is that the water / air in ... is very polluted.
It's said to be caused by sewage / rubbish / farmers / traffic / industry / ...
It's dangerous for people / animals / fish / ...
It can cause infections / breathing problems / problems with ...

What can be done
People / Farmers / Companies should be banned from putting / throwing / using / ...
People / Farmers / Companies should suffer serious disadvantages when ...
We can all stop using / throwing away / ...
We can protest about this issue to ...
We can make a website / posters / a post on social media about ...

Unit 1

1 Indigenous inventions Unit 1 | p. 11 after Ex. 2

You know indigenous Australians invented the boomerang. But they also invented other cool things. Look at the pictures, read about two inventions and choose the correct words.

The didgeridoo is a very old *sport / instrument / type of art*. It is made of *a bag / fruit / a branch* which is *empty / full / light* inside. When a musician *talks / blows / shouts* into it, it makes a very special sound.

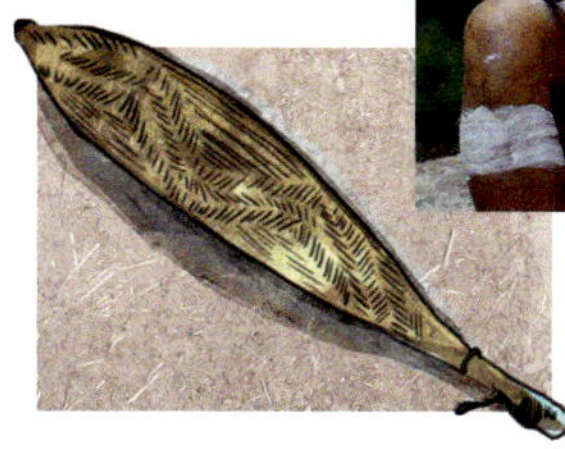

The woomera is *a fish-catcher / a spear[1]-thrower / a camel-holder*. Indigenous Australians took a long thin piece of *wood / metal / dried grass* and tied *an egg / a ball / a stone* to the end to hold the spear. With this invention, hunters could *catch / throw / hold* the spear much higher.

2 Read for fun Unit 1 | p. 15 after Ex. 4

Vegemite – Aussies love it!

For all you out there who haven't heard of Vegemite – you definitely don't live in Australia! So what is it? Well, it contains yeast[2] from making beer, vegetables and spices. Aussies spread this thick, black stuff on toast and sandwiches. Vegemite doesn't contain fat or sugar or any animal products. However, it does contain a lot of salt and it has a very strong, salty taste. It also contains lots of extra vitamins which means it can't be sold in some countries. In the UK you can buy a similar product which is called Marmite.

3 Bruce Lee Unit 1 | p. 19 after Ex. 3b

Match the information about Bruce Lee.

1 He was born
2 He grew up
3 He was a
4 He moved back to the US
5 He developed
6 His martial arts films
7 He has a star
8 He died
9 He didn't

a when he was 18.
b from an allergic reaction when he was 32.
c his own style of martial arts[3].
d on the Hollywood Walk of Fame.
e play badminton.
f in Hong Kong.
g in 1940 in Chinatown in San Francisco.
h are popular all over the world.
i child actor.

Lösung zu Fast finishers 1: *instrument* • *a branch* • *empty* • *blows* • *spear-thrower* • *wood* • *a stone* • *throw*

Lösung zu Fast finishers 3: 1g • 2f • 3i • 4a • 5c • 6h • 7d • 8b • 9e

[1]**spear** [spɪə] *Speer* [2]**yeast** [jiːst] *Hefe* [3]**martial arts** *(pl)* [mɑːʃl ˈɑːts] *Kampfsport*

Unit 2

4 Read for fun Unit 2 | p. 29 after Ex. 3a

Germany is different

On my first birthday in Germany, I got lots of handshakes and birthday wishes from my colleagues in the office ... but no cake! I was very disappointed. Later in the day, after a few colleagues had given ME disappointed looks, I asked a colleague how birthdays are celebrated in Germany.
Apparently[1] you buy cake for your friends and colleagues and buy them a drink if you go to a cafe or restaurant. In England it is the opposite – you get the cake and the drinks because it is YOUR birthday.
Another thing which I find strange (but in a good way) is that in cafes and restaurants everybody pays for their own food and drinks (when it's not your birthday, of course). The waiter or waitress is quite happy to take money from each person for their share. In the UK, you have to pay the whole bill and then split[2] it.
One last thing: I was very surprised when I went to the toilets in a German restaurant and I had to pay somebody who was sitting there. Sometimes in England you have to put money in a machine, but usually toilets are free.

5 Job descriptions Unit 2 | p. 31 after Ex. 3

Read the job descriptions. Then choose a job and write your own description.

ice cream taster
toy designer
video game tester
...

CLOWN WANTED!
Must have a red nose and big feet and be good at throwing cream cakes in people's faces.

Snowman wanted!
Must have a hat and a scarf and enjoy standing around in cold weather.

Crossword writer wanted!
Must know lots of words and like the colours black and white.

SUPERHERO WANTED!
Must have a cape and a tight suit, be able to fly and like saving people.

... wanted!
Must have ... / ...be able to ...
Must be good at ...
Must enjoy / like / know / ...

6 *I, Robot* Unit 2 | p. 35 after Ex. 4

Put the description of the film in the right order.

a In the film, Will Smith plays Del Spooner, a cop who doesn't like technology.
b It seems the scientist had built a robot with feelings and dreams. The question is: are there others out there?
c This is because Spooner once nearly died. He was saved by a robot, but the robot left a young girl to die.
d *I, Robot* is quite an old film (2004), but it is set in 2035 when robots have taken over lots of jobs.
e The film is inspired by a collection of stories with the same name by Isaac Asimov.
f Spooner gets the murder case[3] of a scientist whose research was into robots and who gave Spooner a new arm after his accident.

Lösung zu Fast finishers 6: d • e • a • c • f • b

[1] **apparently** [əˈpærəntli] *anscheinend* [2] (to) **split** [splɪt] **split, split** *aufteilen* [3] **case** [keɪs] *Fall*

Unit 3

7 Read for fun Unit 3 | p. 45 after Ex. 3

Fake person generator

If you don't want to give real details online, you can use a fake person generator. This is a legal way to generate[1] an avatar and personal information which looks real, but which is completely fake. All the information is generated randomly[2]. You can use this information to set up social media accounts which are not in your name – to avoid[3] bullying, for example, or to avoid attention.

8 Electric windmills Unit 3 | p. 52 after Ex. 4b

Look at the picture and put the sentences in the right order to explain how the windmills produce electricity.

a Generators create electricity.
b You use the electricity.
c The blades of the windmill turn.
d The wind blows.
e It reaches your home.
f The electricity is sent over power lines.

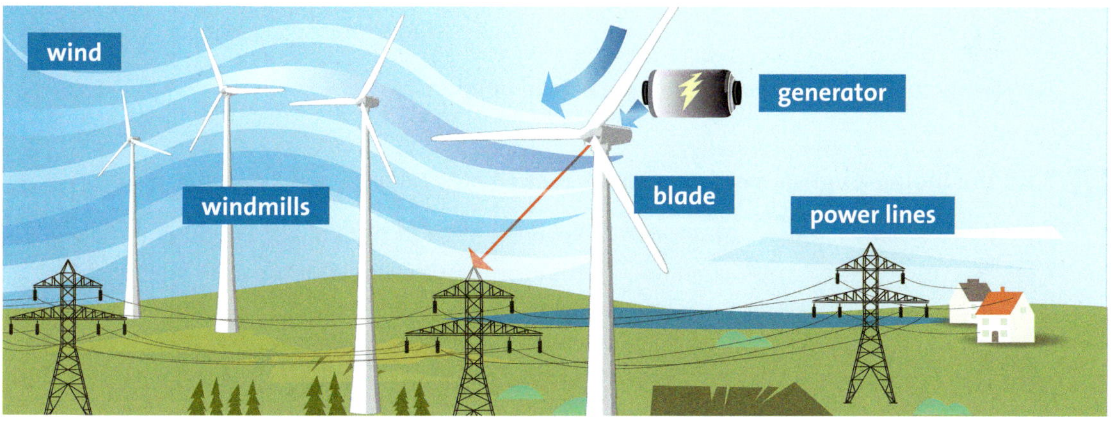

9 Unusual interview questions Unit 3 | p. 55 after Ex. 4a

Choose one or two of these interview questions and think about your answer(s).

1 What's the best film title to describe your life? Why?
2 If you were a company boss, what would you ban in the company? What would you make everybody do?
3 Who would you have dinner with if you could choose anyone in the world? Why?

Lösung zu Fast finishers 8: d • c • a • f • e • b

[1] (to) **generate** [ˈdʒenəreɪt] *erzeugen, generieren* [2] **random** [ˈrændəm] *zufällig, beliebig*
[3] (to) **avoid** [əˈvɔɪd] *(ver)meiden, verhindern*

Unit 4

10 Read for fun Unit 4 | p. 62 after Ex. 2b

A popular Indian film

Dangal (which is translated as *Wrestling*[1] *Competition*) is a film from 2016 about a father who trains his daughters to become top female wrestlers. It is based on a true story about a father who dreams of becoming a wrestler, but who is forced to give up the sport and get a job. He decides that his sons will become wrestlers instead and is disappointed when he has four daughters. But when two of his daughters beat up some boys for calling them names, he realizes they could be great wrestlers. He trains them and his daughter Geeta wins gold at the Commonwealth Games.

female wrestlers in Kolkata

11 #Unpopular opinions Unit 4 | p. 64 after Ex. 3b

a Match these unpopular food opinions from the internet with the correct ending.

1	Chicken hearts are the most	a	that great.
2	I really don't like pizza with	b	better than dessert.
3	In my opinion, vegetables are	c	really wrong.
4	I hate avocados	d	tomato sauce.
5	I think salt in chocolate is	e	but I love guacamole.
6	In my view, cake is not	f	underrated[2] food ever.

b Do you agree? Now write your #unpopular food opinion.

12 Find the Indian-English words Unit 4 | p. 68 after Ex. 3

Read the start of this story. Can you find the eight words that come from Hindi but are used in English?

I was sitting on the veranda of our bungalow. I was wearing my pink pyjamas and, of course, my silver bangles[3]. My hair was wet from the shower and smelled of rose shampoo. I was eating my breakfast (vegetables with rice and chutney) and looking out at the jungle. Suddenly I saw it! A cheetah[4]! And it was looking right at me ...

13 Amar's day Unit 4 | p. 69 after Ex. 5b

Think about Amar's day again. Work out how many journeys on his bike Amar made in that one day.

Lösung zu Fast finishers 12: veranda • bungalow • pyjamas • bangles • shampoo • chutney • jungle • cheetah

Lösung zu Fast finishers 11: 1 f • 2 d • 3 b • 4 e • 5 c • 6 a

[1]**wrestling** ['reslɪŋ] *Ringen (Kampfsport)* [2](to) **underrate** [ʌndə'reɪt] *unterschätzen* [3]**bangle** ['bæŋgl] *Armreif, Armspange* [4]**cheetah** ['tʃiːtə] *Gepard*

Wordbank 1: Sports and rules

Types of sport

It's a/an ...

individual[1] sport / team sport

ball sport

endurance[2] sport (e.g. marathon)

equestrian[3] sport (e.g. showjumping)

extreme sport (e.g. highlining)

martial sport (e.g. judo)

motor sport (e.g. Formula One[4] racing)

mountain sport (e.g. skiing, hiking)

track and field[5] sport/ athletics (e.g. long jump)

water sport (e.g. canoeing)

You play/do this sport

indoors/outdoors

in a ...
gym
pool
...

on a ...
court
field/pitch[6]
race course
track
...

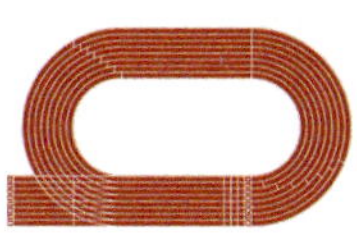

Rules

You can / are allowed to ...

You can't / aren't allowed to ...

You should/shouldn't ...

	the ball
catch	the bike
drive	the car
hit	the horse
hold	the motorbike
kick	the player
ride	the puck[7]
run	the racket[8]
throw	the shuttlecock[9]
touch	the stick
	...

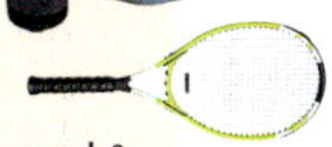

How to win

finish first / in a time of/under ...

get a score of ...

score the most goals

score the most points

the judges decide

the referee[10] / umpire[11] decides

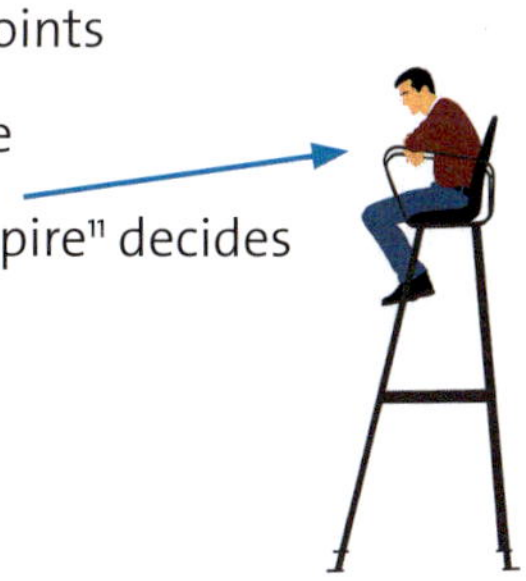

[1] **individual** [ɪndɪˈvɪdʒʊəl] *einzeln, Einzel-* [2] **endurance** [ɪnˈdjʊərəns] *Ausdauer* [3] **equestrian** [ɪˈkwestriən] *Reit-, Reiter-* [4] **Formula One** [fɔːmjələ ˈwʌn] *Formel Eins* [5] **track and field** *(AE)* [træk ən ˈfiːld] / **athletics** *(BE) Leichtathletik* [6] **pitch** [pɪtʃ] *Platz, Spielfeld* [7] **puck** [pʌk] *Puck (Eishockey)* [8] **racket** [ˈrækɪt] *Schläger (Tennis, Squash)* [9] **shuttlecock** [ˈʃʌtlkɒk] *Federball (Ball)* [10] **referee** [refəˈriː], *infml auch:* **ref** *Schiedsrichter/in* [11] **umpire** [ˈʌmpaɪə] *Schiedsrichter/in (Tennis)*

Wordbank 2: Jobs and volunteering

Unit 2 | p. 25 Ex. 4

Part-time jobs

JOB	DESCRIPTION
barista[1]	makes coffee in a cafe
car washer	washes cars by hand and cleans them inside
cleaner	tidies and cleans people's houses
fast food server	takes orders and makes fast food like burgers
lawn mower[2] / gardener	cuts the grass and tidies up gardens
lifeguard	makes sure there are no accidents at a pool
newspaper boy/girl	delivers[3] newspapers to people's houses
office assistant	puts papers in files, answers the phone
pet sitter	looks after people's pets in their own homes when the owners are away
shelf-stacker	fills up the shelves in a supermarket / food shop
tutor[4]	helps other students to understand a school subject they have problems with
video game designer	designs new games
website designer	designs websites

Volunteer jobs

JOB	DESCRIPTION
charity shop helper	works in a charity shop and sells second-hand clothes and household items[5]
child care assistant	looks after children in day care[6]
civil protection volunteer	assists people after accidents and catastrophes
conservation volunteer	helps conserve forests and landscapes and protect wildlife
volunteer firefighter	puts out fires and helps people (and animals) in difficult situations
food pantry *(AE)* / food bank *(BE)*[7] helper	gives out donated[8] food to people in need[9]
helper in a care home	talks and reads to old people
homeless shelter volunteer	serves[10] food and gives out clothes
library assistant	helps people find books, puts books on shelves
literacy[11] tutor	helps children and adults with reading
community garden volunteer	helps grow flowers, vegetables and fruit in the city
youth club helper	organizes games, prepares food
youth sports coach	plays football and other sports with children and teenagers

[1] **barista** [bəˈriːstə] *Barista (Kaffeezubereiter/in in einer Kaffeebar)* [2] **lawn mower** [ˈlɔːn məʊə] *jd., der Rasen mäht* [3] (to) **deliver** [dɪˈlɪvə] *(aus)liefern* [4] **tutor** [ˈtjuːtə] *Nachhilfelehrer/in* [5] **item** [ˈaɪtəm] *Gegenstand* [6] **day care** [ˈdeɪ keə] *(Kinder-)Tagesbetreuung* [7] **food pantry** *(AE)* [ˈfuːd pæntri] / **food bank** [ˈfuːd bæŋk] *Tafel (karitative Essensausgabe)* [8] (to) **donate** [dəʊˈneɪt] *spenden* [9] **in need** *in (der) Not* [10] (to) **serve** [sɜːv] *servieren; bedienen* [11] **literacy** [ˈlɪtərəsi] *Alphabetisierung (Fähigkeit zu lesen und zu schreiben)*

Unit 3 | p. 45 Ex. 5

media verbs

download • log on/in/into • log off/out • post • program • scroll down/up • switch sth. on/off • unplug • upload

digital activities

chatting • creating playlists • gaming • making/posting videos • messaging • surfing the internet • using digital creation[1] tools

social media

account (set up / shut down an account) • addict • comment • do a digital detox / stay off social media • following/followers • hashtag# • influencer • like • network • selfie • tweet

online issues

advertising • (cyber)bullying[2] • digital footprint • fake news • fake profiles • netiquette • pornography[3] • privacy

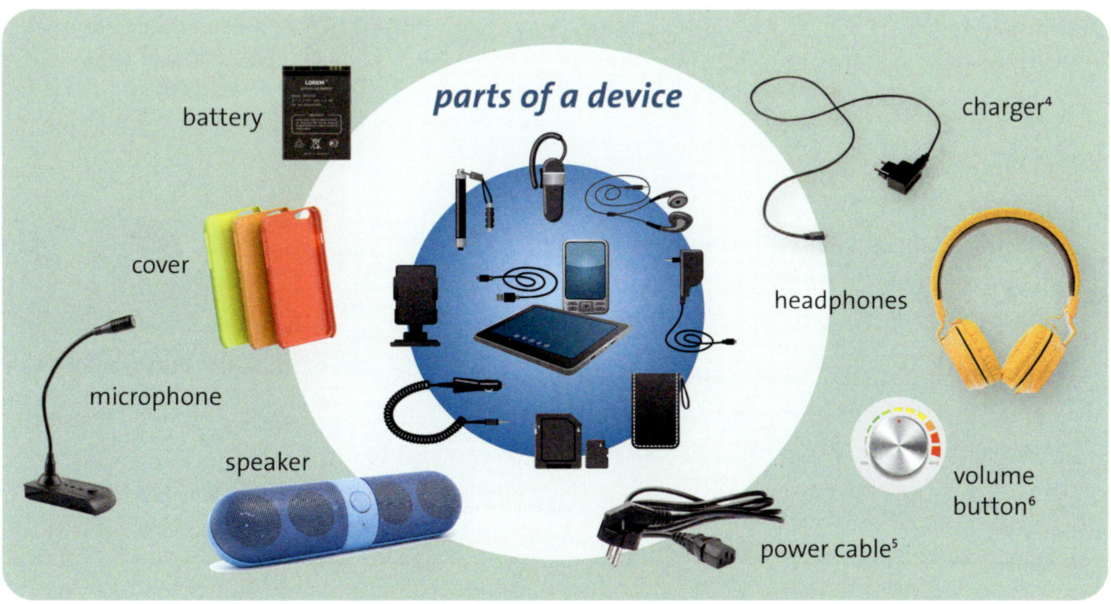

[1]**creation** [kriˈeɪʃn] *Erstellung; Schaffung* [2]**cyberbullying** [saɪbəˈbʊliŋ] *Cybermobbing* [3]**pornography** [pɔːˈnɒgrəfi] *Pornografie* [4]**charger** [ˈtʃɑːdʒə] *Ladegerät* [5]**cable** [ˈkeɪbl] *Kabel* [6]**button** [ˈbʌtn] *Schaltfläche, Knopf*

Wordbank 4: Describing and evaluating adverts

Unit 3 | p. 54 Ex. 3

PRODUCT / AIM

This is an advert for ...
The advert promotes ...
The aim / objective[1] of the ad is to ...
The advert suggests that ... / tries to persuade[2] people that ...

GRAPHICS

The model/s in the advert look/s attractive / strong / friendly / ...
(Think about age, gender, ethnicity[3], looks, hairstyle and colour, clothes and style)
The product looks natural / luxurious /
We connect ... in the ad with (beauty / health / ...)
It tries to grab attention through ...
The colours are fresh / bright / moody[4] / ...

LANGUAGE

The name of the product is ...
It's clever / boring / eye-catching / ... because ...
The language is simple / descriptive[5] / vague[6] / emotional / humorous[7] / ...
It's appealing[8] because ...

AUDIENCE

I think the target audience of this advert is (teenagers / girls and women / people who are interested in ... / people who worry about ...)
I think this advert will / won't appeal to ...

MESSAGE

It promises that ...
The message of this advert is ...
The ad sends the reader the message that ...
It addresses concerns about (health/attractiveness) ...
I think it reinforces[9] stereotypes about ...

COMPARING AND CONTRASTING ADVERTS

What they both have in common is ...
They are similar to each other because ...
... is like ... because ...
This advert is ..., whereas / while that advert is ...
In contrast to ...
Unlike the soap advert ..., this one ...

[1]**objective** *(n)* [əbˈdʒektɪv] *Ziel* [2](to) **persuade** [pəˈsweɪd] *überzeugen* [3]**ethnicity** [eθˈnɪsəti] *Volkszugehörigkeit*
[4]**moody** [ˈmuːdi] *stimmungsvoll; trüb* [5]**descriptive** [dɪˈskrɪptɪv] *beschreibend* [6]**vague** [veɪg] *unbestimmt*
[7]**humorous** [ˈhjuːmərəs] *humorvoll* [8](to) **appeal to sb.** [əˈpiːl] *für jn. attraktiv sein, jn. ansprechen*
[9](to) **reinforce** [riːɪnˈfɔːs] *(ver)stärken, verfestigen* [10]**cosy** [ˈkəʊzi] *gemütlich*

Wordbank 5: Saying what you have done

Personal care

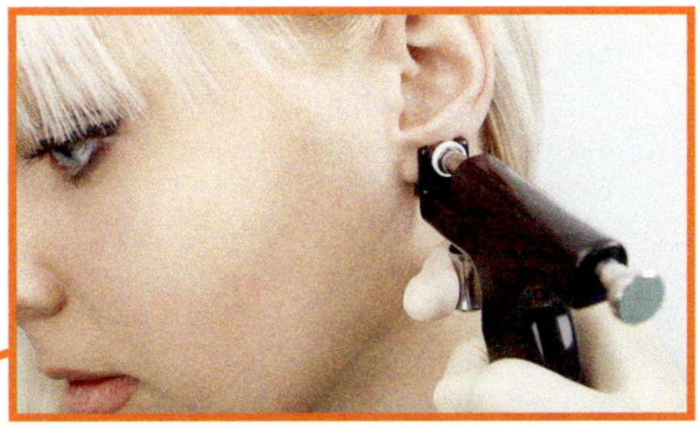

have your hair cut / styled / dyed[1] / shaved / brushed[2]

have your nails done / manicured / varnished[3]

have your eyebrows[4] plucked[5] / dyed

have your eyelashes[6] dyed

have your ears / nose / ... pierced[7]

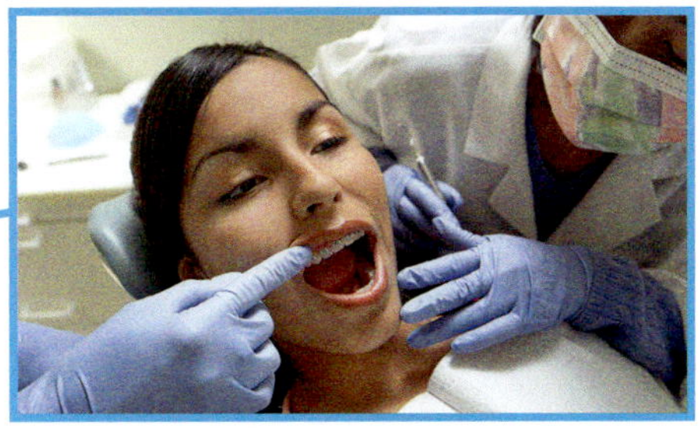

have your teeth checked / fixed[8] / cleaned

have a tooth filled / pulled out[9]

have braces[10] / a brace fitted[11]

have your braces checked / adjusted

have your eyes / eyesight[12] / glasses checked

have your ears / hearing aid checked

Clothes and shoes

have your clothes washed / dry cleaned / mended[13] / altered[14]

have your shoes repaired

In the home

have pizza / sushi / takeaway food / groceries[15] delivered

have your room painted

have your flat / windows cleaned

have your computer / phone repaired

---

[1] (to) **dye** [daɪ] *färben* [2] (to) **brush** [brʌʃ] *bürsten* [3] (to) **varnish** [ˈvɑːnɪʃ] *lackieren* [4] **eyebrow** [ˈaɪbraʊ] *Augenbraue* [5] (to) **pluck** [plʌk] *zupfen* [6] **eyelash/es** [ˈaɪlæʃ] *Wimper/n* [7] (to) **pierce** [pɪəs] *piercen* [8] (to) **fix sth.** *(infml)* [fɪks] = *to repair sth.* [9] (to) **pull sth. out** [pʊl ˈaʊt] *etwas herausziehen* [10] **brace/s** [breɪs] *Zahnspange* [11] (to) **fit** [fɪt] *einsetzen, anpassen* [12] **eyesight** [ˈaɪsaɪt] *Sehkraft* [13] (to) **mend** [mend] *reparieren* [14] (to) **alter** [ˈɔːltə] *(ab)ändern (Kleidung)* [15] **groceries** *(pl)* [ˈgrəʊsəriz] *Lebensmittel*

Country/Continent	Adjective	Person	People
Afghanistan [æf'gænɪstæn] *Afghanistan*	**Afghan** ['æfgæn]	**an Afghan**	**the Afghans**
Africa ['æfrɪkə] *Afrika*	**African** ['æfrɪkən]	**an African**	**the Africans**
America [ə'merɪkə] *Amerika*	**American** [ə'merɪkən]	**an American**	**the Americans**
Asia ['eɪʃə, 'eɪʒə] *Asien*	**Asian** ['eɪʃn, 'eɪʒn]	**an Asian**	**the Asians**
Australia [ɒ'streɪliə] *Australien*	**Australian** [ɒ'streɪliən]	**an Australian**	**the Australians**
Austria ['ɒstriə] *Österreich*	**Austrian** ['ɒstriən]	**an Austrian**	**the Austrians**
Bangladesh [bæŋglə'deʃ] *Bangladesch*	**Bangladesh**	**a Bangladeshi** [bæŋglə'deʃi]	**the Bangladeshis**
Barbados [bɑː'beɪdɒs] *Barbados*	**Barbadian** [bɑː'beɪdiən]	**a Barbadian**	**the Barbadians**
Belgium ['beldʒəm] *Belgien*	**Belgian** ['beldʒən]	**a Belgian**	**the Belgians**
Bhutan [buː'tɑːn] *Bhutan*	**Bhutanese** [buːtə'niːz]	**a Bhutanese**	**the Bhutanese**
Brazil [brə'zɪl] *Brasilien*	**Brasilian** [brə'zɪliən]	**a Brasilian**	**the Brasilians**
Bulgaria [bʌl'geəriə] *Bulgarien*	**Bulgarian** [bʌl'geəriən]	**a Bulgarian**	**the Bulgarians**
Canada ['kænədə] *Kanada*	**Canadian** [kə'neɪdiən]	**a Canadian**	**the Canadians**
China ['tʃaɪnə] *China*	**Chinese** [tʃaɪ'niːz]	**a Chinese**	**the Chinese**
Costa Rica [kɒstə 'riːkə] *Costa Rica*	**Costa Rican** [kɒstə 'riːkən]	**a Costa Rican**	**the Costa Ricans**
Croatia [krəʊ'eɪʃə] *Kroatien*	**Croatian** [krəʊ'eɪʃn]	**a Croatian**	**the Croatians**
the Czech Republic [ˌtʃek rɪ'pʌblɪk] *Tschechien, die Tschechische Republik*	**Czech** [tʃek]	**a Czech**	**the Czechs**
Denmark ['denmɑːk] *Dänemark*	**Danish** ['deɪnɪʃ]	**a Dane** [deɪn]	**the Danes**
England ['ɪŋglənd] *England*	**English** ['ɪŋglɪʃ]	**an Englishman/-woman**	**the English**
Europe ['jʊərəp] *Europa*	**European** [ˌjʊərə'piːən]	**a European**	**the Europeans**
Finland ['fɪnlənd] *Finnland*	**Finnish** ['fɪnɪʃ]	**a Finn** [fɪn]	**the Finns**
France [frɑːns] *Frankreich*	**French** [frentʃ]	**a Frenchman/-woman**	**the French**
Germany ['dʒɜːməni] *Deutschland*	**German** ['dʒɜːmən]	**a German**	**the Germans**
(Great) Britain ['brɪtn] *Großbritannien*	**British** ['brɪtɪʃ]	**a Briton** ['brɪtn]	**the British**
Greece [griːs] *Griechenland*	**Greek** [griːk]	**a Greek**	**the Greeks**
Hungary ['hʌŋgəri] *Ungarn*	**Hungarian** [hʌŋ'geəriən]	**a Hungarian**	**the Hungarians**
India ['ɪndiə] *Indien*	**Indian** ['ɪndiən]	**an Indian**	**the Indians**
Iran [ɪ'rɑːn] *Iran*	**Iranian** [ɪ'reɪniən]	**an Iranian**	**the Iranians**
Iraq [ɪ'rɑːk] *Irak*	**Iraqi** [ɪ'rɑːki]	**an Iraqi**	**the Iraqis**
Ireland ['aɪələnd] *Irland*	**Irish** ['aɪrɪʃ]	**an Irishman/-woman**	**the Irish**
Italy ['ɪtəli] *Italien*	**Italian** [ɪ'tæliən]	**an Italian**	**the Italians**
Japan [dʒə'pæn] *Japan*	**Japanese** [ˌdʒæpə'niːz]	**a Japanese**	**the Japanese**
Malawi [mə'lɑːwi] *Malawi*	**Malawian** [mə'lɑːwiən]	**a Malawian**	**the Malawians**
Myanmar [mjæn'mɑː] **(= Burma** [bɜːmə]**)**	**Burmese** [bɜːmiːz]	**a Burmese**	**the Burmese**
Nepal [nə'pɔːl] *Nepal*	**Nepalese** [nepə'liːz]	**a Nepalese**	**the Nepalese**
the Netherlands ['neðələndz] *die Niederlande, Holland*	**Dutch** [dʌtʃ]	**a Dutchman/-woman**	**the Dutch**
New Zealand [ˌnjuː 'ziːlənd] *Neuseeland*	**New Zealand** [ˌnjuː 'ziːlənd]	**a New Zealander**	**the New Zealanders**
Norway ['nɔːweɪ] *Norwegen*	**Norwegian** [nɔː'wiːdʒən]	**a Norwegian**	**the Norwegians**
Pakistan [pækɪ'stæn] *Pakistan*	**Pakistani** [pækɪ'stæni]	**a Pakistani**	**the Pakistanis**
Poland ['pəʊlənd] *Polen*	**Polish** ['pəʊlɪʃ]	**a Pole** [pəʊl]	**the Poles**
Portugal ['pɔːtʃʊgl] *Portugal*	**Portuguese** [ˌpɔːtʃʊ'giːz]	**a Portuguese**	**the Portuguese**
Romania [ru'meɪniə] *Rumänien*	**Romanian** [ru'meɪniən]	**a Romanian**	**the Romanians**
Russia ['rʌʃə] *Russland*	**Russian** ['rʌʃn]	**a Russian**	**the Russians**
Scotland ['skɒtlənd] *Schottland*	**Scottish** ['skɒtɪʃ]	**a Scotsman/-woman,**	**the Scots**
Serbia ['sɜːbiə] *Serbien*	**Serbian** ['sɜːbiən]	**a Serb** [sɜːb]	**the Serbs**
Slovakia [slə'vækiə] *die Slowakei*	**Slovak** ['sləʊvæk]	**a Slovakian** [slə'vækiən]	**the Slovakians**
Slovenia [slə'viːniə] *Slowenien*	**Slovene** ['sləʊviːn]	**a Slovenian** [slə'viːniən]	**the Slovenians**
Spain [speɪn] *Spanien*	**Spanish** ['spænɪʃ]	**a Spaniard** ['spænɪəd]	**the Spaniards**
Sweden ['swiːdn] *Schweden*	**Swedish** ['swiːdɪʃ]	**a Swede** [swiːd]	**the Swedes**
Switzerland ['swɪtsələnd] *die Schweiz*	**Swiss** [swɪs]	**a Swiss**	**the Swiss**
Syria ['sɪriə] *Syrien*	**Syrian** ['sɪriən]	**a Syrian**	**the Syrians**
Turkey ['tɜːki] *die Türkei*	**Turkish** ['tɜːkɪʃ]	**a Turk** [tɜːk]	**the Turks**
the United Kingdom (the UK) [juˌnaɪtɪd 'kɪŋdəm, ˌjuː'keɪ] *das Vereinigte Königreich (Großbritannien und Nordirland)*	**British** ['brɪtɪʃ]	**a Briton** ['brɪtn]	**the British**
the United States of America (the USA) *die Vereinigten Staaten von Amerika*	**American** [ə'merɪkən]	**an American**	**the Americans**
Wales [weɪlz] *Wales*	**Welsh** [welʃ]	**a Welshman/-woman**	**the Welsh**

TF1 ARTICLES Convict colonies

1 The early history of Australia

Read this online encyclopedia[1] entry. Explain what role convicts played in the history of Australia.

Convicts from Britain on their way to Australia

Indigenous Australians lived in Australia about 50,000 years ago. The first Europeans that came to Australia were the Dutch in 1606. They named the continent '**New Holland**' and explored[2] the northern and western coast, but they did not settle there. In 1770 the British explorer **Captain James Cook** landed in Sydney with his ship *Endeavour*[3]. Cook named the land in the area '**New South Wales**' and Britain founded the first European colony at **Sydney** in 1788. Many of the first settlers were criminals[4]. Prisons in Britain were full and **convicts** were sent to the Australian colony as punishment[5]. When convicts became free, the British government gave them land for farming. Around 160,000 convicts were sent to Australia between 1788 and 1868.

Five other **British colonies** were founded in Australia. In 1851 gold was discovered in **Victoria** and thousands of new immigrants came to Australia from different countries, especially from China. In 1901 the six colonies joined together[6] to become one country.

Australia's national day, ***Australia Day***, is 26th January – the date of the founding of the first colony. However, indigenous Australians often call this day *Day of mourning*[7]. Their ancestors suffered greatly from the arrival of the Europeans: many died from diseases and they lost much of their land and their traditional way of life.

2 Ned Kelly

Read the article about Ned Kelly. Who was he and why do people see him as a hero?

This day in AUSTRALIAN history: June 28, 1880

On June 28, 1880, famous outlaw[8] Ned Kelly was in his last gun battle[9] with the police. To protect himself, he had made heavy armour[10] – but only for the top half of his body. When the police finally discovered this, they shot him in the legs and took him prisoner[11]. Later Ned Kelly was hanged as a thief[12] and a murderer.

The background: Ned Kelly's father was a convict from Ireland who was sent to Australia for stealing two pigs. As a teenager, Ned himself was arrested several times for crimes he probably didn't commit. These arrests marked the start of Ned's criminal career and his conflicts with the police. In 1878, after Ned shot and injured a policeman, his mother was sent to prison for the crime – probably unfairly. Ned ran away with his brother Dan and two friends. Six months later, hearing about a group of policemen who were looking for them, Ned and his gang found and killed them. After this, they continued to hide, steal money from banks and shoot people who got in their way … until the police finally found them.

The legend: Ned Kelly was a criminal, but he was also strong and brave. He fought for his freedom and against injustice towards his family. That is why people often call him the "Australian Robin Hood" and up to today he is still seen by some as an Australian hero.

---

[1] **encyclopedia** [ɪnsaɪklə'piːdiə] *Lexikon* [2] (to) **explore** [ɪk'splɔː] *erforschen* [3] **endeavour** [ɪn'devə] *Bemühung, Anstrengung* [4] **criminal** ['krɪmɪnl] *Verbrecher/in, Kriminelle/r* [5] **punishment** ['pʌnɪʃmənt] *Strafe, Bestrafung* [6] (to) **join together** *sich zusammenschließen* [7] (to) **mourn** [mɔːn] *trauern* [8] **outlaw** ['aʊtlɔː] *Gesetzlose/r, Bandit/in* [9] **battle** ['bætl] *Kampf, Schlacht* [10] (to) **make armour** ['ɑːmə] *(eine) Rüstung herstellen* [11] **prisoner** ['prɪzənə] *Strafgefangene/r* [12] **thief** [θiːf] *Dieb/in*

TF2 QUIZ The Commonwealth of Nations

1 What is the Commonwealth?

Look at the map on page 99, read the information on this page and then do the quiz.

teenZone

THE COMMONWEALTH OF NATIONS

Meet our members!

Hi, my name's Celeste and I live in Jamaica. Jamaica is a small island in the Caribbean with beautiful beaches – a lot of tourists visit our country. Do you know reggae music? It comes from Jamaica. And have you heard of the sprinter Usain Bolt? He comes from Jamaica too. Music and sport are really important to me and my country. In 1962 Jamaica got independence from Britain and joined the Commonwealth. My parents say the Commonwealth helps fight corruption[1] in Jamaica.

I'm Lim, I'm from Singapore. If I had to describe Singapore, I'd say multicultural, 24-hour, clean, green, safe and wired[2]! Tech is big here. And if I had to describe my life I'd say study, study, study – good grades are really important. I do lots of sport too, though. I took part in the Commonwealth Youth Games last year and met other teenagers from all over the world. I think the Commonwealth brings people together.

Get the facts!

- The Commonwealth is a family of 53 countries. It includes Australia, New Zealand, Canada and India and was created in the first half of the 20th century. Most countries in the Commonwealth were British colonies and part of the British Empire.
- Queen Elizabeth II of the UK is the head of state of 16 Commonwealth countries (for example in Jamaica). Commonwealth countries work together to support economic development, democracy and peace.
- The Commonwealth has 30% of the world's people and 60% of the Commonwealth's citizens are under 30 years old!
- Many of the fastest growing global cities are in the Commonwealth (for example Mumbai and Nairobi).
- The Commonwealth Games (athletics) take place every four years. They include Youth[3] Games for athletes[4] aged 14–16 and games for athletes with a disability.

Take our quiz! True or false?

1. The Commonwealth is all about building stronger economies.
2. All Commonwealth countries belonged to the British Empire.
3. The Commonwealth Games have special competitions for teenagers.
4. South Africa is part of the Commonwealth.
5. The Commonwealth has mostly young citizens.
6. Nearly a third of the world's people live in the Commonwealth.
7. The UK is the only European country in the Commonwealth.
8. Most Commonwealth countries are in Asia.

[1]**corruption** [kəˈrʌpʃn] *Korruption, Bestechlichkeit* [2]**wired** [ˈwaɪəd] *verdrahtet, verkabelt* [3]**youth** [juːθ] *Jugend(-)* [4]**athlete** [ˈæθliːt] *(Leicht-)Athlet/in*

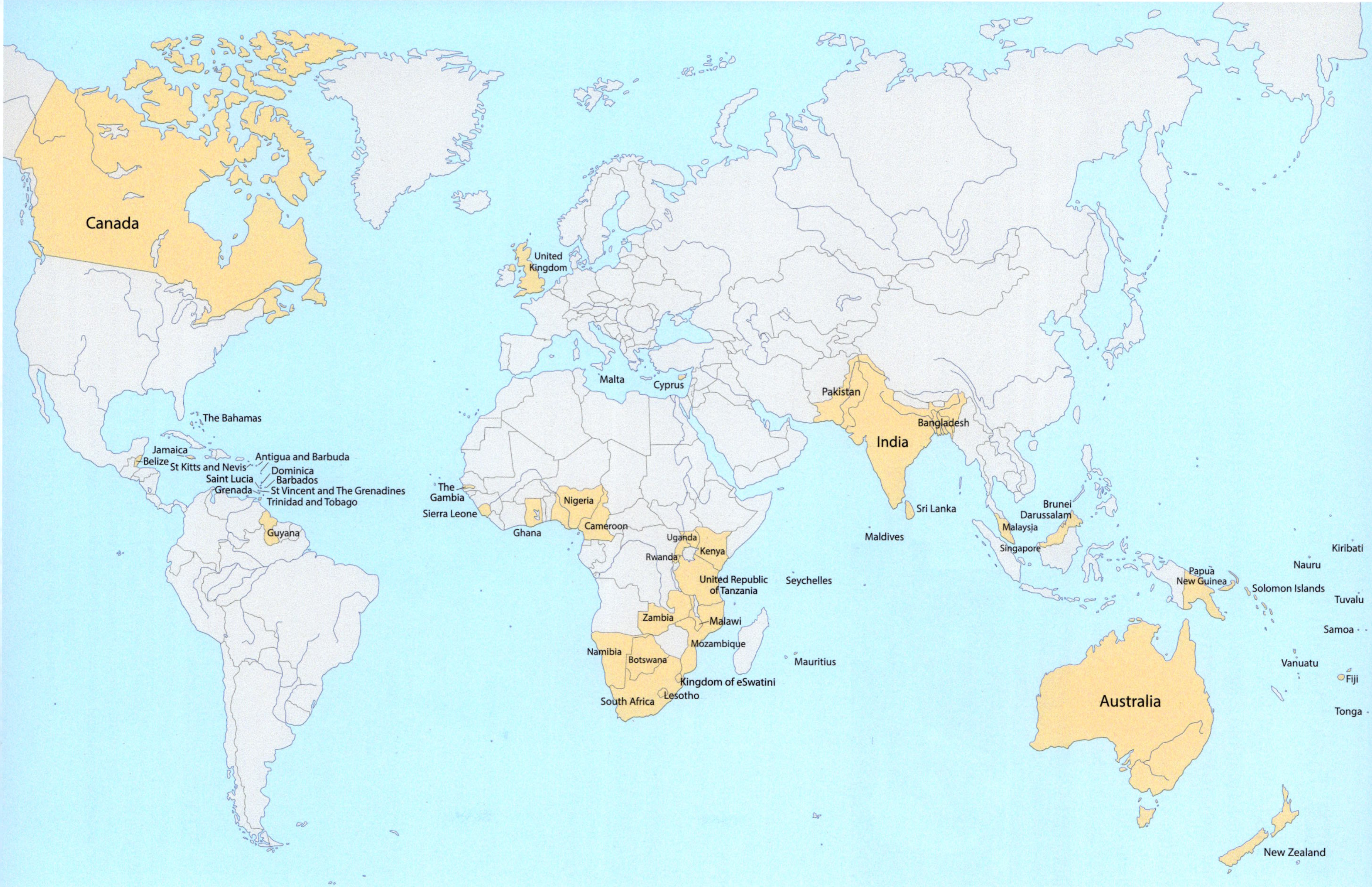

Member states of the Commonwealth of Nations

TF3 SONG Took the children away *(by Archie Roach)*

2.1

1 The lyrics

a Listen to and read the song lyrics. What event in Australian history does the song refer to? What do the lyrics say about how the children were treated?

b What lyrics are repeated? Explain what effect this has.

2.1

2 The music

Listen again to the song and then describe the style of the music. How does it fit with the lyrics?

Archie Roach

This song is by **Archie Roach**, an Australian singer-songwriter. When he was four, Archie and his sisters were taken from their family and put in a children's home. He found out his mother had died when he was fourteen years old and for the next fourteen years he lived on the streets.

This story's right, this story's true
I would not tell lies to you
Like the promises they did not keep
And how they fenced[1] us in like sheep
Said to us 'Come take our hand'
Set us up[2] on mission[3] land
Taught us to read, to write and pray
Then they took the children away

Took the children away
The children away
Snatched[4] from their mother's breast[5]
Said 'This is for the best'
Took them away

The welfareman, the policeman
Said you've got to understand
We'll give to them what you can't give
Teach them how to really live
'Teach them how to live', they said
Humiliated[6] them instead
Taught them that and taught them this
And others taught them prejudice[7]

You took the children away
The children away
Breaking their mothers' heart
Tearing us all apart
Took them away

One dark day on Framlingham
Came and didn't give a damn[8]
My mother cried 'Go get their dad'
He came running, fighting mad[9]
Mother's tears were falling down
Dad shaped up and stood his ground
He said, 'You touch my kids and you
fight me'
And they took us from our family

Took us away
They took us away
Snatched from our mother's breast
Said this was for the best
Took us away
Told us what to do and say
Taught us all the white man's way
Then they split us up[10] again
And gave us gifts[11] to ease[12] the pain
Sent us off to foster homes[13]
As we grew up we felt alone
'Cause we were acting white
Yet feeling black
One sweet day all the children
came back

The children came back
The children came back
Back where their hearts
grow strong
Back where they all belong
The children came back

Said the children came back
The children came back
Back where they understand
Back to their mother's land
The children came back

Back to their mother
Back to their father
Back to their sister
Back to their brother
Back to their people
Back to their land

All the children came back
The children came back
The children came back
Yes, I came back

---

[1] (to) **fence sb. in** [fens ˈɪn] *einengen, einzäunen* [2] (to) **set sb. up** [set ˈʌp] *hier: unterbringen* [3] **mission** [ˈmɪʃn] *Mission(sstation)* [4] (to) **snatch** [snætʃ] *schnappen* [5] **breast** [brest] *Brust* [6] (to) **humiliate** [hjuːˈmɪlieɪt] *demütigen, erniedrigen* [7] **prejudice** [ˈpredʒudɪs] *Vorurteil(e)* [8] (to) **not give a damn (about)** [dæm] *sich einen Dreck scheren (um)* [9] **mad** [mæd] *verrückt, wütend* [10] (to) **split (people) up** [splɪt ˈʌp] *(Menschen) (voneinander) trennen* [11] **gift** [gɪft] *Geschenk* [12] (to) **ease (pain)** [iːz] *(Schmerzen) lindern* [13] **foster home** [ˈfɒstə həʊm] *Pflegeheim, Pflegefamilie*

Lost in the outback

Sam and his mother

1 Sam's story

2.2

a Read the magazine article. Explain how Sam got lost[1] and how he was found.

b What did Sam do wrong? What outback survival tips didn't he follow?

British student Sam Woodhead, 18, was working on a cattle farm in the outback in Queensland during a gap year in Australia. A fan of extreme sports and hoping to go into the army, he went for a run near the farm every day. One Tuesday, after being there for only eight days, he decided to run in the outback and set off with a rucksack full of clothes.

As it was very hot, Sam left at about 4 p.m. His plan was to run for two hours through the scrubland[2]. What he didn't know was that this area with bushes[3] and small trees looked the same for hundreds of kilometres. After running for ninety minutes and then walking for four or five hours to find the way back, he knew he was lost. He had already drunk all his water – he had only taken one litre. He decided to sleep and find his way back the next day.

When he woke up, he started walking and tried to find water. However, all the streams[4] in the area were dry and it was getting hotter and hotter. He spent the night outdoors again, but found it hard to sleep: he heard dingoes and was worried about an attack. Flies were also collecting in his mouth which he couldn't close because his lips and tongue were swollen[5].

Sam then remembered the box of contact lenses[6] in his rucksack. Each one was in a small amount[7] of salt water. He drank the water and immediately felt better. Then he found his own footprints from his run and realized he had been walking in the wrong direction. He began to walk back. Meanwhile[8], his boss at the cattle farm had started a search and planes were looking for him. Sam saw the planes, but they couldn't see him because of the trees.

By Thursday[9] night Sam was very thirsty[10] again. He decided to collect his own urine[11] in his water bottle and drink it, but the terrible taste meant he couldn't drink more than a little bit.

By Friday morning Sam wasn't able to walk and he decided to use some of the clothes from his rucksack to make an SOS sign. Two helicopters flew past without seeing it. In the afternoon another helicopter flew past ... and then suddenly came back. The wind from the helicopter had blown Sam's shorts up in the air and the pilot had seen them!

Sam Woodhead (second left) in rescue helicopter

Sam was taken back to the cattle farm and then to hospital. He had lost 12 kilos in three days. Doctors said he was lucky – he wouldn't have survived another day without water.

Local people asked themselves if Sam had really got lost. Maybe he had actually wanted to do a survival test in the outback like his hero, British adventurer and TV survival expert Bear Grylls, and that was also the reason why he took the rucksack of clothes. Sam said it was just a run that went wrong. Fortunately for him, his story had a happy ending – many others who weren't so lucky have died in the outback.

---

[1] (to) **be/get lost** *sich verlaufen/verirren* [2] **scrubland** [ˈskrʌblənd] *Buschland* [3] **bush, bushes** [bʊʃ] *Busch, Büsche* [4] **stream** [striːm] *Bach, Strom* [5] **swollen** [swəʊlən] *(an)geschwollen* [6] **contact lens** [ˈkɒntækt lenz] *Kontaktlinse* [7] **amount** [əˈmaʊnt] *Menge* [8] **meanwhile** [ˈmiːnwaɪl] *inzwischen, unterdessen* [9] **by Thursday** *bis Donnerstag* [10] (to) **be thirsty** [ˈθɜːsti] *Durst haben* [11] **urine** [ˈjʊərɪn] *Urin*

TF5 BLOG How to manage[1] your money

HARLEY'S blog

Hi guys! My topic today is MONEY.
Maybe you get pocket money from your parents every month or money for your birthday or for Christmas. Or maybe you have a part-time job. I have three tips which can help you manage your money. I also have an inspiring story about an American 16-year-old who has made a big profit by buying stocks[1].

Top three tips to manage your money

1 Get a bank account

If you haven't got a bank account, it's a good idea to open one to manage your money. A **current account** is for money you spend. You can use a **debit card** or a mobile phone app to pay in shops, cafes or online. Or you can use your card to get **cash** out of **cash machines / ATMs**.

2 Check what you spend

You can follow what you spend and **check your balance** online or on a paper **bank statement**. If you didn't buy things on your statement, contact your bank. If you're trying to save money, look what you don't really need.

3 Save when you can

Open a **savings account** to save money in a safe place. You might get a small amount of **interest** from the bank. Put money into your account when you can. You can **transfer** money from your current account.

How a 16-year-old made thousands by investing in stocks

Chongan Wong's grandfather wanted him to learn about money. On his sixteenth birthday he gave Chongan $5,000. But there was a condition: he had to spend it on **stocks**. If he made money, his grandfather would give him another $5,000.
First Chongan spent six months buying stocks with virtual money on a virtual **stock exchange**. Then he started buying real stocks with real money. In two years he earned $57,000. Even Chongan's grandfather was surprised!
Not everybody has a rich grandfather, but this story can inspire everybody to manage money successfully.

1 Managing money

Read Harley's blog. Then match the words in bold with the correct definitions.

a shares[3] in companies
b an account[4] for saving money
c coins and banknotes
d a place where stocks are bought and sold
e money you get from the bank when you save money in an account
f move money from one account to another
g a piece of plastic that you can pay with
h an account for money that you spend
i a machine that gives you money from your account
j a list of money you have taken out of your account
k see how much money is in your account

2 NOW YOU Talking about money

Explain how you manage your money and what other tips you have.
Do you think buying stocks is a good idea? Why or why not?

[1] (to) **manage sth.** [ˈmænɪdʒ] *etwas verwalten* [2] **stock** [stɒk] *Aktie, Anleihe* [3] **share** [ʃeə] *Anteil*
[4] **(bank) account** [əˈkaʊnt] *(Bank-)Konto*

1 Lyra's letter

a Read the information about Lyra McKee.

b 2.3 Read the letter she wrote when she was 24. What was her secret and what effect did it have on her? How did her life change between the ages of 14 and 24? Make a list.

Lyra McKee was a journalist from Northern Ireland. In April 2019 she was reporting from Derry when she was shot and killed by a member of a terrorist organization which is fighting for a united[1] Ireland. She was only 29.
In 2014 McKee wrote an open letter to her teenage self about her future. She wanted to show other teenagers with problems that life can get better.

A letter to my 14-year-old self

Lyra McKee

Kid,

It's going to be OK.

I know you're not feeling that way right now. You're sitting in school. The other kids are making fun of you. You told the wrong person you had a crush[2] and soon, they all knew your secret. They make your life hell[3]. They laugh at you and call you names. Every day, you wake up wondering[4] who else will hate you.

It won't always be like this. It's going to get better.

In a year's time, you're going to join a scheme that trains people your age to be journalists. I know the careers teacher suggested that as an option and you said no because it sounded boring, but go with it. For the first time in your life, you will feel like you're good at something useful. You'll have found your calling[5].

In two years' time, you will leave school and go to a local technical college. Don't worry – you're going to make friends. These will be your first real friends, the people who will answer your calls at 4 o'clock in the morning. When you're 17, you'll tell them your secret and they won't mind. It will take courage[6] but you will do it.

You'll go to university, like you always planned to, but you'll drop out. The campus is just too big and scary. But this experience will be the making of[7] you. Through this, you will meet your best friends. They'll help you replace all the bad memories[8] with good ones. For the first time in your life, you will like yourself.

Before your 21st birthday, you will tell Mum the secret. You can't get the words out so she says it: "Are you gay?" And you will say, "Yes Mummy, I'm so sorry." She tells you how could you ever think that anything would make her love you any less? You will feel like a prisoner who has been given their freedom.

You will tell your siblings[9]. They will all say "I love you," "I'm so proud of you," "This doesn't change a thing."

You will fall in love[10] for the first time. You will have your heart broken for the first time, and you will feel like you might die of the pain. You won't. You will get over it.

Life will not only get easier, it will get so much better. People will use words like "awesome" and "cool" to describe you. You will fall in love again. You will smile every day, knowing that someone loves you as much as you love them.

Keep hanging on[11], kid. It's worth it[12]. I love you.

[1] **united** [ju'naɪtɪd] *vereint* [2] (to) **have a crush (on sb.)** [krʌʃ] *verknallt sein (in jn.)* [3] (to) **make sb.'s life hell** [hel] *jm. das Leben zur Hölle machen* [4] (to) **wonder** ['wʌndə] *sich fragen* [5] **calling** *Berufung* [6] **courage** ['kʌrɪdʒ] *Mut* [7] (to) **be the making of sb.** *jn. zu dem machen, was er/sie ist* [8] **memory** ['meməri] *Erinnerung; Gedächtnis* [9] **siblings** *(pl)* ['sɪblɪŋz] *Geschwister* [10] (to) **fall in love (with sb.)** *sich (in jn.) verlieben* [11] **Keep hanging on!** *≈ Gib nicht auf!* [12] **It's worth it.** [wɜːθ] *Das ist es wert.*

TF7 STORY Oliver Twist *(by Charles Dickens)* Unit 2

1 Oliver goes to work

2.4 **a** Read the information in the box. Then listen to an introduction to the story.

b Look at the first picture: Who are the four people in the foreground?

Charles Dickens This story was written by the famous British writer. It was first published as a series in a newspaper, but there have also been many films and TV series of the story, as well as a popular musical.
In this part of the story, Oliver Twist runs away to London, where he meets a boy called the Dodger who takes him to live with an old man called Fagin and the Dodger's friend Charley Bates.

2 A surprise for Oliver

2.5 **Read the story and look at the second picture. Explain what the Dodger and Charley do, and how Oliver reacts.**

For many days, Oliver stayed in the old man's room, picking the initials[1] out of the handkerchiefs[2]. After a while, he began to miss fresh air and asked to go out to work with the other two boys.

Oliver wanted to work because of the old man's strict character. Whenever the Dodger or Charley Bates came home at night empty-handed, he complained[3] about their lazy[4] habits and sent them to bed without dinner. On one night, he even kicked them both down the stairs[5].

Finally, one morning, Oliver got permission. There had been no handkerchiefs for two or three days, and the dinners had been poor. Maybe this was why the old man told Oliver he might go with Charley Bates and the Dodger.

The three boys went out: the Dodger wearing his hat as usual, Master[6] Bates walking with his hands in his pockets and Oliver between them.

It was a very lazy walk and Oliver soon began to think they were not going to work at all. The Dodger pulled the caps from the heads of small boys while Charley Bates stole apples from the stalls[7] and put them into pockets which were surprisingly big.

They were just coming out of a narrow[8] street when the Dodger made a sudden stop and putting his finger on his lips, pulled the other two boys back.

'What's the matter?' asked Oliver.

'Hush!' replied the Dodger. 'Do you see that old man at the book stall?'

'The old gentleman over there?' said Oliver. 'Yes, I see him.'

'He'll do,' said the Dodger.

'A perfect victim,' said Master Charley Bates.

Oliver looked from one to the other with the greatest surprise.

The two boys walked across the road, and moved close behind the old gentleman. Oliver walked a few steps after them and watched in amazement[9].

The old gentleman was a very respectable[10]-looking person with gold glasses. He had taken a book from the stall, and there he stood reading as if he were in his chair in his own study. He neither saw the book stall, nor the street, nor the boys – just the book itself which he was reading with the greatest interest.

With horror, Oliver saw the Dodger put his hand into the old gentleman's pocket and pull out a handkerchief! He gave it to Charley Bates and

---

[1] **initial** [ɪ'nɪʃl] *Initiale (Anfangsbuchstabe)* [2] **handkerchief** ['hæŋkətʃɪf] *Taschentuch* [3] (to) **complain** [kəm'pleɪn] *sich beklagen, jammern* [4] **lazy** ['leɪzi] *faul* [5] **stairs** *(pl)* [steəz] *Treppe; (Treppen-)Stufen* [6] **Master** ['mɑːstə] *Titel für einen Jungen, der zu jung ist, um Mr genannt zu werden* [7] **stall** [stɔːl] *(Verkaufs-)Stand* [8] **narrow** ['nærəʊ] *eng, schmal* [9] **amazement** [ə'meɪzmənt] *Erstaunen, Verwunderung* [10] **respectable** [rɪ'spektəbl] *ehrenwert*

they both ran away round the corner at full speed!
Oliver stood for a moment in terror. Then, puzzled and frightened, he ran off as fast as he could.
The old gentleman, putting his hand to his pocket, and missing his handkerchief, turned around. Seeing the boy running away at such a speed, he shouted 'Stop thief[1]!' and ran off after him, book in hand.

When the Dodger and Charley Bates heard the cry[2], and saw Oliver running, they suddenly appeared. Shouting 'Stop thief!' too, they ran after him like good citizens.
'Stop thief! Stop thief!' The crowd gets bigger.
Poor Oliver is breathing hard, has terror in his eyes and sweat running down his face.
Stopped at last! He is down upon the pavement and the crowd collect round him. 'Where's the gentleman?' 'Here he is.' 'Is this the boy, sir?'
Oliver lay covered with mud and bleeding from the mouth, looking wildly[3] at the faces around him.
'Yes,' said the gentleman, 'I am afraid it is the boy. Poor fellow[4]! He has hurt himself.'
'I did that, sir,' said a fellow, coming forward. 'I stopped him, sir.'
The fellow touched his hat with a grin[5], expecting something for his actions, but the old gentleman looked at him with dislike.
A police officer at that moment made his way through the crowd and grabbed Oliver by the collar[6].
'Come, get up,' said the man, roughly[7].
'It wasn't me, sir. It was two other boys,' said Oliver, looking round. 'They are here somewhere.'
'Oh no, they aren't,' said the officer. 'Get up!'
'Don't hurt him,' said the old gentleman, kindly.
'Oh no, I won't hurt him,' replied the officer, tearing his jacket half off his back. 'Stand on your legs, you young devil!'
Oliver tried to get up and was at once[8] pulled along the streets by his jacket collar. The gentleman walked on with them. The Dodger and Charley Bates shouted happily and continued on their way.

3 True or false?

Decide if the sentences are true or false. Correct the false sentences.

1. The boys make wallets and handkerchiefs.
2. Fagin treats the boys kindly.
3. The old gentleman thinks Oliver is the thief.
4. The Dodger and Charley Bates help Oliver.
5. The old gentleman is worried about Oliver.
6. The police officer believes Oliver.

4 Imagine you are Oliver

You are Oliver. Explain ...

- what it was like to be an orphan[9] and live in a children's home.
- how you felt when the Dodger offered to help you.
- how you felt when your new 'friends' called you a thief.
- how you felt when the police officer took you away.

5 What will happen to Oliver?

Discuss what you think will happen to Oliver after he is taken away by the police officer. Then find out what happened: look for information online or watch the musical or one of the films.

[1] **thief,** *pl* **thieves** [θiːf, θiːvz] *Dieb/in* [2] **cry** [kraɪ] *Schrei* [3] **wildly** *(adv.)* [ˈwaɪldli] *verzweifelt; unkontrolliert*
[4] **fellow** *(infml)* [ˈfeləʊ] *Mann, Junge* [5] **with a grin** [ɡrɪn] *mit einem Grinsen* [6] **collar** [ˈkɒlə] *Kragen (Mantel, Hemd)*
[7] **rough** [rʌf] *grob, brutal* [8] **at once** *sofort, augenblicklich* [9] **orphan** [ˈɔːfn] *Waise*

TF8 PLAY Get a life!

In this play there are:
- Dad (Joel) and Mum (Alice)
- a son, Luke
- a daughter, Bella
- Luke's friend, Owen

2.6 **1 A short play**

Read this short play. What is it about?

2 NOW YOU

Make groups. Choose who plays which person and what other roles are necessary (for example a director). Practise the play (and film it). Then act the play or show your film to the class. You can also change the scenes or write more stage directions[1].

Scene 1

(Dad knocks and comes into Luke's room. Luke is lying on his bed and is on his phone.)

Dad: *(irritated[2])* Are you on your phone again, Luke?

Luke: Yeah, just watching some videos.

Dad: What a waste of time! Get a life, son! Why don't you start on that German homework you have?

Luke: I'll do it in a minute. ... Look at this video, it's really cool.

Dad: *(sighs)* Do I have to? What is it?

Luke: It's this experiment with cola ... Look! *(shows video)*

Dad: *(reluctantly)* Hmm, OK ... *(watches video)* Wow, that is cool. Hey, what's that video there? Can we watch that one ...

Luke: Well, all right ... *(after watching the video)* Dad, can you go out of my room now please, I need to do my homework.

Dad: Oh, yeah, sorry, those videos were great. Maybe I'll watch some on my phone.

Scene 2

(Mum knocks and comes into Bella's room. The daughter is lying on her bed and is on her phone.)

Mum: *(sighing)* Are you on your phone again? On that photo app? Oh Bella – get a life!

Bella: I'm just looking what my friends have been doing.

Mum: *(not understanding)* But you see them at school all the time.

Bella: Well, Serenity has just been on holiday and she posted some amazing photos. Look!

Mum: Hmm, yes, those mountains are beautiful.

Bella: And Violet is learning to waterski ... this is her first time on water skis.

Mum: Ow! I bet[3] that hurt!

Bella: Well, it was her first try. And this is Sam's latest painting. I think it's really good.

Mum: *(surprised)* Yes, it is, it's fantastic. Your friends are doing some really interesting things, Bella ...
Oh, look at that cake your friend Gavin made! ... And Anna has done a sponsored bike ride to raise money for charity. Very impressive[4].

Bella: Er, Mum, can I have my phone back?

Mum: What? *(reluctantly)* Oh, yes, sorry, here you are.

[1] **stage direction(s)** [steɪdʒ] *Regieanweisung(en)* [2] (to) **irritate sb.** [ˈɪrɪteɪt] *jn. (ver)ärgern, irritieren*
[3] (to) **bet, bet, bet** [bet] *wetten* [4] **impressive** [ɪmˈpresɪv] *beeindruckend, eindrucksvoll*

Scene 3

(Luke is playing a video game with his friend Owen in his room.)

Luke: Oh, that is amazing. Yes!

Owen: Go faster! There, there, there ... Yes!

Dad: *(comes in without knocking, looking at his phone)* Hey, guys, you have to see this video with this baby dancing, it's so funny ... and this one with the cat and the hamster ...

Luke: Er, Dad, we're in the middle of a game.

Owen: Oh no, you missed that one!

Luke: Sorry! ... OK now! Yeesss!

Dad: Oh, sorry. *(walks out looking disappointed)*

Scene 4

(Mum is on the sofa in the living room, looking at photos on a phone app. Bella comes in.)

Bella: Mum, have you been stalking me online?

Mum: Stalking? No, sweetheart. I've just been looking at a few of your pictures.

Bella: Mum, you've liked nearly all my pictures. I know I said you could follow me, but you can't spy[1] on me like this. And my friends said you've followed them as well and written comments. That is so embarrassing[2].

Mum: Why? I'm just interested in what you and your friends are doing.

Bella: It's stalking. And they're my friends, not yours. I'm sorry, Mum, but please stop.

Mum: *(disappointed)* Ok Bella, got it.

Scene 5

(Mum and Dad are on the sofa in the living room, each looking at their phone.)

Dad: *(shaking his head)* Those kids, they're always on their phones.

Mum: Yeah, they really need to get a life.

Luke: *(coming into room)* Hey, I'm going out to meet the boys and maybe watch a film or go bowling.

Mum: *(not really listening)* OK, Luke. ... Joel, look at this here. Bella's friend Sheena is visiting her grandparents in India. ... Their house is amazing.

Bella: *(coming into room)* I'm going to Serenity's flat. We're going to have a meeting of the school party committee to choose the theme of the next school party and sort out[3] who does what.

Dad: *(not really listening)* OK Bella. ... Alice, just look at this video ... *(laughing)* ... how silly can you be?

Mum: *(laughing)* Yes, that's a good one.[4]

Luke: *(rolling his eyes at his sister)* Hey, parents. Get off those screens and get a life!

---

[1] (to) **spy on sb.** [spaɪ] *jm. nachspionieren* [2] **embarrassing** [ɪmˈbærəsɪŋ] *peinlich* [3] (to) **sort sth. out** [sɔːt] *etwas klären, lösen*
[4] **That's a good one.** *Der ist gut. (z. B. Witz)*

TF9 STORY Robinson Crusoe *(by Daniel Defoe; adapted by David Fermer)* Unit 3

1 On a desert island

a Imagine you have to go and live on a desert island. You can take five things with you, but you can't take any electronics. What would you take? Use some of the ideas below or your own ideas.

b Compare ideas. Explain why you chose your five things.

2 A famous story

Read the information about *Robinson Crusoe*. What do you know about the story?

Most people know the story of **Robinson Crusoe**: a man who is shipwrecked[1] in 1659 and lives on a desert island for 28 years. He takes supplies[2] and tools from the ship before it sinks, builds a home, plants seeds[3] and finds wild goats[4], birds and turtles for food. For most of the years on the island he is alone, with only the ship's dog, a parrot and the goats for company. When he finally escapes from the island, he tells his story to Daniel Defoe.
The book was published in 1719. Defoe was inspired by the true story of a man called Alexander Selkirk who spent over four years on a desert island in the South Pacific after his captain left him there in 1704.

3 On the island

2.7

Read this part from the story and answer the questions.

1. What do you think is Robinson's biggest problem?
2. At the end of this part, does Robinson feel optimistic or pessimistic about the future? Explain how and why his attitude changed.

Now that I was well settled in my daily life, my thoughts had more space, and my emotions would often overcome me.[5] Just the thought that my life might end in this place brought tears to my eyes. I would cry like a child, but then I would stop myself and talk to myself, for[6] I had no one to correct me.

"Wait," I would say, "you are right: you are here in a most terrible place, but where are the rest of your comrades? Where are the thirteen men with whom[7] you set sail[8] from Brazil? They are dead, and you are alive."

[1](to) **be shipwrecked** [ˈʃɪprekt] *Schiffbruch erleiden* [2]**supplies** *(pl)* [səˈplaɪz] *Vorräte* [3]**seed** [siːd] *Samen; Saat* [4]**goat** [gəʊt] *Ziege* [5]**my emotions would often overcome me ...** *meine Gefühle überwältigten mich (früher) oft* [6]**for** *denn* [7]**with whom** [huːm] *mit denen, mit dem/der (Relativpronomen)* [8](to) **set sail** [set ˈseɪl] *in See stechen, lossegeln*

At first, this logic helped comfort[1] me, but in the bitterest moments of loneliness, I wondered if it wasn't better to be dead than to be alive.

I couldn't ignore the fundamental difference between these two fates[2] – my own and that of my comrades. The difference was: I had a choice. If I wanted to die, then I could die any time. And if I wanted to live, then I could live. This was a choice my comrades at the bottom of the sea no longer had. That choice had been taken from them.

The more I thought about this, the more[3] I realized that I was lucky, not unlucky, and that happiness is a question of perspective and can be navigated by its owner, much like a captain steers his ship at sea. To have choice is to be human. To have choice is to be alive.

Having a chance at happiness – even if it seemed so far away – is always better than death. My life, although difficult, was still very much in my own hands. There was no immediate threat to my existence. I had plenty of food. I had all the provisions[4] from the ship, which was truly a miracle. Without those provisions, I would certainly have died.

To help me evaluate my situation, and in order to organize my thoughts clearly, I took pen and ink[5], which I had also rescued from the ship, and drew up[6] a table of Good against Evil.

Would you like to see it, sir? I kept a diary for many years. It is the only thing I took with me from the island. I only wrote a few words every day, because I wanted to save ink, but I am glad[7] I still have it. Here, this is my first entry, from the end of October:

Evil	Good
I am stranded on a horrible, desolate[8] island without any prospect[9] of being rescued.	I am alive and did not drown like my comrades on the ship.
I am alone and miserable.	As long as I am alive, there is a chance of happiness.
I have no one to talk to, no friends. I'm not part of any society.	I have plenty to eat and will never go hungry.
I have no clothes to cover me.	It is hot. If I had clothes, I would hardly wear them.
I cannot defend myself[10] against man or beast.	I have seen no wild beasts, unlike during my experience in Africa.

In those months on the island, I often thought of my time on the coast of Africa. I would not have survived there for more than two days in the wild. Here there were no lions, no murdering natives. I was lucky. After making that list, I stopped looking out to sea every day. I was expecting to be on this island for some time, though not forever, for I believed a ship would pass by some day.

After making that list, I stopped waiting for it. Instead, I chose to live.

4 True, false or not in the text?

Choose the correct statements and correct the false ones.

1 At the beginning Robinson thought he was in a terrible place.
2 He was worried about not having enough food in the future.
3 He wrote a list of Good and Evil in order to find out whether he was lucky or unlucky.
4 He missed having clothes.
5 In Africa, wild animals or natives would probably have killed him.
6 Finally, one day, Robinson saw a ship pass by.

5 I chose to live

a Think: Look at the last two sentences. What do you think Robinson meant?

b Pair: Discuss your ideas.

c Share: Tell the class.

[1] (to) **comfort** [ˈkʌmfət] *trösten, beruhigen* [2] **fate** [feɪt] *Schicksal* [3] **the more ..., the more ...** *je mehr ..., desto mehr ...* [4] **provisions** *(pl)* [prəˈvɪʒnz] *Vorräte, Proviant* [5] **ink** [ɪŋk] *Tinte, Tusche* [6] (to) **draw sth. up, drew, drawn** *etwas abfassen, erstellen* (z. B. Text) [7] (to) **be glad** [glæd] *froh sein* [8] **desolate** [ˈdesələt] *trostlos, öde, verlassen* [9] **prospect** [ˈprɒspekt] *Aussicht, Perspektive* [10] (to) **defend yourself (against)** [dɪˈfend] *sich verteidigen (gegen)*

TF10 COMPILATION[1] The world of Shakespeare Unit 4

1 The famous playwright[2]

Read about William Shakespeare. Work in pairs and answer the questions in each section.

Dates and numbers: What is new for you?

The world's most famous playwright, William Shakespeare, was born in Stratford-upon-Avon in England in 1564. His plays have been translated into more than 100 languages and are performed every day around the world.

- He married Anne Hathaway when he was 18 and she was 26. They had three children.
- He wrote at least 37 plays (comedies, tragedies and historical plays) and over 150 sonnets (a type of poem). Some people have questioned whether these plays and sonnets were all actually written by him.
- He died in Stratford-upon-Avon in 1616 when he was 52, which was quite old in those days. It is unclear why he died, but stories suggest that he became ill after drinking too much with friends.

The Globe Theatre: What is special about it?

Shakespeare was a part owner in an acting company. When the company could no longer perform in their old theatre, they took it down and used the materials to build a new theatre in South London in 1559. The theatre was a round open-air theatre for 3,000 people, with the stage[3] in the middle. In 1644 the theatre was pulled down[4]. In 1997, a new Globe Theatre opened in London near the site of Shakespeare's old one. It looks nearly the same as the old theatre and most of the audience stand near the stage to watch the plays. Check out the theatre and plays online!

Shakespeare and India: What's the connection?

Some say that Shakespeare is Bollywood's most successful screenplay[5] writer. The Indian film industry has produced many film versions of his plays and many modern films have storylines[6] based on his works. The themes in Shakespearean tragedies are especially popular in India: romance[7], problems in love, friendship and family issues. His plays are full of deaths and funerals[8], parties and weddings. These are all topics and events which are relevant today.

Performers in a musical adapted from a play by Shakespeare in New Delhi, India, 27/05/2018

1 **compilation** [kɒmpɪˈleɪʃn] *Zusammenstellung* 2 **playwright** [ˈpleɪraɪt] someone who writes plays 3 **stage** [steɪdʒ] *Bühne* 4 (to) **pull down** [pʊl ˈdaʊn] *(Gebäude) abreißen* 5 **screenplay** [ˈskriːnpleɪ] *Drehbuch* 6 **storyline** [ˈstɔːrilaɪn] *Handlung (z. B. Film/Geschichte)* 7 **romance** [ˈrəʊmæns] *Romantik, romantische Liebesgeschichte* 8 **funeral** [ˈfjuːnərəl] *Beerdigung*

Three Shakespeare plays: Which would you like to see?

Hamlet: The ghost of the King of Denmark tells his son Hamlet to kill the new king, Hamlet's uncle. Hamlet pretends[1] to be crazy so he can do this, but his uncle also tries to kill Hamlet. In the end everybody dies.

A Midsummer Night's Dream: Two girls and two boys go to the forest. Puck the fairy uses magic to make both boys fall in love with the same girl. But there is a happy ending and both couples get married.

Twelfth Night: Viola and her twin Sebastian think each other are dead. Viola dresses as a boy but falls in love with Duke Orsino. Orsino is in love with Olivia – but she falls in love with Viola. After much excitement, Sebastian marries Olivia and Viola marries Orsino.

Shakespeare's words and phrases: Which of them do you know?

Many English words and phrases that we use today come from the plays and sonnets that Shakespeare wrote over 400 years ago. He probably invented about 1,700 words.

Words	Phrases
bedroom	Too much of a good thing
gossip[2]	The clothes make the man.
hurry[3]	He has eaten me out of house and home.
kissing	It's Greek to me.
lonely	Jealousy is the green-eyed monster.
skim milk[4]	All that glitters is not gold.

Five famous quotes: What do they mean?

1 'To be, or not to be: that is the question.'
– Hamlet

2 'Some are born great, some achieve greatness, and some have greatness thrust upon[5] them.'
– Twelfth Night

3 'Good night, good night! Parting[6] is such sweet sorrow[7],That I shall say good night till it be morrow.'
– Romeo and Juliet

4 'All the world's a stage,
And all the men and women merely[8] players.'
— As You Like It

5 'It is not enough to speak, but to speak true.'
– A Midsummer Night's Dream

Five good insults[9]: Which do you like best?

1 'Would thou wert[10] clean enough to spit upon[11].'
– Timon of Athens

2 'I am sick when I do look on thee[12].'
– A Midsummer Night's Dream

3 'You have such a February face, so full of frost, of storm and cloudiness.'
– Much Ado about Nothing

4 'Thou hast no more brain than I have in mine elbows.'
– Troilus and Cressida

5 'You kiss by the book[13].'
– Romeo and Juliet

[1](to) **pretend (to be sth.)** [prɪˈtend] *so tun, als ob (man etwas wäre)* [2]**gossip** [ˈɡɒsɪp] *Klatsch, Tratsch* [3]**hurry** [ˈhʌri] *Eile* [4]**skim milk** *Magermilch* [5](to) **thrust sth. upon sb.** [ˈθrʌst əpɒn] *jm. etwas aufdrängen, aufbürden* [6](to) **part (from/with)** [pɑːt] *sich trennen (von)* [7]**sorrow** [ˈsɒrəʊ] *Kummer, Leid* [8]**merely** [ˈmɪəli] *= only* [9]**insult** [ˈɪnsʌlt] *Beleidigung* [10]**Would thou wert ...** [ˈwʊd ðaʊ wɜːt] *= If only you were ...* [11](to) **spit upon** [ˈspɪt əpɒn] *spucken auf* [12]**thee** [ðiː] *dich, dir* [13]**by the book** *streng nach Vorschrift*

TF11 STORY Lion *(by Saroo Brierley)*

Unit 4

1 Going home

Read the end of the story. What is it about?

Saroo was adopted by a kind Australian family, but he never forgot where he was from. One day he started looking for his home using Google Earth. He remembered the train tracks and some features of the nearby town. When he was thirty, after three years of looking, he found his home – and he went back to India to find his mother. Saroo found out his real name was Sheru, which means 'lion'. His story has been made into a film with this name.

My heart was in my mouth[1] as I came to the place where I remembered the old flat to be. And before I could think about what I was expecting, I found myself standing right in front of it.

It looked so small to me, but it was unmistakable[2]. It was also unmistakably empty.

The brick[3] walls were familiar, though the ground level was now covered with cheap concrete[4]. The door to the corner room was in exactly the right place – but the door itself was broken. It was the size of a window in Australia. I couldn't see much through the holes in the door, so around the corner I looked in through the only window, only thirty centimetres square. I couldn't believe that my mother, sister, brothers and I had lived in the small dark space inside. It was perhaps three metres square. The little fireplace was still there, clearly not used for some time, but the water tank had gone. Some of the wall's bricks had fallen out, letting in light. The mud floor, which my mother had always kept clean, was now dusty[5].

While I looked in, a goat[6] ate some hay on a rock by the door. I'd told myself again and again that I couldn't expect to just fly to India and find my family safe and well in the same place after all this time. But it was hard to understand that I'd found the flat without any of them in it. Secretly I had been sure that they'd be here waiting. I watched the goat eat, full of disappointment[7].

I had no idea what to do next. My search was over.

As I stood there, a young Indian woman holding a baby came out of the next door. She spoke to me in Hindi and I understood she was asking if she could help me. I replied, 'I don't speak Hindi, I speak English.' She said, 'I speak English, a little.' Quickly, I said, 'This house ...' and then said the names of my family: 'Kamla, Guddu, Kallu, Shekila, Saroo.' The woman didn't reply, so I repeated the names and pulled out the photos Mum had given me. That was when she told me that no one lived there any more.

It was then that two men walked over to see what was happening, and it was the second – perhaps in his mid-thirties and with good English – who looked at the photos, told me to wait, and then walked off down an alley[8]. I didn't have much time to think about what was happening – other people had begun standing near us, wanting to know what was going on, and why there was a foreigner[9] in these streets where tourists would never visit.

After a couple of minutes the man came back and said those words I'll never forget: 'Come with me. I'm going to take you to your mother.'

He said it very directly, like an official making an announcement. I didn't understand what he'd said until I'd begun to follow him down an alley. Then I got goosebumps and my head began to spin – just moments ago I'd given up twenty-five years of hoping for exactly this. Could it possibly be true that this stranger knew where my mother was? It seemed too unlikely and too fast.

[1] **My heart was in my mouth.** *Mir schlug das Herz bis zum Hals.* [2] **unmistakable** [ʌnmɪˈsteɪkəbl] *unverwechselbar, unverkennbar* [3] **brick** [brɪk] *Ziegel(stein), Backstein* [4] **concrete** [ˈkɒŋkriːt] *Beton* [5] **dusty** [ˈdʌsti] *staubig* [6] **goat** [gəʊt] *Ziege* [7] **disappointment** [dɪsəˈpɔɪntmənt] *Enttäuschung* [8] **alley** [ˈæli] *Gasse* [9] **foreigner** [ˈfɒrənə] *Ausländer/in*

After only about fifteen metres, the man stopped in front of three women who were standing outside a door, all of them looking in my direction. 'This is your mother,' he said. I was too shocked to ask which one – I half asked myself whether this was a trick.

I looked from one woman to the next. The first was certainly not her. There was something familiar about the woman in the middle and the third woman was a stranger. It was the woman in the middle.

She was small and thin, with greying hair, and she was wearing a bright-yellow dress. Despite the years, I knew the fine bone structure of her face the moment I looked back at her, and in that moment she seemed to know me too.

We looked at each other for a second longer. I felt a feeling of sadness that it took a mother and son so long to recognize each other, and then great happiness. She stepped forward, took my hands and held them, and stared into my face with complete surprise. I was thinking clearly enough to understand that whatever I was feeling, at least I'd had some chance to prepare. For my mother, twenty-five years after losing him, her son had simply appeared again. ◈

2 Finding his mother

Read 1–6. Then read the story again and choose the best ending for each sentence.

1 When Saroo found his old flat ...
- A he didn't recognize it.
- B he couldn't believe it was so small.
- C he broke the door to get in.
- D it was exactly as before.

2 When he realized his family weren't there, Saroo ...
- A started to cry.
- B was angry.
- C felt disappointed.
- D didn't feel anything.

3 The young Indian woman next door ...
- A didn't speak English.
- B recognized the photo of his mother.
- C said she couldn't help him.
- D said nobody lived there.

4 When Saroo followed the man, he ...
- A felt happy.
- B didn't really believe what was happening.
- C felt ill.
- D thought it was definitely a trick.

5 Saroo and his mother ...
- A recognized each other immediately.
- B needed a moment to recognize each other.
- C didn't recognize each other.
- D needed help to recognize each other.

6 After so many years, Saroo's mother ...
- A was upset to see him.
- B felt sad and happy at the same time.
- C was amazed to see him.
- D didn't know how to feel.

3 A happy day

Choose one of these tasks.

1 Write interview questions for Saroo and his mother (imagine she can speak English).
2 Write a short conversation between Saroo and his mother.
3 Write a diary entry for this day by Saroo or his mother.
4 Make a drawing of the scene where Saroo and his mother meet.

LF 1 Wiederholung: Zeiten der Gegenwart und der Vergangenheit — Revision: Present and past tenses

Unit 1
p. 12

Present tenses

Simple present: für alles, was **regelmäßig** stattfindet (Gewohnheiten, Hobbys, Routinen), für **Dauerzustände** (alles, was immer so ist).
Signalwörter: *always, usually, often, never, sometimes, today, every day, on Fridays, ...*

Indigenous Australians often pass on their culture and history through art. They usually draw sacred designs in the sand.

Present progressive: für alles, was **gerade im Gang** (noch nicht abgeschlossen) ist.
Signalwörter: *now, at the moment, today, ...*

Today younger artists are interpreting their stories in different ways.
The artist in the photo is working on a picture.

Past tenses

Simple past: um zu sagen, **wann in der Vergangenheit etwas geschehen ist** oder **wann jemand etwas getan hat**; die Handlung / das Ereignis ist abgeschlossen.
Signalwörter: *yesterday, last month, two weeks/years ago, in the 1970s, in 2017, ...*

Thousands of years ago the first Australians painted on rocks and on tree bark.
The artists used natural materials for the colours.

Past progressive: um zu sagen, dass etwas **zu einer bestimmten Zeit in der Vergangenheit im Gang** (noch nicht abgeschlossen) war.
Das *past progressive* steht oft nach *while*.

In the 1970s a teacher noticed their designs while he was teaching near Alice Springs and watching the storytellers.

Past perfect: um zu sagen, dass eine Handlung **vor einer anderen Handlung** oder **vor einem bestimmten Zeitpunkt in der Vergangenheit** stattgefunden hatte.

The elders talked to the teacher because he had asked children to paint things from their culture.
They began to paint on canvas after the teacher had encouraged them to make permanent pictures.

⚠ Wenn die Reihenfolge der Ereignisse klar ist, steht oft das *simple past* statt des *past perfect*.

After James Cook (had) landed in Australia, lots of indigenous Australians were killed.

LF 2 *used to* + Infinitiv — *used to* + infinitive

Unit 1 p. 13

Die Konstruktion ***used to*** [ˈjuːst tə] + **Infinitiv** wird verwendet, wenn man **über einen früheren Zustand oder eine frühere regelmäßige Handlung (eine Gewohnheit)** spricht. Der Zustand bzw. die Gewohnheit besteht heute nicht mehr.

Elders used to put a ring in the boy's ears or nose.
Früher haben die Stammesältesten einen Ring durch die Ohren oder die Nase des Jungen gezogen.

Verneinungen werden mit ***didn't use to*** [ˈjuːs tə] + **Infinitiv** gebildet.

There didn't use to be discipline problems.
Früher gab es normalerweise keine Disziplinprobleme.

Fragen werden mit ***Did … use to*** + **Infinitiv** gebildet.

Did you use to walk to school as a kid, Mum?
Bist du als Kind zu Fuß zur Schule gegangen?

What did you use to do for fun after school?
Was hast du in deiner Freizeit gemacht?

LF 3 *be/get used to* + *-ing*-Form — *be/get used to* + *-ing* form

Unit 2 p. 27

- Die Konstruktion ***be used to*** + ***-ing*-Form** wird verwendet, wenn man ausdrücken will, dass man an etwas gewöhnt ist.

Artem is used to travelling alone.
Artem ist daran gewöhnt, allein zu reisen. / Artem ist es gewohnt, allein zu reisen.

- Die Konstruktion ***get used to*** + ***-ing*-Form** entspricht dem deutschen „sich an etwas gewöhnen".

It was hard for Marina to get used to living with her host family.
Es war schwierig für Marina, sich daran zu gewöhnen, mit ihrer Gastfamilie zu leben / sich an das Leben … zu gewöhnen.

After a while she got used to being a part of the family.
Nach einer Weile gewöhnte sie sich daran, ein Teil der Familie zu sein.

You'll soon get used to speaking English.
Du wirst dich bald daran gewöhnen, Englisch zu sprechen.

⚠ Du darfst *used to* + Infinitiv nicht mit *be/get used to* + -ing-Form verwechseln – vergleiche die Beispiele rechts.

We used to get up early on Saturdays.
Früher sind wir … (immer) früh aufgestanden.
We are used to getting up early.
Wir sind daran gewöhnt, früh aufzustehen. / Wir sind es gewohnt, früh aufzustehen.

LF 4 Wiederholung: Das *simple past* und das *present perfect*

Revision: The simple past and the present perfect

a **Das *simple past***

Unit 2 p. 28

Du verwendest das ***simple past*** für abgeschlossene Handlungen **in der Vergangenheit**. Das ***simple past*** sagt aus, wann etwas geschehen ist oder wann jemand etwas getan hat.
Das ***simple past*** steht oft mit genauen Zeitangaben wie *yesterday, last month, on May 5th, three weeks ago, in 2017*.

The simple past

Marina spent a year in Brighton.

What did Victoria notice in Bamberg?

Ivan didn't go to Amberg. He went to Augsburg.

Ellen moved to Germany a few weeks ago.

b **Das *present perfect***

Unit 2 p. 28

Du verwendest das ***present perfect***, um zu sagen, dass jemand etwas irgendwann getan hat oder dass etwas irgendwann geschehen ist. Der Zeitpunkt wird nicht genannt, weil er unwichtig oder unbekannt ist. Oft hat die Handlung Auswirkungen auf die Gegenwart oder die Zukunft.
Das ***present perfect*** steht häufig mit unbestimmten Zeitangaben wie *already, always, ever, just, never, often, recently, not ... yet*.

The present perfect

People have sometimes told Ivan that his clothes don't look good.

Have you ever noticed that Germans are very direct?

Mila has recently started waiting for the green light when she wants to cross the road.

Harvey has just started drinking coffee. He thinks German coffee is very good.

⚠ **Simple past**
abgeschlossen; genaue Zeitangabe

She spent a month in Italy in 2019.
Sie verbrachte 2019 einen Monat in Italien. (Der Aufenthalt ist vorüber, sie ist zurück.)

Present perfect
Handlung mit Auswirkung auf die Gegenwart; unbestimmte Zeitangabe

I've already packed. We can go now.
Ich habe schon gepackt. Wir können gehen.

⚠ Im Deutschen sind Perfekt und Präteritum oft austauschbar, aber im Englischen nicht:

- Der Interviewer möchte wissen, **ob** (nicht wann!) Melanie schon einmal im Ausland war. → *present perfect*
- Melanie bejaht als Erstes die Frage. → *present perfect*
  Dann fügt sie hinzu, **wann** und **wo** das war:
  I spent the summer holidays in Brighton in 2019. → *simple past*

Interviewer: Have you ever been abroad?
Melanie, warst du schon mal im Ausland? / Bist du schon mal im Ausland gewesen?

Melanie: Yes, I have. I spent the summer in Brighton in 2019.
Ja. Ich habe den Sommer im Jahr 2019 in Brighton verbracht.

LF 5 Wiederholung: Das Futur mit *will* und das Futur mit *going to* — Revision: The *will*-future and the *going to*-future

a Das Futur mit *will*

Unit 2 p. 29

Das **Futur mit *will*** wird verwendet,

- wenn man sagen will, was **in Zukunft geschehen wird**.
  Oft geht es um **Vermutungen oder Vorhersagen** (häufig eingeleitet mit *I think, I'm sure, probably* oder *definitely*) oder um Dinge, die wir nicht beeinflussen können.

- wenn man **spontan** (also ohne es im Voraus geplant zu haben) **eine Entscheidung fällt**. Oft geht es dabei um **Hilfsangebote** oder **Versprechen**.

The *will*-future

I think your presentation will be a big success.

I'm sure you'll like it in Augsburg.

Don't panic, we will definitely find a solution.

My grandmother will be 80 next month.

This exercise looks really difficult.
– Don't worry, I'll help you.

b Das Futur mit *going to*

Unit 2 p. 29

Das **Futur mit *going to*** wird verwendet,

- um über **Vorhaben** und **Pläne** für die Zukunft zu sprechen.

- um auszudrücken, dass etwas gleich geschehen wird, weil es bereits **Anzeichen** dafür gibt.

The *going to*-future

What are you going to do this summer?
Are you going to travel abroad?
– No. I'm not. I'm going to stay at home this year.

LF 6 Indirekte Rede — Reported speech

a Direkte und indirekte Rede

Unit 3 pp. 46–48

- Wenn wir miteinander reden, verwenden wir die sogenannte **direkte Rede**.
- Wenn wir **berichten, was jemand sagt, schreibt oder denkt**, verwenden wir die **indirekte Rede** (*reported speech* oder *indirect speech*).

⚠ Im Englischen steht vor der indirekten Rede kein Komma, und das Wort ***that*** (deutsch: „**dass**") wird oft weggelassen.

Direct speech and reported speech

Ava: "Dad, I'm going to Milo's flat."
Ava says, "I'll be back soon."

Ava says that she's going to Milo's flat.
or Ava says she's going to Milo's flat.

Ava tells her dad that she'll be back soon.
or Ava tells her dad she'll be back soon.

Ava says that Isla Lopez doesn't sell things.
or Ava says Isla Lopez doesn't sell things.

b Indirekte Rede: Aussagen

Unit 3 pp. 46–47

Wenn wir **berichten, was jemand gesagt, geschrieben oder gedacht hat** – also mit Verben im *simple past* wie etwa *said, told me, wrote, thought* –, dann werden die Zeitformen der direkten Rede meist um eine Zeitstufe in die Vergangenheit „zurückverschoben" *(backshift of tenses)*.
Vergleiche:
Direkte Rede: "I have to go."
Indirekte Rede: Ava said she had to go.

Reported speech: statements

Ava said that she was going to Milo's flat.
or Ava said she was going to Milo's flat.

Ava told her dad that she would be back soon.
or Ava told her dad she would be back soon.

Ava said that Isla Lopez didn't sell things.
or Ava said Isla Lopez didn't sell things.

Verschiebung der Zeitformen nach Verben im *simple past* (*Backshift of tenses*)

	direct speech	reported speech
present progressive → past progressive	I'm following Isla Lopez.	Ava said she was following Isla Lopez.
simple present → simple past	Isla doesn't sell things.	She said Isla didn't sell things.
simple past → past perfect	Ava's dad heard about influencers.	Ava told Milo that her dad had heard about influencers.
present perfect → past perfect	Most kids have already used social media.	Milo told me that most kids had already used social media.
can → *could*	We can meet on Friday.	She said we could meet on Friday.
will → *would*	I'll show you one of Tex's videos.	Milo said he would show Ava one of Tex's videos.
am/are/is going to → *was/were going to*	We're going to do a project on social media.	Our teacher told us we were going to do a project on social media.

Beachte:

- Wie im Deutschen werden in der indirekten Rede die **Pronomen** verändert, je nachdem, wer wem berichtet.

Milo *(to Ava)*: "I'll call you when we're back."

Ava *(to Hanita)*: Milo said he would call me when they were back.

Milo *(to his dad)*: I told Ava I would call her when we were back.

- Auch **Zeitangaben** werden in der indirekten Rede aus der Sicht der Berichtenden gewählt. Sie können sich also, je nach Situation, gegenüber der direkten Rede verändern.
- Dasselbe gilt ggf. für Ortsangaben: Aus *here* wird *there*, wenn es die Situation erfordert.

Ava *(to Milo, on Thursday morning)*: "I'm going to call you tomorrow."

Milo *(later the same day)*: Ava said she was going to call me tomorrow.

Milo *(on Friday)*: Ava told me she was going to call me today.

Milo *(on Saturday)*: Ava told me on Thursday that she was going to call me the next day / the following day / on Friday.

Typische Veränderungen von Zeitangaben in der indirekten Rede

now →	*then, at that time*	*next month* →	*the following month, a month later, in May/...*
today →	*(on) that day, yesterday, last Monday/...*	*yesterday* →	*the day before, on Monday/...*
this week →	*that week*	*last week* →	*the week before*
tomorrow →	*today, the next day, the following day, on Monday/...*	*six days ago* →	*six days before, six days earlier, on Monday/...*

c Indirekte Rede: Fragen

Unit 3 p. 48

Auch bei **indirekten Fragen** erfolgt der ***backshift of tenses***, wenn das einleitende Verb im *simple past* steht *(asked, wanted to know)*.

Reported speech: questions

- Wenn die direkte **Frage mit einem Fragewort** beginnt, dann bleibt das Fragewort in der indirekten Frage erhalten.

"How long were you on your phone last night?"

Ava's dad **asked** Ava how long she had been on her phone.

- Ist die direkte Frage eine **Frage ohne Fragewort** *(yes/no question)*, dann wird die indirekte Frage mit ***if*** oder ***whether*** (deutsch: „**ob**") eingeleitet.

"Do you have a strong password?"

Ava's dad **wanted to know** if/whether Ava had a strong password.

Beachte:
- Die **Wortstellung** in indirekten Fragen ist **wie in Aussagesätzen**:
  S – V – ...
  Vergleiche die Wortstellung in den Beispielen rechts.

Statement	I have a strong password.
Direct question	Do you have a strong password**?**
Indirect question	Dad wanted to know **if** I had a strong password. *..., ob ich ein starkes Passwort habe.*

- Wie in der direkten Frage steht eine **Präposition am Satzende**.

Direct question	Who are you talking to?
Indirect question	Mum asked who I was talking to. *..., mit wem ich redete.*

d Indirekte Rede: Bitten, Anordnungen, Ratschläge

Unit 3 p. 48

Reported speech: requests, orders, advice

Bitten, **Anordnungen** und **Ratschläge** werden in der Regel durch eine **Infinitivkonstruktion** wiedergegeben:

- Für die Wiedergabe von **Bitten** verwendet man meist ***ask sb. to do sth.*** (bzw. ***ask sb. not to do sth.***). **(1)**

(1) "Please listen to me. And don't look so angry, please."

Ava's dad asked her to listen to him. And he also asked her not to look so angry.
Avas Vater bat sie, ihm zuzuhören. ...

- Für die Wiedergabe von **Anordnungen** verwendet man meist ***tell sb. to do sth.*** (bzw. ***tell sb. not to do sth.***). **(2)**

(2) "Don't download films from illegal sites. Rent or buy them digitally instead."

My father told me not to download films from illegal sites. He told me to rent or buy them digitally instead.
Mein Vater sagte mir, ich solle keine Filme ... herunterladen. / Mein Vater forderte mich auf, keine Filme ... herunterzuladen.

- Für die Wiedergabe von **Ratschlägen** verwendet man meist ***advise sb. to do sth.*** (bzw. ***advise sb. not to do sth.***). **(3)**

(3) "You should be careful online."

Ava's dad advised her to be careful online.
Avas Vater riet ihr, im Netz vorsichtig zu sein.

LF 7 Wiederholung: Das Passiv — Revision: The passive

a Wiederholung: Aktiv und Passiv

Unit 4 pp. 62–63

- Ein **Aktivsatz** betont, **wer (oder was) etwas tut.** Im Beispiel geht es um professionelle Sänger/innen und was sie tun.
- In einem **Passivsatz** steht im Vordergrund, **was** mit einer Sache oder Person **getan wird** oder **passiert ist**. Das Subjekt des Satzes (*The songs*) handelt nicht.

Revision: Active and passive

Active — Professional singers record the songs.

Passive — The songs are recorded by professional singers.

b Wiederholung: Gebrauch

Unit 4 pp. 62–63

Mit einem **Passivsatz** kann man Handlungen beschreiben, ohne zu sagen, wer die Handlung ausführt. (Wer die Handlung ausführt, ist oft nicht bekannt, unwichtig oder offensichtlich.)

Das Passiv wird oft in Nachrichten und Zeitungsberichten, in technischen Beschreibungen und auf Schildern verwendet, wenn man den „Täter" oder „Verursacher" nicht nennen kann oder nicht nennen will.

Wenn man den „Täter", „Verursacher" oder „Urheber" nennen will, verwendet man die Präposition ***by*** („von", „durch").

Revision: Use

The first Indian film was made over 100 years ago.

About a thousand films are made every year.

Indian films are often filled with colourful song and dance scenes.

Thirteen people were killed in a train crash near Mumbai this morning.

The songs aren't sung by the dancers.

In the first films, women's roles were played by men.

c Form

Unit 4 pp. 62–63

Das Passiv wird mit einer **Form von *be* + Partizip Perfekt *(past participle)*** gebildet.

Form

simple present	*am/are/is* + past participle	English **is spoken** here.
simple past	*was/were* + past participle	This film **was made** in 2018.
present perfect	*have/has* + *been* + past participle	It **has been watched** by millions.
past perfect	*had* + *been* + past participle	The film **had been shown** before.
going to-future	*am/are/is going to* + *be* + past participle	Look, the ticket office **is going to be opened** soon.
will-future	*will* + *be* + past participle	This film **will** never **be forgotten**.
modals	*can/must/...* + *be* + past participle	Tickets **can** also **be bought** online.

d **Wiederholung: Das Passiv von Verben mit zwei Objekten**

Unit 4 pp. 62–63

Auch von Verben mit zwei Objekten kann ein Passiv gebildet werden.

Im Englischen wird meist das **Personenobjekt** des Aktivsatzes (hier: *her*) zum **Subjekt des Passivsatzes** (hier: *She*). Diese Art des Passivs nennt man ***personal passive*** („persönliches Passiv").

⚠ Im Deutschen ist das persönliche Passiv nicht möglich. Stattdessen verwenden wir eine unpersönliche Passivkonstruktion oder einen Aktivsatz (oft mit „man"). Das Subjekt des englischen Passivsatzes *(I/he/she/they)* kann also einem deutschen Dativobjekt *(mir/ihm/ihr/ihnen)* entsprechen.

Revision: The passive of verbs with two objects

Active — Her uncle **offered** her a role in his new film.

Passive — She **was offered** a role in her uncle's new film.
Ihr wurde eine Rolle ... angeboten.

I **was told** about the new film last year.
Mir wurde ... von dem neuen Film erzählt.

He **has been given** a job in Mumbai.
Ihm ist ein Job in Mumbai gegeben worden. / Man hat ihm einen Job ... gegeben. / Er hat einen Job ... bekommen.

They **should be paid** decent wages.
Ihnen sollten anständige Löhne gezahlt werden. / Sie sollten anständige Löhne bekommen. / Man sollte ihnen ... zahlen.

LF 8 Kurzsätze mit *so* und *neither/nor* — Short sentences with *so* and *neither/nor*

a ***So do I.***

Unit 4 p. 64

Mit ***So do I.*** bringst du zum Ausdruck, dass etwas <u>auch für dich</u> gilt.

Statt ***do*** können auch andere Hilfsverben auf ***so*** folgen, z. B. *can, have, am, did*.

Wenn du sagen möchtest, dass etwas <u>auch für jemand anders</u> gilt, kannst du ***So does Leo. / So has Ava. / So can he. / So did she.*** u. Ä. verwenden.

So do I.

I **think** Indian films are great. – So do I.
... – *Ich auch.*

My brother **can play** the guitar. – So can I.

Jonathan **has got** a hamster. – So have I.

Emily **is** very clever. – So am I.

We **went** to India last year. – So did I.

Ava **likes** Bollywood films, and so does Leo.

Leo **has watched** many Bollywood films. – So has Ava.

Jeremy's sister **can speak** Hindi, and so can he.

He **went** to India last summer, and so did she.

b *Neither do I.*

Unit 4
p. 64

Mit ***Neither do I.*** bringst du zum Ausdruck, dass etwas **für dich ebenfalls nicht gilt**.

Statt ***do*** können auch andere Hilfsverben auf ***neither*** folgen, z.B. *can, have, am, did*.

Neither do I.

I **don't like** Indian films. – Neither do I.
... – *Ich auch nicht.*

Jeremy **can't play** the piano. – Neither can I.

Lucy **hasn't got** time. – Neither have I.

Leon **isn't** stupid. – Neither am I.

Mike **didn't do** the shopping. – Neither did I.

Wenn du sagen möchtest, dass etwas **für jemand anders ebenfalls nicht gilt**, kannst du ***Neither has Leo.*** / ***Neither can your boss.*** / ***Neither did their neighbours.*** u.Ä. verwenden.

Ava **has never been** to India, and neither has Leo.

I **can't speak** Hindi. – Neither can your boss.

The Boltons **didn't watch** the late film last night, and neither did their neighbours.

Statt ***neither*** wird auch das etwas förmlichere ***nor*** verwendet: ***Nor do I.*** / ***Nor has Leo.*** / ***Nor can your boss.*** usw.

Grammatische Fachbegriffe (Grammatical terms)

active ['æktɪv]	Aktiv	*We took lots of photos.*
adverb of frequency [ˌædvɜːb əv 'friːkwənsi]	Häufigkeitsadverb	*always, usually, often, sometimes, never*
adverb of manner [ˌædvɜːb əv 'mænə]	Adverb der Art und Weise	*badly, carefully, tidily, well, ...*
adverbial phrase [ædˌvɜːbiəl 'freɪz]	adverbiale Bestimmung	*at school, in town, on Saturday, at the weekend, ...*
article ['ɑːtɪkl]	Artikel	*the, a/an*
auxiliary verb [ɔːg'zɪliəri]	Hilfsverb	*be, do, have, will, can, must, ...*
backshift of tenses ['bækʃɪft]	Rückverschiebung der Zeitformen	*I'**m** tired. → She said she **was** tired.*
comparative [kəm'pærətɪv]	Komparativ	*younger, more famous*
comparison [kəm'pærɪsn]	Steigerung	*old – older – oldest*
contact clause ['kɒntækt klɔːz]	Relativsatz ohne Relativpronomen	*We need a flat **we can afford**.*
direct speech [ˌdaɪrekt 'spiːtʃ]	direkte Rede	*"I'm tired."*
emphatic pronoun [ɪmˌfætɪk 'prəʊnaʊn]	verstärkendes Pronomen	*myself, yourself, ...; ourselves, yourselves, ...*
going to-future ['gəʊɪŋ tʊ fjuːtʃə]	Futur mit *going to*	*I'm **going to stay** at home tomorrow.*
if-clause ['ɪf klɔːz]	Nebensatz mit *if*	*If the rain stops, ...*
imperative [ɪm'perətɪv]	Befehlsform, Imperativ	*go, sing, don't play*

indirect speech [ˌɪndərekt 'spiːtʃ]	indirekte Rede	*She said (that)* ***she was tired****.*
irregular verb [ɪˌregjʊlə 'vɜːb]	unregelmäßiges Verb	*go – went – gone*
main clause ['meɪn klɔːz]	Hauptsatz	*We'll have a picnic.*
modal verb [ˌməʊdl 'vɜːb]	modales Hilfsverb, Modalverb	*can, must, should, ...*
object ['ɒbdʒɪkt]	Objekt	*Ben has* ***an idea****.*
participle construction ['pɑːtɪsɪpl kənˌstrʌkʃn]	Partizipialkonstruktion	*He hurt himself* ***while working in the garden****.*
passive ['pæsɪv]	Passiv	*Lots of photos* ***were taken****.*
past participle [ˌpɑːst 'pɑːtɪsɪpl]	Partizip Perfekt, 3. Form des Verbs	*happened, eaten, gone, ...*
past perfect [ˌpɑːst 'pɜːfɪkt]	Vorvergangenheit, Plusquamperfekt	*John* ***had*** *already* ***left*** *the party*
past progressive [ˌpɑːst prə'gresɪv]	Verlaufsform der Vergangenheit	*We* ***were having*** *breakfast.*
personal passive [ˌpɜːsənl 'pæsɪv]	persönliches Passiv	*She was offered a job.*
personal pronoun [ˌpɜːsənl 'prəʊnaʊn]	Personalpronomen (persönliches Fürwort)	*I, you, he, she, it, we, they; me, you, him, her, it, us, them*
possessive adjective [pəˌzesɪv 'ædʒɪktɪv]	Possessivbegleiter	*my, your, his, her, its; our, your, their*
possessive pronoun [pəˌzesɪv 'prəʊnaʊn]	Possessivpronomen	*mine, yours, his, hers, its; ours, yours, theirs*
preposition [ˌprepə'zɪʃn]	Präposition	*after, at, in, into, near, next to, ...*
present participle [ˌpreznt 'pɑːtɪsɪpl]	Partizip Präsens	*doing, eating, going, ...*
present perfect [ˌpreznt 'pɜːfɪkt]	*Present perfect*	*I* ***have visited*** *Hollywood.*
present perfect progressive [ˌpreznt ˌpɜːfɪkt prə'gresɪv]	Verlaufsform des *present perfect*	*Olivia* ***has been working****.*
present progressive [ˌpreznt prə'gresɪv]	Verlaufsform der Gegenwart	*I'****m playing*** *computer games.*
question tag ['kwestʃn tæg]	Frageanhängsel	*You live in Bamberg,* ***don't you?***
reflexive pronoun [rɪˌfleksɪv 'prəʊnaʊn]	Reflexivpronomen (rückbezügliches Pronomen)	*myself, yourself, ...; ourselves, yourselves, ...*
relative clause [ˌrelətɪv 'klɔːz]	Relativsatz	*I have an aunt* ***who lives in Italy****.*
relative pronoun [ˌrelətɪv 'prəʊnaʊn]	Relativpronomen	*who, which, that, whose, where*
reported speech [rɪˌpɔːtɪd 'spiːtʃ]	indirekte Rede	*She said (that)* ***she was tired****.*
simple past [ˌsɪmpl 'pɑːst]	einfache Form der Vergangenheit	*Kinga* ***flew*** *to Poland last summer.*
simple present [ˌsɪmpl 'preznt]	einfache Form der Gegenwart	*Ben* ***plays*** *football every Saturday.*
subject ['sʌbdʒɪkt]	Subjekt	***My mum*** *is working.*
subject question	Frage nach dem Subjekt	*Who lives here? What happened?*
suffix ['sʌfɪks]	Nachsilbe	*-able, -ful, -ish, ...*
superlative [suː'pɜːlətɪv]	Superlativ	*youngest, the most famous*
verb ['vɜːb]	Verb; Prädikat	
wh-question	Frage mit Fragewort	***What*** *is it? /* ***Who*** *do you love?*
will-future ['wɪl fjuːtʃə]	Futur mit *will*	*I'm sure you* ***will like*** *Plymouth.*
word order ['wɜːd ɔːdə]	Wortstellung	
yes/no question [jes'nəʊ kwestʃən]	Entscheidungsfrage	*Are you 12? Do I look OK?*

Kommunikative Kompetenzen

Listening and viewing skills

SF 1 Listening

Unit 1 p. 9, **Unit 3** p. 49, **Unit 4** p. 59

Es gibt in der Begegnung mit dem Englischen viele Situationen, in denen es darauf ankommt zu verstehen, was gesagt wurde. Ab und zu musst du nur verstehen, worum es generell geht *(listening for gist)*, wie z. B. in Filmen oder Hörbüchern. Manchmal jedoch ist es wichtig, Details zu verstehen *(listening for detail)*, z. B. bei Durchsagen oder in Gesprächen.

Strategien fürs Hörverstehen

1 Listening for gist

Wenn du verstehen sollst, worum es generell geht *(global listening)*, dann mach dir keine Sorgen, wenn du nicht alles verstehst. Du brauchst nicht jedes Wort zu kennen, um den wesentlichen Aussagen folgen zu können.
Überlege dir vorher, um was es gehen könnte, z. B. anhand der Überschrift, der Abbildungen, des Themas. Was erfährst du über die Situation und die Anzahl der Sprecher?
Versuche zunächst grob zu verstehen, worum es in dem Text geht. Konzentriere dich beim Zuhören auf die Schlüsselwörter aus der Aufgabenstellung. Achte auf den Kontext. Manchmal gibt der Text weitere Informationen, die verdeutlichen, was gemeint ist.
So kannst du Wörter erschließen, die du nicht kennst. Mache dir kurze Notizen (ggf. zunächst mit Bleistift). Achte auch auf die Intonation der Sprecher, die dir dabei helfen kann, ihre Stimmung und Absicht einzuschätzen.

Obwohl aus Gründen der Lesbarkeit im Text die männliche Form gewählt wurde, beziehen sich die Angaben auf Angehörige aller Geschlechter.

2 Listening for detail
Wenn du Details und spezifische Informationen heraushören sollst (*detailed* oder *selective listening*), dann überlege dir vorher, welche Informationen du verstehen musst.
Um welche Textsorte geht es und welche englischen Begriffe könnten vorkommen?
Bei Verkehrsnachrichten sind das z.B. Wörter wie *accident* oder *traffic*, bei Durchsagen am Bahnhof oder Flughafen Wörter wie *passenger* oder *first class* oder auch Orte und Uhrzeiten bzw. Gate- oder Bahnsteignummern.
Höre gezielt auf solche Wörter und notiere sie.
Achte auch auf Signalwörter, die dir helfen, dem Inhalt zu folgen und dich auf Einzelheiten zu konzentrieren, z.B. *because, so that, however, then, later, ...*

3 Worauf soll ich achten?
Vervollständige deine Notizen sofort. Auch das, was du nicht aufgeschrieben hast, ist wahrscheinlich noch in deinem Gedächtnis. Dann lies noch einmal genau durch, was du geschrieben hast. Passen deine Antworten zu den Fragen?
Vergleiche nach dem Hören mit einem Partner, was ihr verstanden habt.
Im Unterricht kannst du Audio-Dateien oft zweimal hören. Konzentriere dich beim zweiten Hören auf das, was du beim ersten Mal nicht verstanden hast.

Tipps zum Hörverstehen

Bei Telefonnummern wird zweimal die gleiche Zahl *double*, dreimal die gleiche Zahl *triple* ausgesprochen. Die Zahl 0 ist im britischen Englisch *oh*, im Amerikanischen *zero*. Bei E-Mail-Adressen gilt: „@“ wird *at* und „.“ wird *dot* ausgesprochen.

Schau dir deine Lieblingsfilme oder -serien auf Englisch an. Blende Untertitel ein, falls du Probleme beim Verstehen hast. Blende sie aus, wenn du dich sicherer fühlst oder eine Episode schon mehrfach gesehen hast.

SF 2 Viewing

Unit 1 pp. 9, 19, **Unit 2** p. 25, **Unit 3** pp. 43, 55, **Unit 4** pp. 59, 69

Bei Aufgaben zum Hörsehverstehen verstehst du vieles über das Hören, aber auch die visuelle Darstellung ist wichtig für das Verständnis der Szenen und aussagekräftig, um beim Publikum z.B. Spannung, Angst oder Freude auszulösen.

1 Vor dem Sehen
Überlege dir vor dem Sehen, welche Art *(genre)* von Film du sehen wirst: Handelt es sich z.B. um einen Dokumentarfilm *(documentary)*, eine Komödie *(comedy)* oder einen (Musik-/ Erklär-/...) Videoclip?
Wo und wann spielt der Film *(setting)*? Welche Figuren gibt es *(characters)*?
Lies sorgfältig die Aufgabenstellung. Worum könnte es gehen und worauf solltest du besonders achten? Betrachte die Filmszenen im Buch vor dem Anschauen.

2 Kameraeinstellungen *(shots)*

Die Einstellungsgröße der Kamera beeinflusst, wie nah die Zuschauer dem Gezeigten sind und wie Szenen dadurch wahrgenommen werden. Sie ist ein Hinweis auf die Wichtigkeit der dargestellten Personen und Gegenstände und ihre Wirkung. Je nachdem, welche Aspekte im Zentrum stehen sollen, können sie z.B. gefilmt werden als:

- **Nahaufnahme *(close-up)***, bei der z.B. Mimik und Gestik im Fokus stehen

close-up

- **Halbtotale *(medium shot)*,** die die Handelnden mit ihrer näheren Umgebung erfasst

medium shot

- **Totale *(long shot)***, die das Ganze einer Szene und ihre Umgebung, z.B. zum Überblick über die Situation, darstellt

long shot

3 Der Soundtrack

Die Tonspur hat großen Einfluss darauf, wie du eine Szene wahrnimmst. Das sind die Unterhaltungen der Personen, der Klang ihrer Stimmen, Begleitkommentare, Geräusche und die Musik. Besonders Musik hat großen Einfluss auf unsere Wahrnehmung. Eine spannende Szene wird eher mit lauter und schneller Musik unterlegt, eine romantische Szene wahrscheinlich mit ruhiger und leiser Musik.
Achte auch auf die Körpersprache *(body language)* und den Gesichtsausdruck *(facial expression)* der Personen.

4 Redewendungen, um über Filme zu sprechen

This film is about/shows/tells the story of ...
It is set in ... *(place and time)*.
The music in this scene is moving/powerful/sad/...
The music creates/builds/supports ...
The actor's body language helps to create a feeling of danger/happiness/...
In this scene the music/effects/camera shot ... supports the plot / ...
The camera work/soundtrack helps to ...

Reading skills

SF 3 Reading a text

Unit 1 pp. 16–18, **Unit 2** pp. 33–35, **Unit 3** pp. 50–52, **Unit 4** pp. 66–68

Du begegnest z. B. im Internet oder auf Reisen häufig englischen Texten. Wenn du effektive Lesestrategien entwickelst, wirst du sicherer mit Texten umgehen können. Lies viele englische Texte, um sie immer schneller und besser zu verstehen und deinen Wortschatz zu vergrößern.

Lesestrategien

1 Reading for gist *(skimming)*

Beim *Reading for gist* geht es darum, dir einen Überblick über einen Text, z. B. eine Zeitungsseite oder eine Website, zu verschaffen und den Kerngedanken zu erfassen. Dabei ist es nicht wichtig, dass du jedes einzelne Wort liest und alle Details verstehst. Meist musst du nur einen kurzen Blick auf den Text werfen *(skimming)*, um die Textsorte und die zentrale Botschaft zu erkennen. Achte dabei vor allem auf

- Überschriften (auch Untertitel und Zwischenüberschriften)
- Bilder, Illustrationen und Bildunterschriften sowie fett gedruckte Wörter
- den ersten Satz von jedem Absatz (oft der *topic sentence*, der den Hauptgedanken nennt)
- den letzten Absatz des Textes (oft eine Zusammenfassung).

2 Reading for specific information *(scanning)*

Beim *Scanning* durchsuchst du einen Text gezielt nach bestimmten Informationen, z. B. Öffnungszeiten, Preisen oder Abfahrtszeiten. Überlege dir passende Schlüsselbegriffe *(keywords)*. Möchtest du zum Beispiel Öffnungszeiten wissen, dann könnten das Wörter wie *open, hours, am–pm* oder Zahlen sein.
Lies nicht Zeile für Zeile, sondern diagonal und überfliege dabei den Text auf der Suche nach den Schlüsselwörtern. Dazu bewegst du die Augen und ggf. einen Finger in breiten Bewegungen von oben nach unten über den Text.

3 Wie finde ich die Hauptaussagen eines Textes?

Willst du Texte wie z. B. Kommentare oder Berichte richtig verstehen, musst du ihre Hauptaussagen erkennen und verstehen. Schau dir die Struktur dieser Texte genauer an.
Jeder Text dreht sich um ein Thema und hat eine Kernaussage. Du findest sie häufig im ersten Absatz. Lies diesen deshalb besonders gründlich durch. Die Hauptaussage wird in der Regel durch weitere Aussagen bzw. Gedanken unterstützt, die du oft im ersten oder letzten Satz der weiteren Absätze findest, zusammen mit Beispielen und Begründungen.
Die folgenden Wörter und Wendungen werden oft im Zusammenhang mit Begründungen und Beispielen verwendet: *because, e.g. / for example, etc., this shows that, that's why ...*

Lies nicht Wort für Wort, sondern vollständige Sätze und versuche, den Sinn zu erfassen.

Falls du Texte im Internet liest, kannst du über deinen Browser mit Strg+F nach deinen Schlüsselwörtern suchen und nur die Textstellen lesen, in denen *keywords* markiert sind.

SF4 Writing a CV

Unit 2 p. 30

1 Allgemeine Tipps

Wenn du dich auf eine Stelle bewirbst, ist es wichtig, dich ansprechend und aussagekräftig vorzustellen. Die Abkürzung CV kommt aus dem Lateinischen *(curriculum vitae)* und bedeutet Lebenslauf. Im CV (oder *résumé* im Amerikanischen) listest du deine bisherige Ausbildung, deine Fähigkeiten und Interessen auf.
Dein Lebenslauf sollte nicht länger als eine Seite und klar gegliedert sein mit fett gedruckten Überschriften, die das Lesen erleichtern. Im Lebenslauf (z.B. im *personal statement*) verwendest du keine Kurzformen, sondern Langformen (z.B. *I am* statt *I'm*).
Denke daran, vor dem Abschicken gründlich zu prüfen, ob in deinem CV noch Rechtschreib- oder Grammatikfehler sind.

CURRICULUM VITAE

Finn Kollmann
Hasenheide 19, 90407 Nürnberg
Mobile: 0162/2090503 Email: finn.kollmann@beispiel.de

> In GB und den USA ist kein Bewerbungsfoto üblich.

> Geburtsdatum und-ort werden in GB und den USA meist nicht erwähnt.

Personal statement
I am a polite and confident person with good communication and computer skills. I am looking forward to getting more practical work experience.

> Beginne mit einem *personal statement*, in dem du kurz beschreibst, warum du dich für den Job oder das Praktikum eignest.

Work experience

May 2019	two weeks at a local IT company, organized by my school
2018–present	Saturday job as a waiter in a local cafe

> Bei der Aufzählung deiner Jobs, Praktika und Schulen usw. steht das Aktuellste oben.

Education and training

2016–present	Olof-Palme-Realschule, Nürnberg
2012–2016	Regenbogen Grundschule, Fürth

> Liste deine bisherigen Schul- und Ausbildungsstationen, auch alle bisher gemachten Abschlüsse.

Personal skills
Languages: First language: German; Foreign languages: English, French

Communication skills: Good communication skills from my experience at school and as a waiter

Organizational skills: Good teamwork skills, good time management

Skills for specific jobs: Ability to deal with computer problems quickly and creatively

Digital skills: Excellent knowledge of Microsoft Office

> Erwähne deine Qualifikationen und deine Fertigkeiten und betone besonders das, was für die Stelle wichtig ist.

Hobbies and interests
Coding, member of school computer club and after-school basketball club

> Wenn es passt, kannst du am Schluss deine Hobbys und Interessen ergänzen.

SF 5 Writing a formal letter or email

Unit 2 p. 31

1 Allgemeine Tipps

Beim Schreiben von förmlichen Briefen und E-Mails, z. B. bei Anfragen, Beschwerden oder bei Bewerbungen, ist es wichtig, bestimmte Regeln zu beachten.

Hasenheide 19
90407 Nürnberg

→ Schreibe deine Adresse in die rechte obere Ecke.

Walker's Electronics
Attn: Alice Dunn
8 Springfield Park
Brighton BN2 7ZA
Great Britain

15th May 20...

→ Die Anschrift des Adressaten steht links und das Datum rechts.

Dear Ms Dunn

→ Beginne dein Schreiben mit *Dear Madam or Sir*, wenn du keine Kontaktperson hast. Üblicherweise steht kein Komma nach der Anrede.

I am writing to apply for the job of part-time shop assistant at Walker's Electronics that I saw on your website yesterday.

→ Nenne den Grund deines Schreibens im ersten Abschnitt.

As I like being with people and have always had a special interest in computers, I would love to work for you this summer.

Last year I did school work experience at an IT company which gave me an excellent understanding of what IT companies require.
I have had a job as a waiter at a local cafe for the last two years and during that time my responsibilities have increased. I am also proud to provide excellent customer service at all times. I am used to working flexible hours and willing to learn new things. As I speak English, French and German, I would also be able to help international visitors.

→ Ergänze weitere wichtige Informationen in den nächsten Abschnitten (z. B. Gründe für deine Bewerbung, Qualifikationen, warum du geeignet bist, wann du Zeit hast, etc.).

Therefore I think I have the skills that are required to be a shop assistant.

During my school holidays in August I could work at any time.
Please find my CV attached, and I can provide references if you require them.

→ Erwähne mögliche Referenzen und ende mit einem freundlichen Ausblick.

I look forward to hearing from you.

Yours sincerely

Finn Kollmann

Finn Kollmann

→ Beende deinen Brief mit *Yours sincerely*, wenn du den Adressaten namentlich kennst, oder mit *Yours faithfully*, wenn du keinen Ansprechpartner hast, und deinem Namen. In amerikanischen Briefen schreibst du *Sincerely (yours)* bzw. *Yours truly*.
Übrigens, informelle Briefe oder E-Mails beendest du mit einem freundlichen Gruß wie *Best wishes, Love, All the best, …*

2 Was muss ich bei einem Bewerbungsschreiben beachten?

Wenn du dich bewirbst, benötigst du neben dem Lebenslauf (→ SF 4) ein Begleitschreiben (*cover letter*, auch *letter of application*), das nicht länger als eine Seite sein sollte. Lege dar, warum du für die Position, auf die du dich bewirbst, geeignet bist und zeige, dass du dich wirklich dafür interessierst. Dabei ist es wichtig, Fehler zu vermeiden und höfliche und formelle Sprache zu verwenden. Erwähne, welche Dokumente du beifügst.

Mediation skills

SF 6 Mediation

Unit 1 p. 14, **Unit 2** p. 36, **Unit 3** p. 53, **Unit 4** p. 70

Bei der Mediation (Sprachmittlung) musst du zwischen unterschiedlichen Sprachen vermitteln und z. B. englische Informationen auf Deutsch wiedergeben oder umgekehrt. Wie und was genau du von der einen in die andere Sprache übertragen musst, hängt von der Situation ab.

1 Worauf musst du achten?

Mediation ist keine wörtliche Übersetzung, sondern das sinngemäße Übertragen von Inhalten in die andere Sprache. Gib also nur die wesentlichen Informationen sinngemäß wieder und lasse Unwichtiges weg. Vergiss dabei aber bedeutungstragende Wörter nicht. Es ist meist nicht nötig, dass du jedes Wort genau verstehst, um die wichtigsten Punkte richtig wiedergeben zu können.

Mündliche Informationen:

- Höre zielgerichtet auf die gesuchten Informationen.
- Verwende einfach strukturierte, eher kurze und klare Sätze.

Schriftliche Informationen:

- Bei Mediationsaufgaben im Unterricht hast du in der Regel eine Aufgabenstellung, die dir sagt, welche Stellen du wiedergeben sollst. Du musst also nicht den ganzen Text verstehen.
- Scanne den Text gezielt nach den gesuchten Informationen (→ SF 3). Markiere die wichtigsten Textstellen und mache dir Notizen am Rand (→ SF 22.1).

2 Paraphrasing

Manchmal fällt es schwer, etwas auf Englisch wiederzugeben, weil du z. B. das genaue Wort nicht kennst oder es dir in der Situation nicht sofort einfällt. Dann **paraphrasiere**. Das bedeutet, etwas mit anderen Worten auszudrücken oder zu umschreiben. Besonders wichtig ist dabei das Prinzip „Keep it simple". Statt nach einer genauen Übersetzung zu suchen, formuliere eine einfache Erklärung.

Diese Strategien helfen dir dabei. Umschreibe mit ...

- Wörtern, die eine ähnliche oder die gleiche Bedeutung haben (Synonyme), gegensätzlichen Wörtern (Antonyme) oder mit Vergleichen.

  > It's very similar to ...
  > It's the opposite of ...

- Definitionen und Erklärungen: Erkläre Eigenschaften des gesuchten Begriffes, z. B. mithilfe von Relativsätzen.

  > It's a thing that you use when ...
  > It's a place where ...

- Oberbegriffen und Unterbegriffen: Umschreibe mit dem Oberbegriff, wenn du die einzelnen Unterbegriffe nicht kennst bzw. mit Unterbegriffen und Beispielen, wenn du das Wort für den Oberbegriff nicht weißt.

  > *Zehen*: They are a part of my foot.
  > *Geschirr*: glasses and plates ...

3 Cultural differences

Es gibt „typisch deutsche" Dinge und Traditionen, die dein Gegenüber vielleicht nicht kennt. Erkläre dann, was du meinst. Frage höflich nach, wenn dein Gegenüber über etwas aus seiner Kultur spricht, was du nicht kennst.

> I'm sorry, I've never heard of this tradition / rule / meal ...
> Could you please explain it?

Speaking skills

SF 7 Having a conversation

Unit 1 p. 15

Unterhaltungen gelingen gut, wenn du freundlich, höflich und aufgeschlossen bist.

1 Worauf musst du achten?

- Beginne die Unterhaltung freundlich und mit allgemeinen Fragen zu etwas, das dich mit deinem Gesprächspartner verbindet, z.B. dem Ort oder der Situation.

> Hi, I'm Emir. How are you? Are you enjoying ...?

- Stelle dich auf deinen Gesprächspartner ein. Wenn du mit einem Gleichaltrigen sprichst, kannst du viel informeller sein und über andere Themen sprechen als mit jemand Älterem.

> Well, ... / So, ...
> You mentioned / talked about ...
> What about you?

- Halte eine Unterhaltung am Laufen, indem du genau zuhörst und dein Interesse durch gezieltes Nachfragen zeigst.

> Really? That's amazing.
> That sounds interesting.

- Vermeide einsilbige Antworten, um nicht unfreundlich zu wirken. Reagiere auf das Gesagte und erzähle auch etwas von dir. Wenn du etwas nicht verstanden hast, kannst du deinen Gesprächspartner bitten, das Gesagte zu wiederholen und zu vertiefen. Formuliere Fragen und Bitten höflich.

> I also like ...
> Sorry, what do you mean?
> Can you say that again, please?

SF 8 Taking part in an interview

Unit 3, p. 55

Oft ist ein Interview ein Bestandteil einer schulischen Situation, einer Prüfung oder Bewerbung. Bereite dich gut darauf vor.

1 Vorbereitung

Bei einem Bewerbungsgespräch solltest du vorher so viel wie möglich über den Job und den Arbeitgeber herausfinden. Notiere dir Fragen, die du stellen möchtest. Überlege dir auch vorher Antworten auf mögliche Fragen, die dir gestellt werden könnten, z.B. warum du für die Stelle geeignet bist. Übe das Interview vorab vor dem Spiegel oder mit einer vertrauten Person. Überlege dir vorher den Weg, damit du pünktlich bist.

2 Während des Interviews

Stelle dich am Anfang freundlich vor. Höre gut zu und sprich deutlich und nicht zu schnell. Lass dir Zeit, Fragen zu beantworten. Antworte nicht nur mit „Yes" oder „No", sondern versuche, höflich und ausführlich zu antworten. Wenn du etwas nicht verstehst, frage nach. Bedanke dich am Ende für das Gespräch.

> Nice to meet you.
> Thank you for inviting me today.
> I'm really interested in this job because ...
> I am not sure if I have understood your question correctly ...

SF 9 Making a formal phone call

Unit 2 p. 32

Telefonate in einer Fremdsprache, z. B. um den Termin für ein Vorstellungsgespräch auszumachen, kannst du gut vorbereiten.

1 Vorbereitung

Notiere dir den Namen deines Gesprächspartners, damit du ihn ansprechen kannst. Lege dir einen Notizzettel und einen Stift bereit, um Notizen zu machen (z. B. wann du wo sein sollst). Notiere dir vorab Stichpunkte, auf die du im Telefonat eingehen möchtest, wie z. B. deine Arbeitszeiten oder die Bezahlung.

2 Während des Telefonats

Nenne deinen Vor- und Nachnamen. Hör gut zu, sprich deutlich und nicht zu schnell.
Über deine Stimme wird viel wahrgenommen. Daher sei mit deiner Stimme und deiner Sprache überzeugend und verstelle dich nicht. Bilde kurze Sätze, damit dein Gegenüber dir gut folgen kann.
Frage nach, wenn du etwas nicht verstehst, egal ob es ein akustisches oder ein inhaltliches Problem ist.
Am Ende des Gesprächs bedanke dich und verabschiede dich freundlich.

> The line is very bad.
> I'm afraid I can't hear you.
> Sorry, I didn't catch that.
> Could you speak more loudly, please?

> I'm sorry, I don't understand. /
> I didn't understand that.
> What do you mean?
> Could you repeat that, please?

SF 10 Describing pictures

Unit 3 p. 54, Unit 4 p. 59

1 Auf den ersten Blick

Stelle die Abbildung vor und sage, woher sie kommt. Beschreibe die Situation allgemein.

> I'd like to talk about this photo of ...
> This picture shows ...

2 Was ist wo? Schau genau!

Sage, wen oder was du siehst und wo etwas zu sehen ist. Ordne die Personen, Orte und Dinge einander zu. Was tun die Personen gerade *(present progressive)*? Beschreibe die Personen und Gegenstände genauer.

> At the top/bottom there is ...
> In the foreground/background/middle I can see ...
> Above / Between / In front of / Next to / Under ...

3 Was denkst du?

Überlege, woher sich die Personen kennen, wie sie sich fühlen, was vielleicht vorher passiert ist oder was gleich geschehen könnte.

> I think they look ...

4 Werbung beschreiben

Wenn du Werbung analysierst, dann beschreibe das Produkt, die Bildsprache und die Wirkung, die damit erzielt werden soll. Wer ist die Zielgruppe und was ist die Botschaft? (→ Wordbank 4 → p. 98)

> The advert contains ...
> colour / language / writing / ...
> The design of the ad suggests ...
> It will appeal to ...
> The ad sends the message that ...

SF 11 Giving a presentation

Unit 2 p. 37

Sowohl in der Schule als auch später im Beruf ist es wichtig, dass du einen guten Vortrag halten kannst. Zu einer gelungenen Präsentation gehören eine sorgfältige Vorbereitung, ein sinnvoller Aufbau und eine ansprechende Veranschaulichung.

1 Sammle Informationen

Nutze verschiedene Medien, um Informationen zu sammeln, z. B.: Internet, Bücher, Zeitschriften, Zeitungen. Prüfe deine Quellen und Informationen sorgfältig (→ SF 21).

2 Notiere und ordne deine Informationen

Du kannst die Informationen in einer Mindmap, als Stichpunkte oder in einer Tabelle sammeln. Auch Karteikarten bieten sich für deine Notizen an. Schreibe nur die wichtigsten Stichworte auf. Strukturiere deine Notizen genauso wie deine Präsentation. Hebe die wichtigsten Begriffe mit verschiedenen Farben hervor. Notiere, wann du welches Medium einsetzt.

3 Strukturiere deinen Vortrag

- Baue deinen Vortrag sinnvoll auf. In der Einleitung weckst du das Interesse der Zuhörer, z. B. mit einem Foto, einem kurzen Film oder auch einem sprachlichen Impuls, der zum Nachdenken anregt (einer Frage, einem Zitat, einer Anekdote oder einer kontroversen Aussage). Gib deinen Mitschülern zu Beginn deines Vortrags einen Überblick, was sie erwartet.
- Im **Hauptteil** stellst du die Informationen vor, angeordnet z. B. nach ihrer Wichtigkeit oder dem zeitlichen Ablauf. Leite jedes neue Thema ein und mache danach eine kurze Pause.
- Am **Schluss** steht eine Zusammenfassung oder ein Ausblick.

Today I am going to talk about ...
Firstly, I'm going to give you some information about ...
Secondly, ... / Finally, ...

On the next slide you can see ...
Now I would like to explain how ...

To sum up, ...

4 Veranschauliche das Gesagte

Um das Interesse deiner Zuhörer zu behalten, gestalte deine Präsentation abwechslungsreich. Du kannst das Gesagte z. B. mit Bildern, Diagrammen oder Gegenständen unterstreichen. Schalte den Bildschirm zwischendurch auch mal aus und bewege dich im Raum. Verwende kurze, verständliche Sätze, gib Beispiele und fasse dich kurz.

Let me explain ...
These statistics show ...

5 Präsentiere deinen Vortrag

- Bereite alles in Ruhe vor und warte, bis es ruhig ist.
- Sprich langsam und deutlich. Lies nicht von deinen (Computer-)Folien ab. Schau nicht nur auf deine Notizen, sondern schau auch dein Publikum an und lächle.
- Bleibe ruhig, wenn du kurz den Faden verlierst oder Zeit benötigst.
- Bedanke dich bei deinen Zuhörern und beantworte Fragen.

Just a moment, please.
Sorry, let me just take a quick look at this slide.

SF 12 Having a discussion

Unit 4 p. 64

Ziel einer Diskussion ist es, Ideen und Meinungen zu einem Thema auszutauschen. Dabei musst du sowohl deinen eigenen Standpunkt begründen als auch auf andere angemessen eingehen. Damit eine Diskussion gut funktioniert, ist es für den Ablauf wichtig, dass du dich höflich, klar und präzise äußerst.

1 Vorbereitung

- Bereite dich auf eine Diskussion vor, indem du Fakten und Beispiele zum Thema recherchierst, dir Gedanken über deine Meinung machst und Notizen erstellst, auf die du während der Diskussion zurückgreifen kannst.
- Überlege dir vorher einen Satz, der deine Meinung gut wiedergibt. So wird der Einstieg in die Diskussion leichter.

2 Rolle der Teilnehmer

- Alle Teilnehmer hören einander gut zu, lassen andere ausreden und bleiben stets höflich und sachlich. Fragt nach bei Unklarheiten.

3 Ablauf einer Diskussion

- Lege deine Position dar und sage zu Beginn der Diskussion klar, was genau du zu diesem Thema denkst. Begründe deine Meinung und nenne Gründe und Argumente, die deinen Standpunkt unterstützen. Habe nützliche Wörter und höfliche Redewendungen parat.

> In my opinion / view, ...
> If you ask me ...
> The problem is that ...
> I strongly believe that ... – So do I.

- Hake in der Diskussion bei den Standpunkten der anderen nach und widersprich mit sachlichen Argumenten. Reagiere angemessen.

> You may be right there, but I don't agree with you / think so too.
> You've got a good point there, but ...

- Falls dich jemand nicht ausreden lässt, dann setze höflich nach, um deinen Gedankengang zu Ende zu bringen.

> Can I just finish what I was going to say?
> Sorry to interrupt you, but ...
> Just let me add one more thing.

- Fasse deine Argumente am Schluss prägnant zusammen. Einigt euch auf eine Lösung oder einen Kompromiss, wenn das nötig ist.

> To sum up, ...
> Our conclusion is ...
> We agreed ...

Methodische Kompetenzen

SF 13 Learning words

Unit 1 p. 20, **Unit 4** p. 68

Wie und wo lerne ich Vokabeln?

1 Führe dein Vokabelheft, deine Vokabelkartei oder Computer-Vokabelliste aus Klasse 8 weiter. Du lernst neue Vokabeln am besten an einem ruhigen und aufgeräumten Platz. Für unterwegs kannst du sie dir aufs Handy sprechen oder per Vokabeltrainer-App üben.

2 **Du merkst dir neue Wörter noch besser, wenn du …**

a sie unter Oberbegriffen sortierst und diese z. B. auf Karteikarten sammelst (Vorderseite: Oberbegriff; Rückseite: passende Wörter dazu, ggf. mit Illustrationen).

b Wörter, die zu einem Wortfeld gehören, in einem *word web* (Wortnetz), einer Tabelle oder einem Diagramm strukturierst.

c **Synonyme**, also Wörter mit der gleichen Bedeutung, und **Gegensatzpaare** sammelst (→ SF 15.2).

Vokabeltrainer-Apps

Vokabeltrainer-Apps bieten neben den abwechslungsreichen Aufgaben mit Informationen über Bedeutung und Aussprache zusätzliche Vorteile:

- Du kannst deinen eigenen Wortschatz eingeben und gezielt üben – auch unterwegs.
- Wortschatz kannst du als Karteikarten anzeigen und vorlesen lassen.
- Es gibt zusätzlich aufeinander aufbauende interaktive Möglichkeiten des Wiederholens und Übens.
- Dein Lernfortschritt wird in Statistiken dokumentiert.

SF 14 Understanding new words

Unit 1 p. 20, **Unit 3** p. 52

Wie kann ich unbekannte Wörter erschließen?

1 **Bilder und Überschriften**
Bilder zeigen dir oft Dinge, deren englische Bezeichnungen du im Text noch nicht kennst.

2 **Erschließen aus dem Kontext**
Manchmal hilft dir der Kontext, also die Wörter oder die Sätze vor und nach dem neuen Wort.

3 **Internationalismen und Ähnlichkeiten zum Deutschen**
Viele englische Wörter sind international gebräuchlich. Du verstehst sie problemlos, z. B. *attachment, audiobook, cyberbullying, human rights, password, (to) pop up, statement, (to) stream, tool,* …
Andere Wörter wiederum sind deutschen Wörtern in Schrift und Klang ähnlich, sodass du sie leicht erschließen kannst, z. B. *adoption* – Adoption, *attractive* – attraktiv, *expert* – Experte, *horoscope* – Horoskop, *(to) panic* – in Panik geraten, *pilot* – Pilot, …

4 Wortfamilien und Wortbildungsgesetze

a Wörter aus der gleichen Wortfamilie lassen sich meist gut erschließen. Kennst du das Verb *make*, verstehst du auch die Nomen *maker* oder *making*. Manchmal sind sogar die Formen für unterschiedliche Wortarten gleich: *(to) name, a name*.

b Manche Nomen sind aus mehreren Teilwörtern (meist zweien) zusammengesetzt *(compound nouns)*. Du kennst *(to) use* und *name* und kannst dir daher *username* erschließen.
Wörter können auch verkürzt werden: aus *application* wird z. B. *app*.

c Oft werden Wörter mithilfe verschiedener Vor- oder Nachsilben gebildet:

Präfixe (Vorsilben)		
dis-/un-	Ein Wort wird in sein Gegenteil verkehrt.	*belief* ⟶ *disbelief*
super-	Ein Nomen oder Adjektiv wird verstärkt.	*fast* ⟶ *superfast*
Suffixe (Nachsilben)		
-able	Aus einem Verb wird ein Adjektiv.	*suit* ⟶ *suitable*
-er	Aus einem Tätigkeitsverb wird eine Person oder ein Gerät.	*sweep* ⟶ *sweeper*
-ful	Aus einem Nomen wird ein Adjektiv.	*help* ⟶ *helpful*
-ing	Aus einem Verb wird ein Adjektiv oder ein Nomen.	*inspire* ⟶ *inspiring*
-less	Mit *-less* verkehrt man Adjektive in ihr Gegenteil oder macht aus einem Nomen ein Adjektiv.	*helpful* ⟶ *helpless* *home* ⟶ *homeless*
-ment	Aus einem Verb wird ein Nomen.	*require* ⟶ *requirement*

SF 15 Increasing your vocabulary

Unit 1 p. 20

Wie kann ich meinen (englischen) Wortschatz erweitern?

1 Kollokationen

Oft ist es hilfreich und sinnvoll, Wörter nicht isoliert, sondern in geläufigen Zusammenhängen zu lernen. Nutze daher (Online-)Wörterbücher, um Kollokationen – gebräuchliche Wortverbindungen, z. B. *do athletics / ... vs. play cricket / ... vs. go snorkeling / ...* – nachzuschlagen und so deinen Wortschatz zu erweitern. Weitere Kollokationen findest du im Vocabulary (S. 163).

2 Synonyme und Antonyme

Um in Texten häufige Wiederholungen eines Wortes zu vermeiden, kannst du Synonyme, also Wörter, die eine ähnliche Bedeutung haben wie andere Wörter, verwenden (z. B. *fast – quick*). Antonyme dagegen sind Wortpaare, deren Bedeutungen in einer Gegensatzbeziehung stehen (z. B. *fast – slow*). Wenn du also zu Wörtern neue Begriffe mit ähnlicher oder gegenteiliger Bedeutung suchst, kannst du diese in speziellen Wörterbüchern nachschlagen, sammeln und lernen.

3 Idioms

Jede Sprache hat spezifische Redewendungen – also Kombinationen aus zwei oder mehr Wörtern, die unabhängig von der Bedeutung der Einzelwörter einen neuen bildhaften Sinn erhalten. Solche *idioms* lassen sich nicht durch einfache 1:1-Übersetzung erschließen, aber du kannst sie unter den zentralen Begriffen im Wörterbuch nachschlagen (gekennzeichnet durch idiom. oder IDM). Eine Spezialform sind die *phrasal verbs*, bei denen durch Kombinieren gebräuchlicher Verben (wie *get, give, take, ...*) mit Präpositionen oder Adverbien eine neue Bedeutung entsteht.

SF 16 Using an online dictionary

Unit 1 p. 15, Unit 4 p. 70

Wie benutze ich ein Online-Wörterbuch?

Englisch ↔ Deutsch

accommodation

1 Suchfeldeingabe
Gib das Wort in das Suchfeld ein und beachte die richtige Schreibweise.

2 Aussprache anhören
Durch einen Klick auf das Lautsprechersymbol [🔊] kannst du dir das Wort anhören. Manchmal gibt es regionale Varianten, d.h. Wörter werden beispielsweise im britischen Englisch anders ausgesprochen als im amerikanischen Englisch.

3 Wortart wählen
Manchmal kann das gleiche Wort ein Substantiv, ein Adjektiv oder ein Verb sein.

4 Unterschiedliche Bedeutungen beachten
Oft sind mehrere Beispiele (auch ganze Sätze) dafür angegeben, wie das Wort verwendet werden kann. Wähle das Beispiel, das dem Satz in deinem Text am nächsten kommt.

SF 17 Giving feedback

Unit 2 pp. 30, 39, 77–78, Unit 4 p. 73

Gegenseitige Rückmeldungen helfen dir und deinen Partnern dabei, eure Leistungen zu verbessern. Dabei solltest du einige grundlegende Dinge beachten.

1 Wie gehe ich vor?
Wenn du zu einem Text oder einer Präsentation Feedback geben sollst, ist es wichtig, dass du
- den Text sorgfältig liest bzw. der Präsentation aufmerksam folgst.
- dir aussagekräftige, sachliche Notizen machst. Ein Feedbackbogen kann dir dabei helfen.
- deine Aussagen stets sachlich begründest.

2 Wie gebe ich positives Feedback?
Es ist einfacher und angenehmer, etwas zu loben, als es zu kritisieren. Deine Rückmeldung sollte allerdings nicht aus oberflächlichen Floskeln bestehen *(It was a nice text/presentation.)*, sondern sich auf konkrete Gesichtspunkte wie Inhalt, Struktur, Wortwahl, Grammatik und Verständlichkeit beziehen.

Feedback checklist

CONTENT: Anna's text / presentation is ...	☺	😐	☹	**comments**
easy to understand		✔		
informative and clear	✔			*many details*
interesting/exciting			✔	
...				
LANGUAGE: You ...				
join ideas with linking words	✔			*because, however, in addition*
use good phrases and different adjectives	✔			*environment-friendly, silky, organic*
use correct grammar (tenses, adverbs, comparisons, ...)			✔	*uses wrong tense (past tense)*
have correct spelling and punctuation		✔		*comfortable, sustainable*
...				
PRESENTATION: You ...				
spoke clearly		✔		
gave interesting information			✔	
used different media	✔			*PC, poster, video*
had a good plan		✔		
...				

3 Wie weise ich auf Dinge hin, die verbessert werden sollten?

Deine Rückmeldung sollte immer **respektvoll** sein. Niemand darf sich persönlich angegriffen oder beleidigt fühlen. Beginne daher mit einem gut gelungenen Aspekt, den du loben kannst. Gesichtspunkte, die du für weniger gelungen hältst, solltest du dann nicht nur konkret und sachlich benennen, sondern auch Vorschläge machen, wie man sie verbessern – z. B. anders formulieren oder ergänzen – kann.

Wenn du selbst **Feedback erhältst**, verbessere deine Fehler. Überdenke die Hinweise und Vorschläge, die dir von anderen gemacht wurden, und arbeite sie wenn möglich ein.

> I'm afraid you did not use many linking words. Include linking words like "therefore", "although" or "overall".
> Maybe a few more visuals would make it easier to understand part 2 of your talk.

SF 18 How to do better in tests

Revision 1 pp. 40–41, **Revision 2** pp. 74–75

Wie kann ich meine Leistungen verbessern?

Mit diesen Tipps kannst du häufige Fehler vermeiden und bessere Ergebnisse in Tests erzielen.

1 Lerne aus deinen Fehlern: Führe ein Fehlerprotokoll

Ein Fehlerprotokoll *(error log)* kann dir helfen, deine typischen Fehler zu erkennen. Lege eine Übersicht an, in der du notierst, welche Fehler du gemacht hast und wie sie verbessert werden müssen – als handgeschriebene Liste, Notizbuch, Schnellhefter, Karteikasten oder Computerdatei. Ergänze sie, wenn du eine korrigierte Arbeit zurückbekommst und nutze diese Kategorien:

GR = *grammar*: Grammatikfehler, z. B. falsche Verbform (~~sayed~~ statt *said*), falsche Präposition (*in* statt *on*) etc. Hier kann dir oft das *Language file* ab S. 114 helfen.

SP = *spelling*: Falsche Schreibweise, z. B. *My father* ~~*new*~~ *I would like it* statt *My father knew* ...

WW = *wrong word*: Du verwechselst Wörter und ihre Bedeutungen bzw. kannst sie nicht korrekt anwenden. Wiederhole die Vokabeln mithilfe des *Vocabulary* ab S. 146.

FF = *false friend*: Leider gibt es einige Wörter, die im Deutschen und Englischen ähnlich klingen oder aussehen, aber eine andere Bedeutung haben (z. B. *rock* = Fels, Rock = *skirt*).

WO = *word order*: Fehler bei der Wortstellung (*Yesterday* ~~*read I*~~ ... statt *Yesterday I read*).
Wenn du die Liste am Computer führst (z. B. als Tabelle), kannst du sie nach der Art der Fehler sortieren lassen. Dann findest du schnell heraus, in welchem Bereich du die größten Schwierigkeiten hast, und kannst dich darauf konzentrieren, indem du z. B. gezielt ein bestimmtes Grammatikkapitel oder ein spezielles Wortfeld wiederholst. Studiere diese Liste vor der nächsten Schulaufgabe gründlich.

My error log			
sentence with error (fehlerhafter Satz)	correct sentence (korrigierter Satz)	type of error (Art des Fehlers)	notes (Hinweise, Tipps und Notizen)
I became a great DVD for Christmas.	I got a great DVD for Christmas.	false friend (FF)	to become = werden to get = bekommen
My father new I would like it.	My father knew I would like it.	spelling (SP)	klingt gleich, hat andere Bedeutung
My brohter also liked it.	My brother also liked it.	spelling (SP)	Buchstaben vertauscht
I saw it in the internet.	I saw it on the internet.	grammar (GR)	falsche Präposition
It gives many great films at the moment.	There are many great films at the moment.	wrong word (WW)	Es gibt = There is / There are!
My dad sayed he wanted to see you.	My dad said he wanted to see you.	grammar (GR)	(to) say, said, said – s. Liste *irregular verbs* (S. 222f.)
If it rains tomorrow, can we go to the cinema.	If it rains tomorrow, we can go to the cinema.	word order (WO)	Wenn ein Nebensatz vorausgeht, ändert sich die Wortstellung *subject – verb* des Hauptsatzes nicht.

2 Tipps für Prüfungen

- Konzentriere dich bei der Arbeit. Es geht nicht um Geschwindigkeit, sondern um gute Ergebnisse!
- Übe neue Wörter und Wendungen der letzten Unit mit dem *Vocabulary*. Wiederhole auch bekannten Wortschatz regelmäßig. Lasse dich am besten von jemandem abfragen.
- Lerne neue Wendungen im Zusammenhang, statt nur Einzelwörter (z.B. *I look forward to Christmas.*). Wiederhole die grammatischen Schwerpunkte der Unit mit den *Introduction*-Seiten im Schülerbuch. Lies die dazugehörigen Teile im *Language file*.
- Wenn du etwas nicht verstehst, schlage im *Language file* oder in deinen Unterlagen nach und frage deine Lehrkraft oder deine Mitschüler/innen.

3 Prüfungsvorbereitung

- Beginne rechtzeitig mit deiner Vorbereitung. Verschaffe dir zunächst einen Überblick über den Prüfungsstoff und teile ihn in überschaubare Abschnitte ein. Hake Erledigtes ab.
- Lerne, deine typischen Fehler zu vermeiden – mithilfe deines *error logs*.
- Informiere dich über die üblichen Aufgabenstellungen und stelle sicher, dass du genau verstehst, was du tun musst.

4 Während der Prüfung

- Bleibe stets konzentriert und optimistisch. Lass dich nicht nervös machen.
- Lies dir die Arbeitsanweisungen genau durch. Wichtiges kannst du markieren (→ SF 22.1).
- Wenn du fertig bist, überprüfe, ob du alle geforderten Punkte abhaken kannst.
- Teile dir die Zeit gut ein. Oft hilft es, mit etwas Leichtem zu beginnen. Wenn du merkst, dass du bei einer Aufgabe nicht weiterkommst, lege sie beiseite und schaue sie später wieder an. Plane am Ende genügend Zeit ein, um deine Antworten noch einmal in Ruhe durchlesen und korrigieren zu können.

SF19 Working with charts and diagrams

Unit 3 p. 57

Tabellen und Diagramme stellen Vergleiche zwischen mindestens zwei Dingen dar. Sie veranschaulichen komplexe Informationen und helfen dabei, sie besser verstehen und vergleichen zu können. Du kannst mit Diagrammen Entwicklungen aufzeigen und Überblicke geben.

1 Arten von Diagrammen

Englisch	Deutsch	verwendet für ...	Beispiel
bar graph / bar chart	Balken-/Säulen-diagramm	Vergleich von Mengen oder Größen	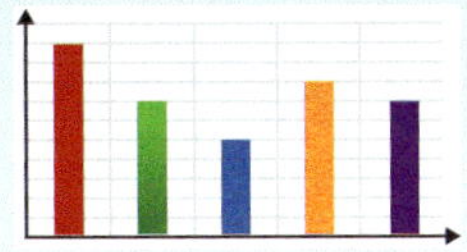
chart/table	Tabelle	Vergleich unterschiedlicher Daten	(siehe Beispieltabelle unten)
infographic	Infografik/ Piktogramm	bildliche Darstellungen mit Symbolen und/oder Bildern	
line graph / line chart	Linien-/Kurven-diagramm	Entwicklungen oder Verläufe	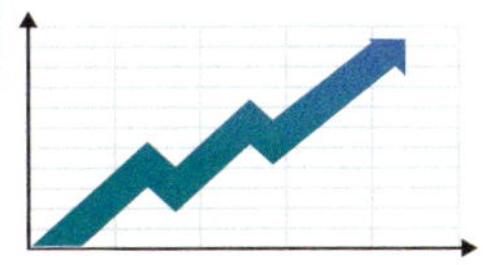
map	Landkarte	Orte oder Entfernungen abbilden	
pie chart	Torten-/ Kreisdiagramm	Überblick über prozentuale Verteilung	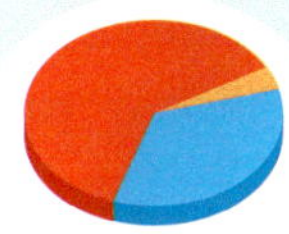
Venn diagram	Venn-/Mengen-diagramm	Beziehungen zwischen Mengen (Gemeinsamkeiten und Unterschiede)	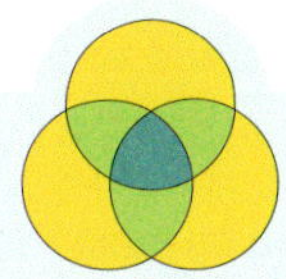

	COLUMN TITLE 1	COLUMN TITLE 2
First Row	140 598	148 564
Second Row	240 452	248 698
Third Row	278 564	283 478
Fourth Row	360 455	364 458
Fifth Row	420 451	422 659
TOTAL	**1 440 520**	**1 467 857**

2 Aufbau

Schritt 1: Schau dir zuerst die Überschrift, die Erklärungen und Beschriftungen an. Sie geben dir Hinweise auf den Inhalt. Schau dann auf die Einheiten der Angaben.
Möglich sind Größen- oder Mengenangaben, Jahreszahlen oder Prozentsätze.
Beschreibe, was das Diagramm aussagt (Thema) und nenne deine Quelle.
Schritt 2: Beschreibe die Hauptaussagen des Diagramms (Inhalt und äußere Gestaltung).
Schritt 3: Fasse die wichtigsten Ergebnisse zusammen.

> This diagram presents/compares/...
> This chart shows the position of / the development of / a trend ...
> The number of ... grows/increases/rises/drops/falls ...
> The number of ... does not change ...
> 25 per cent / One quarter of ...
> The horizontal/vertical axis shows ...

3 Eigene Diagramme erstellen

Schau dir die Tabelle mit den Arten von Diagrammen in **1** an. In der mittleren Spalte findest du einige typische Verwendungsbeispiele für Torten-, Balken oder Kurvendiagramme sowie Infografiken, Karten etc. Diese helfen dir zu entscheiden, in welcher Form du die von dir erhobenen Zahlen, Daten oder Informationen am übersichtlichsten darstellen kannst. Nutze einen Computer und finde geeignete kostenlose Online-Tools, um dein Diagramm zu gestalten.

Text- und Medienkompetenzen

SF20 Making a podcast

Unit 4 p. 73

Als Podcast wird zumeist eine Serie von Audiodateien zu einem bestimmten Thema (z. B. aus Politik, Kultur, Sport etc.) bezeichnet. Podcasts haben meistens einen oder zwei Sprecherinnen und Sprecher.
In einem Podcast kannst du z. B. Rechercheergebnisse oder deine Meinung und Erfahrungen zu einem bestimmten Thema vorstellen.

1 Vorbereitung

Sammle Informationen zu deinem Thema. Nutze das Internet, Bücher und Zeitungen. Prüfe deine Informationen sorgfältig. Trage deine Informationen in Stichpunkten, als Mindmap oder auf Karteikarten zusammen und ordne sie.

2 Schreibe deinen Text

Es hilft, wenn du aufschreibst, was du sagen möchtest. Ein Podcast ist meistens so aufgebaut:

- **Begrüßung:** Die Sprecher begrüßen die Zuhörer, nennen das Thema und geben einen knappen Überblick, worum es in dem Podcast gehen wird.
- **Hauptteil:** Hier werden die wichtigsten Informationen zum Thema vorgestellt. Manchmal findet anschließend auch eine kurze Diskussion zum Thema statt.
- **Schluss:** Abschließend verabschieden sich die Präsentatoren von den Hörern, meist verbunden mit einem Ausblick auf das Thema der nächsten Folge und wann sie erscheint. Manchmal bitten sie auch um Rückmeldung und Meinungen zum Thema, die z. B. in sozialen Netzwerken geäußert werden können.

Die Sprache in Podcasts unterscheidet sich stark. Oft hängt es vom Thema ab, ob eine formelle oder eher informelle Stilebene gewählt wird. Wichtig ist allerdings, dass du die Hörer immer direkt ansprichst. Wie bei anderen Textsorten (z. B. Präsentationen) auch, machen gut aufgebaute und präzise formulierte Texte es deinen Hörern leichter, deine Gedanken nachzuvollziehen. Daher solltest als Basis für deinen Podcast immer einen schriftlichen Entwurf verfassen, diesen kritisch überprüfen (z. B. indem du ihn laut vorliest) und dann überarbeiten.

3 Aufnahme

Nimm deinen Podcast mithilfe eines Smartphones, Tablets oder Computers auf. Wenn du unsicher bist, lies deinen Text einfach vor. Achte dabei auf eine lebendige Betonung!

Sprich langsam, laut und deutlich und mache zwischendurch kurze Pausen. So können dir deine Zuhörer besser folgen.

Wenn du dich versprichst, nimm den Absatz mit dem Versprecher neu auf. Mithilfe von Schnittprogrammen kannst du deine Aufnahme hinterher ganz einfach bearbeiten und nur die gelungenen Abschnitte zusammenschneiden.

SF 21 Doing internet research

Unit 4 p. 71

Im Internet kannst du schnell und einfach Informationen zu allen Themen finden. Aber sei bei deiner Recherche vorsichtig, denn nicht alles, was du im Netz findest, ist wichtig und richtig. Benutze auch Lexika und (Fach-)Bücher aus der Bücherei, Zeitungen und (Fach-)Zeitschriften.

1 Verwende Suchmaschinen

- Formuliere präzise Suchbegriffe, die dein Thema genau beschreiben. Gibst du beispielsweise *tea* in eine Suchmaschine ein, erhältst du u.a. viele kommerzielle Angebote. Kombinierte Suchbegriffe wie z.B. *tea production in India* grenzen die Ergebnisse deutlich ein.
- Die Reihenfolge der Suchbegriffe verändert die Ergebnisse. Verwendest du zusätzlich eine weitere Suchmaschine, erhältst du z.T. unterschiedliche Ergebnisse.
- Nutze die erweiterte Suche, um die Sprache deiner Ergebnisse, die Länder oder auch die Domänen (z.B. *.edu* oder *.gov*) einzugrenzen.

2 Überprüfe deine Ergebnisse und Quellen kritisch

- Das erste Suchresultat muss nicht das Beste sein und auch nicht unbedingt richtig. Wikipedia-Seiten können Fehler enthalten, da die Artikel von freiwilligen Helfern geschrieben werden.
- Analysiere die Ergebnisse kritisch und überprüfe die Endung der Seite. Eher vertrauenswürdig sind die Endungen *.gov, .org* und *.edu*; weniger vertrauenswürdig sind Websites von Firmen *(.com)*, persönliche Blogs, Fanseiten oder Websites von Interessengruppen. Diese verwenden oft weniger neutrale Sprache, um subjektive Meinungen und Einstellungen auszudrücken. Auch hier kannst du Interessantes finden, solltest aber kritisch bei der Verwendung von Inhalten sein.
- Es ist leicht, Bilder zu verfälschen, zu manipulieren oder aus dem Zusammenhang zu reißen. Führe eine umgekehrte Bildersuche durch, indem du das gefundene Bild wieder hochlädst und weitere Fundorte überprüfst.
- Um die Glaubwürdigkeit einer Nachricht zu prüfen, führe eine Gegenprobe in anderen Quellen durch. Unseriöse Nachrichten erkennst du an Merkmalen wie reißerischen oder unpassenden Überschriften, polarisierender Sprache, fehlenden Angaben zum Autor, fehlenden Belegen oder an einem veralteten Datum. Überprüfe auch das Impressum der Webseite. Verwende im Zweifel auch eine URL-Prüfseite.

3 Organisiere deine Internetrecherche

- Speichere die besten Ergebnisse deiner Suche als Lesezeichen ab. Übersichtlich wird es, wenn du sie thematisch sortierst.
- Drucke die wichtigsten Informationen aus, markiere sie und mache dir Notizen (→ SF 22.1).
- Notiere bei jeder deiner Informationen die URL mit Datum des Seitenabrufs und den Autor.

4 Beachte das Copyright

- Schreibe Texte nicht einfach wörtlich ab. Gib stets die exakte Quelle an.
- Bilder sind in der Regel urheberrechtlich geschützt. Verwende daher eigene oder lizenzfreie Bilder *(creative commons)*. Überprüfe die Lizenz sorgfältig: Sind die Bilder gemeinfrei (CC0) oder gibt es Einschränkungen (z.B. Nennung der Urheber)?

SF 22 How to write good texts

Unit 1 p. 21

Gut aufgebaute und präzise formulierte Texte machen es deinen Lesern leichter, deine Gedanken nachzuvollziehen – egal, um welche Textsorte es sich handelt. Auch bei Präsentationen und Projekten sind gute Texte wichtig.

Plane deine Texte, bevor du einen **ersten Entwurf** erstellst. Diesen **überarbeitest** und verbesserst du dann, bis du mit dem Ergebnis zufrieden bist. Das ist zwar zeitaufwändig, aber deine Belohnung sind gelungene, gut lesbare Texte.

1 Planungsphase

Mache dir zunächst klar, über welches **Thema** du schreiben willst.
Welche **Textsorte** ist verlangt? Sollst du eine Geschichte schreiben, eine Zusammenfassung, einen Bericht oder eine Rezension? Jede Textsorte hat unterschiedliche Merkmale. Dementsprechend musst du dabei unterschiedliche Regeln beachten.
Während eine Geschichte z.B. lebendig und anschaulich sein sollte, muss eine Beschreibung, wie z.B. einer Sportart, sachlich formuliert werden (siehe A).

Dann **recherchiere oder sammle** die Informationen, die du für dein Thema benötigst.
Ordne und **strukturiere** deine Materialien
- durch sinnvolle Markierungen (siehe B)
- mithilfe von Mindmaps
- mit Klebezetteln, die du leicht neu anordnen, austauschen oder ergänzen kannst.

Mache **Notizen** (siehe C), **sammle** Ideen, Argumente und ggf. benötigten Wortschatz.
Lege eine **Gliederung** an in Einleitung, Hauptteil und Schluss. Der Hauptteil kann mehrere Unterpunkte mit Unterüberschriften haben (siehe D). Ordne deine Materialien diesen Bestandteilen des Textes zu.

A

Textsorte: description of a sport
- informativ und detailliert: enthält genaue Informationen über die Sportart und ihre Regeln
- relevant: bezieht sich auf die Sportart allgemein, nicht auf einzelne berühmte Sportler oder Teams
- objektiv geschrieben: keine persönliche Bewertung der Sportart, sondern sachliche Schilderung der Regeln und Besonderheiten *(fact file)*

B

Texte markieren
Du kannst wichtige Textstellen
- mit Textmarker hervorheben
- unterstreichen
- umkreisen
- mit Symbolen und Abkürzungen markieren (?, !, ☺, ☹, →)
- durch Notizen am Rand hervorheben.

C

Notizen erstellen
☺ Notiere nur die wichtigsten Wörter, die Schlüsselwörter *(key words)*. Das sind in der Regel Substantive oder Verben.
☺ Mit *wh*-Fragewörtern *(what, where, when, who, why)* kannst du deine Notizen strukturieren und wichtige Antworten notieren.
☺ Benutze Abkürzungen und Symbole:

=	the same as	≠	not the same as
+, &	and	/	or
!	important	?	open question
x	no or wrong	✔	yes or right
→	becomes / will be		
e.g.	for example		

2 Schreibe deinen Text

Jetzt schreibe einen ersten Entwurf. Strukturiere deine Sätze gut. Ergänze passende **linking words**, also Konjunktionen (z.B. *because, however, therefore*). Verwende auch Relativpronomen (z.B. *that, who, where*) und Adjektive, die Personen und Dinge genauer beschreiben, um den Text zu einem stimmigen und zusammenhängenden Ganzen zu machen.

Beginne für jede Idee einen neuen Absatz.

D

Aufbau *description of a sport*

A Einleitung
allgemeine Informationen über die Sportart

B Hauptteil: Beschreibung der Regeln
– Angaben zu Spielort, Anzahl der Spieler, Zubehör, ...
– Spieldauer und Regeln

C Schluss
Ermittlung des Siegers

verwendete Zeitform: *present tense*

3 Überprüfe und korrigiere deinen Text

Wenn der Entwurf fertig ist, lies ihn mehrfach selbstkritisch durch und prüfe ihn unter mehreren Aspekten, am besten in getrennten Durchgängen, mit Pausen dazwischen:

- Aufbau und Lesbarkeit: Hat der Text eine logische Struktur? Ist er verständlich und liest sich flüssig?
- Sprache: Untersuche den Text nach verschiedenen formalen Aspekten wie Rechtschreibung, Zeichensetzung, Grammatik, *linking words, ...*
- Ausdruck: Ist der Text abwechslungsreich und lebendig gestaltet? Verwendest du treffende Adjektive und Adverbien ebenso wie abwechslungsreiche Verben? Gibt es Wortwiederholungen?
- typische Fehlerquellen: Groß- und Kleinschreibung, unregelmäßige Pluralformen (z.B. *child – children, shelf – shelves*), gleicher Klang, aber unterschiedliche Schreibweisen (z.B. *to – two – too, there – their – they're*) und unregelmäßige Verben (s. Liste auf S. 222f.).

Describing sports: Rugby

Überschrift: Name der Sportart

Rugby is a very physical ball sport which is played between two teams of 15 players.
Each team has two groups known as forwards (8) and backs (7).
Rubgy is played outside with an oval ball. The rugby field has three sections: one main playing area which is 100 metres long and 70 metres wide and two goal areas from 10 to 20 metres. The goal posts at the end of the field are H-shaped and stand 5 to 6 meters apart.

Einleitung: kurze Erklärung / Definition der Sportart

Players of each team wear polos of the same colour with matching shorts and socks. They usually wear mouthguards, head guards and special boots.
A rugby match lasts 80 minutes with a break after the first half of 40 minutes. The team with the ball must move the ball up the field. The ball can never be passed forwards, but players can run forwards with the ball or kick the ball forward. The opposing team needs to stop the attacking team by tackling and trying to get the ball.

Hauptteil: Beschreibung der Regeln, z.B.:
- Spielort / -feld
- Zahl und Ausrüstung der Sportler
- Spielregeln

The aim of the game is to score more points than the other team. There are four different ways to score points. The team with more points is the winner.

Schluss: Ziel des Spiels, Ermittlung des Siegers

Das **Vocabulary (S. 146–180)** enthält alle neuen Wörter und Wendungen des Buches, die du lernen musst. Sie stehen in der Reihenfolge, in der sie im Buch zum ersten Mal vorkommen.

Hier siehst du, wie das Vocabulary aufgebaut ist:

quota ['kwəʊtə]	Quote	Let's discuss female **quotas**. Do you think **quotas** will stop discrimination against women?
		the money that your employer pays you for doing your job
		adjective: **pharmaceutical** – *noun:* **pharmaceutical** (Arzneimittel) Das Substantiv steht meist im Plural: **pharmaceuticals**.
biotechnology [baɪəʊtek'nɒlədʒi]		That stuff you're eating isn't natural at all! It's a product of **biotechnology**.
multinational [mʌl		►► in or from different countries *adjective:* **multinational** – *noun:* **multinational** (multinationaler Konzern, Multi)
positive discrimination [pɒzətɪv dɪˌskrɪmɪ'neɪʃn]		a policy that helps people who normally have certain disadvantages (e.g. because of gender, colour of skin or social background) to be treated more fairly
among [ə'mʌŋ]		**among** ◄► **between**
p. 61 **position** [pə'zɪʃn]		
almost ['ɔ:lməʊst]		►► nearly
employee [ɪm'plɔɪi:]		**employment** ◄► **unemployment** **employed** ◄► **unemployed** **self-employed** ◄► **employed by a company** An **employer** gives people work. An **employee** works for a company / an **employer**.
majority [mə'dʒɒrəti]	Mehrheit, Mehrzahl	**majority** ◄► **minority** [maɪ'nɒrəti] (Minderheit) There are 16 girls and 13 boys in my class. The girls are in the **majority**. The boys are in the **minority**. (= There are more girls than boys in our class.)

among the green apples

between the green apples

Die Lautschrift zeigt dir, wie ein Wort ausgesprochen wird. Eine Übersicht über die Lautschriftzeichen findest du auf Seite 225.

Das rote **Warnschild mit Ausrufezeichen** bedeutet: Vorsicht, hier kannst du leicht Fehler machen!

Dies ist das Gegenteil-Zeichen: **among** ◄► **between** bedeutet: „**among** ist das Gegenteil von **between**"

Dies ist das Zeichen für ein Synonym: ►► **nearly** bedeutet: „**nearly** ist ein Synonym von **almost**"

Diese Zahl gibt die **Seite** an, auf der die Wörter zum ersten Mal vorkommen. p. 61 = Seite 61

Die orangen Kästen solltest du dir immer besonders gut ansehen. Dort stehen wichtige Hinweise zu den neuen Wörtern.

Im **Vocabulary** werden folgende Abkürzungen und Symbole verwendet:
p. = *page* (Seite) • *sb.* = *somebody* (jemand) • *AE* = *American English* • *BE* = *British English*
sth. = *something* (etwas) • *pl* = *plural* (Mehrzahl) • *no pl* = es gibt das Wort nicht in der Mehrzahl

Tipps zum Wörterlernen findest du im **Skills file 13–15** auf den Seiten 136ff.

Wenn du nachschlagen möchtest, was ein englisches Wort bedeutet oder wie man es ausspricht, dann solltest du das **Dictionary** auf den Seiten 181–221 verwenden.

Unit 1 – Life in Australia

pp. 8/9	(to) **explore** [ɪk'splɔː]	erforschen, erkunden	Let's go for a walk and **explore** this village.
	parrot ['pærət]	Papagei	
	kangaroo [kæŋgə'ruː]	Känguru	
	crocodile ['krɒkədaɪl]	Krokodil	Betonung auf der 1. Silbe: **croc**odile ['krɒkədaɪl] 
	Tasmanian devil [tæzmeɪniən 'devl]	Beutelteufel *(Tierart)*	**devil** = Teufel 
	camel ['kæml]	Kamel	Betonung auf der 1. Silbe: **ca**mel ['kæml]
	the outback ['aʊtbæk]	*das Hinterland Australiens*	Australia's **outback** is far away from the coast and the towns.
	(to) **bite** [baɪt], **bit** [bɪt], **bitten** ['bɪtn]	beißen; stechen *(z. B. Insekten)*	*verb:* (to) **bite** Careful! That dog **bites**. – *noun:* **bite** (Biss; (Insekten-)Stich) It can give you nasty **bites**.
	insect repellent ['ɪnsekt rɪpelənt]	Insektenschutzmittel	**insect** ['ɪnsekt] = Insekt **repellent** [rɪ'pelənt] = Schutzmittel
	continent ['kɒntɪnənt]	Kontinent	Europe, Africa and Asia are **continents**. Betonung auf der 1. Silbe: **con**tinent ['kɒntɪnənt]
	convict ['kɒnvɪkt]	Sträfling	somebody who has been sent to prison
	scuba-diving ['skuːbə daɪvɪŋ]	Sporttauchen	
	snorkelling ['snɔːkəlɪŋ]	Schnorcheln	
	coral ['kɒrəl]	Koralle/n	**coral reef** [kɒrəl 'riːf] = Korallenriff **reef** = Riff

Text 1

p. 10	**testimony (to)** ['testɪməni]	(Zeugen-)Aussage; Beweis (für), Zeugnis	Thousands of happy customers are **testimony to** the high quality of our products.

(to) **identify** [aɪ'dentɪfaɪ]	erkennen; (sich) identifizieren	Do you think you'll be able to **identify** the man who attacked you? (to) **identify yourself (as)** = sich zu erkennen geben (als)
Aboriginal [æbə'rɪdʒənl]	Aborigine- *(die Ureinwohner/innen Australiens betreffend)*	**Aboriginal** artists/culture; the **Aboriginal** population/flag; **Aboriginal** Australian (australische/r Ureinwohner/in) 
people ['pi:pl], *pl* **peoples**	Volk	**people** = **1.** Menschen – A lot of **people** are afraid of dogs. **2.** Volk – the Zulu **people** (das Volk der Zulu) the native **peoples** of Africa (die Urvölker Afrikas)
(to) **dream (of/about** sth.**)** [dri:m]	träumen (von etwas)	According to Aboriginal culture, the 'Dreamtime' is the period in which life was created. 'Dreaming' is the word used to explain how life began. *verb:* (to) **dream** – *noun:* **dream** (Traum)
plant [plɑ:nt]	Pflanze	*noun:* **plant** – *verb:* (to) **plant** (pflanzen)
(to) **pass** sth. **on (to** sb.**)**	etwas weitergeben (an jn.)	(to) **pass** sth. **down** = etwas weitergeben, überliefern
present ['preznt]	Gegenwart	the **past** – the **present** – the **future** yesterday – today – tomorrow **present** = **1.** Geschenk; **2.** Gegenwart
fellow ['feləʊ]	Mit-	Our **fellow** passengers on the plane were very patient when our baby cried. your **fellow** students = the other students from your class (deine Mitschüler/innen)
(to) **integrate** ['ɪntɪgreɪt]	(sich) integrieren	Betonung auf der 1. Silbe: integrate ['ɪntɪgreɪt]
community [kə'mju:nəti]	Gemeinschaft, Gemeinde	Bayern Munich has a big **community** of fans all over Europe.
(to) **bring** sb. **up**	jd. aufziehen, großziehen	Her parents are from Jamaica, but she was born and **brought up** in London. a **well/badly brought up** child = ein gut/schlecht erzogenes Kind
generation [dʒenə'reɪʃn]	Generation	Betonung auf der vorletzten Silbe: generation [dʒenə'reɪʃn]
(to) **apologize (to** sb. **for** sth.**)** [ə'pɒlədʒaɪz]	sich (bei jm. für etwas) entschuldigen	*verb:* (to) **apologize** – *noun:* **apology** [ə'pɒlədʒi] (Entschuldigung)
(to) **suffer (from)** ['sʌfə]	leiden (an), erleiden	I often **suffer from** headaches. (leiden an) He **suffered** a heart attack. (Er erlitt einen Herzinfarkt.) *verb:* (to) **suffer** – *noun:* **suffering** = *(das)* Leid, Leiden
hurt [hɜ:t]	Schmerz; Kränkung	*noun:* **hurt** – *verb:* (to) **hurt**
(to) **break** sth. **up**	etwas zerbrechen, zerstören; auflösen	Let's **break** the chocolate **up** into small pieces, so each of us can have some. (to) **break up (with** sb.**)** = sich von jm. trennen She **broke up** with her boyfriend.
indignity [ɪn'dɪgnəti]	Demütigung, Erniedrigung	Aboriginal people had to suffer many **indignities** for years and years.
(to) **inflict** sth. **on** sb. [ɪn'flɪkt]	jm. etwas zufügen, etwas bei jm. verursachen	Do you have any idea how much hurt and pain your behaviour **inflicts on** black people?
proud (of) [praʊd]	stolz (auf)	*adjective:* **proud of** sb./sth. – *noun:* **pride** [praɪd] (Stolz)
prime minister [praɪm 'mɪnɪstə]	Premierminister/in	The British **prime minister** lives at 10 Downing Street. Betonung: prime **min**ister [praɪm 'mɪnɪstə]

p. 11	**welfare** ['welfeə]	Sozialhilfe; Wohlfahrt, Fürsorge; Wohl(ergehen)	He doesn't have a job and lives on **welfare**. (... lebt von Sozialhilfe) We need more social **welfare** programmes to support poorer families. (Fürsorge, Wohlfahrt) As parents we want to protect our kids. Their **welfare** is the most important thing to us. (Wohlergehen)
	(to) **separate** ['sepəreɪt]	trennen	*verb:* (to) **separate** ['sepəreɪt] It's not right to **separate** children from their parents. *adjective:* **separate** ['seprət] (getrennt, separat) The library has a **separate** room for children's books. They didn't drive there together (= in the same car), they drove there **separately** (= in different cars).
	nursery ['nɜːsəri]	Kinderzimmer; Kinderkrippe	**1.** a room in a house where young children play and sleep **2.** a place where young children are looked after during the day
	(to) **cut** sth. **out** *(infml)*	mit etwas aufhören	►► (to) stop (doing) sth.
	life expectancy ['laɪf ɪkspektənsi]	Lebenserwartung	the time a person is likely to live
	unemployment [ʌnɪm'plɔɪmənt]	Arbeitslosigkeit	**unemployment** ◄► **employment** [ɪm'plɔɪmənt] (Arbeit, Anstellung)

Introduction

p. 12	**canvas** ['kænvəs]	Leinwand; Segeltuch	You can paint on **canvas** ... 
	(tree) bark [bɑːk]	Baumrinde	... or on tree **bark**. 
	(back) then	damals ⚠	My grandma was born in 1952. Life was a lot slower **(back) then**, she says. **then** = **1.** dann, danach; **2.** damals
	(to) **encourage** [ɪn'kʌrɪdʒ]	ermutigen, ermuntern; unterstützen	*verb:* (to) **encourage** My friends **encouraged** me to apply for the job. – *noun:* **encouragement** [ɪn'kʌrɪdʒmənt] (Ermunterung, Ermutigung; Unterstützung) My friends supported me and gave me lots of **encouragement**.
	permanent ['pɜːmənənt]	dauerhaft, Dauer-; fest; (be)ständig	This isn't a **permanent** tattoo. I can wash it off. After I graduated, I got my first **permanent** job.
	dot [dɒt]	Punkt, Pünktchen	**dot painting** = Punktmalerei; Punktgemälde
	bright [braɪt]	hell, freundlich; leuchtend	The light from my smartphone is very **bright**. I like **bright** colours: orange, yellow, red, ... **bright** ◄► **dark**
	use [juːs]	Gebrauch, Verwendung ⚠	*verb:* (to) **use** [juːz] – *noun:* **use** [juːs]
	(to) **be in progress** ['prəʊgres]	im Gange sein	The blinking sign said: "Quiet please! Recording **in progress**!"

	regular ['regjələ]	regelmäßig; gewohnt, normal	Is "arrive" a **regular** verb? I do sport **regularly**. (regelmäßig) the **regular** person in the street (normal) **regular** ◄► **irregular** [ɪ'regjələ] (unregelmäßig; ungleichmäßig)
p. 13	(to) **come of age**	volljährig werden	►► (to) become an adult by law
	(to) **confirm** [kən'fɜːm]	konfirmieren; firmen	*verb:* (to) **confirm** – *noun:* **confirmation** [kɒnfə'meɪʃn] (Konfirmation; Firmung) ⚠ (to) **confirm** = **1.** bestätigen; **2.** konfirmieren; firmen **confirmation** = **1.** Bestätigung; **2.** Konfirmation; Firmung
	Jewish ['dʒuːɪʃ]	jüdisch	*adjective:* **Jewish** – *noun:* **Jew** (Jude/Jüdin)
	Muslim ['mʊzlɪm]	Muslim/Muslima; muslimisch	I'm a **Muslim**. My religion is Islam.
	ceremony ['serəməni]	Feier, Zeremonie	⚠ Betonung auf der 1. Silbe: ceremony ['serəməni]
	discipline ['dɪsəplɪn]	Disziplin	*noun:* **discipline** – *verb:* (to) **discipline** (disziplinieren) ⚠ Betonung auf der 1. Silbe: discipline ['dɪsəplɪn]
	they used to make ... ['juːst tə]	sie haben (früher) immer ... gemacht	I **used to do** a lot of sport, but I don't have the time now.
	mark [mɑːk]	Markierung; Zeichen	*noun:* **mark** – *verb:* (to) **mark** (kennzeichnen, markieren)
	(to) **return** [rɪ'tɜːn]	zurückkehren, zurückkommen	*verb:* (to) **return** – *noun:* **return** (Rückkehr)

Skills training

p. 14	**venom** ['venəm]	Gift	the dangerous chemical that some insects, snakes, etc. produce when they bite you – it can harm or kill you *noun:* **venom** – *adjective:* **venomous** ['venəməs] (giftig)
	creature ['kriːtʃə]	Geschöpf, (Lebe-)Wesen	⚠ Betonung auf der 1. Silbe: creature ['kriːtʃə]
	snail [sneɪl]	Schnecke	a **snail** 
	backyard *(AE)* [bæk'jɑːd]	(Hinter-)Hof; Garten hinter dem Haus	⚠ *AE* **yard** = *BE* garden *AE* **backyard** = the area behind the house
	anti- ['ænti]	Anti-, Gegen-	**anti-**discrimination laws = laws against discrimination an **antivenom** = ein Gegengift
	jellyfish ['dʒelifɪʃ], *pl* **jellyfish**	Qualle	some **jellyfish** in the sea 
	sting [stɪŋ]	(Insekten-)Stich	*noun:* **sting** – *verb:* (to) **sting, stung, stung** [stʌŋ] (stechen *(Insekt)*; brennen)
	immediately [ɪ'miːdiətli]	sofort, umgehend, unmittelbar	When I call my dog, she comes **immediately**. *adverb:* **immediately** – *adjective:* **immediate** (sofortige/r/s)

	vinegar ['vɪnɪgə]	Essig	Here's some oil and **vinegar** for your salad. 
	octopus ['ɒktəpəs], *pl* **octopuses**	Oktopus, Tintenfisch	a sea creature with eight arms
	paralysis [pə'ræləsɪs], *pl* **paralyses** [pə'ræləsiːz]	Lähmung	She has to use a wheelchair because she suffered **paralysis** in her legs.
	tick [tɪk]	Zecke	a **tick** 
	oval ['əʊvl]	oval	⚠ Betonung auf der 1. Silbe: oval ['əʊvl]
	(to) **suck** [sʌk]	saugen	Mosquitoes bite you and **suck** your blood.
	tweezers *(pl)* ['twiːzəz]	Pinzette	
p. 15	**friendliness** ['frendlinəs]	Freundlichkeit	*noun:* **friendliness** – *adjective:* **friendly**
	informal [ɪn'fɔːml]	informell, locker	**formal ◄► informal** When you apply for a job, your letter should be quite **formal**, but your emails to your friends can be **informal**.
	(to) **shorten** ['ʃɔːtn]	(ver)kürzen	*verb:* (to) **shorten** I need to **shorten** this text. – *adjective:* **short** But I don't want to make it too **short**.
	mate *(infml)* [meɪt]	Freund/in, Kumpel	Weekends are a good time to hang out with your **mates**.
	cheers *(infml)* [tʃɪəz]	tschüs; danke	"Here's your drink." – "**Cheers**, mate!" (danke) "**Cheers**, then, Dave! See you tomorrow!" (tschüs)
	cereal(s) ['sɪəriəlz]	Getreide-, Frühstücksflocken	breakfast **cereals** 

Text 2

p. 16	**detention centre** [dɪ'tenʃn sentə]	Auffanglager, Haftanstalt *(für Abschiebehaft)*	⚠ **detention** = **1.** Haft; Inhaftierung; **2.** Nachsitzen *(in der Schule)* *noun:* **detention** – *verb:* (to) **detain** [dɪ'teɪn] (in Haft nehmen; aufhalten)
	(to) **criticize** ['krɪtɪsaɪz]	kritisieren	If you **criticize** the way I do it, then please also tell me how we could do it differently. ⚠ Betonung auf der 1. Silbe: **cri**ticize ['krɪtɪsaɪz]
	(to) **drown** [draʊn]	ertrinken	(to) die because you're underwater for too long and can't breathe
	conflict ['kɒnflɪkt]	Konflikt, Auseinandersetzung, Streit	⚠ Betonung auf der 1. Silbe: **con**flict ['kɒnflɪkt]
	corner ['kɔːnə]	Ecke	There's a statue in each of the four **corners** of this square.

policy ['pɒləsi]	Politik, Richtlinie(n), Bestimmung(en)	There's a "no junk food"-**policy** at my school.
whatever [wɒt'evə]	was (auch) (immer)	We will help you, **whatever** happens. = It doesn't matter what happens – we will help you.
illegal [ɪ'liːgl]	illegal, verboten; Illegale/r	**illegal** [ɪ'liːgl] ◄► **legal** ['liːgl] (legal)
forever [fər'evə], **for ever**	für immer, ewig (lange)	The terrible accident and her paralysis changed her life **forever** / **for ever**. I hope Simon arrives soon. We can't wait **forever** / **for ever**.
difficulty ['dɪfɪkəlti]	Schwierigkeit(en)	*adjective:* **difficult** – *noun:* **difficulty**
hut [hʌt]	Hütte	►► a small and very simple house 
(to) **dry** [draɪ]	(ab)trocknen	*verb:* (to) **dry** – *adjective:* **dry** (trocken)
expert ['ekspɜːt]	Experte, Expertin	⚠ Betonung auf der 1. Silbe: <u>ex</u>pert ['ekspɜːt]
operation [ɒpə'reɪʃn]	Operation, Einsatz	*noun:* **operation** It was a secret **operation**. – *verb:* (to) **operate** ['ɒpəreɪt] (bedienen *(z. B. Maschine)*, arbeiten *(in Betrieb sein)*, operieren) They **operated** in secret.
(to) **get rid of** sth. [rɪd]	etwas loswerden	I never drive any more, I ride my bike everywhere. I should **get rid of** my car.
textbook ['tekstbʊk]	Schulbuch, Lehrbuch	This is the **textbook** for your English lessons at school.
(to) **photocopy** ['fəʊtəʊkɒpi]	fotokopieren	*verb:* (to) **photocopy** – *noun:* **photocopy** (Fotokopie)
p. 17 **current affairs** *(pl)* [kʌrənt ə'feəz]	Tagespolitik, aktuelle Ereignisse	**current** ['kʌrənt] = aktuell, gegenwärtig **affair** [ə'feə] = Angelegenheit, Sache; Affäre, Verhältnis
course [kɔːs]	Kurs(us)	**crash course** ['kræʃ kɔːs] = Intensivkurs
(to) **realize** sth. ['rɪəlaɪz]	etwas erkennen, sich einer Sache bewusst werden	*verb:* (to) **realize** When I got home, I **realized** that I had left my bag on the train. – *noun:* **realization** [riːəlaɪ'zeɪʃn] (Erkenntnis) The **realization** that my bag was still on the train hit me.
council ['kaʊnsl]	Ausschuss; Rat *(z. B. Gemeinderat, Stadtrat)*	the town **council** = the government of the town
false [fɔːls]	falsch, unrichtig	►► not true, not real
long-term [lɒŋ 'tɜːm]	langfristig, Langzeit-	**medium-term** [miːdiəm 'tɜːm] = mittelfristig **short-term** [ʃɔːt 'tɜːm] = kurzfristig, Kurzzeit-
We recommend that you **go** ... [rekə'mend]	Wir empfehlen, dass Sie ... gehen.	

The verb (to) **recommend** can take ...

1. a noun:	I would **recommend**	**a visit** to your doctor.
2. the *-ing*-form:	I would **recommend**	**seeing** a doctor about this problem.
3. the infinitive with "to", when you recommend another person something:	You should **recommend**	<u>**your dad**</u> **to see** his doctor.
4. "that" + verb:	I would **recommend**	**that you see** your doctor.

authority [ɔː'θɒrəti]	Behörde	**local authority** = Gemeinde(behörde), Kommune/Kommunalbehörde

a while [waɪl]	eine Weile, einige Zeit	⚠ **while** = **1.** während – **while** we were waiting; **2.** Weile – for a **while** (eine Weile lang)
(to) **soak** sth. **up** [səʊk 'ʌp]	etwas aufsaugen, in sich aufnehmen	When young children learn their first language, they will **soak up** everything they hear.
(to) **squint** [skwɪnt]	blinzeln, *(die Augen)* zusammenkneifen, spähen	(to) look at something with your eyes only half open, e.g. because the light is too bright
campaign [kæm'peɪn]	Aktion, Kampagne	*noun:* **campaign** We started a **campaign** against the new factory in our town. – *verb:* (to) **campaign (for/against)** (sich einsetzen (für/gegen), kämpfen (für/gegen)) We **campaigned** against the new factory in our town.
Lord Mayor [lɔːd 'meə]	Oberbürgermeister/in	the title of the mayor in some cities, e.g. in Great Britain, Australia or Canada
a mate of mine	ein/e Freund/in von mir	**a friend of Cooper's / of hers / of mine** • Jack is **a friend of Cooper's**. (= einer von Coopers Freunden) • Kate is **Cooper's friend**. (Coopers (beste) Freundin) ⚠ a friend of **mine/his/hers/ours** *(nicht: of ~~me/him/her/us~~)*
(to) **deny** [dɪ'naɪ]	leugnen, bestreiten	*verb:* (to) **deny** He **denied** having committed the crime. – *noun:* **denial** [dɪ'naɪəl] (*(das)* Leugnen, Dementi) But his **denial** of the crime didn't help him.
(to) **ignore** [ɪg'nɔː]	nicht beachten, ignorieren	*verb:* (to) **ignore** They **ignored** all the safety signs. – *noun:* **ignorance (of/about** sth.**)** ['ɪgnərəns] (Unwissenheit (über etwas), Unkenntnis (einer Sache), Ignoranz) They showed complete **ignorance of** the dangers of venomous jellyfish.
accent ['æksent]	Akzent	Duncan is from Glasgow and speaks with a strong Scottish **accent**. ⚠ Betonung auf der 1. Silbe: accent ['æksent]
p. 18 **riddle** ['rɪdl]	Rätsel	It's a **riddle** how the cat managed to get onto the roof. These **riddles** are really difficult to solve.
direct [də'rekt]	direkt, unmittelbar	**direct** ◄► **indirect** [ɪndə'rekt] (indirekt)
plains *(pl)* [pleɪnz]	Ebene	
(to) **bear** [beə], **bore** [bɔː], **borne** [bɔːn]	ertragen, aushalten; tragen	I can't **bear** this pain much longer. (ertragen, aushalten) Who **bore** the responsibility for this project? (tragen)
perfect ['pɜːfɪkt]	perfekt	**perfectly** still = ganz/völlig ruhig/still ⚠ Betonung auf der 1. Silbe: perfect ['pɜːfɪkt]
calm [kɑːm]	ruhig, besonnen	*adjective:* **calm** Please stay **calm**. – *verb:* (to) **calm (down)** (sich beruhigen) / (to) **calm** sb. **down** (jn. beruhigen) Please **calm down**. Please **calm** the children **down**.

	point of view [pɔɪnt əv 'vjuː]	Standpunkt, Meinung; Perspektive	►► way of seeing things; opinion

Skills training

p. 19	**tournament** ['tʊənəmənt]	Turnier, Wettkampf	a sports competition where a number of teams or players take part in different disciplines/games
	congratulations (on sth.**)** [kəngrætʃə'leɪʃnz]	herzlichen Glückwunsch (zu etwas)	*noun:* **congratulations** **Congratulations on** your good grades! – *verb:* (to) **congratulate** sb. **on** sth. [kən'grætʃuleɪt] (jm. zu etwas gratulieren) I **congratulated** her **on** her good grades.

verbs + -*ing*-form:

You should	**apologize for**	**saying**	such nasty things.
They	**campaigned for**	**making**	bus and train tickets cheaper.
She	**congratulated** us **on**	**getting**	such good results.
He	**denied**	**having**	anything to do with her death.
They	**detained** him **for**	**making**	threats of violence against his boss.
Do you ever	**dream of**	**sailing**	around the world?

⚠ **With some verbs you can use the -*ing*-form or the infinitive with "to":**

I couldn't	**bear**	**seeing / to see**	my dog suffer.
We will	**continue**	**fighting / to fight**	until we get what we want.

	anyway ['eniweɪ]	trotzdem	⚠ **anyway** = **1.** trotzdem It's cold, windy and rainy, but I'll go by bike **anyway**.; **2.** sowieso; jedenfalls, wie dem auch sei I can take you to York in my car. I'm driving there **anyway**. (sowieso)

Study skills

p. 20	**collocation** [kɒlə'keɪʃn]	Kollokation *(inhaltlich kombinierbare sprachliche Einheiten)*	It's not really wrong to say "heavy wind" or "strong rain" in English. But the correct **collocations** are "strong wind" and "heavy rain".
	athletics [æθ'letɪks]	Leichtathletik	sports in which competitions are held, such as running, jumping and throwing
	amateur ['æmətə]	Amateur/in; Amateur-, Hobby-	**amateur** ◄► **professional** ⚠ Betonung auf der 1. Silbe: amateur ['æmətə]
	venue ['venjuː]	Veranstaltungsort, Veranstaltungsstätte	a place where concerts, sports competitions or other big events take place
	antonym ['æntənɪm]	Antonym, Gegenteil	**Antonyms** of "difficult" are "easy" or "simple". **synonym** ◄► **antonym**
	idiom ['ɪdiəm]	Redewendung	a phrase whose meaning you don't know even if you know what all the words in it mean "That's not my cup of tea." is a nice English **idiom**. It means "I'm not a great fan of it."
	It's your turn. [tɜːn]	Du bist dran. / Du bist an der Reihe.	**It was my turn** to ask a question, but I didn't know what to ask.

Skills training

p. 21	**explanation** [eksplə'neɪʃn]	Erklärung	*verb:* (to) **explain** – *noun:* **explanation**
	spectator [spek'teɪtə]	Zuschauer/in	►► somebody who watches a (sports) event
	goalpost ['gəʊlpəʊst]	Torpfosten	**post** = Pfosten, Pfahl

mouthguard *(AE)* ['maʊθɡɑːd]	Mundschutz *(Sport)*	►► *BE* **gumshield** ['ɡʌmʃiːld]
headguard ['hedɡɑːd]	Kopfschutz *(Sport)*	
(to) **kick** [kɪk]	treten; *(Sport)* schießen	*verb:* (to) **kick** – *noun:* **kick** (Tritt, Stoß, Kick)
fist [fɪst]	Faust	

Unit 2 – My world of work

p. 24/25

part-time [pɑːt 'taɪm]	Teilzeit-, Halbtags-	He has a **part-time** job. ◄► He has a **full-time** job. = He works **part-time**. = He works **full-time**. [fʊl 'taɪm]
abroad [ə'brɔːd]	im/ins Ausland	►► in or to another country
job advertisement [dʒɒb əd'vɜːtɪsmənt] *(kurz auch:* **job advert***)*	Stellenanzeige	"I saw your **job advert** and would like to apply for the job."
CV [siː 'viː] **(= curriculum vitae** [kərɪkjələm 'viːtaɪ]**)**	Lebenslauf	At the age of 15, your **CV** is probably not very long.
cover letter ['kʌvə letə]	Anschreiben, Begleitschreiben, Motivationsschreiben	a letter that you send with your CV
automation [ɔːtə'meɪʃn]	Automatisierung	My uncle lost his job. The work he used to do is now done by a machine. He's a victim of **automation**.
technique [tek'niːk]	Methode, Technik	I've learned some good **techniques** for being less nervous before tests. ⚠ Betonung auf der 2. Silbe: tech**nique** [tek'niːk]
work experience ['wɜːk ɪkspɪəriəns]	Arbeitserfahrung(en), Praxiserfahrung(en); Praktikum	She has a strong computer background and a lot of **work experience**. Last year I did some **work experience** at our local supermarket.
high school *(AE)* ['haɪ skuːl]	*(USA) Schule für 14- bis 18-Jährige*	*(in the USA)* a school for young people between the ages of 14 and 18
fee [fiː]	Gebühr; Honorar; (Mitglieds-)Beitrag	money you pay e.g. for club membership, advice or services
fund [fʌnd]	Fonds; Geldmittel	*noun:* **fund** – *verb:* (to) **fund** (finanzieren)
expenses *(pl)* [ɪk'spensɪz]	Kosten; Spesen	**living expenses** = Lebenshaltungskosten **travelling expenses** = Reisekosten
loan [ləʊn]	Darlehen, Kredit	(to) **take out a loan** = ein Darlehen / einen Kredit aufnehmen
training course ['treɪnɪŋ kɔːs]	Ausbildung(sgang)	When you finish school, do you want to go to university or start a **training course**?
cashier [kæ'ʃɪə]	Kassierer/in	the **cashier** 

	(to) **walk a dog**	mit einem Hund spazieren gehen	**dog walking** = Hunde ausführen **dog walker** = Hundeausführer/in (to) **go for a walk** = einen Spaziergang machen (to) **take a dog for a walk** = mit einem Hund spazieren gehen *verb:* (to) **walk** – *noun:* **walk** (Spaziergang; Wanderung; Fußweg *(Weg zu Fuß)*)

Text 1

p. 26	**secondary school** ['sekəndri sku:l]	weiterführende Schule	a school for young people between the ages of 11 and 16 or 18
	childcare ['tʃaɪldkeə]	Kinderbetreuung	We really love working for this company. For example, it offers **childcare** for our children.
	conservation [kɒnsə'veɪʃn]	(Natur-)Schutz; Erhaltung, Bewahrung	*noun:* **conservation** – *verb:* (to) **conserve** [kən'sɜ:v] (schützen, erhalten; schonen)
	internship ['ɪntɜ:nʃɪp]	Praktikum	►► work experience someone who does an internship = **intern** (Praktikant/in)
	apprenticeship [ə'prentɪʃɪp]	Ausbildung, Lehre	My brother is doing an **apprenticeship** as a hairdresser. **apprentice** [ə'prentɪs] = Lehrling, Auszubildende/r
	(to) **jump at** sth. [dʒʌmp]	bei etwas sofort zugreifen, *(Gelegenheit)* sofort ergreifen	If somebody offered you this job, would you think about it for a while or **jump at** the offer?
	accommodation [əkɒmə'deɪʃn]	Unterkunft; Wohnung, Zimmer	We need cheap **accommodation** in Paris for three days.
	host [həʊst]	Gastgeber/in	**host family** = Gastfamilie
	(to) **get along (with** sb.**)**	(gut) auskommen (mit jm.), sich (gut) verstehen (mit jm.)	I **get along** well **with** my sister. = My sister and I **get along** well. (kommen gut miteinander aus / verstehen uns gut)
	(to) **get used to** ['ju:st tə]	sich gewöhnen an	When we were in England, it was difficult to drive on the left, but we soon **got used to** it. ⚠ *English*: We **got used** <u>**to driving**</u> on the left. *German*: Wir **gewöhnten uns daran**, links <u>**zu fahren**</u>. Now I'**m used to** driving on the left. (Ich bin daran gewöhnt, ... zu fahren.)
	(to) **give** (sth.) **up**	(etwas) aufgeben, aufhören (mit etwas)	Times may be hard, but I always try not to **give up**. I want to **give up** buying things I don't really need. (to) **give** sth. **up (to** sb.**)** = auf etwas verzichten, jm. etwas übergeben (to) **give up your seat to** sb.: = für jn. aufstehen (z. B. im Bus)
	(to) **keep /** (to) **stay in contact (with)** ['kɒntækt]	in Kontakt bleiben (mit)	We really wanted to **keep/stay in contact with** each other, but I've never heard from them again.
p. 27	**sloth** [sləʊθ]	Faultier	
	deforestation [di:fɒrɪ'steɪʃn]	Abholzung, Entwaldung	There's a lot of **deforestation** in this area. = Lots of trees are destroyed.

rainforest ['reɪnfɒrɪst]	Regenwald	thick forests in hot parts of the world where there is a lot of rain
(to) **convince** [kən'vɪns]	überzeugen	She had good arguments and was very **convicing**. Still, she couldn't **convince** us. We were **convinced** that it wasn't a good idea.
(to) **let** [let]**, let, let**	lassen	His parents **let** him go to Costa Rica. = They allowed him to go ... = He was allowed to go ...
even though	auch wenn, obwohl *(betont)*	**Even though** it was already 9 am, it was still dark outside. *English:* He's world-famous, **even though** he isn't really an artist. *German:* ... weltberühmt, **und das, obwohl** er gar kein wirklicher Künstler ist.
vaccination [væksɪ'neɪʃn]	(Schutz-)Impfung	These **vaccinations** will protect you against several dangerous diseases.
both ... and ...	sowohl ... als auch ...	I like **both my sisters**. (meine beiden Schwestern) I like **both** Anne **and** Julia. (sowohl Anne als auch Julia)
(to) **check** sb./sth. **out** *(infml)*	sich etwas anschauen, anhören; etwas ausprobieren	They say the band's new CD is awesome. I must **check** it **out** / **check** the band **out**.
scam [skæm]	Schwindel, Betrug	A bike like this for £300? Sold online? Forget it. I'm sure it's a **scam**.
welcome ['welkʌm]	Empfang; Willkommen	(to) give sb. a warm/great **welcome** = jn. herzlich begrüßen (to) get a warm/great **welcome** = herzlich begrüßt werden *noun:* **welcome** – *verb:* (to) **welcome** sb. **(to)** (jn. begrüßen (in), jn. willkommen heißen (in))
(to) **carry on with** sth. **/ doing** sth. [kæri 'ɒn]	weitermachen, fortfahren (mit etwas)	I didn't feel very well, but I **carried on with** my work. ... but I **carried on working**.
occasional [ə'keɪʒənl]	gelegentliche(r, s)	*adjective:* **occasional** We only make **occasional** visits to the zoo. – *adverb:* **occasionally** (gelegentlich, ab und zu) We only go to the zoo **occasionally**. – *noun:* **occasion** [ə'keɪʒn] (Gelegenheit; Ereignis, Anlass) We've only been to the zoo on a few **occasions**.
donkey ['dɒŋki]	Esel	

Introduction

p. 28 **expat** ['ekspæt] *(infml)* **(= expatriate** [eks'pætriət]**)**	im Ausland Lebende/r; im Ausland lebend	They're German, but they live in Scotland. = They're German **expats** in Scotland.
(to) **attract** [ə'trækt]	anziehen, anlocken	London **attracts** millions of tourists every summer. *verb:* (to) **attract** – *adjective:* **attractive** [ə'træktɪv] (attraktiv) – *noun:* **attraction** [ə'trækʃn] (Attraktion; Anziehungskraft)

	certain ['sɜːtn]	gewiss, bestimmt; sicher	*adjective:* **certain** It is **certain** that ... (sicher) A **certain** Mr Miller phoned. (ein gewisser ...) – *adverb:* **certainly** This is **certainly** no easy task, but I'll do my best. (sicher(lich), gewiss)
	honest ['ɒnɪst]	ehrlich	*adjective:* **honest** Thank you for being so **honest** with me. To be **honest**, I don't know the answer. (Um ehrlich zu sein, ...) *adverb:* **Honestly**? Why not? (Ehrlich? / Echt?) – *noun:* **honesty** ['ɒnəstɪ] (Ehrlichkeit) Thank you for your **honesty**.
	punctual ['pʌŋktʃuəl]	pünktlich	►► on time
	teabag ['tiːbæg]	Teebeutel	**teabags** 
	habit ['hæbɪt]	(An-)Gewohnheit	►► something you do regularly Eating too many sweets is a bad **habit**.
p. 29	**photography** [fə'tɒgrəfi]	Fotografie *(Hobby), (das)* Fotografieren	Betonung auf der 2. Silbe: pho**to**graphy [fə'tɒgrəfi]
	Good luck. [lʌk]	Viel Glück!	*noun:* **luck** (Glück *(glückliche Fügung)*) – *adjective:* **lucky** (Glücks-, glücklich) – *adverb:* **luckily** ['lʌkɪli] (glücklicherweise) ►► fortunately
	prediction [prɪ'dɪkʃn]	Vorhersage, Voraussage	*noun:* **prediction** Can you **make a prediction** about how much time this will take? – *verb:* (to) **predict** [prɪ'dɪkt] (vorhersagen, voraussagen) Can you **predict** how much time this will take?
	spontaneous [spɒn'teɪniəs]	spontan	It was a **spontaneous** decision to go to Brighton for the day. = We went to Brighton **spontaneously**.

Skills training

p. 30	**first aid** [fɜːst 'eɪd]	Erste Hilfe	**first aid** = Erste Hilfe **first-aid certificate** = Erste-Hilfe-Schein
	foreign ['fɒrən]	ausländisch; fremd	►► from another country **foreign language** = Fremdsprache
	(to) **deal with** sb./sth. [diːl], **dealt, dealt** [delt]	sich um jn./etwas kümmern, sich mit jm./einer Sache befassen, etwas behandeln *(z. B. Thema)*	Let's **deal with** this problem first and think about everything else later. The film **deals with** the life of John Lennon.
	helpful ['helpfl]	hilfsbereit; hilfreich, nützlich	I had huge problems, so I phoned my best friend. She was really **helpful**. Here are some **helpful** tips for your exam.
	organizational [ɔːgənaɪ'zeɪʃənl]	organisatorisch	*adjective:* **organizational** – *verb:* (to) **organize** – *nouns: (what you do / a company)* **organization**; *(person)* **organizer**
	personal statement [pɜːsənl 'steɪtmənt]	persönliche Beschreibung, Selbstbeschreibung	**statement** = Aussage(satz)

communication [kəmju:nɪ'keɪʃn]	Kommunikation, Verständigung	*noun:* **communication** – *verb:* (to) **communicate** – [kə'mju:nɪkeɪt] (kommunizieren)
decision-making [dɪ'sɪʒn meɪkɪŋ]	Entscheidungsfindung	**decision-making skills** *(pl)* = Entscheidungsfähigkeit
tool [tu:l]	Werkzeug; (Hilfs-)Mittel	**tools** 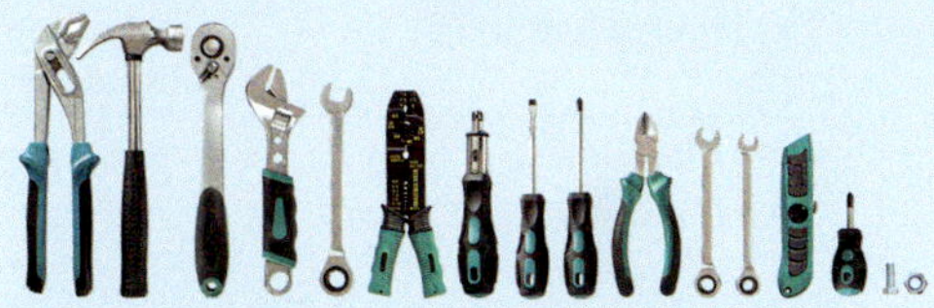
strength [streŋθ]	Stärke, Kraft	One of my **strengths** is that I speak three languages. **strength ◄► weakness** **strong ◄► weak**
p. 31 **flexible** ['fleksəbl]	flexibel	Betonung auf der 1. Silbe: **flex**ible ['**fleks**əbl]
(working) hours *(pl)*	Arbeitszeit(en)	Cooks have long **working hours** – sometimes 14 hours a day. **opening hours** *(pl)* = Öffnungszeiten (to) **work long hours** = lange arbeiten, Überstunden machen (to) **work nights** = nachts arbeiten
reservation [rezə'veɪʃn]	Reservierung, Buchung	*noun:* **reservation** – *verb:* (to) **reserve** [rɪ'zɜ:v] (reservieren)
staff [stɑ:f]	Personal, Belegschaft; Kollegium *(Schule)*	all the people working for a company, organization, etc. **staff manager** = Personalchef/in
attn (= for the attention of)	zu Händen / z. Hd. *(in einer Adresse, an eine bestimmte Person in einer Firma)*	You can write to your local council, **attn** Ms Eve Miller, Mayor.
(to) **require** [rɪ'kwaɪə]	erfordern, benötigen	This isn't an easy task. It **requires** a lot of thinking. *verb:* (to) **require** – *noun:* **requirement** [rɪ'kwaɪəmənt] (Voraussetzung, Anforderung)
patience ['peɪʃns]	Geduld	*noun:* **patience** – *adjective:* **patient**
(to) **attach (to)** [ə'tætʃ]	anfügen; anhängen (an) *(Brief, E-Mail)*	Can you send me an email and **attach** the photos? I'm **attaching** some photos of Ashley's party. *verb:* (to) **attach** – *noun:* **attachment** [ə'tætʃmənt] (Anhang *(E-Mail)*)
(to) **provide** [prə'vaɪd]	(an)bieten, zur Verfügung stellen	Food and accommodation **provided**. (Essen/ Verpflegung und Unterkunft werden (zur Verfügung) gestellt.)
reference ['refrəns]	Referenz, Empfehlung; jd., der eine Referenz erteilt	I gave my coach and my maths teacher as **references**.
greeting ['gri:tɪŋ]	Gruß(formel), Begrüßung	"**Greetings** from Inverness! We're having a great time." "Hi" and "hello" are informal **greetings**.
(to) **sign** [saɪn]	unterschreiben	*verb:* (to) **sign** – *noun:* **signature** **sign** = **1.** Schild, Zeichen; **2.** unterschreiben
introductory [ɪntrə'dʌktəri]	einführend, einleitend	*adjective:* **introductory** – *noun:* **introduction** – *verb:* (to) **introduce** (sb. **to** sb./sth.)
available [ə'veɪləbl]	verfügbar; erhältlich; *(Stelle)* frei	These dresses are **available** in six different colours. If a person is **available**, they have time to see you or to speak to you. (to) be **available** = zur Verfügung stehen, Zeit haben

	lifeguard ['laɪfgɑːd]	Rettungsschwimmer/in; Bademeister/in	The **lifeguards** at a beach watch people who are swimming in the sea and help them if they are in danger.
	life-saving ['laɪf seɪvɪŋ]	Rettungsschwimmen	the skills you need to save people who are in water from drowning
p. 32	(to) **arrange** [ə'reɪndʒ]	arrangieren, planen; (an)ordnen	*verb:* (to) **arrange** – *noun:* **arrangement** [ə'reɪndʒmənt] (Abmachung, Vereinbarung)
	(job) interview ['dʒɒb ɪntəvjuː]	Vorstellungsgespräch	⚠ **interview** = **1.** Interview; **2. (= job interview)** Vorstellungsgespräch *noun:* **(job) interview** – *verb:* (to) **interview** (befragen, interviewen; ein Vorstellungsgespräch führen)
	approximately [ə'prɒksɪmətli] *(kurz auch:* **approx** [ə'prɒks]*)*	ungefähr	**approximately** three hours = about three hours
	(to) **attend** [ə'tend]	(hin)gehen zu, teilnehmen (an); besuchen	(to) **attend** (a) school = (to) go to (a) school
	(to) **ensure** [ɪn'ʃʊə]	sicherstellen, gewährleisten	►► (to) make sure
	(to) **inform** sb. **(about/of** sth.**)** [ɪn'fɔːm]	jn. (über etwas) informieren	We'd like to **inform** you **of/about** some changes in our company which will be introduced in July.
	(to) **receive** [rɪ'siːv]	erhalten, empfangen	a more formal word for **get** **receive a letter ◄► send a letter**
	suitable (for) ['suːtəbl]	geeignet, passend (für)	Shorts aren't **suitable** clothes for a job interview. Who is the most **suitable** person for this job? = Who will do this job best?
	(to) **catch** sth.	verstehen *(hören können)*, mitbekommen	There was so much noise, I didn't **catch** half of what she was saying. ⚠ (to) **catch** = **1.** verstehen *(hören können)*, mitbekommen; **2.** (ein)fangen; erwischen; nehmen *(z. B. Zug, Bus)*

Text 2

p. 33	**professor (of)** [prə'fesə]	Professor/in (für)	She's a **professor of** medicine at Edinburgh University.
	biochemistry [baɪəʊ'kemɪstri]	Biochemie	*nouns: (science:)* **biochemistry**; *(person:)* **biochemist** (Biochemiker/in) – *adjective:* **biochemical** (biochemisch) ⚠ Betonung auf der 3. Silbe: [baɪəʊ'kemɪstri], [baɪəʊ'kemɪst], [baɪəʊ'kemɪkl]
	diary ['daɪəri]	Tagebuch; Kalender	Friday? OK. Let me put this in my **diary**. (Kalender) I **keep a diary**. = I write something in my **diary** every day, for example special things that happened. (Tagebuch, Tagebuch führen)
	(to) **turn (over)** the page(s) [tɜːn]	umblättern (in einem Buch)	**turning over** the pages in a diary 
	crinkly ['krɪŋkli]	zerknittert; faltig *(Haut)*	 **crinkly** paper

(to) **be supposed to** be/do sth. [sə'pəʊzd]	etwas sein sollen / etwas tun sollen	We**'re** not **supposed to** eat in class, but some of us do. I haven't heard their new CD yet, but it**'s supposed to** be really good.
waste [weɪst]	Verschwendung	*noun:* **waste** This is a **waste** of time. I'm leaving. – *verb:* (to) **waste** (verschwenden) I don't want to **waste** my time like this.
(to) **guess** [ges]	(er)raten	

(to) **guess / guess**

verb: (to) **guess**
Guess what I did! (Rate mal, was ...)
I guess I'll leave school next year.
(Ich nehme an, ... / Ich glaube, ...)
Guess what! (Stell dir / Stellt euch (mal) vor!)

noun: **guess** (Vermutung)
Make/Have/Take a **guess**! (Rate mal!)
My **guess** is that he'll leave school next year.
I'll give you three **guesses**. (Dreimal darfst du raten.)

television ['telɪvɪʒn]	Fernsehen	►► TV
attic ['ætɪk]	Dachboden ⚠	*English:* **in the attic** *German:* **auf** dem Dachboden
more than ever	mehr als jemals zuvor	We need environment-friendly forms of transport **more than ever**! We have to change our habits NOW!
mechanical [mɪ'kænɪkl]	mechanisch, Maschinen-	The plane had **mechanical** problems and had to stay on the ground.
inspector [ɪn'spektə]	Inspektor/in, Kontrolleur/in	The safety **inspector** checked the plane and found the problem.
He knew how to put it together again **all right.**	Er wusste sehr wohl / nur zu gut, wie man es wieder zusammenbaut.	Do you think I'm stupid? I know how to do this **all right**, thank you!
large [lɑːdʒ]	groß ⚠	Eight brothers and sisters? What a **large** family! You don't use **large** to describe people. People are **tall** *(groß)*, **big** *(dick, schwer)* or **great** *(bedeutend, angesehen)*.
ugly ['ʌgli]	hässlich	►► not nice to look at, not pretty/beautiful
slot [slɒt]	Schlitz, Öffnung; (Karten-)Einzug	putting a card in a **slot** 
test paper ['test peɪpə]	Prüfungsarbeit	At the end of the lesson our teacher collected all our **test papers**.
(to) **write** sth. **out**	etwas ausstellen, (ins Reine) schreiben	We've reserved the room for next Tuesday and will **write out** a confirmation for you.
(to) **punch** [pʌntʃ]	lochen, stanzen	**punch code** = Stanzcode *(Code mit Lochkarten)*
(to) **calculate** ['kælkjuleɪt]	berechnen, kalkulieren	Let's **calculate** how much money we'll need for a two-week camping holiday.
mark [mɑːk]	(Schul-)Note, Zensur ⚠	**mark** = **1.** (Schul-)Note, Zensur; **2.** Markierung; Zeichen; **3.** (to) **mark** = kennzeichnen, markieren
sector ['sektə]	Sektor, Bereich	►► a part, a (certain) area
p. 34 (to) **slow** sb./sth. **down** [sləʊ 'daʊn]	jn./etwas langsamer machen, jn. aufhalten, etwas verlangsamen	►► (to) make (sb./sth.) slower *verb:* (to) **slow** sth. **down** – *adjective:* **slow**
satisfactory [sætɪs'fæktəri]	zufriedenstellend	►► OK; good enough

	altogether [ɔːltəˈgeðə]	insgesamt	£2.50 and £3.50, that's £6 **altogether**. (macht zusammen ...)
	superior (to sb./sth.**)** [suːˈpɪəriə]	(jm./einer Sache) überlegen; hervorragend	**superior** apartments = Luxuswohnungen *(Werbesprache)* The new phone is **superior** to the older model in so many ways.
	(to) **adjust (to)** [əˈdʒʌst]	(sich) einstellen (auf); (sich) anpassen (an)	I have to **adjust to** living without a car. (... mich einstellen auf ...) Would you **adjust** your behaviour to help the environment? (... dein Verhalten anpassen, um ...)
	just the same / all the same	trotzdem	►► anyway It's raining, but I'll go by bike **all the same / just the same**.
	this way / that way	so, auf diese/jene Art	

way ("Art und Weise")

Try to present your topic **in an interesting way**.	auf eine interessante Art und Weise
In this way, you will make sure that everyone enjoys your talk.	auf diese Weise
I like **the way** Oliver ended his talk.	die Art und Weise, wie ...
John is like his father **in some/many ways**.	in mancher/vielerlei Hinsicht

	right next to ...	gleich/direkt neben ...	**right** from the start = gleich/direkt von Anfang an **right** then = genau dann ⚠ **right** = **1.** richtig; **2.** (nach) rechts; **3.** *(das)* Recht; **4.** gleich, direkt *(Adverb)*
	(to) **be on**	an sein *(eingeschaltet)*	The light is still **on**. Please **turn** it **off**. (ausschalten) It's too dark when the lights are **off**. Please **turn** them **on**. (einschalten)
	(to) **light** [laɪt]**, lit, lit** [lɪt]	anzünden	(to) **light up** = aufleuchten (to) **light a fire** = (ein) Feuer machen
p. 35	**fraction** [ˈfrækʃn]	Bruch(zahl); Bruchteil	1/2, 1/3 and 1/4 are **fractions**. If you buy it online, it sometimes costs only a **fraction** of what it costs in the shops. (= much less than what it costs in the shops)
	sigh [saɪ]	Seufzer	*noun:* **sigh** "All right," she said with a **sigh**. – *verb:* (to) **sigh** (seufzen) "All right," she **sighed**.
	schoolyard *(AE)* [ˈskuːljɑːd]	Schulhof	►► *BE* **(school) playground** [ˈpleɪgraʊnd]
	in the old days	früher	**In the old days** there were no cars. People walked or rode horses.
	human [ˈhjuːmən]	menschlich; Mensch	**human rights** *(pl)* = Menschenrechte

Skills training

p. 36	(to) **translate** [trænsˈleɪt]	übersetzen	*verb:* (to) **translate** – *noun:* **translation** [trænsˈleɪʃn] (Übersetzung)
	self-employed [self ɪmˈplɔɪd]	selbstständig, freiberuflich	not employed by a company, but working for yourself
	graphic designer [græfɪk dɪˈzaɪnə]	Grafiker/in, Grafikdesigner/in	Which **graphic designer** designed your brochures? They're great!
	(to) **motivate** [ˈməʊtɪveɪt]	motivieren	*verb:* (to) **motivate** – *noun:* **motivation** [məʊtɪˈveɪʃn] (Motivation)
	discussion [dɪˈskʌʃn]	Diskussion	*noun:* **discussion** – *verb:* (to) **discuss**

Study skills

p. 37	(to) **get** sb.'s **attention** [ə'tenʃn]	js. Aufmerksamkeit erregen, gewinnen	(to) **keep** sb.'s **attention** = js. Aufmerksamkeit aufrecht erhalten

Collocations: Which verb?

You **bear**	something **in mind**.	You **have**	**breakfast/lunch/dinner** / a **shower**.
You **come**	**of age.**	You **keep**	sb.'s **attention**.
You **do**	an **apprenticeship** / an **internship** / a **training course** / **work experience**.	You **make**	a **decision** / a **prediction** / a **reservation**.
You **get**	sb.'s **attention** / a **warm welcome**.	You **take**	a **break** / a **photo** / sb.'s **temperature**.
You **give**	sb. a **warm welcome**.	You **work**	long **hours**.

	audience ['ɔːdiəns]	Publikum; Zuschauer/innen, Zuhörer/innen	At the end of the concert the **audience** stood up and cheered for a long time.
	statistic [stə'tɪstɪk]	statistische Tatsache, statistische Größe	⚠ **statistic** = statistische Tatsache, statistische Größe; **statistics** *(pl)* = Statistik(en)
	unusual [ʌn'juːʒʊəl]	ungewöhnlich	**usual** ◄► **unusual**
	rhetorical question [rɪtɒrɪkl 'kwestʃən]	rhetorische Frage	a question to which no answer is expected
	(to) **expect** [ɪk'spekt]	erwarten	I'm surprised. I wouldn't have **expected** this result. You can't **expect** small children to be able to read.
	quote [kwəʊt]	Zitat	*noun:* **quote** – *verb:* (to) **quote** (zitieren)
	pilot ['paɪlət]	Pilot/in	⚠ Achte auf Betonung und Aussprache: ['paɪlət]
	(to) **succeed** [sək'siːd]	Erfolg haben	*verb:* (to) **succeed** – *noun:* **success** – *adjective:* **successful** (to) **succeed in doing** sth. = es schaffen, etwas zu tun
	anonymous (= anon.) [ə'nɒnɪməs]	anonym	an **anonymous** person = his/her name is not known ⚠ Betonung auf der 2. Silbe: anonymous [ə'nɒnɪməs]
	focus (on) ['fəʊkəs], *pl* **focuses** *or* **foci** ['fəʊsaɪ]	Mittelpunkt, Hauptpunkt, Schwerpunkt	*noun:* **focus** – *verb:* (to) **focus** (on) (sich konzentrieren (auf)) **focus of attention** = Zentrum der Aufmerksamkeit
	prop [prɒp]	Requisite	

Your task

p. 39	**colleague** ['kɒliːg]	Kollege/Kollegin	⚠ Betonung auf der 1. Silbe: colleague ['kɒliːg]
	sustainability [səsteɪnə'bɪləti]	Nachhaltigkeit	*noun:* **sustainability** – *adjective:* **sustainable**

Unit 3 – The digital age

pp. 42/43	**critical (of)** ['krɪtɪkl]	kritisch (gegenüber)	*adjective:* **critical** – *verb:* (to) **criticize** – *nouns:* (person) **critic**; (what you express when criticizing) **criticism** ['krɪtɪsɪzəm] *English:* **critic** = *German:* **Kritiker/in** *English:* **criticism** = *German:* **Kritik**

(to) **evaluate** [ɪ'væljueɪt]	beurteilen, bewerten, einschätzen	*verb:* (to) **evaluate** – *noun:* **evaluation** [ɪvælju'eɪʃn] (Beurteilung, Bewertung, Einschätzung)
device [dɪ'vaɪs]	Gerät, Apparat	A clock is a **device** that tells you the time.
irony ['aɪrəni]	Ironie	Betonung auf der 1. Silbe: irony ['aɪrəni] *noun:* **irony** – *adjective:* **ironic** [aɪ'rɒnɪk] (ironisch) – *adverb:* **ironically**
(to) **address** sth. [ə'dres]	etwas angehen, sich mit etwas befassen; etwas zur Sprache bringen	Even if you don't like it, I really want to **address** this problem. (= talk about this problem)
issue ['ɪʃuː]	Thema, Anliegen; Problem, (Streit-)Frage	Bullying is a big **issue** at a lot of schools. **issue** = **1.** Thema, Anliegen; Problem, (Streit-)Frage; **2.** Ausgabe, Ausstellung *(z. B. Dokument)*; **3.** (to) **issue** = ausgeben, ausstellen *(z. B. Dokument)*

Text 1

p. 44 (to) **log on/off** [lɒg 'ɒn], [lɒg 'ɒf]	(sich) ein-/ausloggen	►► (to) **log in(to)/out**
(to) **exist** [ɪg'zɪst]	existieren	Do you believe that life **exists** on Mars? *verb:* (to) **exist** – *noun:* **existence** [ɪg'zɪstəns] (Existenz)
detox *(infml)* ['diːtɒks]	Entzug(sprogramm)	**detox** is short for **detoxification** [diːtɒksɪfɪ'keɪʃn] (Entgiftung)
(to) **be tired of** sth. ['taɪəd]	die Nase voll haben von etwas	**I'm** really **tired of** your stupid excuses! Just get the job done.
version ['vɜːʃn]	Version	Betonung auf der 1. Silbe: version ['vɜːʃn]
(to) **get** / (to) **be** / (to) **feel fed up (with)** [fed 'ʌp]	genervt sein, die Nase voll haben (von)	►► (to) be tired of sth.
(to) **pop up** [pɒp 'ʌp]	aufpoppen *(z. B Computer-Fenster)*; (plötzlich) auftauchen; aus dem Boden schießen	I hate it when I just want to look up something online, and lots of ads **pop up**.
inappropriate [ɪnə'prəʊpriət]	unangemessen, unpassend, ungeeignet	**inappropriate** ◄► **appropriate** (angemessen, passend, geeignet) You need **appropriate** clothes for a job interview. Your behaviour was **inappropriate**. You should apologize.
(to) **go to sleep**	einschlafen; schlafen gehen	►► (to) fall asleep; (to) go to bed
(to) **scroll (up/down)** [skrəʊl]	(hoch-/runter)scrollen	"For the French version, please **scroll down** to the bottom of the page."
way more interesting *(infml)*	viel interessanter, weit(aus) interessanter	I think live music is **way** cooler than MP3 music.
(to) **lose touch (with** sb./sth.**)**	den Kontakt (zu jm./etwas) verlieren	**in touch with** = in Kontakt mit (to) **get in touch** (with) = (sich) in Verbindung setzen (mit), Kontakt aufnehmen (zu) If you come to York, **get in touch with** me. (to) **keep** / (to) **stay in touch** (with) = in Verbindung/ Kontakt bleiben (mit) We live 600 miles apart, but we've **stayed/kept in touch**.
(to) **go on**	geschehen, vor sich gehen	Someone was shouting, but I didn't know what was **going on**.
membership ['membəʃɪp]	Mitgliedschaft	►► when you're a member *(e.g. of a club)*

	(to) **build up** [bɪld 'ʌp]	(sich) aufbauen	A storm **built up**. (baute sich auf) My grandpa **built up** this company. (baute ... auf)
	following ['fɒləʊɪŋ]	Anhängerschaft	►► all the supporters; all the people who follow sb., e.g. on social media
p. 45	(to) **hack** [hæk]	hacken	(to) **hack into a system / a computer** = in ein System eindringen; sich in einen Computer einhacken
	sort (of) [sɔːt]	Art (von)	►► kind (of); type (of) What **sort of** music do you like? They had some **sort of** problem. (... irgendwie ein Problem) all **sorts of** things (lauter Dinge, alles mögliche)
	jealous (of) ['dʒeləs]	neidisch (auf); eifersüchtig	You get so much pocket money! I'm really **jealous**. She was **jealous of** her baby brother. She thought her parents loved him more.
	(to) **shut** [ʃʌt], **shut, shut**	schließen, verschließen	(to) **shut** sth. **down** = etwas schließen, stilllegen, abschalten
	(to) **speak out**	sich äußern, seine Meinung äußern	You can't change things if you don't **speak out**.
	despite [dɪ'spaɪt]	trotz	**despite** the dangers = **although/though** it is/was dangerous
	(to) **keep up with**	sich auf dem Laufenden halten über; Schritt halten mit	I've stopped going jogging with my older brother. He's too fast for me, and I can't **keep up with** him.
	It's me that tells her ...	und (ausgerechnet/nur) ich sage ihr ... *(**me** betont)*	**It's** always **me that** helps Jim with his homework! **It was** because of **Jackie that** we had these problems.
	(to) **sign in** [saɪn 'ɪn] (to) **sign out** [saɪn 'aʊt]	sich anmelden, sich ein-tragen sich abmelden, sich aus-tragen	"Click here to set up an account. If you're a customer already, click here to **sign in**." 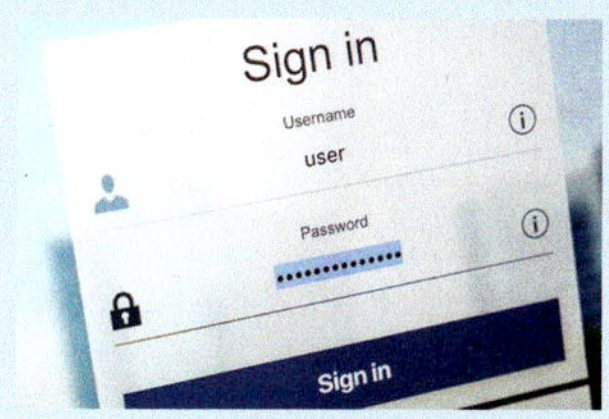
	status ['steɪtəs]	Status	Do you provide personal information, e.g. hometown or relationship **status**, on social media?

Introduction

p. 46	(to) **influence** ['ɪnfluəns]	beeinflussen	Even today, the Beatles still **influence** musicians all over the world. *verb:* (to) **influence** – *nouns:* **influence** (Einfluss) / *(person:)* **influencer**
p. 47	(to) **promote** [prə'məʊt]	Werbung machen für; fördern, unterstützen	These products have been **promoted** in online pop-up ads. (Werbung machen für) We should **promote** people's interest in environ-mental issues. (fördern, unterstützen) She was **promoted** to CEO last year. (befördern)
	(to) **whisper** ['wɪspə]	flüstern	He was scared. "There's someone at the door," he **whispered**. *verb:* (to) **whisper** – *noun:* **whisper** (*(das)* Flüstern, Geflüster)

p. 48	**whether** ['weðə]	ob	►► if I don't know **whether** this is correct. (= if this is correct)
	password ['pɑːswɜːd]	Passwort	"To sign in, please enter your name and **password**."
	request [rɪ'kwest]	Wunsch, Bitte; Anfrage	*noun:* **request** – *verb:* (to) **require**
	order ['ɔːdə]	Befehl ⚠	*noun:* an **order** = **1.** ein Befehl; **2.** eine Bestellung – *verb:* (to) **order** = **1.** bestellen; **2.** (to) **order** sth./sb. **to do** = sth. etwas anordnen; jm. befehlen, etwas zu tun
	(to) **advise** [əd'vaɪz]	empfehlen; (be)raten; informieren	*verb:* (to) **advise** – *noun:* **advice**
	sensible ['sensəbl]	vernünftig; praktisch, zweckmäßig	**sensible shoes** = vernünftige (= bequeme, robuste) Schuhe *adjective:* **sensible** – *noun:* **sense** (Sinn; Vernunft)

Skills training

p. 49	**electronic** [ɪlek'trɒnɪk]	elektronisch	*adjective:* **electronic** – *adverb:* **electronically** – *noun:* **electronics** *(pl)*
	(to) **set** sth. **(to)** [set]	etwas einstellen (auf)	If you don't want your phone to wake you up at night, switch it off or at least **set it to** "quiet".
	airplane ['eəpleɪn]	Flugzeug	►► plane
	mode [məʊd]	Modus; Art	Don't leave your devices on standby **mode** at night – switch them off to save electricity. (Modus) Which **mode** of communication do you prefer? (Art)
	take-off ['teɪk ɒf]	Start *(Flugzeug)*	**take-off**   **landing**
	20% **off** (on) headphones [ɒf]	20% Preisnachlass auf Kopfhörer	Only today! 50% **off** all T-shirts! = All T-shirts **(at) half price**! (zum halben Preis)
	electronics *(pl)* [ɪlek'trɒnɪks]	Elektronik; elektronische Geräte	
	department [dɪ'pɑːtmənt]	Abteilung	A department store is a huge shop with many different **departments**.
	sale [seɪl]	Verkauf; Schlussverkauf *(Verkauf zu ermäßigten Preisen)*	They want to **sell** their house. = Their house is **for sale**. (zu verkaufen) 
	coach [kəʊtʃ]	(Eisenbahn-)Wagen ⚠	**coach** = **1.** (Eisenbahn-)Wagen; **2.** (Reise-)Bus; **3.** Trainer/in
	context ['kɒntekst]	Zusammenhang	What does 'get' mean? – It has lots of meanings. Show me the word in **context**.

Text 2

p. 50	(to) **harness** ['hɑːnɪs]	nutzen, nutzbar machen	We can **harness** water, wind or sunlight as sources of energy.

official [ə'fɪʃl]	offiziell	You can see the logo of the **official** sponsor of a team on the team shirts. **official language** = Amtssprache
(to) **be based on** [beɪst]	basieren auf, beruhen auf, sich stützen auf	Is this statement just your personal opinion or is it **based on** facts?
annual ['ænjuəl]	jährlich	an **annual** fee = a fee which you have to pay once a year an **annual** event = an event that takes place once a year
windmill ['wɪndmɪl]	Windmühle, Windrad	**mill** = Mühle 
(to) **pump** [pʌmp]	pumpen	*verb:* (to) **pump** – *noun:* **pump** (Pumpe)
scrapyard ['skræpjɑːd]	Schrottplatz	
bicycle ['baɪsɪkl]	Fahrrad	►► bike
clothes line ['kləʊðz laɪn]	Wäscheleine	When the weather is nice, we hang washed clothes on the **clothes line** in the garden to dry.
handle ['hændl]	Griff, Handgriff	a **door handle** 
rung [rʌŋ]	Sprosse *(einer Leiter)*	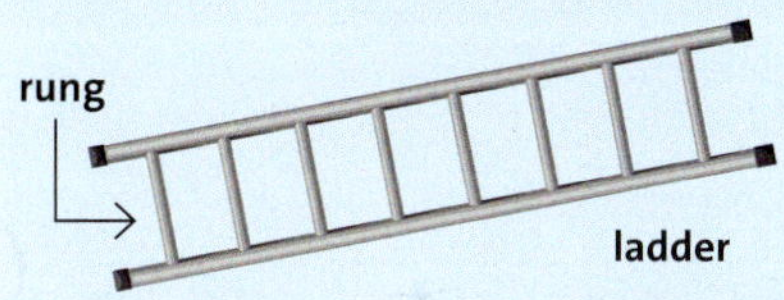
ladder ['lædə]	*(die)* Leiter	
(to) **guide** [gaɪd]	führen, leiten	*verb:* (to) guide – *noun:* **guide** = **1.** *(person)* **(tour guide)** Reiseleiter/in, Fremdenführer/in; **2.** *(book)* Reiseführer; Ratgeber
p. 51 (to) **reply (to)** [rɪ'plaɪ]	antworten (auf)	►► (to) answer *verb:* (to) **reply** – *noun:* **reply** (Antwort)
(to) **swing** [swɪŋ], **swung, swung** [swʌŋ]	schwingen	There were strong winds, and the plane **swung** from side to side as we were landing. I was terrified!
blade [bleɪd]	(Rotor-)Blatt, (Turbinen-)Schaufel	Small planes have engines with two or more **blades**.
close (to) [kləʊs]	nahe (bei, an)	Many people don't like it if you stand too **close to** them. ⚠ Aussprache: (to) **close** (Verb: *schließen*) [kləʊz] – **close** (Adjektiv: *nahe*) [kləʊs]
(to) **secure** sth. [sɪ'kjʊə]	(sich) etwas sichern; sicherstellen	*verb:* (to) **secure** – *adjective:* **secure** (sicher, gesichert)

in place	an Ort und Stelle	I put the note on the table in the garden and a stone on top to keep it **in place**. (= so that the wind couldn't blow it away)
wooden ['wʊdn]	Holz-, hölzern	►► made of **wood**
(to) **tighten** ['taɪtn]	anziehen (z. B Schraube), straff ziehen; verschärfen (z. B. Maßnahme)	►► (to) make (sth.) **tighter** *verb:* (to) **tighten** – *adjective:* **tight: 1.** fest, straff; streng – **2.** knapp, eng (anliegend) *(Kleidung)*
within [wɪ'ðɪn]	innerhalb (von), in	We have to finish our project **within** two weeks. The station is **within walking distance**. (in fußläufiger Entfernung, fußläufig erreichbar)
dozen ['dʌzn], *pl* **dozen**	Dutzend ⚠	two **dozen** eggs = zwei Dutzend Eier *but* **dozens** of people = dutzende Leute
base [beɪs]	Basis; Sockel, Fuß; Boden *(Kuchen, Pizza)*	the bottom part (e.g. of a lamp, ladder, cake); what something is based on
electric [ɪ'lektrɪk]	elektrisch, Elektro-	I play the **electric** guitar in our rock band.
impossible [ɪm'pɒsəbl]	unmöglich	It's **impossible** to run a mile in two minutes. **impossible** ◄► **possible**
(to) **stand back (from)**	zurücktreten (von) *(Schritte nach hinten machen)*	"The train is arriving. Please **stand back from** the platform edge."
copper ['kɒpə]	Kupfer	a pot made of **copper** 
socket ['sɒkɪt]	Steckdose, Anschluss(dose)	a British power **socket** 
wide [waɪd]	breit, weit; weit geöffnet *(Augen)*	The river is too **wide**. We can't get across. Her eyes were **wide**. = Ihre Augen waren weit geöffnet/aufgerissen.
second ['sekənd]	Sekunde	There are 60 **seconds** in a minute.
just as many children [dʒʌst]	genauso viele Kinder	You look **just like** your father. (genau wie ...)
(to) **beg** [beg]	flehen, (eindringlich) bitten; betteln	(to) **beg** sb. **to do** sth. = jn. anflehen, etwas zu tun (to) **beg for** sth. (**from** sb.) = (bei jm.) um etwas betteln
(to) **free** [friː]	befreien	*verb:* (to) **free** – *adjective:* **free** – *noun:* **freedom**
p. 52 **miracle** ['mɪrəkl]	Wunder	What a terrible accident! It's a **miracle** that nobody was seriously hurt.
(to) **flicker** ['flɪkə]	flackern; flimmern	These lamps aren't broken. They always **flicker** at first when you switch them on.
(to) **burst** [bɜːst], **burst, burst**	brechen, bersten, platzen	The kids were frightened when the balloon **burst**.
dizzy ['dɪzi]	schwindelig	**I feel dizzy.** = Mir ist schwindelig.
disbelief [dɪsbɪ'liːf]	Unglaube(n), Ungläubigkeit	*nouns:* **disbelief** ◄► **belief** (Glaube, Überzeugung) *verbs:* (to) **not believe** sth. ◄► to **believe** sth.
(to) **clap (your hands)** [klæp]	(in die Hände) klatschen	It was a great concert. At the end everyone **clapped**.

(to) **doubt** [daʊt]	(be)zweifeln	*verb:* (to) **doubt** – *noun:* **doubt** (Zweifel) I don't **doubt** that you're right. No **doubt** you're right. (ohne Zweifel, zweifellos)
(to) **go bigger**	größer werden	After a while their business **went bigger**. (= grew bigger, became more successful)

German "werden"

Man verwendet am häufigsten (to) **get** und (to) **become**. Das Verb (to) **get** ist etwas umgangssprachlicher.	(to) **get** / (to) **become** angry/tired/nervous/old/ill/... cold/windy/dark/... exciting/boring/funny/more interesting/...	
⚠ Vor Nomen kann nur (to) **become** stehen:	She **became** a doctor / a singer / a successful boxer / ...	
(to) **go** wird oft verwendet: – bei Farbveränderungen: – bei Verschlechterungen:	 (to) **go** red/brown/green/... (to) **go** bad *(food)* (to) **go** hard *(bread)* (to) **go** crazy	 rot/braun/grün/... werden schlecht werden hart werden verrückt werden
(to) **come** bedeutet in einigen feststehenden Ausdrücken „werden":	(to) **come** of age (to) **come** true: Will your dreams **come true**? (to) **come** alive: History **comes alive** in our museum!	volljährig werden wahr werden lebendig werden, (wieder) aufleben
(to) **grow** bedeutet „allmählich werden"	(to) **grow** old, (to) **grow** bigger, (to) **grow** closer to sb.	

Skills training

p. 53	(to) **turn** (sth.) **on/off**	(etwas) ein-/ausschalten; sich ein-/ausschalten	►► (to) switch (sth.) on/off
	(to) **stream** [striːm]	streamen	**streaming service** = Streamingdienst
	stereo ['steriəʊ]	Stereo-; Stereoanlage	 a **stereo**
	(to) **press** [pres]	drücken	**pressing** a **button** 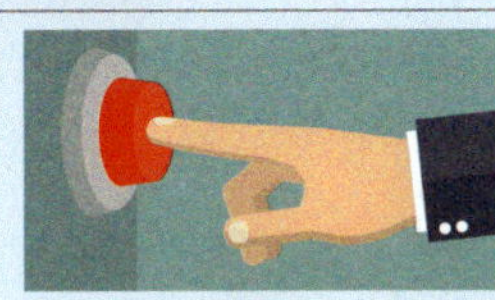
	button ['bʌtn]	Button; Schaltfläche; Knopf	
	warranty ['wɒrənti]	Garantie, Gewährleistung	The device has a one-year **warranty**. = The company which sells the device will repair or replace it if it breaks within one year after you bought it.
	(to) **affect** [ə'fekt]	beeinflussen, betreffen, sich auswirken auf	Climate change will **affect** all of us. ... doesn't **affect** your consumer rights. = ... berührt nicht Ihre Rechte als Verbraucher/in. (to) **be affected by** sth. = von etwas betroffen, beeinflusst sein
	(to) **consume** [kən'sjuːm]	verbrauchen, konsumieren	*verb:* (to) **consume** – *noun:* **consumer** (Konsument/in, Verbraucher/in)
	(to) **unplug** sth. [ʌn'plʌg]	den Stecker von etwas herausziehen, etwas ausstöpseln	►► (to) pull out the plug of sth. (to) **unplug** sth. ◄► (to) **plug** sth. **in**
	(to) **reset** [riː'set], **reset, reset**	zurücksetzen; resetten	I'll delete all my data and **reset** my laptop before I sell it.

p. 54

(to) **aim to do** sth. [eɪm]	bestrebt sein etwas zu tun, etwas tun wollen	"Thank you for your message. We **aim to reply** to all emails within 24 hours."

verbs + infinitive with "to"

I would **advise** you	**to be** careful.	Nobody **expects** you	**to know** everything.
We **aim**	**to reduce** pollution even more.	Let's **motivate** the kids	**to do** more sport.
They **arranged**	**to meet** at the theatre.	Can your boss **order** you	**to work** long hours?
Who **convinced** you	**to become** vegetarian?	We **require** you	**to fill in** and **sign** this form.
We **encouraged** him	**to apply** for the job.		

target ['tɑːɡɪt]	Ziel	I am the **target** of a lot of fashion adverts. If you want to sell something, you have to know your **target group**. **target group** = **target audience** (Zielgruppe, Zielpublikum)
lemon ['lemən]	Zitrone	
(to) **suggest** [sə'dʒest]	suggerieren	⚠ (to) **suggest** = **1.** vorschlagen; **2.** suggerieren
(to) **appeal to** sb. [ə'piːl]	für jn. attraktiv sein, jn. ansprechen	**appealing** = ansprechend *verb:* (to) **appeal** (to) – *noun:* **appeal** (Anziehungskraft, Reiz)

verbs + preposition

(to) **adjust to** sth.	sich **auf** etwas **einstellen**, sich **an** etwas **anpassen**	(to) **get along with** sb.	**gut zurechtkommen mit** jm., sich **mit** jm. **gut verstehen**
(to) **appeal to** sb.	**für** jn. **attraktiv sein**, jn. **ansprechen**	(to) **get rid of** sth.	etwas **loswerden**
(to) **attach** sth. **to** an email	etwas **an** eine E-Mail **anhängen, anfügen**	(to) **inform** sb. **of/about** sth.	jn. über etwas **informieren**
(to) **beg for** sth. **from** sb.	**bei** jm. **um** etwas **betteln**	(to) **jump at** sth.	**bei** etwas **sofort zugreifen**, eine Gelegenheit **sofort ergreifen**
(to) **care for** sb./sth.	sich **um** jn./etwas **kümmern, auf** jn./etwas **aufpassen**	(to) **keep up with** sb./sth.	sich **über** etwas **auf dem Laufenden halten; Schritt halten mit** jm./etwas
(to) **focus on** sth.	sich **auf** etwas **konzentrieren**	(to) **reply to** sth.	**auf** etwas **antworten**

sb./sth. **lacks** sth. [læk]	jm./einer Sache fehlt/mangelt es an etwas	*verb:* (to) **lack** He's good at his job, but he's still young and **lacks** experience. – *noun:* **lack** (Mangel) The way he does certain things shows a **lack** of experience. **for lack of** ... = aus Mangel an ... I'm using this thing **for lack of** the appropriate tool.
eye-catching ['aɪ kætʃɪŋ]	auffallend, ins Auge springend	I love clothes in bright, **eye-catching** colours.
concern [kən'sɜːn]	Befürchtung, Bedenken, Sorge; Angelegenheit, Sache	*noun:* **concern** = **1.** Befürchtung, Bedenken, Sorge Workers expressed their **concern** that the factory might close. **2.** Angelegenheit, Sache This is **none of your concern**. (Das geht dich/Sie nichts an.) *verb:* (to) **concern** = **1.** beunruhigen, bekümmern Workers are **concerned** that the factory might close. **2.** betreffen, angehen Please listen carefully. This **concerns** you all.

luxury ['lʌkʃəri]	Luxus	*noun:* **luxury** – *adjective:* **luxurious** [lʌg'ʒʊəriəs] (luxuriös)
whereas [weər'æz]	während, wohingegen	We're very different. Sam loves meat, **whereas** I'm a vegetarian.
ingredient [ɪn'gri:diənt]	Bestandteil, Inhaltsstoff; Zutat	Look at the cake recipe and make sure you have all the **ingredients**. (= the things you need to make the cake)
basic ['beɪsɪk]	einfach, elementar	*adjective:* **basic** We stayed at a cheap, **basic** hotel. *adverb:* **basically** (im Prinzip, grundsätzlich) **Basically** I like your idea. But I'd like to discuss some of the details. *noun:* the **basics** *(pl)* I only know the **basics** of coding.
Why pay ...?	Warum sollte man ... bezahlen?	**Why pay** more than necessary for a new scooter? **Why not buy** from us and save money?
this good / that bad	so gut / so schlecht	►► so good/bad; as good/bad as this/that

Study skills

p. 55	**firm** [fɜ:m]	Firma	►► company
	knowledge (of/about) ['nɒlɪdʒ]	Wissen (von/über), Kenntnis(se) (von/in)	**knowledge** of art (Wissen auf dem Gebiet der Kunst), **knowledge** of geography (Kenntnisse der Geografie, geografische Kenntnisse), **knowledge** about nature (Wissen über die Natur) *noun:* **knowledge** – *verb:* (to) **know, knew, known**
	(to) **analyze** ['ænəlaɪz]	analysieren, untersuchen	*verb:* (to) **analyze** – *noun:* **analysis** [ə'næləsɪs], *pl* **analyses** [ə'næləsi:z] (Analyse)

Unit 4 – Indian images

pp. 58/59	**image** ['ɪmɪdʒ]	Bild, Abbildung	►► a picture or a photo Africa is much more than just **images** of slums and poor people.
	contrast ['kɒntrɑ:st]	Kontrast, Gegensatz	*noun:* **contrast** ['kɒntrɑ:st] Coming home to London from a holiday in the Caribbean ... what a **contrast**! – *verb:* (to) **contrast** [kən'trɑ:st] (vergleichen, (einander) gegenüberstellen) Please compare and **contrast** the living conditions of Indian children with your own.
	currency ['kʌrənsi]	Währung	Until 2001, the **currency** used in Germany was the Deutsche Mark.
	Hinduism ['hɪndu:ɪzəm]	Hinduismus	⚠ The main religion in India is **Hinduism**. A person whose religion is Hinduism is a **Hindu**. One of India's official languages is **Hindi**.
	cow [kaʊ]	Kuh	 a **cow**
	rule [ru:l]	Herrschaft	*nouns:* **rule** / *(person:)* **ruler** (Herrscher/in) India was under British **rule** for many years. – *verb:* (to) **rule** herrschen (über) The British **ruled** India for many years.

equality [i'kwɒləti]	Gleichberechtigung, Gleichheit	*nouns:* **equality** ◄► **inequality** [ɪnɪ'kwɒləti] (Ungleichheit) *adjectives:* **equal** ◄► **unequal** [ʌn'i:kwəl] (ungleich)
region ['ri:dʒən]	Region	*noun:* **region** ['ri:dʒən] – *adjective:* **regional** ['ri:dʒənl] (regional)
middle class [mɪdl 'klɑ:s]	Mittelstand, Mittelschicht	a **middle-class** family
literacy ['lɪtərəsi]	*Fähigkeit, lesen und schreiben zu können*	*nouns:* **literacy** ◄► **illiteracy** [ɪ'lɪtərəsi] (Analphabetismus) *adjectives:* (to) be **literate** ['lɪtərət] ◄► **illiterate** (lesen/schreiben können ◄► nicht lesen/schreiben können, Analphabet/in sein)

Text 1

p. 60 **caste** [kɑ:st]	Kaste, Gesellschaftsklasse	each of the traditional social classes in India
warrior ['wɒriə]	Krieger/in	someone who fights in a war
labour ['leɪbə]	Arbeit; Arbeitskräfte	**labourer** = Arbeiter/in **child labour** = Kinderarbeit
servant ['sɜ:vənt]	Diener/in; Bedienstete/r	someone who works in a (richer) person's house and does their cooking, cleaning, etc. *noun:* **servant** – *verb:* (to) **serve**
(to) **sweep** [swi:p], **swept, swept** [swept]	fegen, kehren	**(street) sweeper** = Straßenfeger/in **sweeping** the floor 
sewer ['su:ə]	Abwasserkanal	**sewers** *(pl)* = Kanalisation(ssystem) inside a **sewer** tunnel 
constitution [kɒnstɪ'tju:ʃn]	Verfassung	*noun:* **constitution** – *adjective:* **constitutional** [kɒnstɪ'tju:ʃənl] (verfassungsgemäß)
marriage ['mærɪdʒ]	Hochzeit, Ehe	Tim and Jack **got married** last month. = Tim **got married to** / **married** Jack last month. = Their **marriage** was last month. = They've been **married** since last month. = Tim has been **married to** Jack since last month. (verheiratet mit) *noun:* **marriage** – *verb:* (to) **marry**
waste [weɪst]	Müll; Abfall; Fäkalien	**animal waste** / **human waste** = tierische/menschliche Fäkalien ⚠ **waste** = **1.** Müll; Abfall; Fäkalien; **2.** Verschwendung; **3.** (to) **waste** = verschwenden
(to) **avoid** [ə'vɔɪd]	(ver)meiden; verhindern	(to) **avoid** sth. = etwas (ver)meiden You should always do your best to **avoid** accidents. (to) **avoid doing** sth. = es vermeiden, etwas zu tun I'd like to **avoid waiting** for hours, so I'll go there early.
well [wel]	Quelle, Brunnen	Centuries ago people had to get water from **wells**. 

quota ['kwəʊtə]	Quote	Let's discuss female **quotas**. Do you think **quotas** will stop discrimination against women?
salary ['sæləri]	Gehalt	the money that your employer pays you for doing your job
pharmaceutical [fɑːmə'suːtɪkl]	Pharma-, pharmazeutisch	*adjective:* **pharmaceutical** – *noun:* **pharmaceutical** (Arzneimittel) ⚠ Das Substantiv steht meist im Plural: **pharmaceuticals**.
biotechnology [baɪəʊtek'nɒlədʒi]	Biotechnologie	That stuff you're eating isn't natural at all! It's a product of **biotechnology**.
multinational [mʌlti'næʃnəl]	multinational	►► in or from different countries *adjective:* **multinational** – *noun:* **multinational** (multinationaler Konzern, Multi)
positive discrimination [pɒzətɪv dɪskrɪmɪ'neɪʃn]	positive Diskriminierung *(gesellschaftspolitische Maßnahmen, die negativer Diskriminierung entgegenwirken)*	a policy that helps people who normally have certain disadvantages (e.g. because of gender, colour of skin or social background) to be treated more fairly
among [ə'mʌŋ]	unter, zwischen *(mehreren Personen oder Dingen)*	**among** ◄► **between**  **among** the green apples  **between** the green apples
p. 61 **position** [pə'zɪʃn]	Position, Standort; Stellung; (Arbeits-)Stelle	From this **position** on the hill you have a great view of the village. She has had the CEO **position** for seven years now. ⚠ Betonung auf der 2. Silbe: po<u>si</u>tion [pə'zɪʃn]
almost ['ɔːlməʊst]	fast, nahezu, beinahe	►► nearly
employee [ɪm'plɔɪiː]	Arbeitnehmer/in	**employment** ◄► **unemployment** **employed** ◄► **unemployed** **self-employed** ◄► **employed by a company** An **employer** gives people work. An **employee** works for a company / an **employer**.
majority [mə'dʒɒrəti]	Mehrheit, Mehrzahl	**majority** ◄► **minority** [maɪ'nɒrəti] (Minderheit) There are 16 girls and 13 boys in my class. The girls are in the **majority**. The boys are in the **minority**. (= There are more girls than boys in our class.)
ahead [ə'hed]	voran; voraus	There's an accident on the road **ahead**! Let's take a different route. (to) **get ahead** = vorankommen, weiterkommen *(auch beruflich)*
stall [stɔːl]	(Markt-)Stand, Bude	**stallholder** ['stɔːlhəʊldə] (Standinhaber/in)  a **stall**
sensitive ['sensətɪv]	einfühlsam, sensibel; heikel *(z. B. Thema)*	⚠ *English:* **sensitive** – *German:* <u>sensibel</u>, einfühlsam *English:* <u>**sensible**</u> – *German:* vernünftig; praktisch
religious [rɪ'lɪdʒəs]	religiös	⚠ Betonung auf der 2. Silbe: **re<u>li</u>gious** [rɪ'lɪdʒəs] *adjective:* **religious** – *noun:* **religion**

	opportunity [ɒpə'tjuːnəti]	Gelegenheit, Möglichkeit, Chance	►► chance ⚠ **German "Gelegenheit"**: **1.** Chance, Möglichkeit = **chance/opportunity** **2.** Ereignis, Anlass = **occasion**
	rate [reɪt]	Rate, Quote, Anteil; Tarif, Preis	How high is the unemployment **rate** / the **rate** of unemployment this month? (die Arbeitslosenquote) I went to the museum with several friends, so we got a group **rate**. (= a special price for groups)

Introduction

p. 62	**blend** [blend]	Mischung	*noun:* **blend** – That's a nice **blend** of colours. *verb:* (to) **blend** ((sich) (ver)mischen) You can't **blend** oil **with** water. = You can't **blend** oil **and** water. = Oil and water don't **blend**.
	role [rəʊl]	Rolle *(Film, Theater)*	The coach plays a key **role** for any sports team.
	romantic [rəʊ'mæntɪk]	romantisch	*adjective:* **romantic** – *adverb:* **romantically** [rəʊ'mæntɪkli]
	tax [tæks]	*(die)* Steuer	Beer, gin and whisky are so expensive in this country because there's a high **tax on** alcohol.
p. 63	**wonderful** ['wʌndəfl]	wunderbar	►► very good, great, amazing, awesome
	(to) **have** sth. **done (by** sb.**)**	etwas (von jm.) machen lassen *(erledigen lassen)*	Your hair looks nice. Did you cut it yourself or did you **have it cut**? There's something wrong with our car. We need to **have it checked**.

German "lassen"

(to) **have** sth. **done (by** sb.**)**	etwas (von jm.) machen lassen *(erledigen lassen)*	We **had** our website **designed by** a web designer.	= We asked/paid them to do it because they're experts, and we're not.
(to) **leave**	(alleine / in Ruhe / liegen- / zurück-) lassen	**Leave** me **alone**. Don't **leave** me **behind**. I **left** my bag in the car.	= I want to be alone. = Don't go without me. = My bag is still in the car.
(to) **let** sb. **do** sth.	jn. etwas tun/machen lassen *(es erlauben)*	My boss **let** me **go** home a bit earlier.	= My boss allowed me to go home a bit earlier.
(to) **make** sb. **do** sth.	jn. etwas machen lassen *(es befehlen)*	My boss **made** me **sweep** the shop floor.	= My boss ordered me to sweep the shop floor.
(to) **stop** sth.	etwas (sein) lassen	**Stop** that, please.	= Don't do that any more.

(to) **massage** ['mæsɑːʒ]	massieren	⚠ Betonung auf der 1. Silbe: **mas**sage ['mæsɑːʒ] *verb:* (to) **massage** – *noun:* **massage** (Massage)
nail [neɪl]	Nagel	red **fingernails** 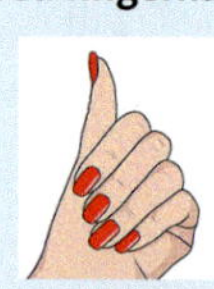 **nails** 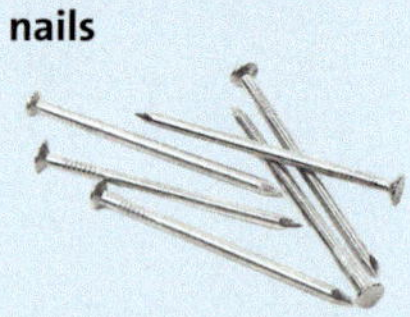 **fingernail** = Fingernagel **toenail** = Zehennagel **toe** = Zehe
(to) **manicure** ['mænɪkjʊə]	maniküren	*verb:* (to) **manicure** – *noun:* **manicure** (Maniküre)
(to) **deliver** [dɪ'lɪvə]	(aus)liefern	*verb:* (to) **deliver** – *noun:* **delivery** [dɪ'lɪvəri] (Lieferung)

Skills training

p. 64	**it is said to be ...**	man sagt, es sei ...	She **is said to be** very rich. (Man sagt, sie sei ...) Sport **is shown to be** good for your health. (Man hat gezeigt / Es wurde gezeigt, dass ... ist.) Green tea **is believed to be** good for you. (Man glaubt, dass ...) He **is known to get up** very early. (Man weiß, dass er ...)

German "man"

There are several ways of expressing the German word "man" in different contexts.

you	**You** never know! **You** can't do it like that.	Man weiß nie! So kann man das nicht machen.
they	**They** say she's rich. In France **they** love cheese.	Man sagt, sie sei/ist reich. In Frankreich liebt man Käse.
one ***(in formal language)***	**One** should not do this in general. **One** should always ask **oneself** if it is necessary.	Man sollte das generell nicht tun. Man sollte sich immer fragen, ob es notwendig ist.
the passive	It **is** not **done**. I **was told** what had happened.	Das macht man nicht. Man sagte mir, was passiert war.
(to) **be expected/said/ thought/... to be/do/...**	Ms Wong **is expected to give** a talk. She **is said to be** rich. There **are thought to be** millions of tonnes of plastic in the oceans.	Man erwartet, dass Frau Wong eine Rede hält. Man sagt, sie sei/ ist reich. Man glaubt, es gebe/gibt Millionen Tonnen Plastik in den Ozeanen.

sin [sɪn]	Sünde	In our religion this is a **sin**. = In our religion this is not allowed.
pilgrim ['pɪlgrɪm]	Pilger/in	somebody who travels to a holy place for religious reasons
(to) **bathe** [beɪð]	baden *(in einem Fluss / dem Meer)*	*verb:* (to) **bathe** – *noun:* **bather** ['beɪðə] (Badende/r *(in einem Fluss / dem Meer)*) ⚠ **German "baden"**: You have a **bath** [bɑːθ] at home in your bathroom. You **bathe** [beɪð] (= go swimming) in the sea or in a river.
(to) **pollute** [pə'luːt]	*(die Umwelt)* verschmutzen	*verb:* (to) **pollute** Cars and factories **pollute** the air. – *noun:* **pollution** Air **pollution** is a serious problem.
sewage ['suːɪdʒ]	Abwasser	dirty water from the sewers
(to) **cremate** [krə'meɪt]	einäschern	*verb:* (to) **cremate** – *noun:* **cremation** (Einäscherung)
So do I.	Ich auch. / Das tue ich auch. / Das gilt auch für mich.	I hate coffee. – **So do I.**
Neither do I. ['naɪðə], [niːðə]	Ich auch nicht.	I don't like coffee. – **Neither do I.** ... – **Nor do I.**
Nor do I. [nɔː]	Ich auch nicht.	

German "auch nicht"

You can use **not ... either** to say the same as you do with **Neither/Nor** + **auxiliary** + **(pro)noun**.

You **don't** own a car?	**Neither/Nor do** I.	= I **don't** (own a car) **either**.
I **haven't bought** bread yet.	**Neither/Nor have** I.	= I **haven't** (bought bread) **either**.
This box **isn't** big enough.	**Neither/Nor is** that one.	= That one **isn't** (big enough) **either**.
Joe **can't** do this.	**Neither/Nor can** Sam.	= Sam **can't** (do this) **either**.

by the way	übrigens	Oh, **by the way**, Grandma called this morning.

	This goes for ... (too).	Dies gilt (auch) für ...	Please be quiet now! **This goes for** all of you!
	(to) **interrupt** [ɪntə'rʌpt]	unterbrechen	It's rude to **interrupt** people when they're talking. *verb:* (to) **interrupt** – *noun:* **interruption** [ɪntə'rʌpʃn] (Unterbrechung)
p. 65	(to) **force** sb. **to do** sth. [fɔːs]	jn. zwingen, etwas zu tun	**forced marriage** = Zwangsheirat (to) **force** sth. = etwas erzwingen verb: (to) **force** – noun: **force** (Zwang; Gewalt; Kraft)
	old-fashioned [əʊld 'fæʃənd]	altmodisch	**old-fashioned ◄► modern**
	(to) **date** sb.	mit jm. gehen, eine Beziehung haben ⚠	**date** = **1.** Datum; **2.** Verabredung, Date; **3.** (to) **date** sb. = mit jm. gehen, eine Beziehung haben
	(to) **have** sth. **in common** ['kɒmən]	etwas gemeinsam haben	We're the same age, but we don't **have** much **in common**.
	horoscope ['hɒrəskəʊp]	Horoskop ⚠	Betonung auf der 1. Silbe: **hor**oscope ['hɒrəskəʊp]
	(to) **match** (sth.) [mætʃ]	zueinander passen; passen zu (etwas), übereinstimmen mit (etwas); (passend) zusammenfügen	*verb:* (to) **match** These socks don't **match**. (zueinander passen) Which translations **match** these sentences? (passen zu, übereinstimmen mit) Can you **match** these sentence parts correctly? (passend zusammenfügen) – *noun:* **match** (Gegenstück, (zusammenpassendes) Paar) (to) be a good **match** = gut zusammenpassen
	personality [pɜːsə'nælәti]	Persönlichkeit; Charakter	Ann has the perfect **personality** to be captain of our team.
	bride [braɪd]	Braut	the **groom**  the **bride**
	groom [gruːm]	Bräutigam	
	divorce [dɪ'vɔːs]	(Ehe-)Scheidung	(to) **get a divorce** = sich scheiden lassen *noun:* **divorce** – *verb:* (to) **divorce** sb. (sich von jm. scheiden lassen) She said that she wanted ... **(to get) a divorce.** **to get divorced (from him).** **to divorce him.** (= sich von ihm scheiden lassen)
	eventually [ɪ'ventʃuəli]	letztendlich, schließlich	

The end!

You use ...	... when:	Examples:
eventually	something happens after a long time or after a series of events	Will this conflict **eventually** lead to war?
finally	you describe the last element in a list or series, sometimes after waiting for a long time	"**Finally**, I'd like to thank my family who supported me so much."
at last	when you're impatient after waiting for a long time	Oh, there you are, **at last**!
in the end	after a long period of time with changes or problems	He thought about emigrating to the US, Ghana or Canada, but **in the end** he just moved to Scotland.
at the end of ...	you speak about the end of something specific	They didn't have much money left **at the end** of the month.
	at the beginning of sth. ◄► at the end	I was fit **at the beginning** of the aerobics class, but I was tired **at the end**.

possibly ['pɒsəbli]	möglicherweise	►► maybe

	logical ['lɒdʒɪkl]	logisch	*adjective:* **logical** – *noun:* **logic** (Logik)

False friends

These words look similar to German words, but they have different meanings.

English	German	German	English	English	German	German	English
also	= auch	also	**= so; Well, …**	**grade**	= Schuljahr; (Schul-)Note	Grad	**= degree**
bald	= glatzköpfig	bald	**= soon**	**kind**	= freundlich	Kind	**= child**
(to) **become**	= werden	bekommen	= (to) **get**	**mode**	= Modus, Art	Mode	**= fashion**
boot	= Stiefel	Boot	**= boat**	**snake**	= Schlange	Schnecke	**= snail**
(to) **build**	= bauen	bilden	= (to) **make,** (to) **form**	**while**	= während	weil	**= because**

Text 2

p. 66	(to) **adopt** [ə'dɒpt]	adoptieren; *(Tier)* bei sich aufnehmen	*verb:* (to) **adopt** – *noun:* **adoption** [ə'dɒpʃn] (Adoption)
	harsh [hɑːʃ]	hart, rau; brutal, harsch	Life is often **harsh** for servants when they work long hours and don't get much money. We had a **harsh** winter – it was very cold and there was lots of snow. To say he never gets anything done is a bit **harsh**.
	reasonable ['riːznəbl]	vernünftig, angemessen	**reasonably** happy = quite happy (ziemlich/durchaus glücklich)
	railway ['reɪlweɪ]	Eisenbahn	**railway station** = Bahnhof **railway line** = Bahnstrecke
	(to) **pass** sb./sth. [pɑːs]	an jm./etwas vorbeigehen, vorbeifahren	I **pass** 14 shops every morning on my way to school. (= walk/cycle/drive past) We **passed through** several small villages. (fahren/reisen durch) Time **passes** so quickly. (vorbeigehen/-ziehen; vorübergehen *(Zeit, Moment, Gelegenheit)*)
	tonight [tə'naɪt]	heute Nacht, heute Abend	It's so hot today, but we can sit in the garden **tonight** when it gets cooler.
	perhaps [pə'hæps]	vielleicht	►► maybe; possibly
	thrilled [θrɪld]	fasziniert, begeistert	►► very excited
p. 67	(to) **hire** ['haɪə]	mieten, leihen; *(Person:)* einstellen	*verb:* (to) **hire** – *noun:* **hire** (Verleih, Vermietung)
	bar [bɑː]	Stange, Balken, (Gitter-)Stab; Riegel *(Schokolade, Müsli)*; Tafel *(Schokolade)*	**bicycle handlebars** *(pl)* (Lenkstange)  *noun:* **bar** – *verb:* (to) **bar** ((ab)sperren, blockieren; vergittern *(z. B. Fenster)*)
	(to) **rest** [rest]	ruhen; sich (auf)stützen; sich ausruhen	*verb:* (to) **rest** Sit down and **rest** your feet. When your feet are **resting** on the ground, you sit comfortably. – *noun:* **rest** (Ruhe, Pause, Erholung) That was hard work. Take a **rest**!
	bumpy ['bʌmpi]	holprig, *(Flug/Schifffahrt)* unruhig	We had to drive slowly along the **bumpy** country road. It was a very **bumpy** flight. I felt so sick!
	bush [bʊʃ]	Busch	⚠ Aussprache: [bʊʃ] **bushes** 

by the time [baɪ]	als; wenn	**By the time** we arrived, the concert had already started. (als) **By the time** you finish school, your English will be very good. (wenn)
sleepy ['sliːpi]	müde; verschlafen	►► a bit tired; needing sleep I sat in the garden and began to feel a bit **sleepy**.
exhausted [ɪg'zɔːstɪd]	erschöpft	►► very tired After ten hours of hard work we were completely **exhausted**.
bench [bentʃ]	Bank *(zum Sitzen)*	**German "Bank":** **1.** where you can sit: **bench** 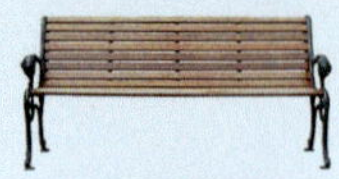 **2.** where you have your money: **bank** 
straightaway [streɪtə'weɪ]	sofort	►► immediately
carriage ['kærɪdʒ]	(Eisenbahn-)Wagen	an old train **carriage** 
(to) **wonder** ['wʌndə]	sich fragen	Do you know that woman over there? I **wonder** who she is. *English:* I **wonder** who ... *(no reflexive pronoun!)* *German:* Ich **frage** mich, wer ...
stairs *(pl)* [steəz]	Treppe; (Treppen-)Stufen	*German:* **Die** Treppe dort ist gefährlich. *English:* Those **stairs** are dangerous.
case [keɪs]	Fall	**In (the) case of** fire, don't panic. Let's take an umbrella, **(just) in case** it rains. ((nur) für den Fall, dass ...)
conductor [kən'dʌktə]	Schaffner/in, Zugbegleiter/in	
(to) **shine** [ʃaɪn], **shone, shone** [ʃɒn]	scheinen *(Sonne)*; leuchten, strahlen, glänzen	Time to get out of bed! The sun is **shining**, and it's a beautiful day.
panic ['pænɪk]	Panik	*noun:* **panic** – *verb:* (to) **panic** (in Panik geraten) **Don't panic.** = Keine Panik. / Immer mit der Ruhe.
(to) **curse** [kɜːs]	fluchen	He **cursed** as he arrived on the platform and saw that his train had just left. *verb:* (to) **curse** – *noun:* **curse** (Fluch)
(to) **keep (on) doing** sth.	etwas immer wieder / immer weiter tun; etwas ständig tun	I tried to speak, but he **kept interrupting** me. **Keep (on) smiling** – and never give up.
p. 70 **golden** ['gəʊldn]	golden, aus Gold	*adjective:* **golden** – *noun:* **gold**
triangle ['traɪæŋgl]	Dreieck	a **triangle** 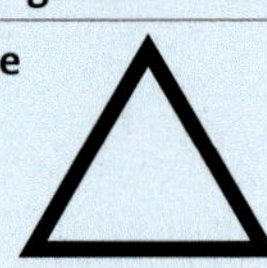
architecture ['ɑːkɪtektʃə]	Architektur	Betonung auf der 1. Silbe: architecture ['ɑːkɪtektʃə]
fabulous ['fæbjələs]	sagenhaft, fabelhaft	►► extremely good; fantastic; awesome

landmark ['lændmɑːk]	Wahrzeichen	The Eiffel Tower is a **landmark** of Paris.
palace ['pæləs]	Palast, Schloss	⚠ Betonung auf der 1. Silbe: palace ['pæləs]  a **palace**
sunrise ['sʌnraɪz]	Sonnenaufgang	**sunrise** ◄► **sunset** ['sʌnset] (Sonnenuntergang)
(to) **impress** [ɪm'pres]	beeindrucken	*verb:* (to) **impress** – *noun:* **impression**
decoration [dekə'reɪʃn]	Dekoration, Schmuck, Verzierung	*noun:* **decoration** – *verb:* (to) **decorate**

Study skills

p. 71 **neutral** ['njuːtrəl]	neutral	⚠ Achte auf Betonung und Aussprache im Gegensatz zum Deutschen: ['njuːtrəl]
reliable [rɪ'laɪəbl]	verlässlich, zuverlässig	She's a very **reliable** person. If she says she will do something, then she will really do it.
plantation [plæn'teɪʃn]	Plantage; Anpflanzung	Sugar **plantation** owners used slave labour to earn a lot of money.
production [prə'dʌkʃn]	Produktion	*verb:* (to) **produce** – *nouns: (what you produce)* **product;** *(the process of producing sth.)* **production** ⚠ Betonung auf der 2. Silbe: production [prə'dʌkʃn]
encyclopedia [ɪnsaɪklə'piːdiə]	Enzyklopädie, Lexikon	⚠ Achte auf Betonung und Aussprache: [ɪnsaɪklə'piːdiə]
item ['aɪtəm]	Artikel, Gegenstand, Punkt *(auf einer Liste)*	I took my **items** to the cash desk. **news item** = Nachrichtenmeldung, Pressemeldung
medical ['medɪkl]	ärztlich, medizinisch; gesundheitlich	⚠ Betonung auf der 1. Silbe: medical ['medɪkl] **medical insurance** = Krankenversicherung
decent ['diːsnt]	anständig, ordentlich, annehmbar	►► good enough; satisfactory You should try to find a **decent** job with **decent** pay.
wage [weɪdʒ], *oft auch:* **wages** *(pl)*	Lohn	Many years ago my dad had a **wage** of £180 per week. Now his **wages** are much higher. **minimum wage** = Mindestlohn

Working for money

pay	money that somebody earns for doing regular work (in general)	Bezahlung
salary	money that employees earn for doing their job, e.g. doctors in hospitals or people working in offices, usually paid every month	Gehalt
wage(s)	money that somebody earns regularly, usually every week or every month, for work or services	Lohn

benefit ['benɪfɪt]	Nutzen, Vorteil	*noun:* **benefit** – *verb:* (to) **benefit** **1.** You **benefit from** sth. = Du profitierst von etwas. **2.** It **benefits** you. = Es nützt dir. ⚠ **benfited/benefiting** *or* **benefitted/benefitting**
caffeine ['kæfiːn]	Koffein	⚠ Betonung auf der 1. Silbe: caffeine ['kæfiːn]
cancer ['kænsə]	Krebs *(Erkrankung)*	He got **cancer**. Luckily he survived after a long treatment.
(to) **claim** [kleɪm]	angeben, behaupten	He looks about 15, but **claims** he's 18. *verb:* (to) **claim** – *noun:* **claim** (Behauptung)
herbal ['hɜːbl]	Kräuter-	**herbal** tea = tea made from **herbs** [hɜːbz] (Kräuter)

mint [mɪnt]	(Pfeffer-)Minze	**mint** leaves 
significant [sɪɡ'nɪfɪkənt]	deutlich, spürbar, erheblich, signifikant	**significant ◄► insignificant** [ɪnsɪɡ'nɪfɪkənt] (unbedeutend, geringfügig)
study ['stʌdi]	Untersuchung, Studie	*noun:* **study** – *verb:* (to) **study** (untersuchen; studieren; lernen *(z. B. für Prüfungen)*)
recent ['riːsnt]	aktuell, jüngst	**recent** history (jüngere/jüngste Geschichte) a **recent** photo of me (ein aktuelles Foto) in **recent** years (in den letzten Jahren)
strike [straɪk]	Streik	*noun:* **strike** Workers **went on strike** for a pay increase. – *verb:* (to) **strike, struck, struck** [strʌk] (streiken; schlagen) We're going to **strike** for a pay increase! Parents should never **strike** their children.
miserable ['mɪzrəbl]	erbärmlich, jämmerlich, trostlos	I felt **miserable**. (= not very well; very unhappy) What **miserable** weather! (= horrible)

Your task

p. 73	**tourism** ['tʊərɪzəm]	Tourismus	⚠ Betonung auf der 1. Silbe: **tou**rism ['tʊərɪzəm]

English-speaking countries

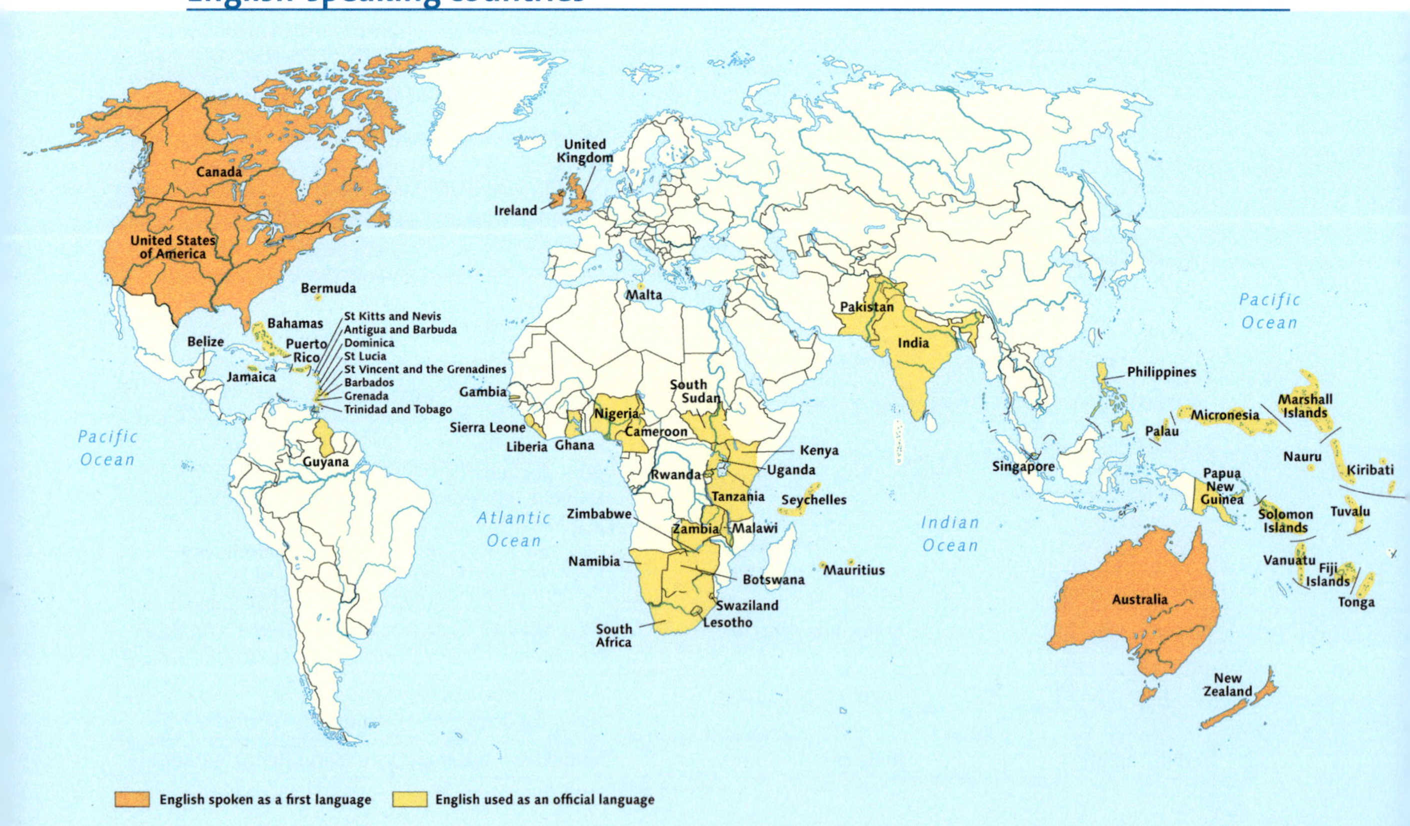

Im **Dictionary** kannst du nachschlagen, wenn du wissen möchtest, was ein englisches Wort bedeutet, wie man es ausspricht oder wie es geschrieben wird.

Im **Dictionary** werden folgende **Abkürzungen** und **Symbole** verwendet:
pl = plural (Mehrzahl) • *AE = American English* • *BE = British English* • *infml = informal* (umgangssprachlich)
sb. = somebody • *sth. = something* • *jn.* = jemanden • *jm.* = jemandem
° Mit diesem Kringel sind Wörter markiert, die nicht zum Lernwortschatz gehören.

Die **Fundstellenangaben** zeigen, wo ein Wort zum ersten Mal vorkommt.
Die Ziffern in Klammern bezeichnen Seitenzahlen:
5 = *Go Ahead 5* • 6 = *Go Ahead 6* • 7 = *Go Ahead 7* • 8 = *Go Ahead 8* • 9: 4 (66) = *Go Ahead 9*, Unit 4, Seite 66

Tipps zur Arbeit mit einem (Online-)Wörterbuch findest du im Skills file 16 auf Seite 138.

A

a [ə] ein, eine 5 **My dad is a teacher.** Mein Papa ist Lehrer (von Beruf). 5 **three times a week** dreimal pro Woche 6
ability [ə'bɪləti] Fähigkeit 8
able ['eɪbl]: **be able to do sth.** etwas tun können, in der Lage sein etwas zu tun 8
Aboriginal [æbə'rɪdʒənl] Aborigine- *(die Ureinwohner/innen Australiens betreffend)* 9: 1 (10) **Aboriginal Australian** australische/r Ureinwohner/in 9: 1 (10)
about [ə'baʊt]:
1. ungefähr 7
2. über 5
about the story über die Geschichte 5 **ask about sth.** wegen etwas (an)fragen 5 **It isn't only about playing games.** Es geht nicht nur darum, Spiele zu spielen. 5 **the good/bad thing about bikes** das Gute/Schlechte an Fahrrädern 5 **What about you?** Und du? / Was ist mit dir? 5
above [ə'bʌv] über, oberhalb (von); oben 8
abroad [ə'brɔːd] im/ins Ausland 9: 2 (24/25)
°Academy Award [əkædəmi ə'wɔːd] *Filmpreis („Oscar")*
accent ['æksent] Akzent 9: 1 (17)
access ['ækses]:
1. **access (to)** Zugang (zu), Zugriff (auf) 8
2. **access sth.** auf etwas zugreifen; Zugang haben zu etwas 8
accessible (to) [ək'sesəbl] erreichbar (für), zugänglich (für) 7 **wheelchair accessible** rollstuhlgerecht *(mit dem Rollstuhl zu erreichen)* 7
accident ['æksɪdənt] Unfall 5
accommodation [əkɒmə'deɪʃn] Unterkunft; Wohnung, Zimmer 9: 2 (26)
according to [ə'kɔːdɪŋ tə] laut, zufolge 7
°account [ə'kaʊnt]: **(bank) account** (Bank-)Konto
accountant [ə'kaʊntənt] Buchhalter/in 7
ache [eɪk] Schmerz(en) 6
achieve [ə'tʃiːv] erreichen, erzielen, schaffen 8
achievement [ə'tʃiːvmənt] Errungenschaft, Leistung 8
across [ə'krɒs] über *(quer über)* 6
act [ækt]:
1. aufführen, spielen 5
2. Theater spielen, schauspielern 8
3. handeln, sich verhalten; so tun, als ob 8
action ['ækʃn] Aktion, Handlung; Action *(z. B. Film)* 7
activist ['æktɪvɪst] Aktivist/in 8
activity [æk'tɪvəti] Aktivität, Tätigkeit 5 **after-school activities** AGs *(freiwillige Veranstaltungen in der Schule nach Unterrichtsschluss)* 6
actor ['æktə] Schauspieler/in 6
actually ['æktʃuəli] eigentlich; tatsächlich 7
AD [eɪ 'diː]: **400 AD** 400 n. Chr. 7
ad [æd] *(infml) siehe* **advertisement**
add [æd] hinzufügen, addieren 7
addict ['ædɪkt] Abhängige/r, Süchtige/r 8
addicted (to) [ə'dɪktɪd] süchtig (nach), abhängig (von) 8
addition [ə'dɪʃn]: **in addition to** außerdem; zusätzlich (zu) ... 8
address [ə'dres]:
1. Adresse 7
2. **address sth.** etwas angehen, sich mit etwas befassen; etwas zur Sprache bringen 9: 3 (43)
adjust (to) [ə'dʒʌst] (sich) einstellen (auf); (sich) anpassen (an) 9: 2 (34)
adobe [ə'dəʊbi] Lehmziegel 8
adopt [ə'dɒpt] adoptieren; *(Tier)* bei sich aufnehmen 9: 4 (66)
adoption [ə'dɒpʃn] Adoption 9: 4 (66)
adult ['ædʌlt] Erwachsene/r 5
advantage [əd'vɑːntɪdʒ] Vorteil 7
adventure [əd'ventʃə] Abenteuer 8
advert ['ædvɜːt] *(infml) siehe* **advertisement**
advertise (sth.) ['ædvətaɪz] Werbung machen (für etwas) 7
advertisement *infml auch* **ad, advert** [əd'vɜːtɪsmənt] Anzeige, Inserat; Werbespot 8
advertising ['ædvətaɪzɪŋ] Werbung, Reklame 7
advice *(no pl)* [əd'vaɪs] Rat, Ratschlag, Ratschläge 7
advise [əd'vaɪz] empfehlen; (be)raten; informieren 9: 3 (48)
affair [ə'feə] Angelegenheit, Sache; Affäre, Verhältnis 9: 1 (17)
affect [ə'fekt] beeinflussen, betreffen, sich auswirken auf 9: 3 (53) **... doesn't affect your consumer rights.** ... berührt nicht Ihre Rechte als Verbraucher/in. 9: 3 (53)
affected (by) [ə'fektɪd] betroffen, beeinflusst (von) 9: 3 (53)
afford sth./to do sth. [ə'fɔːd] sich etwas leisten können / sich leisten können, etwas zu tun 6
afraid [ə'freɪd]: **be afraid (of)** Angst haben (vor), sich fürchten (vor) 8 **I'm afraid** leider, ich fürchte 8
African American [æfrɪkən ə'merɪkən] Afroamerikaner/in; afroamerikanisch 8
after [ɑːftə] nach *(zeitlich)* 5

after-school activities [ɑːftə skuːl æk'tɪvətiz] AGs *(freiwillige Veranstaltungen in der Schule nach Unterrichtsschluss)* 6
afternoon [ɑːftə'nuːn] Nachmittag 5
again [ə'gen] wieder, noch einmal 5
against [ə'genst] gegen 6
age [eɪdʒ]:
1. Alter 5
at any age in jedem Alter 7 **at the age of 12** im Alter von 12 (Jahren) 5 **come of age** volljährig werden 9: 1 (13)
2. Zeitalter 9: 3 (43)
ago [ə'gəʊ]: **many years ago** vor vielen Jahren 6
agree (with sb./sth.) [ə'griː] jm. zustimmen; mit etwas einverstanden sein 6
ahead [ə'hed]: **get ahead** vorankommen, weiterkommen *(auch beruflich)* 9: 4 (61) **Go ahead.** Nur zu! / Dann mal los! 5
aim [eɪm]:
1. Ziel 7
2. aim at sth. zielen auf etwas 7 **aim to do sth.** bestrebt sein etwas zu tun, etwas tun wollen 9: 3 (54)
air [eə] Luft 5
airplane ['eəpleɪn] Flugzeug 9: 3 (49)
airport ['eəpɔːt] Flughafen 6
aka (= also known as) [eɪ keɪ 'eɪ] alias, auch bekannt als 7
alcohol ['ælkəhɒl] Alkohol 8
alert [ə'lɜːt]:
1. Warnung, Alarm 8
2. alert (to sth.) aufmerksam; sich einer Sache bewusst 8
3. alert sb. (to sth.) jn. alarmieren, jn. (vor etwas) warnen 8
alive [ə'laɪv] lebendig, am Leben 8 **come alive** lebendig werden, (wieder) aufleben 9: 3 (52)
all [ɔːl] alle(s) 5 **all over the world** überall auf der Welt, auf der ganzen Welt 7 **all the same** trotzdem 9: 2 (34) **all year** das ganze Jahr (über) 5 **(not) at all** überhaupt (nicht) 6
all-in-one [ɔːl ɪn 'wʌn] Komplett-, alles in einem 8
all right [ɔːl 'raɪt] in Ordnung, OK 8 **know how to do sth. all right** sehr wohl / nur zu gut wissen, wie man etwas macht 9: 2 (33)
allergic (to) [ə'lɜːdʒɪk] allergisch (gegen) 8
allergy (to) ['ælədʒi] Allergie (gegen) 8
alliance [ə'laɪəns] Bündnis, Allianz 8
allowed [ə'laʊd] erlaubt 7 **be allowed to do sth.** etwas tun dürfen 7
almost ['ɔːlməʊst] fast, nahezu, beinahe 9: 4 (61)
alone [ə'ləʊn] allein 6
along [ə'lɒŋ]: **along the path** den Weg entlang 6
alphabet ['ælfəbet] Alphabet 5
already [ɔːl'redi] schon 6
also ['ɔːlsəʊ] auch 5
although [ɔːl'ðəʊ] obwohl 7
altogether [ɔːltə'geðə] insgesamt 9: 2 (34)
always ['ɔːlweɪz] immer 5
am [æm]: **I'm (= I am)** ich bin 5
am [eɪ'em]: **9 am** 9 Uhr morgens/vormittags 6
amateur ['æmətə] Amateur/in; Amateur-, Hobby- 9: 1 (20)
amazed [ə'meɪzd]: **be amazed at/by sth.** über etwas staunen, erstaunt sein 8
amazing [ə'meɪzɪŋ] erstaunlich; großartig 6
among [ə'mʌŋ] unter, zwischen *(mehreren Personen oder Dingen)* 9: 4 (60)
an [ən] ein, eine 5
analyses [ə'næləsiːz] *Plural von* **analysis**
analysis [ə'næləsɪs], *pl* **analyses** Analyse 9: 3 (55)
analyze ['ænəlaɪz] analysieren, untersuchen 9: 3 (55)
ancestor ['ænsestə] Vorfahr/in 8
ancient ['eɪnʃənt] (ur)alt, historisch 7
and [ænd], [ənd] und 5 **go on and on** immer weiter gehen 8 **more and more** immer mehr 8
Angles ['æŋglz] Angeln *(germanisches Volk)* 7
angry ['æŋgri] wütend 5
animal ['ænɪml] Tier 5
animal waste ['ænɪml weɪst] tierische Fäkalien 9: 4 (60)
announcement [ə'naʊnsmənt] Durchsage, Ansage; Bekanntgabe, Ankündigung 8
annoy sb. [ə'nɔɪ] jn. ärgern 7
annoyed [ə'nɔɪd] verärgert, ärgerlich 7
annoying [ə'nɔɪɪŋ] ärgerlich *(unangenehm)* 7
annual ['ænjuəl] jährlich 9: 3 (50)
anonymous (= anon.) [ə'nɒnɪməs] anonym 9: 2 (37)
another [ə'nʌðə] ein/e andere/r/s; noch ein/e 6
answer ['ɑːnsə]:
1. answer (to) Antwort (auf) 5
2. (be)antworten 5
answer the door aufmachen, zur/an die Tür gehen 7 **answer the phone** ans Telefon gehen 7
anti- ['ænti] Anti-, Gegen- 9: 1 (14)
antibiotic [æntibaɪ'ɒtɪk] Antibiotikum 8
antivenom [ænti'venəm] Gegengift 9: 1 (14)
antonym ['æntənɪm] Antonym, Gegenteil 9: 1 (20)
any ['eni]: **Are there any ...?** Gibt es (irgendwelche) ...? 5 **at any age** in jedem Alter 7 **at any time** jederzeit 9: 2 (31) **not (...) any more** nicht mehr 7 **there aren't any ...** es gibt keine ... 5
anybody ['enibɒdi] irgendjemand; jede/r (beliebige) 6 **not (...) anybody** niemand 6
anyone ['eniwʌn] irgendjemand; jede/r (beliebige) 6 **not (...) anyone** niemand 6
anything ['eniθɪŋ] *(in Fragen)* irgendetwas 6 **anything else** sonst noch etwas 6 **not (...) anything** nichts 6
anyway ['eniweɪ]:
1. sowieso; jedenfalls, wie dem auch sei 8
2. trotzdem 9: 1 (19)
anywhere [eniweə] irgendwo(hin); überall 6 **anywhere else** irgendwo anders, sonst irgendwo 6 **not (...) anywhere** nirgends 6
apart [ə'pɑːt] auseinander, getrennt 8 **come apart** auseinandergehen, auseinanderfallen 8
apartment [ə'pɑːtmənt] *(AE)* Wohnung 5
apologize (to sb. for sth.) [ə'pɒlədʒaɪz] sich (bei jm. für etwas) entschuldigen 9: 1 (10)
apology [ə'pɒlədʒi] Entschuldigung 9: 1 (10)
appeal [ə'piːl]:
1. Anziehungskraft, Reiz 9: 3 (54)
2. appeal to sb. für jn. attraktiv sein, jn. ansprechen 9: 3 (54)
appealing [ə'piːlɪŋ] ansprechend 9: 3 (54)
appear [ə'pɪə] auftauchen, erscheinen 7 **appear to be/do** zu sein/zu tun scheinen 7
apple ['æpl] Apfel 5

appliance [ə'plaɪəns] (Haushalts-)Gerät 8
applicant ['æplɪkənt] Antragsteller/in, Bewerber/in 8
application [æplɪ'keɪʃn]:
1. Antrag; Bewerbung 7
2. Anwendung, Programm 8
application form [æplɪ'keɪʃn fɔːm] Bewerbungsformular, Antragsformular 7
apply (to sb. for sth.) [ə'plaɪ] sich (bei jm. um etwas) bewerben 8
appointment [ə'pɔɪntmənt] Termin *(Verabredung)* 8 **by appointment only** nur mit Termin 8 **make an appointment** einen Termin vereinbaren 8
appreciate [ə'priːʃieɪt] schätzen, zu schätzen wissen 8
apprentice [ə'prentɪs] Lehrling, Auszubildende/r 9: 2 (26)
apprenticeship [ə'prentɪʃɪp] Ausbildung, Lehre 9: 2 (26)
appropriate [ə'prəʊpriət] angemessen, passend, geeignet 9: 3 (44)
approximately [ə'prɒksɪmətli], [ə'prɒks] *(kurz auch:* approx*)* ungefähr 9: 2 (32)
April ['eɪprəl] April 5
aquarium [ə'kweəriəm] Aquarium 5
Arabic ['ærəbɪk] arabisch; Arabisch 6
architecture ['ɑːkɪtektʃə] Architektur 9: 4 (70)
Arctic ['ɑːktɪk] die Arktis; arktisch, Polar- 8
are [ɑː] bist, sind, seid 5 **The shirts are £6.** Die Hemden kosten 6 Pfund. 5 **they are** sie sind 5
area ['eəriə] Gegend, Bereich 5
argument ['ɑːgjumənt]:
1. Argument 7
2. Streit 7
get into an argument with sb. in Streit geraten mit jm. 7
arm [ɑːm] Arm 6
armed [ɑːmd] bewaffnet 8
army ['ɑːmi] Armee 7
around [ə'raʊnd]: **around ...** um (... herum) 5 **around the clock** rund um die Uhr 9: 1 (16) **go around and around** sich (immer wieder) drehen 6 **turn around** (sich) umdrehen 5 **walk around** umhergehen 6
arrange [ə'reɪndʒ] arrangieren, planen; (an)ordnen 9: 2 (32)
arrangement [ə'reɪndʒmənt] Abmachung, Vereinbarung 9: 2 (32)
arrest [ə'rest]:
1. Festnahme 8
2. arrest sb. jn. festnehmen, verhaften 8
arrival [ə'raɪvl] Ankunft 6
arrive [ə'raɪv] ankommen 7
art [ɑːt] Kunst 5
article ['ɑːtɪkl] Artikel 7
artist ['ɑːtɪst] Künstler/in 6
°arvo ['ɑːvəʊ] *(Austr., infml)*, *pl* **arvos** Nachmittag *(kurz für „afternoon")*
as [æz], [əz] wie; als, während 7 **as a singer** als Sänger/in 6 **as good as** genauso gut wie 6 **not as good as** nicht so gut wie 6
ask [ɑːsk] fragen 5 **ask for sth.** um etwas bitten, nach etwas fragen 7 **ask sb. to do sth.** jn. bitten, etwas zu tun 5
asleep [ə'sliːp]: **be asleep** schlafen 8 **fall asleep** einschlafen 8
aspect ['æspekt] Aspekt 8
assembly [ə'sembli] Schulversammlung 5
assembly line [ə'sembli laɪn] Montageband, Fließband 8 **on the assembly line** am Fließband 8
assistant [ə'sɪstənt]: **(= shop assistant)** Verkäufer/in 5
at [æt], [ət] an; in; bei; auf 5 **at 7 o'clock** um 7 Uhr 5 **at any age** in jedem Alter 7 **at Ben's house** bei Ben zu Hause, bei Ben daheim 5 **at home** zu Hause, daheim 5 **at least** wenigstens, zumindest 8 **at night** nachts, in der Nacht 5 **at school** in der Schule 5 **at the cinema** im Kino 5 **at work** bei der Arbeit, am Arbeitsplatz 5 **be good at sth.** etwas gut können; gut in etwas sein 5
ate [eɪt], [et] *siehe* **eat**
athletics [æθ'letɪks] Leichtathletik 9: 1 (20)
Atlantic Ocean [ətlæntɪk 'əʊʃn] atlantischer Ozean, Atlantik 6
attach (to) [ə'tætʃ] anfügen; anhängen (an) *(Brief, E-Mail)* 9: 2 (31)
attachment [ə'tætʃmənt] Anhang *(E-Mail)* 9: 2 (31)
attack [ə'tæk]:
1. angreifen 7
2. Angriff 7
attacker [ə'tækə] Angreifer/in 8
attend [ə'tend] (hin)gehen zu, teilnehmen (an); besuchen 9: 2 (32)
attention [ə'tenʃn] Aufmerksamkeit 7 **for the attention of (= attn)** zu Händen / z. Hd. *(in einer Adresse, an eine bestimmte Person in einer Firma)* 9: 2 (31) **get sb.'s attention** js. Aufmerksamkeit erregen, gewinnen 9: 2 (37) **keep sb.'s attention** js. Aufmerksamkeit aufrecht erhalten 9: 2 (37) **pay attention (to)** achten (auf), aufpassen (auf) 7
attic ['ætɪk] Dachboden 9: 2 (33) **in the attic** auf dem Dachboden 9: 2 (33)
attitude (to/towards) ['ætɪtjuːd] Einstellung, (Geistes-)Haltung (zu/gegenüber) 8
attract [ə'trækt] anziehen, anlocken 9: 2 (28)
attraction [ə'trækʃn] Attraktion; Anziehungskraft 9: 2 (28)
attractive [ə'træktɪv] attraktiv 9: 2 (28)
audience ['ɔːdiəns] Publikum; Zuschauer/innen, Zuhörer/innen 9: 2 (37)
audiobook ['ɔːdiəʊbʊk] Audiobuch, Hörbuch 9: 1 (16)
August ['ɔːgəst] August 5
aunt [ɑːnt] Tante 5
°Aussie ['ɒzi]:
1. Australier/in
2. australisch
°Australian paralysis tick [ɒstreɪliən pə'ræləsɪs tɪk] Weiße Zecke
°Australian Rules football [ɒstreɪliən ruːlz 'fʊtbɔːl] Australian Rules football *(australische Football-Variante)*
author ['ɔːθə] Autor/in 8
authority [ɔː'θɒrəti] Behörde 9: 1 (17) **local authority** Gemeinde(behörde), Kommune/Kommunalbehörde 9: 1 (17)
automatic [ɔːtə'mætɪk] automatisch 8
automatically [ɔːtə'mætɪkli] automatisch *(Adv.)* 8
automation [ɔːtə'meɪʃn] Automatisierung 9: 2 (24/25)
autumn ['ɔːtəm] Herbst 8
available [ə'veɪləbl] verfügbar; erhältlich; *(Stelle)* frei 9: 2 (31) **be available** zur Verfügung stehen, Zeit haben 9: 2 (31)
avenue ['ævənjuː] Allee 8
°avo ['ævəʊ] *(Austr., infml)* Avocado *(kurz für „avocado")*
avoid [ə'vɔɪd] (ver)meiden; verhindern 9: 4 (60)
awake [ə'weɪk] wach 8 **shake sb. awake** jn. wachrütteln 8

award [ə'wɔːd]:
1. Preis *(Auszeichnung)* 7
2. *(Preis)* verleihen 8

award-winner [ə'wɔːd wɪnə] Preisträger/in 7
award-winning [ə'wɔːd wɪnɪŋ] preisgekrönt 7
aware [ə'weə]: **be aware of sth.** etwas wissen, sich einer Sache bewusst sein 8
awareness [ə'weənəs] Bewusstsein, Aufmerksamkeit 8 **raise awareness of sth.** die Aufmerksamkeit für etwas erhöhen, das Bewusstsein für etwas schaffen 8
away [ə'weɪ] weg, fort 5
awesome ['ɔːsəm] *(AE, infml)* klasse, stark, großartig 6
axe [æks] Axt, Beil 7

B

back [bæk]:
1. zurück 5
2. Rücken; Rückseite, hinterer Teil 5
at the back hinten 5

background ['bækgraʊnd] Hintergrund 7
backpack ['bækpæk] Rucksack 6
backyard [bæk'jɑːd] *(AE)* (Hinter-)Hof; Garten hinter dem Haus 9: 1 (14)
bacon ['beɪkən] Speck 5
bad [bæd] schlecht; schlimm 5
badge [bædʒ] Dienstmarke *(Polizei)*; Anstecknadel, Button 8
bag [bæg] Tasche 5
baggage ['bægɪdʒ] *(AE)* Gepäck 6
baggy ['bægi] weit (geschnitten), sackig *(Kleidung)* 6
bagpipes *(pl)* ['bægpaɪps] Dudelsack 6
bake [beɪk] backen 7
baking sheet ['beɪkɪŋ ʃiːt] Backblech 7
baking soda ['beɪkɪŋ səʊdə] Back-Natron, Backsoda 7
balcony ['bælkəni] Balkon 5
bald [bɔːld] kahl, glatzköpfig 6
ball [bɔːl] Ball 5
balloon [bə'luːn] Ballon 5
ban [bæn]:
1. verbieten 7
be banned verboten sein/werden 7
2. **ban (on)** Verbot (von) 7

banana [bə'nɑːnə] Banane 5
bank [bæŋk] Bank *(Geldinstitut)* 7
bar [bɑː]:
1. (ab)sperren, blockieren; vergittern *(z. B. Fenster)* 9: 4 (67)
2. Stange, Balken, (Gitter-)Stab; Riegel *(Schokolade, Müsli)*; Tafel *(Schokolade)* 9: 4 (67)

bar chart ['bɑː tʃɑːt] Balkendiagramm, Säulendiagramm 8
barbecue ['bɑːbɪkjuː] Grillfest, Grillen 5
°barbie ['bɑːbi] *(Austr., infml)* Grillparty *(kurz für „barbecue")*
bark [bɑːk] Rinde *(vom Baum)* 9: 1 (12)
bark (at sb.) [bɑːk] (jn. an)bellen 6
barrel ['bærəl] Fass 8
base [beɪs] Basis; Sockel, Fuß; Boden *(Kuchen, Pizza)* 9: 3 (51)
based [beɪst]: **be based on** basieren auf, beruhen auf, sich stützen auf 9: 3 (50)
basic ['beɪsɪk] einfach, elementar 9: 3 (54)
basically ['beɪsɪkli] im Prinzip, grundsätzlich 9: 3 (54)
basics *(pl)* ['beɪsɪks] Grundlagen; *(das)* Wesentliche 9: 3 (54)
°basket ['bɑːskɪt] Korb
basketball ['bɑːskɪtbɔːl] Basketball 5
bat [bæt] Fledermaus 6
bath [bɑːθ] Bad; Badewanne 7 **have/take a bath** baden, ein Bad nehmen *(in der Badewanne)* 7
bathe [beɪð] baden *(in einem Fluss / dem Meer)* 9: 4 (64)
bather ['beɪðə] Badende/r *(in einem Fluss / dem Meer)* 9: 4 (64)
bathroom ['bɑːθruːm]:
1. Bad(ezimmer) 5
2. *(AE)* Toilette *(in Privathäusern)* 8

battery ['bætri] Batterie; Akku 8
Bavaria [bə'veəriə] Bayern 6
bay [beɪ] Bucht 8
°bazaar [bə'zɑː] Basar
BC [biː 'siː]: **750 BC** 750 v. Chr. 7
be [biː], **was/were, been** sein 5
beach [biːtʃ] Strand 5 **on the beach** am Strand 5
bead [biːd] (Holz-/Glas-)Perle 8
bear [beə] Bär 6
bear [beə], **bore, borne** (er)tragen 9: 1 (18)
beard [bɪəd] Bart 7
beat [biːt], **beat, beaten** schlagen, besiegen 6 **°beat sb. up** jn. zusammenschlagen
beaten ['biːtn] *siehe* **beat**
beautiful ['bjuːtɪfl] wunderschön 6
°beauty ['bjuːti] Schönheit
beaver ['biːvə] Biber 8
became [bɪ'keɪm] *siehe* **become**
because [bɪ'kɒz] weil 5
because of [bɪ'kɒz əv] wegen 7
become [bɪ'kʌm], **became, become** werden 5
bed [bed] Bett 5 **go to bed** ins Bett gehen 5
bedroom ['bedruːm] Schlafzimmer 5
bedtime ['bedtaɪm] Schlafenszeit 7
bee [biː] Biene 8
beef [biːf] Rindfleisch 6
been [biːn] *siehe* **be**
beer [bɪə] Bier 7
beetroot ['biːtruːt] Rote Beete 6
before [bɪ'fɔː]:
1. bevor; vor *(zeitlich)* 5
2. zuvor; vorher 6

beg [beg] flehen, (eindringlich) bitten; betteln 9: 3 (51) **beg for sth. (from sb.)** (bei jm.) um etwas betteln 9: 3 (51) **beg sb. to do sth.** jn. anflehen, etwas zu tun 9: 3 (51)
began [bɪ'gæn] *siehe* **begin**
begin [bɪ'gɪn], **began, begun** anfangen, beginnen 8
beginner [bɪ'gɪnə] Anfänger/in 9: 2 (30)
beginning [bɪ'gɪnɪŋ] Anfang 7
begun [bɪ'gʌn] *siehe* **begin**
behave [bɪ'heɪv] sich benehmen; sich verhalten 7
behaviour [bɪ'heɪvjə] Verhalten; Benehmen 8
behind [bɪ'haɪnd] hinter 5
belief [bɪ'liːf] Glaube, Überzeugung 9: 3 (52)
believe (in) [bɪ'liːv] glauben (an) 6
bell [bel] Glocke 6
belong [bɪ'lɒŋ] (hin)gehören 7 **belong to sb./sth.** jm./zu etwas gehören 8
below [bɪ'ləʊ] unter(halb von); unten 7
bench [bentʃ] Bank *(zum Sitzen)* 9: 4 (67)
benefit ['benɪfɪt]:
1. Nutzen, Vorteil 9: 4 (71)
2. nützen 9: 4 (71)
benefit from profitieren von 9: 4 (71)

best [best] beste(r, s); am besten 5 **Best wishes** Viele Grüße *(Briefschluss)* 5 **All the best** Mit besten Grüßen, Alles Gute *(Briefschluss)* 8 **like sth. best** etwas am liebsten mögen 5
better ['betə] besser 6 **do better** besser abschneiden 7 **like sth. better** etwas lieber mögen 7

between [bɪ'twiːn] zwischen 5
bicycle ['baɪsɪkl] Fahrrad 9: 3 (50)
big [bɪg]:
1. groß 5
2. schwer, dick *(Person)* 6
big wheel [bɪg 'wiːl] Riesenrad 6
bike [baɪk] Fahrrad 5
biking ['baɪkɪŋ] *(das)* Radfahren 7
°**bikkie** ['bɪki] *(Austr., infml)* Keks, Plätzchen *(kurz für „biscuit")*
bilingual [baɪ'lɪŋgwəl] zweisprachig 8
bilingualism [baɪ'lɪŋgwəlɪzm] Zweisprachigkeit 8
bill [bɪl] Rechnung 8
°**billboard** ['bɪlbɔːd] *(AE)* Plakatwand, Werbeplakat
billion ['bɪliən] Milliarde 7
bin [bɪn] (Müll-)Eimer 5
biochemical [baɪəʊ'kemɪkl] biochemisch 9: 2 (33)
biochemist [baɪəʊ'kemɪst] Biochemiker/in 9: 2 (33)
biochemistry [baɪəʊ'kemɪstri] Biochemie 9: 2 (33)
biotechnology [baɪəʊtek'nɒlədʒi] Biotechnologie 9: 4 (60)
bird [bɜːd] Vogel 5
birth [bɜːθ] Geburt 7 **date of birth** Geburtsdatum 7 **give birth (to)** gebären, entbinden, zur Welt bringen 9: 4 (70)
birth certificate ['bɜːθ sətɪfɪkət] Geburtsurkunde 8
birthday ['bɜːθdeɪ] Geburtstag 5 **Happy birthday.** Herzlichen Glückwunsch zum Geburtstag. 5
biscuit ['bɪskɪt] Keks, Plätzchen 5
bisexual [baɪ'sekʃuəl]:
1. bisexuell 8
2. Bisexuelle(r) 8
bit [bɪt] *siehe* **bite**
bit [bɪt] Teil, Stück(chen) 7 **a bit** ein bisschen 7
bite [baɪt]:
1. Biss; (Insekten-)Stich 9: 1 (8/9)
2. **bite, bit, bitten** beißen; stechen *(z. B. Insekten)* 9: 1 (8/9)
bitten ['bɪtn] *siehe* **bite**
black [blæk] schwarz 5
blade [bleɪd] (Rotor-)Blatt, (Turbinen-)Schaufel 9: 3 (51)
blanket ['blæŋkɪt] Decke *(zum Zudecken u. Ä.)* 8
blazer ['bleɪzə] Blazer *(Jackett, oft Teil der Schuluniform)* 5
bled [bled] *siehe* **bleed**
bleed [bliːd], **bled, bled** bluten 8
blend [blend]:
1. (ver)mischen 9: 4 (62)
2. Mischung 9: 4 (62)
blew [bluː] *siehe* **blow**
blink [blɪŋk]: **blink (your eyes)** blinzeln, (mit den Augen) zwinkern 8
block [blɒk] Block; Klotz 7
blood [blʌd] Blut 8
blood pressure ['blʌd preʃə] Blutdruck 8 **take sb.'s blood pressure** bei jm. Blutdruck messen 8
bloodline ['blʌdlaɪn] Stammbaum 8
blow [bləʊ], **blew, blown** blasen; wehen 5
blown [bləʊn] *siehe* **blow**
blue [bluː] blau 5
°**blue-ringed octopus** [bluː rɪŋd 'ɒktəpəs] blaugeringelte Krake
board [bɔːd]:
1. Tafel 5
2. Brett 6
board [bɔːd]:
1. an Bord gehen 6
2. einsteigen *(z. B. Zug)* 9: 4 (67)
board game ['bɔːd geɪm] Brettspiel 7
boarder ['bɔːdə] Internatsschüler/in 7
boarding card ['bɔːdɪŋ kɑːd] Bordkarte 6
boarding house ['bɔːdɪŋ haʊs] Wohngebäude eines Internats 7
boarding school ['bɔːdɪŋ skuːl] Internat 7
boat [bəʊt] Boot; Schiff 5
body ['bɒdi]:
1. Körper 6
2. Leiche; Kadaver 9: 4 (64)
3. *(of a car)* (Auto-)Karosserie 8
body language ['bɒdi læŋgwɪdʒ] Körpersprache 7
boil [bɔɪl] kochen *(in Wasser)*; sieden 7
boiled [bɔɪld] gekocht 6
°**bold** [bəʊld] fett (gedruckt)
°**bolt** [bəʊlt] (Metall-)Schraube
bone [bəʊn] Knochen 7
boneless ['bəʊnləs] knochenlos 7
book [bʊk]:
1. Buch 5
2. buchen; reservieren 8
booking ['bʊkɪŋ] Buchung, Reservierung 8
bookmark ['bʊkmɑːk]:
1. Lesezeichen 8
2. markieren; zu den Lesezeichen hinzufügen *(Computer)* 8
boom [buːm] boomen *(Wirtschaft, Geschäft)* 7
boomerang ['buːməræŋ] Bumerang 9: 1 (13)
boot [buːt] Stiefel 6
bore [bɔː] *siehe* **bear**
bored [bɔːd] gelangweilt 5 **I'm bored** mir ist langweilig 5
boring ['bɔːrɪŋ] langweilig 5
born [bɔːn]: **he was born** er wurde geboren 5 **Russian-born** in Russland geboren 9: 2 (33)
borne [bɔːn] *siehe* **bear**
borough ['bʌrə] *(AE)* (Stadt-)Bezirk 8
borrow ['bɒrəʊ] (aus)leihen, sich borgen 5
both [bəʊθ] beide 6 **both ... and ...** sowohl ... als auch ... 9: 2 (27)
bottle ['bɒtl] Flasche 6 **message in a bottle** Flaschenpost 6
bottom ['bɒtəm] unteres Ende 6
bought [bɔːt] *siehe* **buy**
bow [bəʊ] Schleife 7
bow tie [bəʊ 'taɪ] Fliege *(Krawatte)* 7
bowl [bəʊl] Schüssel, Schale 7
box [bɒks] Kasten, Kiste, Kästchen 5
box [bɒks] boxen 8
°**box jellyfish** ['bɒks dʒelifɪʃ], *pl* **box jellyfish** Würfelqualle
boxing ['bɒksɪŋ] *(das)* Boxen 8
boy [bɔɪ] Junge, Bub 5
boyfriend ['bɔɪfrend] (fester) Freund 7
bracelet ['breɪslət] Armband 7
braces *(pl)* ['breɪsɪz] Zahnspange, Zahnklammer 6
braid [breɪd] (geflochtener) Zopf 8
°**brainstorm** ['breɪnstɔːm] Ideen (ungeordnet) sammeln
branch [brɑːntʃ] Ast, Zweig, (Neben-)Arm 8
brand [brænd] Marke *(bei Produkten)* 8
brave [breɪv] mutig 6
bread [bred] Brot 5
break [breɪk] Pause 5 **take a break** Pause machen 7
break [breɪk], **broke, broken** (zer)brechen; kaputtgehen; kaputtmachen 5 **break away (from), broke, broken** sich trennen (von), sich abspalten (von) 8 **break down** eine Panne haben, kaputtgehen *(Auto)* 8 **break sth. up** etwas zerbrechen, zerstören; auflösen 9: 1 (10)
breakfast ['brekfəst] Frühstück 5 **have breakfast** frühstücken 5
breathe (in/out) [briːð] (ein-/aus-)atmen 7
°**brekkie** ['breki] *(Austr., infml)* Frühstück *(kurz für „breakfast")*

bride [braɪd] Braut 9: 4 (65)
bridge [brɪdʒ] Brücke 6
bright [braɪt] hell, freundlich; leuchtend 9: 1 (12)
bring [brɪŋ], **brought, brought** bringen, mitbringen 5 **bring sb. up** jd. aufziehen, großziehen 9: 1 (10)
Brit [brɪt] *(infml)* Brite/Britin 8
Britain ['brɪtn] Großbritannien 5
British ['brɪtɪʃ] britisch 5
Briton ['brɪtn] Brite/Britin 7
brochure ['brəʊʃə] Broschüre, Prospekt 8
broke [brəʊk] *siehe* **break**
broken ['brəʊkən] *siehe* **break** **be broken** zerbrochen, kaputt, sein 6
brother ['brʌðə] Bruder 5
brought [brɔːt] *siehe* **bring** **a well/ badly brought up child** ein gut/ schlecht erzogenes Kind 9: 1 (10)
brown [braʊn] braun 5
buck [bʌk] bocken *(Pferd)* 8
bucket ['bʌkɪt] Eimer 7
buffet ['bʊfeɪ] Büfett 6
build [bɪld], **built, built** bauen 6 **build up** (sich) aufbauen 9: 3 (44)
builder ['bɪldə] Bauarbeiter/in 6
building ['bɪldɪŋ] Gebäude 6
built [bɪlt] *siehe* **build** **built-in** eingebaut 8
bulb [bʌlb] Glühbirne 8
bullet ['bʊlɪt] (Gewehr-)Kugel 8
bully ['bʊli]:
1. Mobber/in, Tyrann/in 7
2. tyrannisieren, mobben 7
bumpy ['bʌmpi] holprig, *(Flug/ Schifffahrt)* unruhig 9: 4 (67)
burglar ['bɜːglə] Einbrecher/in 5
burn [bɜːn], **burnt, burnt** brennen, verbrennen 6 **burn sth. down** etwas abbrennen, niederbrennen 8
burnt [bɜːnt] *siehe* **burn**
burst [bɜːst], **burst, burst** brechen, bersten, platzen 9: 3 (52)
bury ['beri] begraben, beerdigen; vergraben 8
bus [bʌs] Bus 5 **by bus** mit dem Bus 5 **on the bus** im Bus 5
bus stop ['bʌs stɒp] Bushaltestelle 6
bush [bʊʃ] Busch 9: 4 (67)
business ['bɪznəs]:
1. Sache, Angelegenheit 8
2. Geschäft, Betrieb 6
start a business ein Geschäft aufmachen, einen Betrieb gründen/eröffnen 7
businessman ['bɪznəsmən], *pl* **businessmen** Geschäftsmann 6
businesswoman ['bɪznəswʊmən], *pl* **-women** Geschäftsfrau 6
businesswomen ['bɪznəswɪmɪn] *Plural von* **businesswoman**
busy ['bɪzi]:
1. hektisch, belebt 6
2. (viel)beschäftigt 6
be busy beschäftigt sein 6
but [bʌt], [bət] aber 5
butter ['bʌtə] Butter 5
buttermilk ['bʌtəmɪlk] Buttermilch 7
button ['bʌtn] Button; Schaltfläche; Knopf 9: 3 (53)
buy [baɪ], **bought, bought** kaufen 5
buzz cut ['bʌz kʌt] Igelfrisur *(extrem kurzer Haarschnitt)* 8
by [baɪ]: **by bus** mit dem Bus 5 **by the sea** am Meer 6 **by the time** als; wenn 9: 4 (67) **by the way** übrigens 9: 4 (64) **step by step** Schritt für Schritt 7
Bye. [baɪ] Tschüs. 5

C

cab [kæb] *(AE)* Taxi 6
cabin ['kæbɪn] Hütte; Kabine 8
cafe ['kæfeɪ] Café 5
caffeine ['kæfiːn] Koffein 9: 4 (71)
cage [keɪdʒ] Käfig 5
cake [keɪk] Kuchen, Torte 5
calculate ['kælkjuleɪt] berechnen, kalkulieren 9: 2 (33)
calendar ['kælɪndə] Kalender 6
California [kælə'fɔːniə] Kalifornien 6
call [kɔːl]:
1. nennen; rufen; anrufen 6
call sb. names jn. beschimpfen 7
be called heißen 7
2. **(= phone call)** Telefonanruf 7
caller ['kɔːlə] Anrufer/in 7
calm [kɑːm]:
1. ruhig, besonnen 9: 1 (18)
2. **calm (down)** sich beruhigen 9: 1 (18)
calm sb. down jn. beruhigen 9: 1 (18)
came [keɪm] *siehe* **come**
camel ['kæml] Kamel 9: 1 (8/9)
camera ['kæmərə] Fotoapparat; Kamera 6
camerawork ['kæmrəwɜːk] Kameraführung 8
camp [kæmp] (Zelt-)Lager 6
campaign [kæm'peɪn]:
1. Aktion, Kampagne 9: 1 (17)
2. **campaign (for/against)** sich einsetzen (für/gegen), kämpfen (für/gegen) 9: 1 (17)
campfire ['kæmpfaɪə] Lagerfeuer 8
camping ['kæmpɪŋ] Camping 5 **go camping** campen/zelten gehen 5
campus ['kæmpəs], *pl* **campuses** Campus, Unigelände 9: 2 (24/25)
can [kæn], [kən] können 5 **I can't (= cannot)** ich kann nicht 5
cancer ['kænsə] Krebs *(Erkrankung)* 9: 4 (71)
candle ['kændl] Kerze 5
candy ['kændi] *(AE)* Süßigkeit(en), Bonbon 6
canoe [kə'nuː]:
1. Kanu, Paddelboot 8
2. Kanu fahren, paddeln 8
canoeing [kə'nuːɪŋ] Paddeln, Kanusport 8
canteen [kæn'tiːn] Kantine, (Schul-)Mensa 5
canvas ['kænvəs] Leinwand; Segeltuch 9: 1 (12)
capital ['kæpɪtl]:
1. **capital (city)** Hauptstadt 6
2. **capital (letter)** Großbuchstabe 7
capsule ['kæpsjuːl] Kapsel 7
captain ['kæptɪn] Kapitän/in 7
caption ['kæpʃn] Bildunterschrift 7
car [kɑː] Auto 5
car park ['kɑː pɑːk] Parkplatz 6
card [kɑːd] Karte 5
care [keə]: **care about sth.** etwas wichtig nehmen 7 **care for** sich kümmern um; aufpassen auf 9: 1 (17) **I care about you.** Du bist mir nicht egal. / Du liegst mir am Herzen. 7 **I don't care.** Es ist mir egal. 7 **Who cares?** Wen interessiert das? / Was soll's? / Na und? 7
career [kə'rɪə] Karriere; (schulischer/beruflicher) Werdegang 7
careful ['keəfl]:
1. aufmerksam; sorgfältig 7
2. vorsichtig 5
be careful of sb./sth. sich in Acht nehmen vor jm./etwas 9: 1 (8/9)
Caribbean [kærɪ'biːən] Karibik; karibisch 7
carnival ['kɑːnɪvl] Karneval 6
carpet ['kɑːpɪt] Teppich 5
carriage ['kærɪdʒ] (Eisenbahn-)Wagen 9: 4 (67)
carrot ['kærət] Möhre, Karotte 6
carry ['kæri] tragen; befördern, transportieren 5 **carry on with sth. / doing sth.** weitermachen, fortfahren (mit etwas) 9: 2 (27)

case [keɪs] Fall 9: 4 (67) **(just) in case ...** (nur) für den Fall, dass ... 9: 4 (67) **in (the) case of** im Falle von 9: 4 (67)
cashier [kæ'ʃɪə] Kassierer/in 9: 2 (24/25)
caste [kɑːst] Kaste, Gesellschaftsklasse 9: 4 (60)
castle ['kɑːsl] Burg 7
cat [kæt] Katze 5
catch [kætʃ], **caught, caught** (ein) fangen; erwischen; nehmen *(z. B. Zug, Bus)* 7 **catch sth.** verstehen *(hören können)*, mitbekommen 9: 2 (32)
cathedral [kə'θiːdrəl] Kathedrale, Dom 6
Catholic ['kæθlɪk] Katholik/in; katholisch 7
cattle *(pl)* ['kætl] Vieh, Rinder 8
caught [kɔːt] *siehe* **catch**
cause [kɔːz]:
1. Ursache 8
2. **cause sth.** etwas bewirken, verursachen 8
cave [keɪv] Höhle 6
cavern ['kævən] Höhle 7
celebrate ['selɪbreɪt] feiern 5
celebrity [sə'lebrəti] Prominente/r, Promi 7
cell (phone) ['sel fəʊn] *(AE)* Handy 8
cellar ['selə] Keller 6
cent [sent] Cent 5
centre ['sentə] Zentrum 5
century ['sentʃəri] Jahrhundert 7
CEO (Chief Executive Officer) [siː iː'əʊ] Geschäftsführer/in 7
cereal(s) ['sɪəriəlz] Getreide-, Frühstücksflocken 9: 1 (15)
ceremony ['serəməni] Feier, Zeremonie 9: 1 (13)
certain ['sɜːtn] gewiss, bestimmt; sicher 9: 2 (28)
certainly ['sɜːtnli] sicher(lich), gewiss 9: 2 (28)
certificate [sə'tɪfɪkət] Urkunde, Bescheinigung 8 **birth certificate** Geburtsurkunde 8
°chai [tʃaɪ] *Gewürztee mit Milch*
chair [tʃeə] Stuhl 5
chairperson ['tʃeəpɜːsn], *pl* **chairpersons** Vorsitzende/r 8
challenge ['tʃælɪndʒ]:
1. Herausforderung 8
2. **challenge sb. (to sth.)** jn. (zu etwas) herausfordern 8
challenging ['tʃælɪndʒɪŋ] anspruchsvoll, (heraus)fordernd 8
championship ['tʃæmpiənʃɪp] Meisterschaft 5
chance [tʃɑːns] Chance, Gelegenheit 6
change [tʃeɪndʒ]:
1. **change (into)** (sich) (ver-) ändern (zu/in); wechseln; (sich) verwandeln (in), werden (zu); sich umziehen 7
change your mind seine Meinung ändern 7 **change (trains)** umsteigen 6
2. Veränderung; Wechsel; Verwandlung 7
3. Wechselgeld 8
channel ['tʃænl] Kanal 7 **the (English) Channel** der Ärmelkanal 7
chapel ['tʃæpl] Kapelle *(kleiner kirchlicher Raum)* 7
character ['kærəktə] Charakter; Figur *(aus einer Geschichte)* 7
charge [tʃɑːdʒ]:
1. Anklage, Beschuldigung 8
2. **charge sb. (with sth.)** jn. anklagen (wegen etwas) 8
charge (a mobile phone) [tʃɑːdʒ] (ein Mobiltelefon) aufladen 6
charity ['tʃærəti] wohltätige Organisation 6
chart [tʃɑːt] Diagramm; Tabelle 6
chase [tʃeɪs]:
1. verfolgen, jagen 8
2. Verfolgung, Verfolgungsjagd 8
chaser ['tʃeɪsə] Jäger/in, Verfolger/in 8
chat [tʃæt]:
1. Unterhaltung, Chat 6
2. **chat (with)** chatten (mit); sich unterhalten (mit) 6
chat show ['tʃæt ʃəʊ] Talkshow 6
cheap [tʃiːp] billig, preiswert 5
check [tʃek]: **check (for)** (über) prüfen (auf), kontrollieren 5 **check in** einchecken 8 **check out** auschecken 8 **check sb./sth. out** *(infml)* sich etwas anschauen, anhören; etwas ausprobieren 9: 2 (27)
check-in ['tʃek ɪn] Check-in, *(das)* Einchecken 8
checklist ['tʃeklɪst] Checkliste 8
checkout ['tʃekaʊt] Abreise, Auschecken *(z. B. Hotel)* 8
cheek [tʃiːk] Wange 8
cheer [tʃɪə] jubeln, *(Sportler/innen)* anfeuern 6
cheers [tʃɪəz] *(infml)* tschüs; danke 9: 1 (15)
cheese [tʃiːz] Käse 5
cheesecake ['tʃiːzkeɪk] Käsekuchen 8
chemical ['kemɪkl]:
1. Chemikalie 8
2. chemisch 8
chess [tʃes] Schach 5
chest of drawers [tʃest əv 'drɔːz], *pl* **chests of drawers** Kommode 5
chew [tʃuː] kauen 7
chewing gum ['tʃuːɪŋ gʌm] Kaugummi 7
chicken ['tʃɪkɪn] Huhn; (Brat-)Hähnchen 5
chief [tʃiːf]:
1. Haupt-; leitende/r 8
2. Häuptling 8
Chief Executive Officer [tʃiːf ɪgzekjətɪv 'ɒfɪsə]: *(kurz auch CEO)* Geschäftsführer/in 7
child [tʃaɪld], *pl* **children** Kind 5
child labour ['tʃaɪld leɪbə] Kinderarbeit 9: 4 (60)
childcare ['tʃaɪldkeə] Kinderbetreuung 9: 2 (26)
children ['tʃɪldrən] *Plural von* **child**
chill out [tʃɪl 'aʊt] *(infml)* sich entspannen, abhängen 7
chips *(pl)* [tʃɪps] Pommes frites 5
chocolate ['tʃɒklət] Schokolade 5 **hot chocolate** Kakao, heiße (Trink-)Schokolade 5
choice [tʃɔɪs] (Aus-)Wahl 7
choir ['kwaɪə] Chor 7
choose [tʃuːz], **chose, chosen** (aus) wählen 5 **choose to do sth.** sich entscheiden, etwas zu tun 7
chore [tʃɔː] (Haus-)Arbeit, *(lästige)* Pflicht 7 **do chores** (Haus-)Arbeiten erledigen 7
chose [tʃəʊz] *siehe* **choose**
chosen ['tʃəʊzn] *siehe* **choose**
Christian ['krɪstʃən]:
1. Christ/in 8
2. christlich 8
Christmas ['krɪsməs] Weihnachten 6
church [tʃɜːtʃ] Kirche 5
cinema ['sɪnəmə] Kino 5 **at the cinema** im Kino 5
circle ['sɜːkl] Kreis 6
citizen ['sɪtɪzn] (Staats-)Bürger/in 8
citizenship ['sɪtɪzənʃɪp] Staatsbürgerschaft 8
city ['sɪti] (Groß-)Stadt 5
civil ['sɪvl] Bürger-, (staats-)bürgerlich 8
civil rights *(pl)* [sɪvl 'raɪts] Bürgerrechte 8
civil war [sɪvl 'wɔː] Bürgerkrieg 8
claim [kleɪm]:
1. angeben, behaupten 9: 4 (71)
2. Behauptung 9: 4 (71)

clap (your hands) [klæp] (in die Hände) klatschen 9: 3 (52)
class [klɑːs] Klasse; Unterricht; Kurs 5
class teacher ['klɑːs tiːtʃə] Klassenlehrer/in 5
classmate ['klɑːsmeɪt] Mitschüler/in 5
classroom ['klɑːsruːm] Klassenraum 5
claw [klɔː] Kralle; Klaue 7
clean [kliːn]:
1. sauber 6
2. sauber machen, putzen 6
cleaner ['kliːnə] Reinigungskraft 6
cleaning ['kliːnɪŋ]: **do the cleaning** putzen 6
clear [klɪə]:
1. klar, deutlich 6
2. **clear sb. (of sth.)** jn. (von etwas) freisprechen 8
clearly ['klɪəli]: **speak clearly** deutlich sprechen 6
clever ['klevə] schlau, klug 6
click (on) [klɪk] klicken (auf) 7
climate ['klaɪmət] Klima 8
climate change ['klaɪmət tʃeɪndʒ] Klimawandel 8
climb [klaɪm]:
1. Aufstieg, Klettertour; Anstieg 8
2. klettern (auf) 8
climber ['klaɪmə] Kletterer/ Kletterin 8
clock [klɒk] (Wand-, Stand-, Turm-)Uhr 5
close [kləʊz] schließen, zumachen 5
close (to) [kləʊs] nahe (bei, an) 9: 3 (51)
close-up ['kləʊs ʌp] Nahaufnahme *(Film)* 8
closed [kləʊzd] geschlossen 5
closet ['klɒzɪt] *(AE)* (Wand-) Schrank 8
cloth [klɒθ] Tuch; Stoff 8
clothes *(pl)* [kləʊðz] Kleidung, Kleidungsstücke 5
clothes line ['kləʊðz laɪn] Wäscheleine 9: 3 (50)
°**clove (of garlic)** [kləʊv] (Knoblauch-)Zehe
club [klʌb] Klub, Verein 5 **join a club** in einen Klub eintreten 7 **school club** AG 5
coach [kəʊtʃ]:
1. (Reise-)Bus 5
2. Trainer/in 6
3. (Eisenbahn-)Wagen 9: 3 (49)
coast [kəʊst] Küste 6
code [kəʊd] kodieren, programmieren *(Computer)* 7
coder ['kəʊdə] Kodierer/in, Programmierer/in 7
coffee ['kɒfi] Kaffee 8
coffin ['kɒfɪn] Sarg 7
coin [kɔɪn] Münze 7
cold [kəʊld]:
1. kalt 5
be cold frieren 6
2. Kälte 6
3. Erkältung 6
have a cold erkältet sein 6
colleague ['kɒliːg] Kollege/ Kollegin 9: 2 (39)
collect [kə'lekt] sammeln 8
collection [kə'lekʃn] Sammlung 8
college ['kɒlɪdʒ] Hochschule 5
collocation [kɒlə'keɪʃn] Kollokation *(inhaltlich kombinierbare sprachliche Einheiten)* 9: 1 (20)
colon ['kəʊlən] Doppelpunkt 8
colour ['kʌlə] Farbe 5 **What colour is ...?** Welche Farbe hat ...? 5
colourful ['kʌləfl] farbig, bunt 8
°**column** ['kɒləm] Spalte
come [kʌm], **came, come** (mit) kommen 5 **come alive** lebendig werden, (wieder) aufleben 9: 3 (52) **come apart** auseinandergehen, auseinanderfallen 8 **come of age** volljährig werden 9: 1 (13) **come true** wahr werden 9: 3 (52)
comfortable ['kʌmftəbl] bequem, gemütlich 7
comma ['kɒmə] Komma 8
comment ['kɒment]:
1. Kommentar 7
2. **comment on sth.** etwas kommentieren 7
commit (a crime) [kə'mɪt] (ein Verbrechen) begehen 8
common ['kɒmən]: **have sth. in common** etwas gemeinsam haben 9: 4 (65)
communicate [kə'mjuːnɪkeɪt] kommunizieren 9: 2 (30)
communication [kəmjuːnɪ'keɪʃn] Kommunikation, Verständigung 9: 2 (30)
community [kə'mjuːnəti] Gemeinschaft, Gemeinde 9: 1 (10)
community college [kə'mjuːnəti kɒlɪdʒ] weiterführende Schule *(BE)* 5
company ['kʌmpəni] Firma, Gesellschaft 6
compare (to/with) [kəm'peə]:
1. vergleichen (mit) 7
2. vergleichbar sein (mit), sich vergleichen lassen (mit) 8
competition [kɒmpə'tɪʃn] Wettbewerb 5
complete [kəm'pliːt]:
1. vervollständigen 7
2. vollständig, komplett 7
complex ['kɒmpleks] komplex, kompliziert 8
concentrate (on) ['kɒnsntreɪt] sich konzentrieren (auf) 7
concentration [kɒnsn'treɪʃn] Konzentration 7
concern [kən'sɜːn]:
1. Befürchtung, Bedenken, Sorge; Angelegenheit, Sache 9: 3 (54)
... is none of your concern. ... geht dich/Sie nichts an. 9: 3 (54)
2. betreffen, angehen; beunruhigen, bekümmern 9: 3 (54)
concert ['kɒnsət] Konzert 7
°**conclusion** [kɒn'kluːʒn] Schluss(folgerung)
condition [kən'dɪʃn] Bedingung; Zustand 8
conditions *(pl)* [kən'dɪʃnz] Bedingungen, Verhältnisse 8 **in/under these conditions** bei/unter diesen Bedingungen 8
conductor [kən'dʌktə] Schaffner/in, Zugbegleiter/in 9: 4 (67)
confident ['kɒnfɪdənt] (selbst-) sicher; zuversichtlich 7
confirm [kən'fɜːm]:
1. bestätigen 8
2. konfirmieren; firmen 9: 1 (13)
confirmation [kɒnfə'meɪʃn]:
1. Bestätigung 8
2. Konfirmation; Firmung 9: 1 (13)
conflict ['kɒnflɪkt] Konflikt, Auseinandersetzung, Streit 9: 1 (16)
°**confusing** [kən'fjuːzɪŋ] verwirrend
congratulate sb. on sth. [kən'grætʃəleɪt] jm. zu etwas gratulieren 9: 1 (19)
congratulations (on sth.) [kəngrætʃə'leɪʃnz] herzlichen Glückwunsch (zu etwas) 9: 1 (19)
connect (to/with) [kə'nekt] (sich) verbinden (mit); verbunden sein (mit) 8
connection [kə'nekʃn] Verbindung 8
conquer ['kɒŋkə] erobern 7
conservation [kɒnsə'veɪʃn] (Natur-)Schutz; Erhaltung, Bewahrung 9: 2 (26)
conserve [kən'sɜːv] schützen, erhalten; schonen 9: 2 (26)
console [kən'səʊl]: **games console** Spielekonsole 6

constitution [kɒnstɪ'tju:ʃn] Verfassung 9: 4 (60)
constitutional [kɒnstɪ'tju:ʃənl] verfassungsgemäß 9: 4 (60)
consume [kən'sju:m] verbrauchen, konsumieren 9: 3 (53)
consumer [kən'sju:mə] Konsument/in, Verbraucher/in 9: 3 (53)
contact ['kɒntækt]:
1. Kontakt 6
keep/stay in contact (with) in Kontakt bleiben (mit) 9: 2 (26)
2. **contact sb.** Kontakt aufnehmen mit jm., sich in Verbindung setzen mit jm. 6
contain [kən'teɪn] enthalten 8
content ['kɒntent] Inhalt 8
context ['kɒntekst] Zusammenhang 9: 3 (49)
continent ['kɒntɪnənt] Kontinent 9: 1 (8/9)
continue [kən'tɪnju:] fortfahren, weitermachen; (sich) fortsetzen, weitergehen 7
contrast [kən'trɑ:st] vergleichen, (einander) gegenüberstellen 9: 4 (58/59)
contrast ['kɒntrɑ:st] Kontrast, Gegensatz 9: 4 (58/59)
control [kən'trəʊl]:
1. Kontrolle 8
lose control (of) die Kontrolle verlieren (über) 8
2. kontrollieren, regulieren 8
controller [kən'trəʊlə] Steuerung, Steuereinheit 8
conversation [kɒnvə'seɪʃn] Gespräch 7
convict ['kɒnvɪkt] Sträfling 9: 1 (8/9)
convince [kən'vɪns] überzeugen 9: 2 (27)
cook [kʊk]:
1. Koch, Köchin 6
2. kochen, *(Essen)* zubereiten 6
cookie ['kʊki] *(AE)* Keks, Plätzchen 8
cool [ku:l]:
1. kühl 6
2. (ab)kühlen 7
copper ['kɒpə] Kupfer 9: 3 (51)
copy ['kɒpi]:
1. Kopie; Exemplar 7
2. kopieren, abschreiben 7
coral ['kɒrəl] Koralle/n 9: 1 (8/9)
coral reef [kɒrəl 'ri:f] Korallenriff 9: 1 (8/9)
°**coriander** [kɒri'ændə] Koriander
corn [kɔ:n] *(BE)* Korn, Getreide; *(AE)* Mais 8
corner ['kɔ:nə] Ecke 9: 1 (16)
correct [kə'rekt]:
1. korrekt 8
2. korrigieren, berichtigen 8
°**correction** [kə'rekʃn] Berichtigung, Korrektur
cosmetics *(pl)* [kɒz'metɪks] Kosmetikprodukte, Kosmetika 8
cost [kɒst], **cost, cost** kosten 6
costume ['kɒstju:m] Kostüm, Verkleidung 6
cotton ['kɒtn] Baumwolle 8
cough [kɒf]:
1. husten 6
2. *(der)* Husten 6
could [kʊd]:
1. **she could** sie konnte 5
2. **I could** ich könnte 5
council ['kaʊnsl] Ausschuss; Rat *(z. B. Gemeinderat)* 9: 1 (17)
count [kaʊnt] zählen 6 **count on sb.** sich auf jn. verlassen 6
counter ['kaʊntə] (Verkaufs-)Schalter, Ladentheke 8
country ['kʌntri] Land 5
couple ['kʌpl] Paar 7 **a couple (of)** ein paar; ein Paar 7
course [kɔ:s]:
1. Kurs(us) 9: 1 (17)
crash course Intensivkurs 9: 1 (17)
2. **main course** Hauptgericht 6
3. **of course** natürlich, selbstverständlich 7
court [kɔ:t] Gericht(shof) 8 **go to court (over sth.)** vor Gericht ziehen, sich (gerichtlich) streiten (um/wegen etwas) 8 **take sb. to court** jn. verklagen 8
cousin ['kʌzn] Cousin/e 5
cover ['kʌvə] bedecken 6
cover letter ['kʌvə letə] Anschreiben, Begleitschreiben, Motivationsschreiben 9: 2 (24/25)
cow [kaʊ] Kuh 9: 4 (58/59)
crab [kræb] Krebs *(Tier)* 5 **hermit crab** Einsiedlerkrebs 5
crack [kræk] lösen *(z. B. Problem)*, knacken *(z. B. Code)* 7
crash [kræʃ]:
1. Zusammenstoß, Unfall; Zusammensturz, Absturz 7
2. abstürzen (lassen), zusammenbrechen 7
crash (into) krachen; einen Unfall haben, zusammenstoßen (mit) 5
3. **Crash!** Krach! *(z. B. in Comics)* 5
crash course ['kræʃ kɔ:s] Intensivkurs 9: 1 (17)
crawl [krɔ:l] kriechen; krabbeln 8
crazy ['kreɪzi] verrückt 6
cream [kri:m] Sahne; Creme 6
create [kri'eɪt] (er)schaffen, erstellen 7
creative [kri'eɪtɪv] kreativ 7
creature ['kri:tʃə] Geschöpf, (Lebe-)Wesen 9: 1 (14)
cremate [krə'meɪt] einäschern 9: 4 (64)
cremation [krə'meɪʃn] Einäscherung 9: 4 (64)
crime [kraɪm] Verbrechen; Kriminalität 6
crime film ['kraɪm fɪlm] Krimi 6
crinkly ['krɪŋkli] zerknittert; faltig *(Haut)* 9: 2 (33)
crisps *(pl)* [krɪsps] (Kartoffel-)Chips 5
critic ['krɪtɪk] Kritiker/in 9: 3 (43)
critical (of) ['krɪtɪkl] kritisch (gegenüber) 9: 3 (43)
criticism ['krɪtɪsɪzəm] Kritik 9: 3 (43)
criticize ['krɪtɪsaɪz] kritisieren 9: 1 (16)
crocodile ['krɒkədaɪl] Krokodil 9: 1 (8/9)
°**crop** [krɒp] Feldfrucht, Anbaupflanze; Ernte
cross [krɒs]:
1. Kreuz 7
2. kreuzen, überqueren 7
crowd [kraʊd] (Menschen-)Menge 7
crowded ['kraʊdɪd] überfüllt, voll *(von Menschen)* 7
cruel [kru:əl] grausam 8
cruelty ['kru:əlti] Grausamkeit 8
crush [krʌʃ] (zer)quetschen; (aus)pressen 8
cry [kraɪ]:
1. weinen 6
2. rufen, schreien 8
cultural ['kʌltʃərəl] kulturell 8
culture ['kʌltʃə] Kultur 7
cup [kʌp] Tasse 5 **a cup of ...** eine Tasse ... 5
cupboard ['kʌbəd] Schrank *(z. B. Küchenschrank)* 5
curfew ['kɜ:fju:] Ausgangssperre; Sperrstunde 8
curly ['kɜ:li] lockig 6
currency ['kʌrənsi] Währung 9: 4 (58/59)
current ['kʌrənt] aktuell, gegenwärtig 9: 1 (17)
current affairs *(pl)* [kʌrənt ə'feəz] Tagespolitik, aktuelle Ereignisse 9: 1 (17)
curse [kɜ:s]:
1. Fluch 9: 4 (67)
2. fluchen 9: 4 (67)

curtain ['kɜːtn] Vorhang, Gardine 5
customer ['kʌstəmə] Kunde, Kundin 7
cut [kʌt], **cut, cut:**
1. schneiden; *(Rasen)* mähen 7
cut sth. out *(infml)* mit etwas aufhören 9: 1 (11)
2. reduzieren, senken, kürzen *(finanzielle Mittel)* 9: 1 (10)
cute [kjuːt] niedlich, süß 7
CV (= curriculum vitae) [siː 'viː], [kərɪkjələm 'viːtaɪ] Lebenslauf 9: 2 (24/25)

D

dad [dæd] Papa, Vati 5
daily ['deɪli] täglich 7
dance [dɑːns] tanzen 5
dancer ['dɑːnsə] Tänzer/in 6
danger ['deɪndʒə] Gefahr 6
dangerous ['deɪndʒərəs] gefährlich 5
dare [deə] wagen, sich trauen 8
dark [dɑːk] dunkel 6
dashboard ['dæʃbɔːd] Armaturenbrett 8
data ['deɪtə] Daten 8
date [deɪt]:
1. Datum 5
2. Verabredung, Date *(auch die Person, mit der man ausgeht)* 6
3. date sb. mit jm. gehen, eine Beziehung haben 9: 4 (65)
date of birth [deɪt əv 'bɜːθ] Geburtsdatum 7
date of death [deɪt əv 'deθ] Todesdatum 7
date of issue [deɪt əv 'ɪʃuː] Ausstellungsdatum, Ausgabedatum *(z. B. Dokument)* 8
daughter ['dɔːtə] Tochter 7
day [deɪ] Tag 5 **in the old days** früher 9: 2 (35) **one day** eines Tages 6
day out [deɪ 'aʊt], *pl* **days out** (Tages-)Ausflug 6
daylight ['deɪlaɪt] Tageslicht 9: 4 (67)
dead [ded] tot 5 **play dead** sich tot stellen 8 **The line went dead.** Die (Telefon-)Leitung war tot. 7
deal [diːl] Geschäft; Vereinbarung 7
deal with [diːl], **dealt, dealt** sich kümmern um, sich befassen mit, behandeln *(z. B. Thema)* 9: 2 (30)
dealt [delt] *siehe* **deal with**
Dear ... [dɪə] Liebe/r ... 5 **Dear Sir or Madam** Sehr geehrte Damen und Herren 8
death [deθ] Tod 7 **date of death** Todesdatum 7
debate [dɪ'beɪt]:
1. debattieren 8
2. Debatte 8
hold/have a debate eine Debatte führen 8
December [dɪ'sembə] Dezember 5
decent ['diːsnt] anständig, ordentlich, annehmbar 9: 4 (71)
decide to do sth. [dɪ'saɪd] beschließen, sich entscheiden (etwas zu tun) 6
decision [dɪ'sɪʒn] Entscheidung 6
decision-making [dɪ'sɪʒn meɪkɪŋ] Entscheidungsfindung 9: 2 (30)
decision-making skills *(pl)* [dɪ'sɪʒn meɪkɪŋ skɪlz] Entscheidungsfähigkeit 9: 2 (30)
deck [dek] Deck 7 **on deck** an Deck 7
decorate ['dekəreɪt] dekorieren, schmücken 7
decoration [dekə'reɪʃn] Dekoration, Schmuck, Verzierung 9: 4 (70)
deep [diːp] tief 7
deer [dɪə], *pl* **deer** Reh; Hirsch 6
red deer Rotwild 6
defence [dɪ'fens] Verteidigung 7
definitely ['defɪnətli] auf jeden Fall; ganz bestimmt 6
definition [defɪ'nɪʃn] Definition 8
deforestation [diːfɒrɪ'steɪʃn] Abholzung, Entwaldung 9: 2 (27)
degree [dɪ'griː] Grad 8
delayed [dɪ'leɪd] verspätet 6
delete [dɪ'liːt] löschen 7
deli ['deli] Feinkostgeschäft 8
deliver [dɪ'lɪvə] (aus)liefern 9: 4 (63)
delivery [dɪ'lɪvəri] Lieferung 9: 4 (63)
demonstrate ['demənstreɪt] demonstrieren, vorführen 8
demonstration [demən'streɪʃn] Vorführung, Demonstration 8
denial [dɪ'naɪəl] *(das)* Leugnen, Abstreiten, Dementi 9: 1 (17)
dentist ['dentɪst] Zahnarzt/-ärztin 6
deny [dɪ'naɪ] leugnen, bestreiten 9: 1 (17)
department [dɪ'pɑːtmənt] Abteilung 9: 3 (49)
department store [dɪ'pɑːtmənt stɔː] Kaufhaus 6
depress [dɪ'pres] deprimieren 8
depressed [dɪ'prest] deprimiert 8
depressing [dɪ'presɪŋ] deprimierend 8
descendant [dɪ'sendənt] Nachfahre/-fahrin, Nachkomme 8
describe (sth. to sb.) [dɪ'skraɪb] (jm. etwas) beschreiben 5
description [dɪ'skrɪpʃn] Beschreibung 7
desert ['dezət] Wüste 6
design [dɪ'zaɪn] entwerfen, gestalten 7
desk [desk] Schreibtisch, Schülertisch 5
despite [dɪ'spaɪt] trotz 9: 3 (45)
dessert [dɪ'zɜːt] Nachspeise, Dessert 5
destroy [dɪ'strɔɪ] zerstören, vernichten 8
detail ['diːteɪl] Detail, Einzelheit 8
in detail im Detail 8
detailed ['diːteɪld] detailliert 8
detain [dɪ'teɪn] in Haft nehmen; aufhalten 9: 1 (16)
detective [dɪ'tektɪv] Detektiv/in 6
detective series [dɪ'tektɪv sɪəriːz], *pl* **detective series** Krimiserie 6
detention [dɪ'tenʃn]:
1. Haft; Inhaftierung 9: 1 (16)
2. Nachsitzen *(in der Schule)* 7
detention centre [dɪ'tenʃn sentə] Auffanglager, Haftanstalt *(für Abschiebehaft)* 9: 1 (16)
detox ['diːtɒks] *(infml)* Entzug(sprogramm) 9: 3 (44)
detoxification [diːtɒksɪfɪ'keɪʃn] Entgiftung 9: 3 (44)
develop [dɪ'veləp]:
1. entwickeln; sich entwickeln 7
2. erschließen *(z. B. Gelände, Bodenschätze)* 8
development [dɪ'veləpmənt]:
1. Entwicklung 8
2. Erschließung *(z. B. Gelände, Bodenschätze)* 8
device [dɪ'vaɪs] Gerät, Apparat 9: 3 (43)
devil ['devl] Teufel 9: 1 (8/9)
diagram ['daɪəgræm] Diagramm 8
dialogue ['daɪəlɒg] Dialog 7
diary ['daɪəri] Tagebuch; Kalender 9: 2 (33) **keep a diary** Tagebuch führen 9: 2 (33)
diary entry ['daɪəri entri] Tagebucheintrag 7
dice [daɪs], *pl* **dice** Würfel 7
dictionary ['dɪkʃənri] Wörterbuch, *(alphabetisches)* Wörterverzeichnis 5
did [dɪd] *siehe* **do I didn't like ... (= did not)** ich mochte ... nicht 5

die [daɪ] sterben 5
diet ['daɪət]:
1. Ernährung, Kost 8
2. Diät 8
go on a diet eine Diät machen 8
difference ['dɪfrəns] Unterschied 5
different ['dɪfrənt] verschieden; anders 5
difficult ['dɪfɪkəlt] schwierig 8
difficulty ['dɪfɪkəlti] Schwierigkeit(en) 9: 1 (16)
dig [dɪg], **dug, dug** graben 7
digital ['dɪdʒɪtl] digital 7
dingo ['dɪŋgəʊ], *pl* **dingoes** Dingo 9: 1 (8/9)
dining room ['daɪnɪŋ ru:m] Esszimmer 5
dinner ['dɪnə] Abendessen 5 **for dinner** zum Abendessen 5 **have dinner** (zu) Abend essen 5
direct [də'rekt] direkt, unmittelbar 9: 1 (18)
direction [də'rekʃn] Richtung 6
directions *(pl)* [də'rekʃnz] Wegbeschreibung(en) 5 **ask for directions** nach dem Weg fragen 5 **give directions** den Weg beschreiben 5
director [də'rektə] Regisseur/in 6
dirty ['dɜ:ti] schmutzig 7
disability [dɪsə'bɪləti] Behinderung 8
disabled [dɪs'eɪbld] (körper)behindert 8
disadvantage [dɪsəd'vɑ:ntɪdʒ] Nachteil 7 **at a disadvantage** im Nachteil 7
disagree [dɪsə'gri:] nicht zustimmen, widersprechen 6
disappear [dɪsə'pɪə] verschwinden 5
disappoint sb. [dɪsə'pɔɪnt] jn. enttäuschen 7
disappointed (with) [dɪsə'pɔɪntɪd] enttäuscht (von) 7
disappointing [dɪsə'pɔɪntɪŋ] enttäuschend 7
disaster [dɪ'zɑ:stə] Katastrophe, Unglück 8
disbelief [dɪsbɪ'li:f] Unglaube(n), Ungläubigkeit 9: 3 (52)
discipline ['dɪsəplɪn]:
1. Disziplin 9: 1 (13)
2. disziplinieren 9: 1 (13)
discover [dɪ'skʌvə] entdecken 7
discriminate against sb. [dɪ'skrɪmɪneɪt] jn. diskriminieren 8
discrimination (against sb.) [dɪskrɪmɪ'neɪʃn] Diskriminierung (eines Menschen) 8
discuss sth. [dɪ'skʌs] über etwas diskutieren; etwas besprechen 7
discussion [dɪ'skʌʃn] Diskussion 9: 2 (36)
disease [dɪ'zi:z] Krankheit 7
disgusted (by/that ...) [dɪs'gʌstɪd] empört (über/dass ...); angewidert (von) 8
disgusting [dɪs'gʌstɪŋ] ekelhaft, widerlich 8
dish [dɪʃ]:
1. Schüssel, Schale 7
2. Gericht *(Mahlzeit)* 6
side dish Beilage 6
dishes *(pl)* ['dɪʃɪz] Abwasch 6
dishwasher ['dɪʃwɒʃə] Geschirrspülmaschine 6 **load the dishwasher** die Spülmaschine einräumen 7
distance ['dɪstəns] Distanz, Entfernung 7 **in the distance** in der Ferne 7
dive [daɪv]:
1. einen Kopfsprung machen, *(ins Wasser)* springen 5
2. (ein)tauchen 8
divide (up) (into) [dɪ'vaɪd] auf-/einteilen (in) 7
divorce [dɪ'vɔ:s]:
1. (Ehe-)Scheidung 9: 4 (65)
get a divorce sich scheiden lassen 9: 4 (65)
2. divorce sb. ich von jm. scheiden lassen 9: 4 (65)
divorced [dɪ'vɔ:st] geschieden 5
dizzy ['dɪzi] schwindelig 9: 3 (52)
I feel dizzy. Mir ist schwindelig. 9: 3 (52)
do [du:], **did, done** machen, tun 5
do better besser abschneiden 7
do sport Sport treiben 5 **do your homework** Hausaufgaben machen 5 **it doesn't help** es hilft nicht 5
dock [dɒk] Hafen, Dock 7
doctor ['dɒktə] Arzt, Ärztin 6
doctor's office [dɒktəz 'ɒfɪs] *(AE)* Arztpraxis; Behandlungszimmer 8
document ['dɒkjumənt] Dokument; Text(datei) 8
documentary [dɒkju'mentri] Dokumentarfilm 6
dog [dɒg] Hund 5 **walk a dog** mit einem Hund spazieren gehen 9: 2 (24/25)
dog walker ['dɒg wɔ:kə] Hundeausführer/in 9: 2 (24/25)
dog walking ['dɒg wɔ:kɪŋ] Hunde ausführen 9: 2 (24/25)
dogs' home [dɒgz 'həʊm] Hundeheim 6
dolphin ['dɒlfɪn] Delfin 7
done [dʌn] *siehe* **do**
donkey ['dɒŋki] Esel 9: 2 (27)
door [dɔ:] Tür 5 **answer the door** aufmachen, zur/an die Tür gehen 7
dot [dɒt] Punkt, Pünktchen 9: 1 (12)
dot painting ['dɒt peɪntɪŋ] Punktmalerei; Punktgemälde 9: 1 (12)
doubt [daʊt]:
1. (be)zweifeln 9: 3 (52)
2. Zweifel 9: 3 (52)
no doubt ohne Zweifel, zweifellos 9: 3 (52)
down [daʊn] hinunter, herunter 5
be down (by) ... % um ... % gesunken sein 7
download [daʊn'ləʊd] herunterladen 6
downstairs [daʊn'steəz] (nach) unten *(die Treppe hinunter)* 5
dozen ['dʌzn], *pl* **dozen** Dutzend 9: 3 (51)
Dr (= Doctor) ['dɒktə] Doktor *(akademischer Titel)* 8
drama ['drɑ:mə] Schauspiel, darstellende Kunst 5
drank [dræŋk] *siehe* **drink**
draw [drɔ:], **drew, drawn** zeichnen 8
drawing ['drɔ:ɪŋ] Zeichnung 5
drawn [drɔ:n] *siehe* **draw**
dream [dri:m]:
1. Traum 5
2. dream (of/about sth.) träumen (von etwas) 9: 1 (10)
dreamcatcher ['dri:mkætʃə] Traumfänger 8
dress [dres]:
1. Kleid 5
2. Kleidung 8
dress code ['dres kəʊd] Kleiderordnung, Dresscode 6
dressed [drest]: **get dressed** sich anziehen 5
drew [dru:] *siehe* **draw**
drink [drɪŋk]:
1. Getränk 5
2. drink, drank, drunk trinken 5
drinking water ['drɪŋkɪŋ wɔ:tə] Trinkwasser 8
drive [draɪv] (Garagen-)Zufahrt 5
drive [draɪv], **drove, driven:**
1. *(mit dem Auto)* fahren 5
2. (an)treiben *(Tiere)* 7
driven ['drɪvn] *siehe* **drive**
driver ['draɪvə] Fahrer/in 6
driving licence ['draɪvɪŋ laɪsns] Führerschein 8

drone [drəʊn] Drohne 8
drop [drɒp]:
1. (sich) fallen lassen 6
2. fallen, sinken 7
3. drop out (of school) (die Schule) abbrechen 8
drought [draʊt] Dürre 8
drove [drəʊv] *siehe* **drive**
drown [draʊn] ertrinken 9:1 (16)
drug [drʌg] Droge, Rauschgift 6
drugstore ['drʌgstɔːː] *(AE)* Drogerie 8
drunk [drʌŋk] *siehe* **drink**
drunk driving [drʌŋk 'draɪvɪŋ] Trunkenheit am Steuer 8
dry [draɪ]:
1. (ab)trocknen 9:1 (16)
2. trocken 9:1 (16)
duck [dʌk] Ente 7
dug [dʌg] *siehe* **dig**
dummy ['dʌmi] Schnuller 7
during ['djʊərɪŋ] während 8
°dynamo ['daɪnəməʊ], *pl* **dynamos** Dynamo

E

e-friend ['iːfrend] E-Mail-Freund/in 6
each [iːtʃ] jeder/jede/jedes (einzelne) 7
each other [iːtʃ 'ʌðə] einander, sich (gegenseitig) 7
ear [ɪə] Ohr 6
earache ['ɪəreɪk] Ohrenschmerzen 6
early ['ɜːli] früh 5 **He's in his early thirties.** Er ist Anfang dreißig. 8
earn [ɜːn] verdienen *(Geld)* 7
earth [ɜːθ] Erde 7
earthquake ['ɜːθkweɪk] Erdbeben 6
east [iːst] Osten; östlich; Ost- 6
eastbound ['iːstbaʊnd] in Richtung Osten *(Zug, Bus)* 6
Easter ['iːstə] Ostern 6
eastern ['iːstən] östlich, Ost- 7
easy ['iːzi] einfach, leicht 5
easy-to-use [iːzi tu 'juːz] benutzerfreundlich, leicht zu bedienen 8
eat [iːt], **ate, eaten** essen; fressen 5
eaten ['iːtn] *siehe* **eat**
economic [iːkə'nɒmɪk] wirtschaftlich, Wirtschafts- 7
economy [ɪ'kɒnəmi] (Volks-)Wirtschaft 7
edge [edʒ] Rand, Kante 8
edit ['edɪt] bearbeiten, editieren 8
education [edʒu'keɪʃn] Erziehung, (Schul-)Bildung 8
effect [ɪ'fekt] (Aus-)Wirkung, Einfluss, Effekt 7
effective [ɪ'fektɪv] effektiv, wirksam 7
e.g. [iː 'dʒiː] *(aus dem Lateinischen)* z. B. (zum Beispiel) 8
egg [eg] Ei 5
eight [eɪt] acht 5
either ['aɪðə]: **either ... or ...** entweder ... oder ... 8 **not ... either** auch nicht 9:4 (64)
elbow ['elbəʊ] Ellbogen 7
electric [ɪ'lektrɪk] elektrisch, Elektro- 9:3 (51)
electricity [ɪlek'trɪsəti] Strom, Elektrizität 8
electronic [ɪlek'trɒnɪk] elektronisch 9:3 (49)
electronics *(pl)* [ɪlek'trɒnɪks] Elektronik; elektronische Geräte 9:3 (49)
elephant ['elɪfənt] Elefant 7
elevator ['elɪveɪtə] *(AE)* Lift *(Aufzug)* 6
eleven [ɪ'levən] elf 5
else [els]: **anything else** sonst noch etwas 6 **anywhere else** sonst irgendwo 6 **everybody/ everyone else** alle anderen; jede/r andere 6
embarrassed [ɪm'bærəst] verlegen 6
emergency [i'mɜːdʒənsi] Notfall 7
emigrant ['emɪgrənt] Auswanderer, Auswanderin 7
emigrate ['emɪgreɪt] auswandern, emigrieren 7
emigration [emɪ'greɪʃn] Auswanderung 7
emperor ['empərə] Kaiser 7
emphases ['emfəsiːz] *Plural von* **emphasis**
emphasis ['emfəsɪs], *pl* **emphases** Betonung, Schwerpunkt, Akzent 8
emphasize ['emfəsaɪz] betonen, deutlich machen 7
empire ['empaɪə] Imperium, Reich 7
employ sb. [ɪm'plɔɪ] jn. anstellen, beschäftigen 8
employee [ɪm'plɔɪiː] Arbeitnehmer/in 9:4 (61)
employer [ɪm'plɔɪə] Arbeitgeber/in 9:2 (31)
employment [ɪm'plɔɪmənt] Arbeit, Anstellung 9:1 (11)
empress ['emprəs] Kaiserin 7
empty ['empti]:
1. leer 6
2. leeren 6
encourage [ɪn'kʌrɪdʒ] ermutigen, ermuntern; unterstützen 9:1 (12)
encouragement [ɪn'kʌrɪdʒmənt] Ermunterung, Ermutigung; Unterstützung 9:1 (12)
encyclopedia [ɪnsaɪklə'piːdiə] Enzyklopädie, Lexikon 9:4 (71)
end [end]:
1. Ende, Schluss 5
in the end schließlich, zum Schluss 9:4 (65)
2. (be)enden 6
°end up (schließlich) enden, landen, gelangen **°end up doing sth.** am Ende / schließlich etwas tun
endless ['endləs] endlos 6
enemy ['enəmi] Feind/in 7
energy ['enədʒi] Energie 8
engine ['endʒɪn] Motor, Maschine 8 **search engine** Suchmaschine 8
engineer [endʒɪ'nɪə] Ingenieur/in; Techniker/in 6
English-speaking ['ɪŋglɪʃ spiːkɪŋ] englischsprachig 7
enjoy [ɪn'dʒɔɪ] genießen 6 **enjoy doing sth.** es genießen, etwas zu tun 6
enough [ɪ'nʌf] genug 6
ensure [ɪn'ʃʊə] sicherstellen, gewährleisten 9:2 (32)
enter sth. (in(to)/on sth.) ['entə] etwas (in etwas) eintragen, eingeben 8
entertain sb. [entə'teɪn] jn. unterhalten 7
entertainment [entə'teɪnmənt] Unterhaltung 8
entrance ['entrəns] Eingang; Zutritt 8
entry ['entri] Eintritt, Zutritt; (Tagebuch-)Eintrag 7
envelope ['envələʊp] (Brief-)Umschlag 5
environment [ɪn'vaɪrənmənt] Umwelt; Umfeld, Umgebung 7
environment-friendly [ɪnvaɪrənmənt 'frendli] umweltfreundlich 8
environmental [ɪnvaɪrən'mentl] Umwelt- 7
equal ['iːkwəl] gleich(berechtigt) 9:4 (58/59)
equality [i'kwɒləti] Gleichberechtigung, Gleichheit 9:4 (58/59)
equipment *(no pl)* [ɪ'kwɪpmənt] Ausrüstung 6
escalator ['eskəleɪtə] Rolltreppe 6

escape [ɪ'skeɪp]:
1. Flucht 7
2. escape (from) entkommen (aus), fliehen (vor/aus) 7
especially [ɪ'speʃəli] insbesondere 7
etc. [et'setərə] *(aus dem Lateinischen)* usw. (und so weiter) 7
EU (= European Union) [iː 'juː] EU (Europäische Union) 7
euro ['jʊərəʊ], *pl* **euros** Euro 5
European Union [jʊərəpiːən 'juːniən] Europäische Union 7
evaluate [ɪ'væljueɪt] beurteilen, bewerten, einschätzen 9: 3 (43)
evaluation [ɪvælju'eɪʃn] Beurteilung, Bewertung, Einschätzung 9: 3 (43)
even ['iːvn] sogar, selbst 6 **not even** (noch) nicht einmal 6 **without even checking ...** ohne überhaupt zu checken ... 7
even though [iːvn 'ðəʊ] auch wenn, obwohl *(betont)* 9: 2 (27)
evening ['iːvnɪŋ] Abend 5 **in the evening** abends, am Abend 5
event [ɪ'vent] Ereignis 5
eventually [ɪ'ventʃuəli] letztendlich, schließlich 9: 4 (65)
ever ['evə] jemals, schon einmal 6 **for ever** für immer, ewig (lange) 9: 1 (16) **more than ever** mehr als jemals zuvor 9: 2 (33)
every ['evri] jede(r, s) 5
everybody ['evribɒdi] jeder; alle 5
everyday ['evrideɪ] alltäglich, Alltags- 8
everyday life [evrideɪ 'laɪf] Alltag 8
everyone ['evriwʌn] jeder; alle 5
everything ['evriθɪŋ] alles 5
everywhere ['evriweə] überall 6
evil ['iːvl] böse; *(das)* Böse 7
exact [ɪg'zækt] genau, exakt 7
exam [ɪg'zæm] *siehe* **examination**
examination [ɪgzæmɪ'neɪʃn], *infml auch* **exam** Prüfung 7 **take/do an exam(ination)** eine Prüfung machen 7
example [ɪg'zɑːmpl] Beispiel 6 **for example** zum Beispiel 6
excellent ['eksələnt] ausgezeichnet, hervorragend 8
except (for) [ɪk'sept] außer, bis auf 8
exception [ɪk'sepʃn] Ausnahme 8
exchange [ɪks'tʃeɪndʒ]:
1. austauschen 7
2. (Aus-)Tausch, Schüleraustausch 7
excited [ɪk'saɪtɪd] aufgeregt, gespannt 5
excitement [ɪk'saɪtmənt] Aufregung, Spannung 7
exciting [ɪk'saɪtɪŋ] aufregend 6
exclamation mark [ekskləˈmeɪʃn mɑːk] Ausrufezeichen 8
excuse [ɪk'skjuːs] Entschuldigung *(Ausrede)*; Vorwand 8 **make an excuse** sich entschuldigen, eine Entschuldigung vorbringen 8
Excuse me, ... [ɪks'kjuːz miː] Entschuldigung, ... / Entschuldigen Sie, ... 5
exercise ['eksəsaɪz] Übung, Aufgabe 6
exercise book ['eksəsaɪz bʊk] (Schul-)Heft 5
exhausted [ɪg'zɔːstɪd] erschöpft 9: 4 (67)
exhibition [eksɪ'bɪʃn] Messe; Ausstellung 8
exist [ɪg'zɪst] existieren 9: 3 (44)
existence [ɪg'zɪstəns] Existenz 9: 3 (44)
exit ['eksɪt] Ausgang; Ausfahrt 6
expat ['ekspæt] siehe **expatriate**
expatriate [eks'pætriət] *(infml auch* **expat***)* im Ausland Lebende/r; im Ausland lebend 9: 2 (28)
expect [ɪk'spekt] erwarten 9: 2 (37)
expectancy [ɪk'spektənsi]: **life expectancy** Lebenserwartung 9: 1 (11)
expenses *(pl)* [ɪk'spensɪz] Kosten; Spesen 9: 2 (24/25)
expensive [ɪk'spensɪv] teuer 5
experience [ɪk'spɪəriəns]:
1. Erfahrung; Erlebnis 8
2. experience sth. etwas erfahren; erleben 8
experiment [ɪk'sperɪmənt] Experiment 6
expert ['ekspɜːt] Experte, Expertin 9: 1 (16)
expiration [ekspə'reɪʃn] *(AE)* Ablauf, Verfall 8
expire [ɪk'spaɪə] ablaufen, verfallen 8
expiry [ɪk'spaɪəri] Ablauf, Verfall 8
explain sth. to sb. [ɪk'spleɪn] jm. etwas erklären 6
explanation [eksplə'neɪʃn] Erklärung 9: 1 (21)
explode [ɪk'spləʊd] explodieren 7
explore [ɪk'splɔː] erforschen, erkunden 9: 1 (8/9)
explorer [ɪk'splɔːrə] Forschungsreisende/r, Entdecker/in 9: 1 (10)
explosion [ɪk'spləʊʒn] Explosion 7
express [ɪk'spres] ausdrücken, zum Ausdruck bringen 7
expression [ɪk'spreʃn] Ausdruck 7
extraordinary [ɪk'strɔːdnri] außergewöhnlich 7
extreme [ɪk'striːm]:
1. extrem 8
2. Extrem 8
eye [aɪ] Auge 6 **take your eyes off sth.** den Blick abwenden von etwas 8
eye-catching ['aɪ kætʃɪŋ] auffallend, ins Auge springend 9: 3 (54)

F

fabulous ['fæbjələs] sagenhaft, fabelhaft 9: 4 (70)
face [feɪs]:
1. Gesicht 6
2. face sb./sth. jm./einer Sache ins Auge sehen, entgegentreten 6
facilities *(pl)* [fə'sɪlətiz] Einrichtungen, Geräte 7
fact [fækt] Tatsache 7
°fact file ['fækt faɪl] Informationsbogen, Steckbrief
factory ['fæktri] Fabrik 7
Fahrenheit (F) ['færənhaɪt] Fahrenheit 8
fairy ['feəri] Fee, Elfe 7
fairy tale ['feəri teɪl] Märchen 7
faithfully ['feɪθfəli]: **Yours faithfully** Mit freundlichen Grüßen *(Briefschluss)* 8
fake [feɪk]:
1. falsch, gefälscht 8
2. Fälschung 8
fall [fɔːl], **fell, fallen** fallen; hinfallen 5
fallen ['fɔːlən] *siehe* **fall**
false [fɔːls] falsch, unrichtig 9: 1 (17)
fame [feɪm] Ruhm 6
family ['fæməli] Familie 5
famine ['fæmɪn] Hungersnot 7
famous (for) ['feɪməs] berühmt (für, wegen) 5
fancy dress *(no pl)* [fænsi 'dres] Kostüm, Verkleidung 5
fancy dress party [fænsi 'dres pɑːti] Kostümparty 5
fantastic [fæn'tæstɪk] fantastisch 8
fantasy ['fæntəsi] Fantasie 7
FAQ (= frequently asked questions) [ef eɪ 'kju] häufig gestellte Fragen 6
far [fɑː] weit (entfernt) 6
fare [feə] Fahrpreis 8

farm [fɑːm] Bauernhof, Farm 6
farmer ['fɑːmə] Bauer, Bäuerin; Landwirt/in 6
farming ['fɑːmɪŋ] Landwirtschaft 7
fashion ['fæʃn] Mode 7
fast [fɑːst] schnell 5
fat [fæt]:
1. dick, fett 8
2. Fett 8
father ['fɑːðə] Vater 5
fault [fɔːlt] Fehler; Schuld 5
favourite ['feɪvərɪt] Lieblings- 5
fear [fɪə]:
1. (be)fürchten; sich fürchten vor 8
2. **fear (of)** Angst (vor) 8
feather ['feðə] Feder *(eines Vogels)* 8
feature ['fiːtʃə]:
1. bieten, haben; vorkommen, eine Rolle spielen 8
2. Merkmal, Eigenschaft 8
February ['februəri] Februar 5
fed [fed] *siehe* **feed** **be/feel/get fed up (with)** genervt sein, die Nase voll haben (von) 9: 3 (44)
fee [fiː] Gebühr; Honorar; (Mitglieds-)Beitrag 9: 2 (24/25)
feed [fiːd], **fed, fed** füttern; ernähren 6
feel [fiːl], **felt, felt** sich fühlen; fühlen 5
feeling ['fiːlɪŋ] Gefühl 6
feet [fiːt] *Plural von* **foot**
fell [fel] *siehe* **fall**
fellow ['feləʊ] Mit- 9: 1 (10)
felt [felt] *siehe* **feel**
female ['fiːmeɪl] weiblich; Frau 7
fence [fens] fechten *(Sport)* 7
ferret ['ferɪt] Frettchen 5
ferry ['feri] Fähre 5
ferryman ['ferimən], *pl* **ferrymen** Fährmann 6
festival ['festɪvl] Fest 5
few [fjuː] wenige 8 **a few** ein paar, einige 7
field [fiːld] Feld; Weide 6 **in the field** auf der Weide 6
fight [faɪt]:
1. Kampf 5
2. **fight, fought, fought** kämpfen, bekämpfen 5
fight back sich wehren 8
fighter ['faɪtə] Kämpfer/in 7
figure ['fɪgə]:
1. Figur 6
2. Ziffer, Zahl 7
°**file** [faɪl] Datei; Ordner, Liste
fill [fɪl] füllen 7 **fill sth. in** etwas ausfüllen; etwas einsetzen 7

final ['faɪnl] Finale 6
finally ['faɪnəli] schließlich, endlich 8
financial [faɪ'nænʃl] finanziell 8
find [faɪnd], **found, found** finden 5
find out (about) herausfinden; sich informieren über 7
fine [faɪn]:
1. gut, in Ordnung; schön 5
I'm fine. Mir geht es gut. 5
2. fein *(z. B. Stoff)*; dünn *(z. B. Haar)* 7
finger ['fɪŋgə] Finger 6 **tap your fingers** mit den Fingern klopfen 7
fingernail ['fɪŋgəneɪl] Fingernagel 9: 4 (63)
finish ['fɪnɪʃ] beenden, zu Ende machen 5
fire ['faɪə] Feuer 6
fireplace ['faɪəpleɪs] Kamin 8
firework ['faɪəwɜːk] Feuerwerkskörper 5 **fireworks** *(pl)* Feuerwerk 5
firm [fɜːm] Firma 9: 3 (55)
first [fɜːst]:
1. erste(r, s) 5
2. zuerst, als Erstes 5
finish first *(im Wettkampf)* Erste/r werden 5
first aid [fɜːst 'eɪd] Erste Hilfe 9: 2 (30)
first-aid certificate [fɜːst 'eɪd sətɪfɪkət] Erste-Hilfe-Schein 9: 2 (30)
first floor [fɜːst 'flɔː] *(AE)* Erdgeschoss 8
first language [fɜːst 'læŋgwɪdʒ] Muttersprache 7
first name ['fɜːst neɪm] Vorname 7
First Nations [fɜːst 'neɪʃnz] Erste Nationen *(indigene Völker Kanadas)* 8
Firstly, ... ['fɜːstli] Erstens ... 7
fish [fɪʃ]:
1. Fisch(e) 5
2. fischen, angeln 8
fish finger [fɪʃ 'fɪŋgə] Fischstäbchen 5
fishing ['fɪʃɪŋ] Fischen, Angeln; Fischerei 8
fist [fɪst] Faust 9: 1 (21)
fit (sth.) [fɪt] passen (zu etwas) 7
five [faɪv] fünf 5
flag [flæg] Fahne, Flagge 5
flash [flæʃ]:
1. Aufblitzen; Blinklicht; Blitz *(Kamera)* 8
2. blinken, leuchten 8
flashing lights *(pl)* [flæʃɪŋ 'laɪts] Warnlicht; Blaulicht 8

flashlight ['flæʃlaɪt] *(AE)* Taschenlampe 8
flat [flæt] Wohnung 5
flesh [fleʃ] Fleisch; *(von Menschen auch)* Haut 8
flew [fluː] *siehe* **fly**
flexible ['fleksəbl] flexibel 9: 2 (31)
flicker ['flɪkə] flackern; flimmern 9: 3 (52)
flight [flaɪt] Flug 6
float [fləʊt] schweben; *(auf der Wasseroberfläche)* treiben 8
flood [flʌd]:
1. Überschwemmung, Hochwasser; Flut 8
2. überschwemmen, überfluten 8
be flooded unter Wasser stehen 8
floor [flɔː]:
1. Fußboden 5
2. Etage, Stock(werk) 6
first floor *(AE:)* Erdgeschoss; *(BE:)* 1. Etage 6
flour ['flaʊə] Mehl 7
flower ['flaʊə] Blume; Blüte 5
flown [fləʊn] *siehe* **fly**
fly [flaɪ], **flew, flown** fliegen 5
flyer ['flaɪə] Flieger/in 7
focus (on) ['fəʊkəs]:
1. sich konzentrieren (auf) 9: 2 (37)
2. **focus (on)**, *pl* **focuses** *or* **foci** Mittelpunkt, Hauptpunkt, Schwerpunkt 9: 2 (37)
focus of attention Zentrum der Aufmerksamkeit 9: 2 (37)
fog [fɒg] Nebel 5
foggy ['fɒgi] nebelig 5
follow ['fɒləʊ] (be)folgen; verfolgen 7
follow-up ['fɒləʊ ʌp] Anschluss-, Folge- 8
follower ['fɒləʊə] Anhänger/in, Fan 7
following ['fɒləʊɪŋ] Anhängerschaft 9: 3 (44)
food [fuːd] Essen, Lebensmittel; Futter 5
fool [fuːl] Idiot, Dummkopf 8
foot [fʊt], *pl* **feet** Fuß 6 **on foot** zu Fuß 8
football ['fʊtbɔːl]:
1. Fußball 5
2. *(AE)* American Football 6
football club (FC) ['fʊtbɔːl klʌb] Fußballverein 5
footprint ['fʊtprɪnt] Fußabdruck 8
for [fɔː] für 5 **for 30 years** 30 Jahre (lang); seit 30 Jahren 5 **for example** zum Beispiel 6 **What's**

for homework? Was haben wir als Hausaufgabe(n) auf? 6
force [fɔːs]:
1. Zwang; Gewalt; Kraft 9: 4 (65)
2. force sth. etwas erzwingen 9: 4 (65)
force sb. to do sth. jn. zwingen, etwas zu tun 9: 4 (65)
forced marriage [fɔːst 'mærɪdʒ] Zwangsheirat 9: 4 (65)
foreground ['fɔːgraʊnd] Vordergrund 7
foreign ['fɒrən] ausländisch; fremd 9: 2 (30)
foreign language [fɒrən 'læŋgwɪdʒ] Fremdsprache 9: 2 (30)
forest ['fɒrɪst] Wald 6
forever, for ever [fər'evə] für immer, ewig (lange) 9: 1 (16)
forget [fə'get]**, forgot, forgotten** vergessen 6
forgot [fə'gɒt] *siehe* **forget**
forgotten [fə'gɒtn] *siehe* **forget**
fork [fɔːk] Gabel 7
form [fɔːm]:
1. Formular 7
2. Form 9: 1 (12)
3. (sich) formen, (sich) bilden 9: 1 (12)
formal ['fɔːml] förmlich, formell 9: 1 (15)
fortunately ['fɔːtʃənətli] zum Glück, glücklicherweise 7
forward ['fɔːwəd] vorwärts, nach vorne 7 **look forward to doing sth.** sich darauf freuen, etwas zu tun 7 **look forward to sth.** sich auf etwas freuen 7
fought [fɔːt] *siehe* **fight**
found [faʊnd]:
1. *siehe* **find**
2. gründen 7
founder ['faʊndə] Gründer/in 7
four [fɔː] vier 5
fox [fɒks] Fuchs 6
fraction ['frækʃn] Bruch(zahl); Bruchteil 9: 2 (35)
°frame [freɪm] Rahmen; Gestell
free [friː]:
1. frei 5
free time Freizeit, freie Zeit 5
2. kostenlos 5
3. befreien 9: 3 (51)
freedom ['friːdəm] Freiheit 8
freeze [friːz]**, froze, frozen** (ge)frieren; erstarren 7
frequently asked questions (FAQ) [friːkwəntli ɑːskt 'kwestʃənz] häufig gestellte Fragen 6
fresh [freʃ] frisch 5
Friday ['fraɪdeɪ], ['fraɪdi] Freitag 5
fridge [frɪdʒ] Kühlschrank 6
fried [fraɪd] frittiert, gebraten 6
friend [frend] Freund/in 5 **make friends** Freunde finden 7
friendless ['frendləs] ohne Freunde 6
friendliness ['frendlinəs] Freundlichkeit 9: 1 (15)
friendly ['frendli] freundlich 5
friendship ['frendʃɪp] Freundschaft 7
frighten ['fraɪtn] Angst einjagen, verängstigen; erschrecken 8
frighten sb./sth. off/away jn./etwas verscheuchen 8
frightened ['fraɪtnd]: **be frightened** Angst haben 8
frightening ['fraɪtnɪŋ] beängstigend, erschreckend 8
frog [frɒg] Frosch 6
from [frɒm] von, aus 5 **Where are you from?** Wo kommst du her? 5
front [frʌnt] vorderer Teil, Vorderseite 5 **at the front** vorne 5 **in front of** vor 5
front page [frʌnt 'peɪdʒ] Titelseite 6
frown [fraʊn]:
1. die Stirn runzeln 7
2. Stirnrunzeln 7
froze [frəʊz] *siehe* **freeze**
frozen ['frəʊzn] *siehe* **freeze**
fruit [fruːt] Obst 5
fry [fraɪ] frittieren, braten 6
°fuel ['fjuːəl] antreiben; anfachen
full [fʊl] vollständig; voll 7 **full of** voll mit/von, voller 7
full stop [fʊl 'stɒp] Punkt *(Satzzeichen)* 8
full-time [fʊl 'taɪm] Vollzeit-, Ganztags- 9: 2 (24/25)
fun [fʌn] Spaß 5 **be fun** Spaß machen 5 **have fun** Spaß haben 5 **it sounds fun** es klingt, als ob es Spaß macht 6 **°for fun** zum Spaß, zum Vergnügen
fund [fʌnd]:
1. finanzieren 7
2. Fonds; Geldmittel 9: 2 (24/25)
funding ['fʌndɪŋ] Finanzierung, *(finanzielle)* Mittel 7
°funnel ['fʌnl] Trichter
funny ['fʌni] witzig, komisch 5
furniture ['fɜːnɪtʃə] Möbel 6
further ['fɜːðə] weiter (entfernt) 6
furthest ['fɜːðəst] am weitesten (entfernt) 6
future ['fjuːtʃə]:
1. Zukunft 7
2. zukünftige(r, s) 7

G

Gaelic ['geɪlɪk] Gälisch *(Sprache)* 7
°gallery ['gæləri] Galerie
gallon ['gælən] Gallone *(= 3,78 l in den USA)* 8
game [geɪm] Spiel 5
games console ['geɪmz kɒnsəʊl] Spielekonsole 6
gap [gæp] Lücke, Abstand 6
garage ['gærɑːʒ] Garage 5
garden ['gɑːdn] Garten 5
garlic ['gɑːlɪk] Knoblauch 6
gas [gæs] *(AE)* Benzin 6
gas station ['gæs steɪʃn] *(AE)* Tankstelle 6
gasp [gɑːsp]:
1. (tiefer) Atemzug 8
2. nach Luft ringen 8
gate [geɪt] Tor, Gatter 6
gave [geɪv] *siehe* **give**
gay [geɪ] schwul 7
°g'day [gə'deɪ] *(Austr., infml)* Hallo! / Guten Tag!
gel [dʒel] Gel 8
gender ['dʒendə] Geschlecht *(als soziales Merkmal)* 7
general ['dʒenrəl] allgemein 8
in general im Allgemeinen, generell 8
generation [dʒenə'reɪʃn] Generation 9: 1 (10)
°generator ['dʒenəreɪtə] Generator
geography [dʒi'ɒgrəfi] Geografie, Erdkunde 5
get [get]**, got, got**:
1. *(sich etwas)* holen/besorgen; bekommen 5
2. werden 6
get wet nass werden 6
3. get sth. etwas verstehen, mitbekommen 7
4. get (to) gelangen, (hin) kommen (nach) 6
get on a plane/bus/train in ein Flugzeug/einen Bus/einen Zug einsteigen 6 **get off a plane/bus/train** aus einem Flugzeug/Bus/Zug aussteigen 6 **get in(to) a car** in ein Auto einsteigen 7 **get out of a car** aus einem Auto aussteigen 7 **get along (with sb.)** (gut) auskommen (mit jm.), sich (gut) verstehen (mit jm.) 9: 2 (26) **get around** sich fortbewegen *(mobil sein)* 9: 4 (66) **get in touch (with)** (sich) in Verbindung setzen (mit), Kontakt aufnehmen (zu) 9: 3 (44) **get up** aufstehen 5
ghost [gəʊst] Geist, Gespenst 6

giraffe [dʒə'rɑːf], *pl* **giraffe** *or* **giraffes** Giraffe 7
girl [gɜːl] Mädchen 5
girlfriend ['gɜːlfrend] (feste) Freundin 7
give [gɪv], **gave, given** geben 5 **give (sth.) up** (etwas) aufgeben, aufhören (mit etwas) 9: 2 (26) **give a talk** einen Vortrag halten 5 **give in (to sb./sth.)** (jm./einer Sache) nachgeben 7 **give sth. up (to sb.)** auf etwas verzichten, jm. etwas übergeben 9: 2 (26)
given ['gɪvn] *siehe* **give**
glass [glɑːs] Glas 7
glasses *(pl)* ['glɑːsɪz] *(eine)* Brille 6
global ['gləʊbl] global, weltweit 8
global warming [gləʊbl 'wɔːmɪŋ] Erderwärmung 8
glove [glʌv] Handschuh 6
go [gəʊ]:
1. **on the go** unterwegs 7
2. **go, went, gone** gehen, fahren 5 **go bigger** größer werden 9: 3 (52) **go off** klingeln *(Wecker)*; losgehen *(Alarm, Waffe)* 7 **go on** geschehen, vor sich gehen 9: 3 (44) **go on** weitergehen; weitermachen, weiterreden; (sich) fortsetzen 8 **go wrong** schiefgehen 6 **go to sleep** einschlafen; schlafen gehen 9: 3 (44) **I'm going to ...** ich werde ... *(Plan, Vorhaben)* 6 **This goes for ... (too).** Dies gilt (auch) für ... 9: 4 (64)
goal [gəʊl] Tor *(im Sport)* 5
goalpost ['gəʊlpəʊst] Torpfosten 9: 1 (21)
gobbledygook ['gɒbldiguːk] *(infml)* Kauderwelsch 7
god [gɒd] Gott 7 **Oh my god!** Oh mein Gott! 7
gold [gəʊld] Gold 5
golden ['gəʊldn] golden, aus Gold 9: 4 (70)
gone [gɒn] *siehe* **go be gone** weg sein 7
good [gʊd] gut 5 **Good morning.** Guten Morgen. 5
Goodbye. [gʊd'baɪ] Auf Wiedersehen! / Servus. 5
goods *(pl)* [gʊdz] Waren, Güter 8
got [gɒt] *siehe* **get have got** haben 6
government ['gʌvənmənt] Regierung 7
grab [græb] packen, greifen (nach), ergreifen 8
grade [greɪd]:
1. (Schul-)Note 6
2. *(AE)* Klasse, Schuljahr 6
graduate (from) ['grædʒueɪt] den Abschluss machen (an) *(Schule, Hochschule)* 8
gram (= g) [græm] Gramm 5
grammar ['græmə] Grammatik 8
grandad ['grændæd] Opa 5
granddaughter ['grændɔːtə] Enkelin 8
grandfather ['grænfɑːðə] Großvater 5
grandma ['grænmɑː] Oma 5
grandmother ['grænmʌðə] Großmutter 5
grandparents *(pl)* ['grænpeərənts] Großeltern 5
grandson ['grænsʌn] Enkel 8
graph [græf], [grɑːf] Graph, Schaubild 6
graphic designer [græfɪk dɪ'zaɪnə] Grafikdesigner/in 9: 2 (36)
graphics *(pl)* ['græfɪks] Grafik 8
grass [grɑːs] Gras; Rasen 6
great [greɪt]:
1. toll, großartig 5
2. groß *(bedeutend, angesehen)* 5
Great Britain [greɪt 'brɪtn] Großbritannien 5
great-grandfather [greɪt 'grænfɑːðə] Urgroßvater 8
great-grandmother [greɪt 'grænmʌðə] Urgroßmutter 8
great-great-grandfather [greɪt greɪt 'grænfɑːðə] Ururgroßvater 8
great-great-grandmother [greɪt greɪt 'grænmʌðə] Ururgroßmutter 8
greedy ['griːdi] gierig, habgierig 7
green [griːn] grün 5
greeting ['griːtɪŋ] Gruß(formel), Begrüßung 9: 2 (31)
grew [gruː] *siehe* **grow**
grey [greɪ] grau 5
gritty ['grɪti] ungeschminkt, schonungslos 8
groom [gruːm] Bräutigam 9: 4 (65)
gross [grəʊs] *(infml)* widerlich 7
ground [graʊnd] (Erd-)Boden 7
group [gruːp] Gruppe 5
grow [grəʊ], **grew, grown**:
1. anbauen 8
2. wachsen 8
grow up aufwachsen; erwachsen werden 8
3. werden 8
grown [grəʊn] *siehe* **grow**
°**guacamole** [gwækə'məʊleɪ] Avocadocreme
guard [gɑːd]:
1. Wärter/in; Wache; Sicherheitsbedienstete/r; Schutz(vorrichtung) 8
2. schützen, bewachen 8
guardian ['gɑːdiən] Vormund 7
guess [ges]:
1. Vermutung 9: 2 (33)
2. (er)raten 9: 2 (33)
Guess what! Stell dir / Stellt euch (mal) vor! 9: 2 (33) **I guess** ich glaube, ich nehme an 9: 2 (33)
guest [gest] Gast 7
guide:
1. *(= tour guide)* Reiseleiter/in, Fremdenführer/in 9: 3 (50)
2. **guide (to)** Ratgeber (für), Reiseführer *(Buch, Broschüre)* 5
3. führen, leiten 9: 3 (50)
guinea pig ['gɪni pɪg] Meerschweinchen 5
guitar [gɪ'tɑː] Gitarre 5
gum [gʌm] Gummi; Zahnfleisch 7
gumshield ['gʌmʃiːld] Mundschutz *(Sport)* 9: 1 (21)
gun [gʌn] Schusswaffe, Pistole 8
gun licence ['gʌn laɪsns] Waffenschein 8
guy [gaɪ] Typ, Kerl 8
guys *(pl)* [gaɪz] Leute *(Anrede)* 5
gym [dʒɪm]:
1. Turnhalle, Sporthalle 5
2. Fitnessstudio 5
gymnast ['dʒɪmnæst] Turner/in 8
gymnastics [dʒɪm'næstɪks] Turnen, Gymnastik 5

H

habit ['hæbɪt] (An-)Gewohnheit 9: 2 (28)
hack [hæk] hacken 9: 3 (45) **hack into a computer / a system** sich in einen Computer einhacken / in ein System eindringen 9: 3 (45)
had [hæd] *siehe* **have**
haggis ['hægɪs] *schottisches Gericht aus gefülltem Schafsmagen* 6
hair [heə] Haar, Haare 5
hairdresser ['heədresə] Friseur/in 6 **hairdresser's** Friseursalon 6
hairstyle ['heəstaɪl] Frisur 7
half [hɑːf] halbe(r, s) 6 **half an apple** ein halber Apfel 6 **half past 6** halb 7 5 **at half price** zum halben Preis 9: 3 (49)
half-brother ['hɑːf brʌðə] Halbbruder 5
half-sister ['hɑːf sɪstə] Halbschwester 5

half-time show ['hɑːftaɪm ʃəʊ] Show in der Halbzeitpause 6
halfway [hɑːf'weɪ] auf halbem Wege, halb(wegs) 7
hall [hɔːl]**:**
1. Flur, Diele 5
2. Halle, Saal 7
ham [hæm] Schinken 5
hamster ['hæmstə] Hamster 5
hand [hænd] Hand 5 **hold hands** Händchen halten 6 **put up your hand** sich melden, aufzeigen 6
handgun ['hændgʌn] Handfeuerwaffe 8
handle ['hændl] Griff, Handgriff 9: 3 (50)
handlebars *(pl)* ['hændlbɑːz] (Fahrrad-)Lenkstange 9: 4 (67)
handover ['hændəʊvə] Übergabe 7
°handshake ['hændʃeɪk] Händedruck, Handschlag
hang [hæŋ]**, hung, hung** hängen 6 **hang out** rumhängen, abhängen 6 **hang sth. out** etwas aufhängen *(Wäsche)* 6 **hang up** auflegen *(Telefon)* 8
happen (to sb.) ['hæpən] (jm.) geschehen, passieren 5
happiness ['hæpinəs] Glück, Zufriedenheit 7
happy ['hæpi] glücklich, froh 5
harbour ['hɑːbə] Hafen 5
hard [hɑːd] schwer, schwierig; hart 5 **train hard** hart trainieren 7
hardly ['hɑːdli] kaum 7
harm [hɑːm]**:**
1. Schaden, Schäden, Verletzung 8
do harm (to) sb. / do sb. harm jm. Schaden zufügen 8
2. schaden, schädigen, verletzen 8
harness ['hɑːnɪs] nutzen, nutzbar machen 9: 3 (50)
harsh [hɑːʃ] hart, rau; brutal, harsch 9: 4 (66)
has [hæz], [həz]: *(er/sie/es)* hat 5
hat [hæt] Hut, Mütze 6
hatchet ['hætʃɪt] Beil 8
hate [heɪt]**:**
1. hassen 5
2. Hass 8
hater ['heɪtə] Verfasser/in von Hasskommentaren 7
have [hæv]**, had, had** haben 5 **have breakfast/lunch/dinner** frühstücken/(zu) Mittag essen/(zu) Abend essen 5 **have sth. done (by sb.)** etwas (von jm.) machen lassen *(erledigen lassen)* 9: 4 (63) **have to do sth.** etwas tun müssen 6 **I'll have ...** ich nehme ... *(im Restaurant)* 5
have got [həv 'gɒt] haben 6
he [hiː] er 5 **he's (= he is)** er ist 5
head [hed] Kopf 6
headache ['hedeɪk] Kopfschmerzen 6
headdress ['heddres] Kopfschmuck 8
headguard ['hedgɑːd] Kopfschutz *(Sport)* 9: 1 (21)
heading ['hedɪŋ] Überschrift 7
headline ['hedlaɪn] Überschrift 8
headphones *(pl)* ['hedfəʊnz] *(ein)* Kopfhörer 8
health [helθ] Gesundheit 6
health care ['helθ keə] Gesundheitsfürsorge, medizinische Versorgung 8
healthy ['helθi] gesund 6
hear [hɪə]**, heard, heard** hören 5
heard [hɜːd] *siehe* **hear**
heart [hɑːt] Herz 6
heavy ['hevi] schwer *(Gewicht)* 6
heck [hek]**: What/Where/... the heck is ...?** *(infml)* Was/Wo/... ist denn nur/bloß ...? 7
heel [hiːl] Absatz *(Schuh)*; Ferse 8
held [held] *siehe* **hold**
helicopter ['helɪkɒptə] Hubschrauber 8 **get a helicopter view of** einen weiten Überblick bekommen über (*wörtlich:* Hubschrauber-Ansicht) 8
Hello. [hə'ləʊ] Hallo. / Grüß Gott. 5
helmet ['helmɪt] Helm 8
help [help]**:**
1. helfen 5
2. Hilfe 5
helper ['helpə] Helfer/in 9: 2 (27)
helpful ['helpfl] hilfsbereit; hilfreich, nützlich 9: 2 (30)
helpless ['helpləs] hilflos 9: 1 (18)
her [hɜː], [hə] sie; ihr 5
her mum [hɜː], [hə] ihre Mutter 5
herbal ['hɜːbl] Kräuter- 9: 4 (71)
herbs *(pl)* [hɜːbz] Kräuter 9: 4 (71)
here [hɪə] hier; hierher 5 **Here you are.** Bitte schön. / Hier, bitte. 5
hermit crab ['hɜːmɪt kræb] Einsiedlerkrebs 5
hero ['hɪərəʊ], *pl* **heroes** Held/in 7
hers [hɜːz] ihrer, ihre, ihres *(zu „she")* 6
herself [hɜː'self] sie/sich selbst *(zu „she")* 6
Hi. [haɪ] Hallo. 5 **Say hi to everyone.** Grüß/t alle. 7
hid [hɪd] *siehe* **hide**
hidden ['hɪdn] *siehe* **hide**
hide [haɪd]**, hid, hidden** verstecken; sich verstecken 7
high [haɪ] hoch 6
high school ['haɪ skuːl] *(AE) Schule für 14- bis 18-Jährige* 9: 2 (24/25)
Highlands *(pl)* ['haɪləndz] schottisches Hochland *(der bergige Norden Schottlands)* 6
highlight ['haɪlaɪt]**:**
1. hervorheben, unterstreichen 7
2. Höhepunkt; Schlaglicht 7
highway ['haɪweɪ] *(AE)* Fernstraße *(oft mit vier oder mehr Spuren)* 6
hike [haɪk]**:**
1. wandern 6
2. Wanderung 8
hiking ['haɪkɪŋ] *(das)* Wandern 6
hill [hɪl] Hügel 6
him [hɪm] ihm, ihn 5
himself [hɪm'self] er selbst, ihn/ihm/sich selbst 6
Hindi ['hɪndi] Hindi 9: 4 (58/59)
Hindu ['hɪndu] Hindu 9: 4 (58/59)
Hinduism ['hɪnduːɪzəm] Hinduismus 9: 4 (58/59)
hire ['haɪə]**:**
1. mieten, leihen; (Person:) einstellen 9: 4 (67)
2. Verleih, Vermietung 9: 4 (67)
his [hɪz]**:**
1. sein/e *(zu „he")* 5
2. seiner, seine, seins *(zu „he")* 6
Hispanic [hɪ'spænɪk] hispanisch *(lateinamerikanischer Herkunft)* 6
history ['hɪstri] Geschichte 5
hit [hɪt]**, hit, hit:**
1. schlagen 5
2. stoßen gegen, zusammenstoßen mit; treffen auf 5
3. *(Sturm)* aufziehen, treffen (auf) 8
hold [həʊld]**, held, held** halten 5 **hold hands** Händchen halten 6 **hold onto sth.** sich an etwas festhalten; etwas festhalten 8 **hold out** *(jm. etwas)* hinhalten 6
hole [həʊl] Loch 6
holiday ['hɒlədeɪ] Urlaub 5 **holidays** Ferien 5 **on holiday** im/in den Urlaub 5
holy ['həʊli] heilig 7
home [həʊm]**:**
1. Heim, Zuhause 5
home to (sb./sth.) js. Heimat, Heimat einer Sache 8 **at home** zu Hause, daheim 5 **dogs' home** Hundeheim 6
2. nach Hause 5
come home nach Hause kommen 5
home-made [həʊm'meɪd] hausgemacht, selbstgemacht 6
homeless ['həʊmləs] obdachlos 6

homelessness ['həʊmləsnəs] Obdachlosigkeit 8
homesick ['həʊmsɪk]: **be/feel homesick** Heimweh haben 7
hometown [həʊm'taʊn] Heimatstadt 8
homework ['həʊmwɜːk] Hausaufgabe(n) 5 **do your homework** Hausaufgaben machen 5 **What's for homework?** Was haben wir als Hausaufgabe(n) auf? 6
honest ['ɒnɪst] ehrlich 9: 2 (28)
honesty ['ɒnəsti] Ehrlichkeit 9: 2 (28)
hood [hʊd] Kapuze 6
hope [həʊp]:
1. hoffen 6
2. Hoffnung 7
hopeful ['həʊpfl] zuversichtlich, hoffnungsvoll 7
hopeless ['həʊpləs] hoffnungslos 6
horn [hɔːn] Horn; Hupe *(Auto)* 8
horoscope ['hɒrəskəʊp] Horoskop 9: 4 (65)
horrible ['hɒrəbl] schrecklich 5
horror ['hɒrə] Horror 6
horse [hɔːs] Pferd 5 **ride a horse** ein Pferd reiten 5
horse riding ['hɔːs raɪdɪŋ] *(das)* Reiten, Reitsport 5
hospital ['hɒspɪtl] Krankenhaus 5
host [həʊst] Gastgeber/in 9: 2 (26)
host family ['həʊst fæməli] Gastfamilie 9: 2 (26)
hostel ['hɒstl] Wohnheim 7
hot [hɒt] heiß, warm 5
hot chocolate [hɒt 'tʃɒklət] Kakao, heiße (Trink-)Schokolade 5
hotel [həʊ'tel] Hotel 5
hour ['aʊə] Stunde 5 **(working) hours** *(pl)* Arbeitszeit(en) 9: 2 (31) **work long hours** lange arbeiten, Überstunden machen 9: 2 (31)
house [haʊs] Haus 5
household ['haʊshəʊld] Haushalt; Haushalts- 8
how [haʊ] wie 5 **How are you?** Wie geht's? / Wie geht es dir/euch/Ihnen? 5 **How much is/are ...?** Was (Wie viel) kostet/kosten ...? 5 **how to do sth.** wie man etwas macht 7 **°How are you going?** *(AE)* Wie geht's? / Wie geht es dir/euch/Ihnen?
however [haʊ'evə] allerdings, jedoch 7
huddle ['hʌdl] sich (zusammen) drängen 8
huge [hjuːdʒ] riesig, Riesen- 8
human ['hjuːmən]:
1. Mensch 9: 2 (35)
2. menschlich 9: 2 (35)
human rights *(pl)* [hjuːmən 'raɪts] Menschenrechte 9: 2 (35)
human waste ['hjuːmən weɪst] menschliche Fäkalien 9: 4 (60)
hundred ['hʌndrəd]: **a hundred** (ein)hundert 5
hung [hʌŋ] *siehe* **hang**
hungry ['hʌŋgri] hungrig 5
hunt [hʌnt]:
1. Jagd 7
2. jagen 7
hunter ['hʌntə] Jäger/in 9: 1 (13)
hurricane ['hʌrɪkən] Hurrikan, Orkan 8
hurt [hɜːt]:
1. Schmerz; Kränkung 9: 1 (10)
2. hurt, hurt, hurt verletzen; wehtun 5
be hurt verletzt sein 6 **get hurt** sich verletzen 6
husband ['hʌzbənd] Ehemann 7
hut [hʌt] Hütte 9: 1 (16)
hyphen ['haɪfn] Bindestrich, Trennstrich 7

I

I [aɪ] ich 5 **I'm (= I am)** ich bin 5
ice [aɪs] Eis *(gefrorenes Wasser)* 6
ice cream [aɪs 'kriːm] (Speise-)Eis 5
idea [aɪ'dɪə] Idee 5
identify [aɪ'dentɪfaɪ] erkennen; (sich) identifizieren 9: 1 (10) **identify yourself (as)** sich zu erkennen geben (als) 9: 1 (10)
identity [aɪ'dentəti] Identität 7
idiom ['ɪdiəm] Redewendung 9: 1 (20)
if [ɪf]:
1. wenn, falls 6
What if? Was wäre, wenn? 6
2. ob 7
ignorance (of/about sth.) ['ɪgnərəns] Unwissenheit (über etwas), Unkenntnis (einer Sache), Ignoranz 9: 1 (17)
ignore [ɪg'nɔː] nicht beachten, ignorieren 9: 1 (17)
ill [ɪl] krank 6
illegal [ɪ'liːgl]:
1. illegal, verboten 9: 1 (16)
2. Illegale/r 9: 1 (16)
illiteracy [ɪ'lɪtərəsi] Analphabetismus 9: 4 (58/59)
illiterate [ɪ'lɪtərət]: **be illiterate** nicht lesen und schreiben können, Analphabet/in sein 9: 4 (58/59)
illness ['ɪlnəs] Krankheit 7
image ['ɪmɪdʒ] Bild, Abbildung 9: 4 (58/59)
imagine sth. [ɪ'mædʒɪn] sich etwas vorstellen 7
immediate [ɪ'miːdiət] sofortige/r/s 9: 1 (14)
immediately [ɪ'miːdiətli] sofort, umgehend, unmittelbar 9: 1 (14)
immigrant ['ɪmɪgrənt] Einwanderer, Einwanderin 7
immigrate ['ɪmɪgreɪt] einwandern, immigrieren 7
immigration [ɪmɪ'greɪʃn] Einwanderung 7
impatient [ɪm'peɪʃnt] ungeduldig 7
important [ɪm'pɔːtnt] wichtig 5
impossible [ɪm'pɒsəbl] unmöglich 9: 3 (51)
impress [ɪm'pres] beeindrucken 9: 4 (70)
impression [ɪm'preʃn] Eindruck 8
improve [ɪm'pruːv] verbessern; sich verbessern 8
improvement [ɪm'pruːvmənt] Besserung, Verbesserung 8
in [ɪn] in 5 **in 1540** (im Jahre) 1540 5 **in English** auf Englisch 5 **in my picture/photo** auf meinem Bild/Foto 5 **in the country** auf dem Land 5 **in the end** schließlich, zum Schluss 9: 4 (65) **in the evening** abends, am Abend 5 **in the field** auf der Weide 6 **in the morning** morgens, am Morgen 5 **in town** in der Stadt 5 **five in 100** fünf von 100 8
inappropriate [ɪnə'prəʊpriət] unangemessen, unpassend, ungeeignet 9: 3 (44)
inch [ɪntʃ] Zoll *(Längenmaß = 2,54 cm)* 8
include [ɪn'kluːd] (mit) einschließen 8
including [ɪn'kluːdɪŋ] einschließlich, inklusive 8
increase ['ɪŋkriːs] Anstieg, Wachstum, Zunahme 8
increase (by) [ɪn'kriːs] steigern, (sich) erhöhen; steigen, zunehmen (um) 8
independence (from) [ɪndɪ'pendəns] Unabhängigkeit (von) 7
Independence Day [ɪndɪ'pendəns deɪ] *(US-amerikanischer)* Unabhängigkeitstag *(4. Juli)* 6
independent (of/from) [ɪndɪ'pendənt] unabhängig (von) 7

indigenous (to) [ɪn'dɪdʒənəs] einheimisch (in) 8 **indigenous people** Einheimische, Ureinwohner/innen 8
indignity [ɪn'dɪgnəti] Demütigung, Erniedrigung 9: 1 (10)
indirect [ɪndə'rekt] indirekt 9: 1 (18)
industry ['ɪndəstri] Industrie 8
inequality [ɪnɪ'kwɒləti] Ungleichheit 9: 4 (58/59)
infect [ɪn'fekt] infizieren; verseuchen 8
infection [ɪn'fekʃn] Infektion 8
inflict sth. on sb. [ɪn'flɪkt] jm. etwas zufügen, etwas bei jm. verursachen 9: 1 (10)
influence ['ɪnfluəns]:
1. beeinflussen 9: 3 (46)
2. Einfluss 9: 3 (46)
infographic [ɪnfə'græfɪk] Infografik 8
inform sb. (about/of) [ɪn'fɔːm] jn. informieren über 9: 2 (32)
informal [ɪn'fɔːml] informell, locker 9: 1 (15)
information [ɪnfə'meɪʃn] Information(en) 5
information technology (IT) [ɪnfə'meɪʃn teknɒlədʒi] IT (Informationstechnologie) 5
ingredient [ɪn'griːdiənt] Bestandteil, Inhaltsstoff; Zutat 9: 3 (54)
injure ['ɪndʒə] (sich) verletzen 8
injured ['ɪndʒəd] verletzt, verwundet 8
injury ['ɪndʒəri] Verletzung 8
injustice [ɪn'dʒʌstɪs] Ungerechtigkeit; Unrecht 8
insect ['ɪnsekt] Insekt 9: 1 (8/9)
insect repellent ['ɪnsekt rɪpelənt] Insektenschutzmittel 9: 1 (8/9)
inside [ɪn'saɪd] innen, auf der Innenseite 6
inside out [ɪnsaɪd 'aʊt] verkehrt herum, auf links *(Kleidung)* 7 **turn your T-shirt inside out** dein T-Shirt auf links ziehen 7
insignificant [ɪnsɪg'nɪfɪkənt] unbedeutend, geringfügig 9: 4 (71)
inspector [ɪn'spektə] Inspektor/in, Kontrolleur/in 9: 2 (33)
inspire [ɪn'spaɪə] begeistern, inspirieren 8
inspiring [ɪn'spaɪərɪŋ] begeisternd, inspirierend 8
install [ɪn'stɔːl] installieren, einbauen 8
installation [ɪnstə'leɪʃn] Installation *(Kunst)* 8
instead [ɪn'sted] stattdessen 8
instead of [ɪn'sted əv] anstatt, anstelle von 8
instruction [ɪn'strʌkʃn] Anweisung 7
instrument ['ɪnstrəmənt] Instrument 5
insurance [ɪn'ʃʊərəns] Versicherung 8 **proof of insurance** Versicherungsnachweis 8 **take out insurance** Versicherungen / eine Versicherung abschließen 8
integrate ['ɪntɪgreɪt] (sich) integrieren 9: 1 (10)
interest (in) ['ɪntrəst] Interesse (an) 7
interested (in) ['ɪntrəstɪd] interessiert (an) 8
interesting ['ɪntrəstɪŋ] interessant 5
intern ['ɪntɜːn] Praktikant/in 9: 2 (26)
international [ɪntə'næʃnəl] international 6
internship ['ɪntɜːnʃɪp] Praktikum 9: 2 (26)
interpret [ɪn'tɜːprɪt]:
1. interpretieren 8
°2. dolmetschen *(gesprochenen Text mündlich wiedergeben)*
interrupt [ɪntə'rʌpt] unterbrechen 9: 4 (64)
interruption [ɪntə'rʌpʃn] Unterbrechung 9: 4 (64)
interview ['ɪntəvjuː]:
1. (= job interview) Vorstellungsgespräch 9: 2 (32)
2. befragen, interviewen; ein Vorstellungsgespräch führen 9: 2 (32)
into ['ɪntu], ['ɪntə] in (... hinein) 5
introduce sb. to sb./sth. [ɪntrə'djuːs] jm. jn./etwas vorstellen, jn. mit jm./etwas bekanntmachen 7
introduction [ɪntrə'dʌkʃn] Einleitung; Vorstellung *(Bekanntmachen)* 7
introductory [ɪntrə'dʌktəri] einführend, einleitend 9: 2 (31)
invade [ɪn'veɪd] einmarschieren (in), eindringen (in) 7
invent [ɪn'vent] erfinden 8
invention [ɪn'venʃn] Erfindung 8
inventor [ɪn'ventə] Erfinder/in 8
invitation (to) [ɪnvɪ'teɪʃn] Einladung (zu, nach) 5
invite (to) [ɪn'vaɪt] einladen (zu, nach) 5
ironic [aɪ'rɒnɪk] ironisch 9: 3 (43)
irony ['aɪrəni] Ironie 9: 3 (43)
irregular [ɪ'regjələ] unregelmäßig; ungleichmäßig 9: 1 (12)
is [ɪz] *(er/sie/es)* ist 5 **The shirt is £2.** Das Hemd kostet 2 Pfund. 5
island ['aɪlənd] Insel 6
issue ['ɪʃuː]:
1. Thema, Anliegen; Problem, (Streit-)Frage 9: 3 (43)
2. ausgeben, ausstellen *(z. B. Dokument)* 8
3. Ausgabe, Ausstellung *(z. B. Dokument)* 8
date of issue Ausstellungsdatum, Ausgabedatum *(z. B. Dokument)* 8
issue date ['ɪʃuː deɪt] Ausstellungsdatum, Ausgabedatum *(z. B. Dokument)* 8
IT (= information technology) [aɪ 'tiː] IT (Informationstechnologie) 5
it [ɪt] er, sie, es 5
item ['aɪtəm] Artikel, Gegenstand, Punkt *(auf einer Liste)* 9: 4 (71) **news item** Nachrichtenmeldung, Pressemeldung 9: 4 (71)
its [ɪts] sein/seine, ihr/ihre *(besitzanzeigend: Dinge und Tiere)* 5
itself [ɪt'self] es/sich selbst (zu *„it"*) 6

J

jacket ['dʒækɪt] Jacke, Jackett 6
January ['dʒænjuəri] Januar 5
jar [dʒɑː] Glasgefäß 8
jealous (of) ['dʒeləs] neidisch (auf); eifersüchtig 9: 3 (45)
jellyfish ['dʒelifɪʃ], *pl* **jellyfish** Qualle 9: 1 (14)
Jew [dʒuː] Jude/Jüdin 9: 1 (13)
jewellery ['dʒuːəlri] Schmuck 8
Jewish ['dʒuːɪʃ] jüdisch 9: 1 (13)
job advertisement [dʒɒb əd'vɜːtɪsmənt] *(kurz auch:* job advert*)* Stellenanzeige 9: 2 (24/25)
job interview ['dʒɒb ɪntəvjuː] Vorstellungsgespräch 9: 2 (32)
jobless ['dʒɒbləs] arbeitslos 6
join a club [dʒɔɪn] in einen Klub eintreten 7
joke [dʒəʊk] Witz, Scherz 6
journey ['dʒɜːni] Reise 5
judge [dʒʌdʒ]:
1. (be)urteilen 7
2. Richter/in 7
judo ['dʒuːdəʊ] Judo 9: 1 (20)
juice [dʒuːs] Saft 5
juicy ['dʒuːsi] saftig 6
July [dʒu'laɪ] Juli 5

jump [dʒʌmp] springen 7 **jump at sth.** bei etwas sofort zugreifen, *(Gelegenheit)* sofort ergreifen 9: 2 (26)
June [dʒuːn] Juni 5
°jungle ['dʒʌŋgl] Dschungel
junior high (school) [dʒuːniə 'haɪ skuːl] *(AE) Schule für Kinder zwischen 12 und 14* 7
just [dʒʌst]:
1. nur, bloß; einfach 6
2. gerade (eben) 6
3. *(adj.)* gerecht 8
4. **just as many children** genauso viele Kinder 9: 3 (51) **just like ...** genau wie ... 9: 3 (51) **just the same** trotzdem 9: 2 (34)
justice ['dʒʌstɪs] Gerechtigkeit 8

K

kangaroo [kæŋgə'ruː] Känguru 9: 1 (8/9)
keep [kiːp], **kept, kept** halten; behalten 7 **keep (on) doing sth.** etwas immer wieder / immer weiter tun; etwas ständig tun 9: 4 (67) **keep in touch (with)** in Verbindung/Kontakt bleiben (mit) 9: 3 (44) **keep sth. out of the oceans** verhindern, dass etwas in die Ozeane gelangt 7 **keep up with** sich auf dem Laufenden halten über; Schritt halten mit 9: 3 (45)
keeper ['kiːpə] Wärter/in, Hüter/in, Bewahrer/in 8
kept [kept] *siehe* **keep**
key [kiː] Schlüssel 8
key card ['kiː kɑːd] Schlüsselkarte 8
key point [kiː 'pɔɪnt] Kernpunkt, wichtigster Punkt 8
keyword ['kiːwɜːd] Stichwort, Schlagwort 8
kick [kɪk]:
1. treten; *(Sport)* schießen 9: 1 (21)
2. Tritt, Stoß, Kick 9: 1 (21)
kid [kɪd] Kind, Jugendliche/r 5
kidney ['kɪdni] Niere 8
kilo(gram) ['kiːləʊ] Kilo(gramm) 8
kilometre (km) ['kɪləmiːtə] Kilometer 6
kind [kaɪnd] nett, freundlich 6
kind (of) [kaɪnd] Art, Sorte 7
king [kɪŋ] König 7
Kingdom ['kɪŋdəm]: **the United Kingdom (= the UK)** das Vereinigte Königreich 5
kiss [kɪs]:
1. (sich) küssen 8
2. Kuss 8
kitchen ['kɪtʃɪn] Küche 5
knead [niːd] kneten 7
knee [niː] Knie 8
kneel [niːl], **knelt, knelt** knien 7
knelt [nelt] *siehe* **kneel**
knew [njuː] *siehe* **know**
knife [naɪf], *pl* **knives** Messer 7
knit [nɪt] stricken 7
knives [naɪvz] *Plural von* **knife**
knock (at sth.) [nɒk] (an)klopfen (an etwas) 6
know [nəʊ], **knew, known** wissen; kennen 5 **you know** nämlich, weißt du 7
knowledge (of/about) ['nɒlɪdʒ] Wissen (von/über), Kenntnis(se) (von/in) 9: 3 (55)
known [nəʊn] *siehe* **know**
koala [kəʊ'ɑːlə] Koala(bär) 9: 1 (8/9)
Kurdish ['kɜːdɪʃ] Kurdisch 6

L

labour ['leɪbə] Arbeit; Arbeitskräfte 9: 4 (60)
labourer ['leɪbərə] Arbeiter/in 9: 4 (60)
lack [læk]:
1. **lack (of)** Mangel (an) 9: 3 (54) **for lack of** aus Mangel an 9: 3 (54)
2. **sb./sth. lacks sth.** jm./einer Sache fehlt/mangelt es an etwas 9: 3 (54)
ladder ['lædə] *(die)* Leiter 9: 3 (50)
lady ['leɪdi] Dame 6
lain [leɪn] *siehe* **lie**
lake [leɪk] (Binnen-)See 6
lame [leɪm] lahm, langweilig 7
lamp [læmp] Lampe 5
land [lænd]:
1. Land *(Grund und Boden)* 7
2. landen 7
landing ['lændɪŋ] Landung *(Flugzeug)* 9: 3 (49)
landmark ['lændmɑːk] Wahrzeichen 9: 4 (70)
landscape ['lændskeɪp] Landschaft; Landschaftsbild 8
°landslide ['lændslaɪd] Erdrutsch
language ['læŋgwɪdʒ] Sprache 5 **foreign language** Fremdsprache 9: 2 (30)
large [lɑːdʒ] groß 9: 2 (33)
lasso [læ'suː], *pl* **lassos** *or* **lassoes** Lasso 7
last [lɑːst] letzte(r, s) 5 **last week** letzte/vorige Woche 5 **at last** schließlich, endlich 7
last (for) [lɑːst] (an)dauern; halten *(von Bestand sein)* 8
last name ['lɑːst neɪm] Nachname, Familienname 7
late [leɪt] spät 5 **He's in his late thirties.** Er ist Ende dreißig. 8 **I'm late.** Ich habe mich verspätet. 5
late-night shopping [leɪt 'naɪt] Einkaufen am späten Abend 6
later ['leɪtə] später 5
latest ['leɪtɪst] neueste/r/s, aktuelle/r/s 8
Latino [læ'tiːnəʊ] *Einwohner/in der USA mit lateinamerikanischen Vorfahren* 8
laugh [lɑːf] lachen 6
law [lɔː] Gesetz; Jura *(Studium)* 8 **by law** per Gesetz, gesetzlich 8
lawyer ['lɔːjə] (Rechts-)Anwalt/Anwältin 8
lay [leɪ] *siehe* **lie**
lead [liːd], **led, led** führen, leiten 8
leader ['liːdə] Leiter/in, (An-)Führer/in 8
leaf [liːf], *pl* **leaves** Blatt *(Pflanze)* 8
leaflet ['liːflət] Faltblatt, Informationsblatt 6
league [liːg] Liga 6
lean [liːn] lehnen 7
learn [lɜːn] lernen 5
least [liːst]: **at least** wenigstens, zumindest 8
leather ['leðə] Leder 7
leave [liːv], **left, left** abfahren; (weg)gehen; *(jemanden)* verlassen 5 **leave out** weglassen 7 **leave sb./sth. behind** etwas/jn. zurücklassen, etwas hinter sich lassen 9: 1 (10) **leave sth.** etwas (zurück)lassen 5 **leave sth. at home** etwas zu Hause lassen 5
leaves [liːvz] *Plural von* **leaf**
led [led] *siehe* **lead**
left [left] *siehe* **leave**
left [left] links; nach links 5 **on the left** links, auf der linken Seite 5
leg [leg] Bein 6
legal ['liːgl] legal 9: 1 (16)
legend ['ledʒənd] Legende, Sage 8
lemon ['lemən] Zitrone 9: 3 (54)
lemonade [lemə'neɪd] Limonade 6
lend [lend], **lent, lent** leihen, verleihen 6
length [leŋθ] Länge; Dauer 7
lent [lent] *siehe* **lend**
°lentil ['lentl] Linse *(Hülsenfrucht)*
lesbian ['lezbiən]:
1. lesbisch 8
2. Lesbe 8
less [les] weniger 8

lesson ['lesn] (Unterrichts-)Stunde 5
let [let], **let, let** lassen 9: 2 (27) **Let's go!** Auf geht's! / Dann mal los! 5
letter ['letə]:
1. Brief 6
2. Buchstabe 6
level ['levl] Grad, Stufe; Niveau, Ebene 8 **at professional level** auf Profi-Ebene 8
liberty ['lɪbəti] Freiheit 8
library ['laɪbrəri] Bücherei, Bibliothek 5
licence ['laɪsns] Genehmigung, Lizenz 8 **driving licence** Führerschein 8
lie [laɪ]:
1. Lüge 7
tell a lie/lies lügen 7
2. lie (to sb.) (jn. an)lügen 7
lie [laɪ], **lay, lain** liegen 8
life [laɪf], *pl* **lives** *(das)* Leben 5 **in real life** im echten Leben 7 **way of life** Lebensweise 8
life expectancy ['laɪf ɪkspektənsi] Lebenserwartung 9: 1 (11)
life-saving ['laɪf seɪvɪŋ] Rettungsschwimmen 9: 2 (31)
lifeguard ['laɪfgɑːd] Rettungsschwimmer/in; Bademeister/in 9: 2 (31)
lift [lɪft]:
1. Lift *(Aufzug)* 6
2. heben, hochheben 8
light [laɪt]:
1. hell 7
2. leicht 7
light [laɪt]:
1. Licht 7
lights out Licht aus 7
2. light, lit, lit anzünden 9: 2 (34)
light a fire (ein) Feuer machen 9: 2 (34) **light up** aufleuchten 9: 2 (34)
light bulb ['laɪt bʌlb] Glühbirne 8
like [laɪk] mögen 5 **I'd (= I would) like ...** Ich hätte gern ... / Ich möchte ... 5 **I'd (= I would) like to talk about ...** Ich würde gern über ... sprechen. 5 **I'd like you to be ...** Ich möchte, dass ihr ... seid. 6 **they like to play ...** sie spielen gern ... 5
like [laɪk] wie 5 **like this** so, auf diese Art 7 **-like** -ähnlich 9: 1 (16) **prison-like conditions** gefängnisähnliche Zustände 9: 1 (16) **something like that** so etwas 8 **What's ... like?** Wie ist ...? / Wie sieht ... aus? 5
likely ['laɪkli] wahrscheinlich 7
line [laɪn]:
1. Reihe 5
2. Telefonanschluss; Telefonleitung 7
The line went dead. Die (Telefon-)Leitung war tot. 7
3. U-Bahn-Linie 6
4. Zeile 5
5. power line Stromleitung 6
line chart ['laɪn tʃɑːt] Liniendiagramm 8
linen ['lɪnɪn] Leinen; Wäsche 7
°lingo ['lɪŋgəʊ] *(infml)* Sprache *(kurz für „language")*
link [lɪŋk]:
1. Verbindung; Link 7
2. link (to/with) verbinden (mit) 7
lion ['laɪən] Löwe 6
lip [lɪp] Lippe 8
°lip-sync ['lɪp sɪŋk] die Lippen synchron bewegen
list [lɪst]:
1. Liste 6
°2. auflisten, aufzählen
listen ['lɪsn]: **listen (to)** (sich etwas) anhören; zuhören 5 **listen for sth.** auf etwas horchen, *(beim Zuhören)* auf etwas achten 7
listener ['lɪsənə] Zuhörer/in 6
lit [lɪt] *siehe* **light**
literacy ['lɪtərəsi] *Fähigkeit, lesen und schreiben zu können* 9: 4 (58/59)
literate ['lɪtərət]: **be literate** lesen und schreiben können 9: 4 (58/59)
litre ['liːtə] Liter 8
litter ['lɪtə] Abfall 6
litter bin ['lɪtə bɪn] Mülleimer 6
little ['lɪtl]:
1. klein 5
2. a little ein wenig, ein bisschen 7
live [lɪv] leben, wohnen 5 **live on sth.** sich von etwas ernähren, von etwas leben 9: 4 (66)
lives [laɪvz] *Plural von* **life**
living ['lɪvɪŋ]: **(sustainable) living** (nachhaltige) Lebensweise 8
living expenses *(pl)* ['lɪvɪŋ ɪkspensɪz] Lebenshaltungskosten 9: 2 (24/25)
living room ['lɪvɪŋ ruːm] Wohnzimmer 5
load [ləʊd] (be)laden 6 **load the dishwasher** die Spülmaschine einräumen 7
loan [ləʊn] Darlehen, Kredit 9: 2 (24/25) **take out a loan** ein Darlehen / einen Kredit aufnehmen 9: 2 (24/25)
local ['ləʊkl] einheimisch, am/vom Ort 8
loch [lɒx] *schottisches Wort für* **lake** 6
lock [lɒk]:
1. abschließen *(z. B. Tür)* 8
2. Schloss *(Türschloss)* 8
locker ['lɒkə] Spind, Schließfach 5
log [lɒg]: **log off/out** (sich) /ausloggen 9: 3 (44) **log on/in(to)** (sich) einloggen 9: 3 (44)
logging ['lɒgɪŋ] Abholzung 8
logic ['lɒdʒɪk] Logik 9: 4 (65)
logical ['lɒdʒɪkl] logisch 9: 4 (65)
lonely ['ləʊnli] einsam 7
long [lɒŋ] lang 5 **as long as** solange 9: 1 (16)
long gun [lɒŋ 'gʌn] Gewehr 8
long shot ['lɒŋ ʃɒt] Totale *(Film)* 8
long-term [lɒŋ 'tɜːm] langfristig, Langzeit- 9: 1 (17)
look [lʊk]:
1. aussehen 5
2. sehen, schauen 5
look after sich kümmern um; aufpassen auf 6 **look at sth.** sich etwas anschauen 5 **look for** suchen; Ausschau halten nach 5 **look forward to doing sth.** sich darauf freuen, etwas zu tun 7 **look forward to sth.** sich auf etwas freuen 7
Lord Mayor [lɔːd 'meə] Oberbürgermeister/in 9: 1 (17)
lorry ['lɒri] Lastwagen, LKW 7
lose [luːz], **lost, lost** verlieren 6 **lose touch (with)** den Kontakt verlieren (zu) 9: 3 (44)
loser ['luːzə] Verlierer/in 9: 1 (19)
lost [lɒst] *siehe* **lose**
lot [lɒt]: **lots (of)** viel/e 5 **a lot (of)** viel/e; sehr 5
loud [laʊd] laut 7
love [lʌv]:
1. lieben, sehr mögen 5
love to do sth. / love doing sth. etwas sehr gern tun 5
2. Liebe 6
Love ... Liebe Grüße, ... *(Briefschluss)* 5 **Lots of love ...** Alles Liebe / Liebe Grüße *(Briefschluss)* 8
lover ['lʌvə]: **music lover** Musikliebhaber/in 9: 3 (53)
low [ləʊ] niedrig, tief 8 **low in sth.** arm an etwas *(z. B. Nahrungsmittel)* 9: 4 (71)
luck [lʌk]: **Good luck.** Viel Glück! 9: 2 (29)

luckily ['lʌkɪli] glücklicherweise 9: 2 (29)
lucky ['lʌki] Glücks-, glücklich 5
ludo ['lu:dəʊ] Mensch ärgere dich nicht *(Spiel)* 7
luggage ['lʌgɪdʒ] Gepäck 6
lunch [lʌntʃ] Mittagessen 5 **have lunch** (zu) Mittag essen 5 **What's for lunch?** Was gibt es zum Mittagessen? 5
°lunchtime ['lʌntʃtaɪm] Mittagszeit
luxurious [lʌg'ʒʊəriəs] luxuriös 9: 3 (54)
luxury ['lʌkʃəri] Luxus 9: 3 (54)
lyrics *(pl)* ['lɪrɪks] Liedtext 8

M

macaroni [mækə'rəʊni] Makkaroni 7
machine [mə'ʃi:n] Automat, Maschine 6
madam ['mædəm]: **Dear Sir or Madam** Sehr geehrte Damen und Herren 8
made [meɪd] *siehe* **make** **... is made with nuts.** ... besteht (zum Teil) aus Nüssen. / ... enthält Nüsse. 8 **be made of** bestehen aus, (gemacht) sein aus 8
mag [mæg] *(infml)* Zeitschrift 8
magazine [mægə'zi:n] Zeitschrift 5
magic ['mædʒɪk]:
1. magisch 7
2. Zauberei, Magie 7
by magic durch Zauberei 7
magic trick [mædʒɪk 'trɪk] Zaubertrick 8
main [meɪn] Haupt-, wichtigste(r, s) 7
main course [meɪn 'kɔ:s] Hauptgericht 6
majority [mə'dʒɒrəti] Mehrheit, Mehrzahl 9: 4 (61)
make [meɪk], **made, made** machen, herstellen 5 **make (money)** (Geld) verdienen 6 **make a difference** etwas bewirken, etwas ausmachen 5 **make an excuse** sich entschuldigen, eine Entschuldigung vorbringen 8 **make friends** Freunde finden 7 **make sb. do sth.** jn. dazu bringen, etwas zu tun 7 **make sth. / it** etwas / es schaffen, (mit etwas) Erfolg haben 8 **make sure that ...** sicherstellen, dass ...; dafür sorgen, dass ... 7
makeup ['meɪkʌp] Make-up 8
male [meɪl] männlich; Mann 7

man [mæn], *pl* **men** Mann 5
manage (to do sth.) ['mænɪdʒ] (es) schaffen (etwas zu tun) 7
manatee ['mænəti:] Seekuh 8
manicure ['mænɪkjʊə]:
1. Maniküre *(Handpflege)* 8
2. maniküren 9: 4 (63)
many ['meni] viele 5 **how many?** wie viele? 5
map [mæp] Landkarte, Stadtplan 6
maple ['meɪpl] Ahorn 8
maple leaf ['meɪpl li:f] Ahornblatt 8
March [mɑ:tʃ] März 5
march [mɑ:tʃ]:
1. Marsch 8
2. marschieren 8
Mardi Gras [mɑ:di 'grɑ:] Faschingsdienstag *(auch: die Karnevalsfeiern in New Orleans)* 8
mark [mɑ:k]:
1. Markierung; Zeichen 9: 1 (13)
2. (Schul-)Note, Zensur 9: 2 (33)
3. kennzeichnen, markieren 9: 1 (13)
market ['mɑ:kɪt] Markt 5
marmot ['mɑ:mət] Murmeltier 8
marriage ['mærɪdʒ] Hochzeit, Ehe 9: 4 (60)
married (to) ['mærid] verheiratet (mit) 9: 4 (60) **get married to sb.** jn. heiraten 9: 4 (60)
marry ['mæri] heiraten 7
mask [mɑ:sk] Maske 7
mass [mæs] Masse(n-) 8
massage ['mæsɑ:ʒ]:
1. Massage 9: 4 (63)
2. massieren 9: 4 (63)
match [mætʃ]:
1. Gegenstück, (zusammenpassendes) Paar 9: 4 (65)
be a good match gut zusammenpassen 9: 4 (65)
2. **match (sth.)** zueinander passen; passen zu (etwas), übereinstimmen mit (etwas); (passend) zusammenfügen 9: 4 (65)
°match with/to zuordnen
match [mætʃ] Spiel, Wettkampf 6
°matchmaker ['mætʃmeɪkə] Heiratsvermittler/in
mate [meɪt] Freund/in, Kumpel 9: 1 (15) **a mate of mine** ein/e Freund/in von mir 9: 1 (17)
material [mə'tɪəriəl] Stoff; Material 7
maths [mæθs] Mathe(matik) 5
matter ['mætə] von Bedeutung sein, wichtig sein 8 **It doesn't matter.** Es/Das ist egal. 8
maximum (= max) ['mæksɪməm] Höchst-, maximal; Maximum 8

May [meɪ] Mai 5
may [meɪ]:
1. dürfen 5
May I ...? Darf ich ...? 5
2. **accidents may happen ...** Unfälle passieren vielleicht; Unfälle können passieren 8
maybe ['meɪbi] vielleicht 6
mayor [meə] Bürgermeister/in 8
me [mi:] mich; mir 5 **It's me.** Ich bin's. 5
meal [mi:l] Mahlzeit, Essen 5
mean [mi:n], **meant, meant** bedeuten; sagen wollen 6
meaning ['mi:nɪŋ] Bedeutung 7
meant [ment] *siehe* **mean**
measure ['meʒə] messen 8
measurement ['meʒəmənt] Abmessung, Maß(einheit) 8
meat [mi:t] Fleisch 5
meatball ['mi:tbɔ:l] Fleischbällchen, Frikadelle 6
mechanical [mɪ'kænɪkl] mechanisch, Maschinen- 9: 2 (33)
medal ['medl] Medaille 8
media ['mi:diə] Medien 6
mediate ['mi:dieɪt] vermitteln *(inhaltlich wiedergeben)* 8
mediation [mi:di'eɪʃn] Vermittlung, Sprachmittlung 8
medical ['medɪkl] ärztlich, medizinisch; gesundheitlich 9: 4 (71)
medical insurance [medɪkl ɪn'ʃʊərəns] Krankenversicherung 9: 4 (71)
medicine *(no pl)* ['medsɪn] Medizin; Medikament(e) 6
medium ['mi:diəm] mittel(groß); mittlere(r, s) 8
medium shot ['mi:diəm ʃɒt] Halbtotale *(Film)* 8
medium-term [mi:diəm 'tɜ:m] mittelfristig 9: 1 (17)
meet [mi:t], **met, met** kennenlernen; (sich) treffen 5 **Nice to meet you.** Freut mich, dich/euch/Sie kennenzulernen. 5
melt [melt] (ab)schmelzen 8
melting pot ['meltɪŋ pɒt] Schmelztiegel 8
member ['membə] Mitglied 8
membership ['membəʃɪp] Mitgliedschaft 9: 3 (44)
meme [mi:m] Internet-Mem, Internetphänomen 7
memorial (to sb./sth.) [mə'mɔ:riəl] Denkmal (für jn./etwas), Gedenkstätte 7
Memorial Day [mə'mɔ:riəl deɪ] Gedenktag *(zur Erinnerung an Kriegsgefallene und -opfer)* 6
men [men] *Plural von* **man**

mention ['menʃn] erwähnen 8
mentor ['mentə]**:**
1. Mentor/in *(Ratgeber/in)* 7
2. betreuen *(als Mentor/in)* 7
menu ['menjuː] Speisekarte 5
message ['mesɪdʒ]**:**
1. Nachricht, Mitteilung 5
message in a bottle Flaschenpost 6
2. message sb. jm. eine *(elektronische)* Nachricht schicken 9: 3 (45)
met [met] *siehe* **meet**
metal ['metl] Metall 7
metre ['miːtə] Meter 6
mice [maɪs] *Plural von* **mouse**
microphone ['maɪkrəfəʊn] Mikrofon 8
mid- [mɪd]**: He's in his mid-thirties.** Er ist Mitte dreißig. 8
middle ['mɪdl] Mitte 5 **in the middle** in der Mitte 5
middle class [mɪdl 'klɑːs] Mittelstand, Mittelschicht 9: 4 (58/59)
Midwest [mɪd'west] Mittlerer Westen *(der USA)* 8
might [maɪt]**: you might find ...** du könntest ... finden, vielleicht findest du ... 7
migrate [maɪ'greɪt] (aus-/ab-)wandern, ziehen 8
migration [maɪ'greɪʃn] Migration, Zu-/Aus-/Abwanderung 8
mile [maɪl] Meile *(ca. 1,6 km)* 8
milk [mɪlk] Milch 5
mill [mɪl] Mühle 9: 3 (50)
million ['mɪljən] Million 6
mime [maɪm] vorspielen, pantomimisch darstellen 7
°**minaret** [mɪnə'ret] Minarett
mind [maɪnd]**: Mind the gap ...** Achten Sie auf den Abstand ... 6 **I don't mind doing sth.** Es macht mir nichts aus, etwas zu tun. 6 **Never mind him.** Kümmer dich nicht um ihn. / Er braucht dich nicht zu interessieren. 5 **Never mind.** (Das) macht nichts. / Nicht (so) schlimm. 5
mind [maɪnd] Geist, Verstand; Gedanken; Kopf *(im übertragenen Sinn)* 8 **change your mind** seine Meinung ändern 7
mind map ['maɪnd mæp] Gedankenkarte, Wörternetz, Mindmap 5
mine [maɪn] meine, meiner, meins 6 **a mate of mine** ein/e Freund/in von mir 9: 1 (17)
mine [maɪn]**:**
1. Bergwerk, Mine 8
2. mine sth. etwas abbauen, fördern *(z. B. Bergbau)* 8
minimum ['mɪnɪməm] Mindest-, minimal; Minimum 8
minimum wage [mɪnɪməm 'weɪdʒ] Mindestlohn 9: 4 (71)
minority [maɪ'nɒrəti] Minderheit 9: 4 (61)
mint [mɪnt] (Pfeffer-)Minze 9: 4 (71)
minus ['maɪnəs] minus 8
minute ['mɪnɪt] Minute 5 **Wait a minute.** Warte mal. / Einen Moment. 5
miracle ['mɪrəkl] Wunder 9: 3 (52)
mirror ['mɪrə] Spiegel 7
miserable ['mɪzrəbl] erbärmlich, jämmerlich, trostlos 9: 4 (71)
miss [mɪs]**:**
1. vermissen 6
miss doing sth. vermissen, etwas zu tun 6
2. auslassen; verpassen 6
mix [mɪks] (ver)mischen 5
mobile (phone) [məʊbaɪl 'fəʊn] Handy 5
mode [məʊd] Modus; Art 9: 3 (49)
model ['mɒdl] (Foto-)Modell 5
modern ['mɒdn] modern 6
mom [mɒm] *(AE)* Mama, Mutti 5
moment ['məʊmənt] Moment 5 **at the moment** im Moment, zurzeit 5 **Just a moment.** Einen Moment. / Moment mal. 8
Monday ['mʌndeɪ], ['mʌndi] Montag 5
money ['mʌni] Geld 5 **pocket money** Taschengeld 8
monk [mʌŋk] Mönch 6
°**monsoon** [mɒn'suːn] Regenzeit; Monsunregen
monster ['mɒnstə] Monster, Ungeheuer 6
month [mʌnθ] Monat 5
monument ['mɒnjumənt] Monument, Denkmal 7
moor [mɔː] Heide(land); Moor 6
more [mɔː] mehr 6 **more than** mehr als 6
morning ['mɔːnɪŋ] Morgen 5 **Good morning.** Guten Morgen. 5 **in the morning** morgens, am Morgen 5
mosaic [məʊ'zeɪɪk] Mosaik 8
mosquito [məs'kiːtəʊ], *pl* **mosquitos** *or* **mosquitoes** Mücke 8
most [məʊst]**: the most ...** die meisten ...; am meisten 5
mostly ['məʊstli] hauptsächlich 8
mother ['mʌðə] Mutter 5
mother tongue ['mʌðə tʌŋ] Muttersprache 8
motivate ['məʊtɪveɪt] motivieren 9: 2 (36)
motivation [məʊtɪ'veɪʃn] Motivation 9: 2 (36)
mountain ['maʊntən] Berg 6
mouse [maʊs], *pl* **mice** Maus 5
mousetrap [maʊstræp] Mausefalle 8
mouth [maʊθ] Mund 6
mouthguard ['maʊθgɑːd] *(AE)* Mundschutz *(Sport)* 9: 1 (21)
move [muːv] (sich) bewegen; *(etwas)* verschieben, verlegen, versetzen 5 **move (to)** (um)ziehen (nach); *(Schule)* wechseln (auf/zu) 5
movement ['muːvmənt] Bewegung 7
movie ['muːvi] Film, Spielfilm 6
movie theater ['muːvi θɪətə] *(AE)* Kino 6
mow [məʊ] mähen 7
°**mozzie** ['mɒzi] *(Austr., infml)* Mücke *(kurz für „mosquito")*
Mr ... ['mɪstə] Herr ... 5
Mrs ... ['mɪsɪz] Frau ... *(Anrede für verheiratete Frauen)* 5
Ms ... [mɪz], [məz] Frau ... *(allgemeine Anrede für Frauen)* 5
much [mʌtʃ] viel 5 **How much is/are ...?** Was (Wie viel) kostet/kosten ...? 5 **How much?** Wie viel? 5
mud [mʌd] Schlamm, Matsch 8
multicultural [mʌlti'kʌltʃərəl] multikulturell 6
multinational [mʌlti'næʃnəl]**:**
1. multinational 9: 4 (60)
2. multinationaler Konzern, Multi 9: 4 (60)
multiplayer [mʌlti'pleɪə] Mehrspieler- 7
mum [mʌm] Mama, Mutti 5
°**mummy** ['mʌmi] Mutti, Mama
murder ['mɜːdə]**:**
1. ermorden 8
2. Mord 8
murderer ['mɜːdərə] Mörder/Mörderin 8
museum [mju'ziːəm] Museum 5
music ['mjuːzɪk] Musik 5
musical ['mjuːzɪkl] musikalisch 6
musician [mju'zɪʃn] Musiker/in 7
Muslim ['mʊzlɪm]**:**
1. muslimisch 9: 1 (13)
2. Muslim/Muslima 9: 1 (13)
must [mʌst]**:**
1. müssen 5
mustn't do nicht tun dürfen 7
2. a must *(infml)* ein Muss, eine Notwendigkeit 8
mustard ['mʌstəd] Senf 8

my [maɪ] mein/e 5
myself [maɪ'self] ich/mich/mir (selbst) 6

N

nail [neɪl] Nagel 9: 4 (63)
°**Namaste.** ['nʌməsteɪ] *unter Hindus verbreitete Grußformel und Grußgeste*
name [neɪm]:
1. Name 5
call sb. names jn. beschimpfen 7
first name Vorname 7 **last name** Nachname, Familienname 7
What's your name? Wie heißt du? 5
2. (be)nennen 8
name day ['neɪm deɪ] Namenstag 5
nasty ['nɑːsti] gemein, fies 8
nation ['neɪʃn] Nation 8 **First Nations** Erste Nationen *(indigene Völker Kanadas)* 8
national ['næʃnəl] national, National- 6
national day [næʃnəl 'deɪ] Nationalfeiertag 7
national park [næʃnəl 'pɑːk] Nationalpark 6
nationality [næʃə'næləti] Nationalität 6
native ['neɪtɪv] einheimisch, Heimat-; Einheimische/r 8
Native American [neɪtɪv ə'merɪkən]: amerikanische/r Ureinwohner/in; indianisch 8
native language [neɪtɪv 'læŋgwɪdʒ] Muttersprache 8
natural ['nætʃrəl] natürlich, Natur- 8
natural disaster [nætʃrəl dɪ'zɑːstə] Naturkatastrophe 8
nature ['neɪtʃə] (die) Natur 8
near [nɪə] nahe (bei), in der Nähe von 5
nearest ['nɪərəst]: **the nearest ...** der/die/das nächstgelegene ... 7
nearly ['nɪəli] fast 5
necessary ['nesəsəri] notwendig, nötig, erforderlich 8
need [niːd] brauchen, benötigen 5
need to do etwas tun müssen 6
needn't do nicht tun brauchen 7
negative ['negətɪv] negativ 7
neighbour ['neɪbə] Nachbar/in 5
neighbourhood ['neɪbəhʊd] Nachbarschaft, Gegend, Viertel 8
neighbourhood watch [neɪbəhʊd 'wɒtʃ] Nachbarschaftswache *(Bürger/innen, die in ihrer Nachbarschaft Kriminalität zu verhindern versuchen)* 8
neither ['naɪðə]: **neither ... nor ...** weder ... noch ... 8 **Neither do I.** Ich auch nicht. 9: 4 (64)
nervous ['nɜːvəs] nervös, aufgeregt 5
nervous system ['nɜːvəs sɪstəm] Nervensystem 9: 1 (14)
net [net] Netz *(Sport)* 7
netball ['netbɔːl] Korbball 5
network ['netwɜːk] Netz; Netzwerk; Wortnetz 8
neutral ['njuːtrəl] neutral 9: 4 (71)
never ['nevə] nie, niemals 5 **Never mind.** (Das) macht nichts. / Nicht (so) schlimm. 5
new [njuː] neu 5
news [njuːz] Nachrichten 6
news item ['njuːz aɪtəm] Nachrichtenmeldung, Pressemeldung 9: 4 (71)
newspaper ['njuːzpeɪpə] (Tages-)Zeitung 6
next [nekst] nächste(r, s) 5
Next ... Als Nächstes ... 7 **the next day/morning** am nächsten Tag/Morgen 6
next to ['nekst tə] neben 5
nice [naɪs] nett, schön 5
nickname ['nɪkneɪm] Spitzname 8
niece [niːs] Nichte 6
night [naɪt] Nacht 5 **at night** nachts, in der Nacht 5 **Good night.** Gute Nacht. 5 **that night** in jener Nacht 6
nine [naɪn] neun 5
no [nəʊ]:
1. nein 5
2. kein, keine; verboten 5
no one ['nəʊ wʌn] niemand 5
nobody ['nəʊbədi] niemand 5
nod [nɒd]:
1. **nod (of your head)** (Kopf-)Nicken 7
2. **nod (your head)** (mit dem Kopf) nicken 7
nod to sb. jm. zunicken 7
noise [nɔɪz] Geräusch; Lärm 5
noisy ['nɔɪzi] laut, voller Lärm 5
nominate ['nɒmɪneɪt] nominieren 8
none [nʌn] keine(r, s) 7
noodles *(pl)* [nuːdlz] Nudeln 5
nor [nɔː]: **Nor do I.** Ich auch nicht. 9: 4 (64) **neither ... nor ...** weder ... noch ... 8
normal ['nɔːml] normal 7
Norman ['nɔːmən] Normanne/Normannin; normannisch 7
north [nɔːθ] Norden; nördlich; Nord- 6
north-east [nɔːθ'iːst] Nordosten, nordöstlich 6
north-west [nɔːθ'west] Nordwesten, nordwestlich 6
northbound ['nɔːθbaʊnd] in Richtung Norden *(Zug, Bus)* 6
northern ['nɔːðən] Nord-, nördlich 7
nose [nəʊz] Nase 6
not [nɒt] nicht 5 **I'm not a boy.** Ich bin kein Junge. 5
note [nəʊt] Notiz; kurzer Brief 7
make a note/notes of sth. sich etwas notieren 8 **make notes** (sich) Notizen machen *(zur Vorbereitung)* 7 **take notes** (sich) Notizen machen *(beim Lesen oder Zuhören)* 7
notebook ['nəʊtbʊk] Notizbuch 7
nothing ['nʌθɪŋ] nichts 6
notice ['nəʊtɪs] (be)merken 7
notification [nəʊtɪfɪ'keɪʃn] Benachrichtigung, Mitteilung 7
November [nəʊ'vembə] November 5
now [naʊ] nun, jetzt 5
nowhere ['nəʊweə] nirgendwo(hin) 7
number ['nʌmbə] Zahl, Ziffer, Nummer 5 **number of** Anzahl (an) 6 **phone number** Telefonnummer 5
nurse [nɜːs] Krankenpfleger/in 6
nursery ['nɜːsəri] Kinderzimmer; Kinderkrippe 9: 1 (11)
nut [nʌt]:
1. Nuss 7
°2. Mutter *(für Schrauben)*

O

object ['ɒbdʒɪkt] Objekt, Gegenstand 7
occasion [ə'keɪʒn] Gelegenheit; Ereignis, Anlass 9: 2 (27)
occasional [ə'keɪʒənl] gelegentliche(r, s) 9: 2 (27)
occasionally [ə'keɪʒənəli] gelegentlich, ab und zu 9: 2 (27)
ocean ['əʊʃn] Ozean 6
o'clock [ə'klɒk]: **at 7 o'clock** um 7 Uhr 5
October [ɒk'təʊbə] Oktober 5
octopus ['ɒktəpəs], *pl* **octopuses** Oktopus, Tintenfisch 9: 1 (14)
°**blue-ringed octopus** blaugeringelte Krake

of [ɒv], [əv] von 5 **a cup of ...** eine Tasse ... 5 **the name of the school** der Name der Schule 5
of course [əv 'kɔːs] natürlich, selbstverständlich 7
off [ɒf]:
1. weg von; hinunter von 8
20% off (on) headphones 20% Preisnachlass auf Kopfhörer 9: 3 (49) **go off** klingeln *(Wecker)*; losgehen *(Alarm, Waffe)* 7 **keep sb. off the streets** jn. von der Straße fernhalten *(= verhindern, dass jd. auf der Straße lebt)* 8
take your eyes off sth. den Blick abwenden von etwas 8
2. be off aus sein *(ausgeschaltet)* 9: 2 (34)
off-peak [ɒf 'piːk] außerhalb der Stoßzeiten 6
offer ['ɒfə]:
1. (an)bieten 7
2. Angebot 7
officer ['ɒfɪsə] Beamter/Beamtin 8
official [ə'fɪʃl] offiziell 9: 3 (50)
official language [əfɪʃl 'læŋgwɪdʒ] Amtssprache 9: 3 (50)
often ['ɒfn], ['ɒftən] oft 5
oh [əʊ] Null *(im gesprochenen Englisch)* 5
oil [ɔɪl] Öl 6
oil rig ['ɔɪl rɪg] Ölbohrinsel 6
oily ['ɔɪli] ölig 6
OK [əʊ'keɪ] okay, gut, in Ordnung 5 **I'm OK.** Es geht mir gut. 5
old [əʊld] alt 5 **in the old days** früher 9: 2 (35)
old-fashioned [əʊld 'fæʃənd] altmodisch 9: 4 (65)
°oldies ['əʊldiz] *(pl, infml)* Oldies; Eltern
Olympic [ə'lɪmpɪk] olympisch 8
Olympics [ə'lɪmpɪks] olympische Spiele 5
on [ɒn]:
1. auf 5
on holiday im/in den Urlaub 5
on the beach am Strand 5 **on the bus** im Bus 5 **on the river** am Fluss 8 **on TV** im Fernsehen 6 **on Wednesday** am Mittwoch 5
2. What's on? Was läuft? / Was findet statt? *(Kino, Theater)* 6
3. be on an sein *(eingeschaltet)* 9: 2 (34)
once [wʌns] einmal; einst; sobald, wenn (erst) 8
once-over ['wʌns əʊvə]: **give sb. a/ the once-over** *(infml)* jn. (kurz) in Augenschein nehmen 8
one [wʌn]:
1. eins 5
one day eines Tages 6
2. the nearest one der/die/das Nächstgelegene 7
the only one der/die Einzige 7
3. man 9: 4 (64)
oneself [wʌn'self] sich: sich (selbst) *(zu „one")* 9: 4 (64)
°onion ['ʌnjən] Zwiebel
only ['əʊnli]:
1. nur, bloß 5
2. erst 5
3. the only student der einzige Schüler / die einzige Schülerin 7
onto the rocks ['ɒntu], ['ɒntə] auf die Felsen (hinauf) 6
open ['əʊpən]:
1. öffnen; aufschlagen *(Buch)* 5
2. sich öffnen, aufgehen 6
3. offen, geöffnet 5
opening hours *(pl)* ['əʊpənɪŋ aʊəz] Öffnungszeiten 9: 2 (31)
opera ['ɒpərə] Oper 6
operate ['ɒpəreɪt] bedienen *(z. B. Maschine)*, arbeiten *(in Betrieb sein)*, operieren 9: 1 (16)
operation [ɒpə'reɪʃn] Operation, Einsatz 9: 1 (16)
opinion [ə'pɪnjən] Meinung 6
in my opinion meiner Meinung nach 6
opportunity [ɒpə'tjuːnəti] Gelegenheit, Möglichkeit, Chance 9: 4 (61)
opposite ['ɒpəzɪt]:
1. Gegenteil 8
2. gegensätzlich, entgegengesetzt, gegenüberliegend 8
3. gegenüber (von) 8
or [ɔː] oder; sonst 5
orange ['ɒrɪndʒ]:
1. orange(farben) 5
2. Orange, Apfelsine 5
orange juice ['ɒrɪndʒ dʒuːs] Orangensaft 5
orchestra ['ɔːkɪstrə] Orchester 7
order ['ɔːdə]:
1. Bestellung 9: 3 (48)
2. order sth. etwas bestellen 5
order ['ɔːdə]:
1. Befehl 9: 3 (48)
2. order sth. / sb. to do sth. etwas anordnen; jm. befehlen, etwas zu tun 9: 3 (48)
ordinary ['ɔːdnri] normal, gewöhnlich 7
organic [ɔː'gænɪk] biologisch (angebaut), Bio- 8
organization [ɔːgənaɪ'zeɪʃn] Organisation 8
organizational [ɔːgənaɪ'zeɪʃənl] organisatorisch 9: 2 (30)
organize ['ɔːgənaɪz] organisieren 8
organizer ['ɔːgənaɪzə] Organisator/in 8
°orphanage ['ɔːfənɪdʒ] Waisenhaus
other ['ʌðə] andere(r, s) 5 **the others** die anderen 5
ought to ['ɔːt tə]: **it ought to be ...** es sollte ... sein 7
our ['aʊə] unser/e 5
ours [ɑːz], ['aʊəz] unserer, unsere, unseres 6
ourselves [aʊə'selvz] wir/uns selbst 6
out (of ...) [aʊt] aus, heraus/ hinaus; aus ... (heraus/hinaus) 5
out-of-school activities [aʊt əv 'skuːl] Aktivitäten außerhalb der Schule 7
outback ['aʊtbæk]: *Hinterland Australiens* 9: 1 (8/9)
outdoor ['aʊtdɔː]: **outdoor (sport)** (Sport) für draußen / im Freien 5
outdoor swimming pool Freibad 5
outdoors [aʊt'dɔːz] im Freien, draußen 8
outside [aʊt'saɪd] draußen; nach draußen 5 **outside (the UK)** außerhalb (des Vereinigten Königreiches) 6
oval ['əʊvl] oval 9: 1 (14)
oven ['ʌvn] Backofen 6
over ['əʊvə] über, hinüber 6 **over here** hier herüber; hier drüben 6
over there da drüben, dort drüben 6 **So it's car over me?** Also das Auto ist dir wichtiger als ich? 7
overall [əʊvər'ɔːl] allgemein, im Großen und Ganzen, (ins)gesamt, Gesamt- 8
overview ['əʊvəvjuː] Überblick, Übersicht 8
overweight [əʊvə'weɪt] übergewichtig 8 **be overweight** Übergewicht haben 8
owe sb. sth. [əʊ] jm. etwas schulden, schuldig sein 6
own [əʊn]:
1. own sth. etwas besitzen 7
2. eigene(r, s) 7
my own room mein/ein eigenes Zimmer 7
owner ['əʊnə] Besitzer/in 7
oyster ['ɔɪstə] Auster 7

P

Pacific Ocean [pəsɪfɪk 'əʊʃn] Pazifischer Ozean, Pazifik 6
page (= p.) [peɪdʒ] (Buch-/Heft-)Seite 5 **front page** Titelseite 6 **turn (over) the page(s)** umblättern *(Buch/Heft)* 9: 2 (33)
paid [peɪd] *siehe* **pay**
pain [peɪn] Schmerz; Plage 8 **be a pain** lästig sein, nerven 8 **be in pain** Schmerzen haben 8 **What a pain!** Wie lästig! / Was für eine Plage! 8
paint [peɪnt]:
1. Farbe, Lack 8
2. lackieren, anstreichen; malen 8
painting ['peɪntɪŋ] Malerei; Gemälde 9: 1 (12) **dot painting** Punktmalerei; Punktgemälde 9: 1 (12)
pair [peə] Paar 6
palace ['pæləs] Palast, Schloss 9: 4 (70)
pan [pæn] Pfanne 6
panic ['pænɪk]:
1. Panik 9: 4 (67)
2. in Panik geraten 9: 4 (67)
Don't panic. Keine Panik. / Immer mit der Ruhe. 9: 4 (67)
panther ['pænθə] Panther; *(AE:)* Puma 8
pants *(pl)* [pænts] *(AE)* (eine) Hose 6 **baggy pants** Schlabberhose 6
paper ['peɪpə] Papier 6 **piece of paper** Stück Papier, Zettel 6
parade [pə'reɪd] Parade, Umzug 6
paragraph ['pærəgrɑːf] (Text-)Abschnitt 7
paralyses [pə'ræləsɪːs] *Plural von* **paralysis**
paralysis [pə'ræləsɪs], *pl* **paralyses** Lähmung 9: 1 (14)
paraphrase ['pærəfreɪz] umschreiben, mit anderen Worten sagen 7
parents *(pl)* ['peərənts] Eltern 5
parking lot ['pɑːkɪŋ lɒt] *(AE)* Parkplatz 6
parliament ['pɑːləmənt] Parlament 6
parrot ['pærət] Papagei 9: 1 (8/9)
part (of) [pɑːt] Teil (von) 6 **take part (in)** teilnehmen (an), mitmachen (bei) 8
part-time [pɑːt 'taɪm] Teilzeit-, Halbtags- 9: 2 (24/25)
pass [pɑːs]:
1. vorbeigehen/-ziehen; vorübergehen *(Zeit, Moment, Gelegenheit)* 9: 4 (66)
pass (a test / an exam) *(einen Test / eine Prüfung)* bestehen, schaffen 8 **pass sb./sth.** an jm./etwas vorbeigehen, vorbeifahren 9: 4 (66) **pass sth. down** etwas weitergeben, überliefern 9: 1 (10) **pass sth. on (to sb.)** etwas weitergeben (an jn.) 9: 1 (10) **pass through (a village)** fahren/reisen durch (ein Dorf) 9: 4 (66)
2. pass a law ein Gesetz verabschieden 8
passenger ['pæsɪndʒə] Passagier/in, Fahrgast 6
passport ['pɑːspɔːt] (Reise-)Pass 6
password ['pɑːswɜːd] Passwort 9: 3 (48)
past [pɑːst]:
1. half past 6 halb 7 5
quarter past 6 viertel nach 6 5
2. past (the wood) (am Wald) vorbei 6
past [pɑːst]:
1. Vergangenheit 6
2. vergangene(r, s) 9: 1 (12)
pat [pæt] klopfen; tätscheln 8 **pat sb. down** jn. abtasten *(bei Polizeikontrolle)* 8
path [pɑːθ] Weg, Pfad 6
patience ['peɪʃns] Geduld 9: 2 (31)
patient ['peɪʃnt] geduldig 7
pattern ['pætn] *(wiederkehrendes)* Muster, Schema 7
pavement ['peɪvmənt] Gehweg, Bürgersteig 6
pay [peɪ]:
1. Bezahlung *(Lohn)* 9: 2 (32)
2. pay (for sth.), paid, paid (etwas be)zahlen 6
PC (= personal computer) [piː 'siː] PC 8
PE (= physical education) [piː 'iː] (Schul-)Sport 5
pea [piː] Erbse 6
peace [piːs] Frieden 7
peaceful ['piːsfl] friedlich 8
pen [pen] Kugelschreiber, Stift; Füller 5
pence [pens] *Plural von* **penny** 5
pencil ['pensl] Bleistift 5
pencil case ['pensl keɪs] Federmäppchen 5
pencil sharpener ['pensl ʃɑːpnə] Bleistiftspitzer 5
penknife ['pennaɪf], *pl* **penknives** Taschenmesser 6
penknives ['pennaɪvz] *Plural von* **penknife**
penny (= p) ['peni] Penny *(kleinste britische Münze)* 5
people ['piːpl]:
1. *(pl)* Leute, Menschen 5
2. *pl* **peoples** Volk 9: 1 (10)
pepper ['pepə]:
1. Paprika, Peperoni 6
2. Pfeffer 6
per [pɜː], [pə] pro 8 **miles per hour (mph)** Meilen pro Stunde 8
per cent (%) [pə 'sent] Prozent 5
perfect ['pɜːfɪkt] perfekt 9: 1 (18)
perfectly (still) ['pɜːfɪktli] ganz/völlig (still) 9: 1 (18)
perform [pə'fɔːm] auftreten *(Künstler/in)*; aufführen; durchführen 8
performance [pə'fɔːməns] Vorstellung, Aufführung 8
performer [pə'fɔːmə] Künstler/in *(der/die etwas aufführt)* 9: 2 (27)
perhaps [pə'hæps] vielleicht 9: 4 (66)
period ['pɪəriəd] (Unterrichts-)Stunde 6
permanent ['pɜːmənənt] dauerhaft, Dauer-; fest; (be)ständig 9: 1 (12)
permission [pə'mɪʃn] Erlaubnis 8
person ['pɜːsn] Person 5
personal ['pɜːsənl] persönlich 8
personal computer (PC) [pɜːsənl kəm'pjuːtə] PC 8
personal statement [pɜːsənl 'steɪtmənt] persönliche Beschreibung, Selbstbeschreibung 9: 2 (30)
personality [pɜːsə'næləti] Persönlichkeit; Charakter 9: 4 (65)
pet [pet] (Haus-)Tier 5
petrol ['petrəl] Benzin 6
petrol station ['petrəl steɪʃn] Tankstelle 6
pharmaceutical [fɑːmə'suːtɪkl]:
1. Pharma-, pharmazeutisch 9: 4 (60)
2. pharmaceuticals *(pl)* Arzneimittel 9: 4 (60)
phone [fəʊn]:
1. anrufen, telefonieren 6
2. Telefon 5
answer the phone ans Telefon gehen 7 **on the phone** am Telefon 5
phone call ['fəʊn kɔːl] *(oft auch kurz:* call*)* (Telefon-)Anruf 7
phone number ['fəʊn nʌmbə] Telefonnummer 5
photo ['fəʊtəʊ] Foto 5 **in the photo** auf dem Foto 5 **take a photo** ein Foto machen 5
photocopy ['fəʊtəʊkɒpi]:
1. Fotokopie 9: 1 (16)
2. fotokopieren 9: 1 (16)

photograph ['fəʊtəgrɑːf] Foto(grafie) 8
photographer [fə'tɒgrəfə] Fotograf/in 6
photography [fə'tɒgrəfi] Fotografie *(Hobby)*, *(das)* Fotografieren 9: 2 (29)
phrase [freɪz] Ausdruck, (Rede-)Wendung 7
physical education (PE) [fɪzɪkl edʒu'keɪʃn] (Schul-)Sport 5
piano [pi'ænəʊ] Klavier 5 **play the piano** Klavier spielen 5
pick sth. up [pɪk 'ʌp] etwas aufheben *(vom Boden)*, etwas hochheben 6
picnic ['pɪknɪk] Picknick 6 **have a picnic** ein Picknick machen 6
picture ['pɪktʃə] Bild 5
pie chart ['paɪ tʃɑːt] Tortendiagramm 6
piece [piːs] Stück, Teil 6 **piece of paper** Stück Papier 6
pigeon ['pɪdʒɪn] Taube 6
pilgrim ['pɪlgrɪm] Pilger/in 9: 4 (64)
pill [pɪl] Tablette, Pille 8
pillow ['pɪləʊ] Kopfkissen 8
pilot ['paɪlət] Pilot/in 9: 2 (37)
pink [pɪŋk] rosa 5
pirate ['paɪrət] Pirat/in 5
place [pleɪs] Ort, Platz 5 **in place** an Ort und Stelle 9: 3 (51)
plains *(pl)* [pleɪnz] Ebene 9: 1 (18)
plan [plæn]:
1. Plan 5
2. planen 5
plan to do sth. planen, etwas zu tun 5
plane [pleɪn] Flugzeug 5
plant [plɑːnt]:
1. Pflanze 9: 1 (10)
2. pflanzen 9: 1 (10)
plantation [plæn'teɪʃn] Plantage; Anpflanzung 9: 4 (71)
plastic ['plæstɪk] Plastik, Kunststoff 7
plate [pleɪt] Teller 7
platform ['plætfɔːm]:
1. Bahnsteig 6
at platform 4 auf Gleis 4 6
2. Plattform 9: 3 (44)
play [pleɪ]:
1. spielen 5
play dead sich tot stellen 8 **play sport(s)** Sport treiben 7 **play the piano** Klavier spielen 5
2. Schauspiel, Theaterstück 6
player ['pleɪə] Spieler/in 5
playground ['pleɪgraʊnd]: **(school) playground** Schulhof 9: 2 (35)
playing field ['pleɪɪŋ fiːld] Sportplatz 7
please [pliːz] bitte 5
pleased [pliːzd] froh, erfreut, zufrieden 7 **Pleased to meet you.** Freut mich Sie kennenzulernen. 7
plot [plɒt] Handlung(sverlauf) *(z. B. Film/Geschichte)* 7
plough [plaʊ]:
1. Pflug 7
2. pflügen 7
plug [plʌg]:
1. Stecker 7
2. **plug sth. in** etwas einstecken, anschließen 7
plum [plʌm] Pflaume 5
plus [plʌs] plus 8
pm [piː'em]: **7 pm** 7 Uhr nachmittags/abends, 19 Uhr 6
pocket ['pɒkɪt] Tasche *(an Kleidungsstücken)* 8
pocket money ['pɒkɪt mʌni] Taschengeld 8
poem ['pəʊɪm] Gedicht 5
point [pɔɪnt]:
1. Punkt 6
2. Komma *(Dezimalzeichen)* 6
3. Argument, Standpunkt 8
make a point ein Argument vortragen 8 **make your point** sagen, wie du darüber denkst 8
take a point einen Standpunkt verstehen 8
point (at/to) [pɔɪnt] zeigen, deuten (auf) 6 **point a gun at sb.** eine Waffe auf jn. richten 8
point sth. out auf etwas hinweisen, aufmerksam machen 7
polar ['pəʊlə] polar 8
polar bear ['pəʊlə beə] Eisbär 8
°pole [pəʊl] Mast, Stange
police *(pl)* [pə'liːs] Polizei 7
police officer [pə'liːs ɒfɪsə] Polizeibeamter/-beamtin 6
policy ['pɒləsi] Politik, Richtlinie(n), Bestimmung(en) 9: 1 (16)
polite [pə'laɪt] höflich 7
°political [pə'lɪtɪkl] politisch
politician [pɒlə'tɪʃn] Politiker/in 8
pollute [pə'luːt] *(die Umwelt)* verschmutzen 9: 4 (64)
pollution [pə'luːʃn] (Umwelt-)Verschmutzung 8
pony ['pəʊni] Pony 6
pool [puːl]:
1. (Wasser-)Becken 8
2. *(= swimming pool)* (Schwimm-)Bad 5
poor [pɔː], [pʊə]:
1. arm 6
2. schlecht, schwach, minderwertig 8
pop up [pɒp 'ʌp] aufpoppen *(z. B. Computer-Fenster)*; (plötzlich) auftauchen; aus dem Boden schießen 9: 3 (44)
popular ['pɒpjələ] beliebt, populär 5
population [pɒpju'leɪʃn] Bevölkerung, Einwohner(zahl) 7
porridge ['pɒrɪdʒ] Haferbrei 6
position [pə'zɪʃn] Position, Standort; Stellung; (Arbeits-)Stelle 9: 4 (61)
positive ['pɒzətɪv] positiv 7
positive discrimination [pɒzətɪv dɪskrɪmɪ'neɪʃn] positive Diskriminierung *(gesellschaftspolitische Maßnahmen, die negativer Diskriminierung entgegenwirken)* 9: 4 (60)
possible ['pɒsəbl] möglich 8
possibly ['pɒsəbli] möglicherweise 9: 4 (65)
post [pəʊst]:
1. Post *(Briefe etc.)* 5
2. Pfosten, Pfahl 9: 1 (21)
post office ['pəʊst ɒfɪs] Post(amt) 5
postcard ['pəʊstkɑːd] Postkarte 6
postcode ['pəʊstkəʊd] Postleitzahl 7
pot [pɒt] Topf 8
potato [pə'teɪtəʊ], *pl* **potatoes** Kartoffel 5
potluck (dinner) [pɒtlʌk 'dɪnə] *(AE)* *(Abend-)Essen, zu dem jeder etwas mitbringt* 7
pound [paʊnd]:
1. Pfund *(Gewichtseinheit; GB: 454 Gramm)* 7
2. **(£)** Pfund *(britische Währung)* 5
pour [pɔː] strömen; gießen, schütten 7
poverty ['pɒvəti] Armut 8
°powder ['paʊdə] Pulver
power ['paʊə]:
1. Kraft, Macht 7
2. Energie, Strom 8
power line ['paʊə laɪn] Stromleitung 6
°powerful ['paʊəfl] kräftig, stark, mächtig
practice ['præktɪs]:
1. Übung(en) 6
2. *(AE)* üben 6
practise ['præktɪs] üben 6
pray [preɪ] beten 7
prayer [preə] Gebet 7
precious ['preʃəs] wertvoll, kostbar 7
precious metal [preʃəs 'metl] Edelmetall 7

predict [prɪ'dɪkt] vorhersagen, voraussagen 9: 2 (29)
prediction [prɪ'dɪkʃn] Vorhersage, Voraussage 9: 2 (29)
prefer sth. to sth. [prɪ'fɜː] etwas einer Sache vorziehen, etwas lieber tun/haben als etwas 7 **I'd prefer ...** ich würde ... vorziehen 7
prepare (for) [prɪ'peə] vorbereiten; sich vorbereiten (auf) 7
prescription [prɪ'skrɪpʃn] Rezept *(vom Arzt)* 8
present [prɪ'zent] präsentieren, vorstellen 6
present ['preznt]:
1. Geschenk 5
wedding present Hochzeitsgeschenk 6
2. Gegenwart 9: 1 (10)
3. gegenwärtig 9: 1 (12)
presentation [prezn'teɪʃn] Referat, Präsentation 6 **give a presentation** ein Referat halten 6
president ['prezɪdənt] Präsident/in 7
press [pres] drücken 9: 3 (53)
pressure ['preʃə] Druck 7 **put pressure on sb.** jn. unter Druck setzen 7
pretty ['prɪti] hübsch 8
prevent [prɪ'vent] verhindern 8
price [praɪs] (Kauf-)Preis 6 **at half price** zum halben Preis 9: 3 (49)
pride [praɪd] Stolz 9: 1 (10)
priest [priːst] Priester/in 7
prime minister [praɪm 'mɪnɪstə] Premierminister/in 9: 1 (10)
prince [prɪns] Prinz 7
principal ['prɪnsəpl] Rektor/in, Schulleiter/in 5
print [prɪnt]:
1. Druck; Schrift(art) 8
2. **print (out)** (aus)drucken 8
printer ['prɪntə] Drucker 8
prison ['prɪzn] Gefängnis 8
privacy ['prɪvəsi] Privatsphäre 8
private ['praɪvət] privat; persönlich 6
prize [praɪz] Preis, Gewinn 6
probably ['prɒbəbli] wahrscheinlich 6
problem ['prɒbləm] Problem 6
process ['prəʊses] Prozess; Verfahren, Ablauf 8
produce [prə'djuːs] produzieren 8
producer [prə'djuːsə] Produzent/in 9: 4 (63)
product ['prɒdʌkt] Produkt 8
production [prə'dʌkʃn] Produktion 9: 4 (71)
professional [prə'feʃənl]:
1. professionell, Profi- 8
2. *infml auch:* **pro** Fachmann/Fachfrau, Profi 8
professor (of) [prə'fesə] Professor/in (für) 9: 2 (33)
profile ['prəʊfaɪl]:
1. Profil; Beschreibung, Portrait 7
2. beschreiben, porträtieren 8
profit ['prɒfɪt] Gewinn *(Profit)* 7
make a profit Gewinn/Profit machen 7
program ['prəʊgræm]:
1. (Computer-)Programm 8
2. *(AE)* (Fernseh-)Sendung 8
3. programmieren 8
programme ['prəʊgræm]
1. (Fernseh-)Sendung 6
2. Programm 9: 1 (9)
programmer ['prəʊgræmə] Programmierer/in 9: 4 (61)
progress ['prəʊgres]: **be in progress** im Gange sein 9: 1 (12)
project ['prɒdʒekt] Projekt 5
promise ['prɒmɪs]:
1. versprechen 8
2. *(ein)* Versprechen 8
promote [prə'məʊt] Werbung machen für; fördern, unterstützen 9: 3 (47) **promote sb.** jn. befördern 9: 3 (47)
pronounce [prə'naʊns] aussprechen 7
pronunciation [prənʌnsi'eɪʃn] Aussprache 7
proof *(no pl)* [pruːf] Beweis(e); Nachweis(e) 8
proof of insurance [pruːf əv ɪn'ʃʊərəns] Versicherungsnachweis 8
prop [prɒp] Requisite 9: 2 (37)
propeller [prə'pelə] Propeller 9: 3 (52)
proper ['prɒpə] anständig, richtig, ordnungsgemäß 8
property ['prɒpəti] Eigentum, Besitz 8
protect (from/against) [prə'tekt] (be)schützen (vor) 7
protest ['prəʊtest] Protest(demonstration) 8
protest [prə'test] protestieren 8
Protestant ['prɒtɪstənt] Protestant/in; protestantisch, evangelisch 7
protester [prə'testə] Demonstrant/in 8
proud (of) [praʊd] stolz (auf) 9: 1 (10)
prove [pruːv] nachweisen, beweisen 6
provide [prə'vaɪd] (an)bieten, zur Verfügung stellen 9: 2 (31) **Food and accommodation provided.** Essen/Verpflegung und Unterkunft werden (zur Verfügung) gestellt. 9: 2 (31)
pub [pʌb] Kneipe 7
public ['pʌblɪk] öffentlich 6
public holiday [pʌblɪk 'hɒlədeɪ] öffentlicher/gesetzlicher Feiertag 6
publish ['pʌblɪʃ] veröffentlichen, herausbringen 8
pueblo ['pwebləʊ], *pl* **pueblos** Pueblo *(indianische Siedlung)* 8
pug [pʌg] Mops *(Hund)* 7
pull [pʊl]:
1. *(das)* Ziehen, Ruck 9: 3 (51)
2. ziehen 8
pull over anhalten, an den Straßenrand fahren 8 **pull sb. over** jn. an den (Straßen-)Rand winken 8
°**pulley** ['pʊli] Flaschenzug
pullover ['pʊləʊvə] Pullover 5
pump [pʌmp]:
1. Pumpe 9: 3 (50)
2. pumpen 9: 3 (50)
punch [pʌntʃ] lochen, stanzen 9: 2 (33)
punch code ['pʌntʃ kəʊd] Stanzcode *(mit Lochkarten)* 9: 2 (33)
punctual ['pʌŋktʃuəl] pünktlich 9: 2 (28)
punctuation [pʌŋktʃu'eɪʃn] Zeichensetzung 8
purple ['pɜːpl] violett, lila 5
push [pʊʃ]:
1. Stoß, Schubs 8
2. schieben, stoßen, schubsen 8
put [pʊt], **put, put** *(etwas wohin)* tun, legen, stellen, stecken 5 **put away** weglegen, zur Seite legen 6 **put in** hineinlegen 5 **put sth. together** etwas zusammensetzen, zusammenstellen 8 **put up your hand** sich melden, aufzeigen 6
puzzled ['pʌzld] verwundert 6
°**pyjamas** *(pl)* [pə'dʒɑːməz] *(ein)* Schlafanzug

Q

quake [kweɪk] *(infml)* Erdbeben 6
quality ['kwɒləti] Qualität, Qualitäts-; Eigenschaft 7 **be better quality** von besserer Qualität sein 7
quarter ['kwɔːtə] Viertel 5
quarter past 6 viertel nach 6 5
quarter to 7 viertel vor 7 5
queen [kwiːn] Königin 5
question ['kwestʃən] Frage 5

question mark ['kwestʃən mɑːk] Fragezeichen 8
quick [kwɪk] schnell 7
quiet ['kwaɪət] ruhig, still, leise 5
quite [kwaɪt] ziemlich, ganz 6
quiz [kwɪz], *pl* **quizzes:**
 1. Quiz 5
 2. Test 7
quota ['kwəʊtə] Quote 9: 4 (60)
quotation marks *(pl)* [kwəʊ'teɪʃn mɑːks] Anführungszeichen 8
quote [kwəʊt]:
 1. Zitat 9: 2 (37)
 2. zitieren 9: 2 (37)

R

rabbit ['ræbɪt] Kaninchen 5
race [reɪs]:
 1. (Wett-)Rennen 8
 2. um die Wette laufen/reiten, Rennen fahren 8
race [reɪs] Rasse 8
racer ['reɪsə] Rennreiter/in; Rennfahrer/in; Wettläufer/in 8
racial ['reɪʃl] Rassen- 8
radio ['reɪdiəʊ] Radio 8
raft [rɑːft] Floß 6
railway ['reɪlweɪ] Eisenbahn 9: 4 (66)
railway line ['reɪlweɪ laɪn] Bahnstrecke 9: 4 (66)
railway station ['reɪlweɪ steɪʃn] Bahnhof 9: 4 (66)
rain [reɪn]:
 1. Regen 5
 2. regnen 5
rain jacket ['reɪn dʒækɪt] Regenjacke 6
rainforest ['reɪnfɒrɪst] Regenwald 9: 2 (27)
rainy ['reɪni] regnerisch 5
raise [reɪz] (er)heben 8 **raise awareness of sth.** die Aufmerksamkeit für etwas erhöhen, das Bewusstsein für etwas schaffen 8 **raise one's eyes from sth.** von etwas aufschauen 8 **raise one's voice** die Stimme erheben 8
ramp [ræmp] Rampe 5
ran [ræn] *siehe* **run**
rang [ræŋ] *siehe* **ring**
ranger ['reɪndʒə] *Aufseher/in in einem Nationalpark* 8
rate [reɪt] Rate, Quote, Anteil; Tarif, Preis 9: 4 (61)
raw [rɔː] roh 6
reach (sb./a place) [riːtʃ] (jn./einen Ort) erreichen 8 **reach for sth.** nach etwas greifen 8 **reach out (your hand)** die Hand ausstrecken 8
react (to) [ri'ækt] reagieren (auf) 7
reaction (to) [ri'ækʃn] Reaktion (auf) 8
read [red] *siehe* **read**
read [riːd], **read, read** lesen 5
reader ['riːdə] Leser/in 7
ready ['redi] fertig, bereit 5 **Get ready.** Bereite dich vor. 5
real [rɪəl] echt, wirklich 6 **in real life** im echten Leben 7
real-life [rɪəl 'laɪf] real *(aus dem echten Leben)* 7
realistic [riːə'lɪstɪk] realistisch 8
realistically [riːə'lɪstɪkli] realistisch *(Adv.)* 8
reality [ri'ælɪti] Realität, Wirklichkeit 6
realization [riːəlaɪ'zeɪʃn] Erkenntnis 9: 1 (17)
realize sth. ['rɪəlaɪz] etwas erkennen, sich einer Sache bewusst werden 9: 1 (17)
really ['riːəli], ['rɪəli] wirklich 5
reason ['riːzn] Grund, Begründung 6 **for this reason** aus diesem Grund 6
reasonable ['riːznəbl] vernünftig, angemessen 9: 4 (66)
reasonably (happy) ['riːznəbli] ziemlich/durchaus (glücklich) 9: 4 (66)
rebuild [riː'bɪld], **rebuilt, rebuilt** wiederaufbauen 8
rebuilt [riː'bɪlt] *siehe* **rebuild**
receive [rɪ'siːv] erhalten, empfangen 9: 2 (32)
recent ['riːsnt] aktuell, jüngst 9: 4 (71) **in recent years** in den letzten Jahren 9: 4 (71)
recently ['riːsntli] in letzter Zeit, neulich 6
reception [rɪ'sepʃn] Empfang *(auch beim Telefon)*; Rezeption 8 **in reception** an der Rezeption 8
receptionist [rɪ'sepʃənɪst] Empfangsmitarbeiter/in 8
recess [rɪ'ses] *(AE)* Pause 6
recipe ['resəpi] (Koch-)Rezept 6
recognize ['rekəgnaɪz] (wieder)erkennen 8
recommend [rekə'mend]: **recommend sth. (to sb.)** (jm.) etwas empfehlen 7 **We recommend that you go ...** Wir empfehlen, dass Sie ... gehen. 9: 1 (17)
record [rɪ'kɔːd] aufnehmen, aufzeichnen; dokumentieren, verzeichnen 8
record ['rekɔːd]:
 1. Rekord 8
 2. Schallplatte 7
record deal ['rekɔːd diːl] Plattenvertrag 7
recording [rɪ'kɔːdɪŋ] Aufnahme 8
recycle [riː'saɪkl] recyceln, wiederverwerten 7
recycling [rɪ'saɪklɪŋ] Recycling 7
red [red] rot 5
red deer [red 'dɪə] Rotwild 6
reduce (by) [rɪ'djuːs] reduzieren, verringern (um) 8
reduction [rɪ'dʌkʃn] Reduzierung, Verringerung 8
°reed [riːd] Schilf(rohr)
reef [riːf] Riff 9: 1 (8/9)
refer to [rɪ'fɜː] sich beziehen auf, Bezug nehmen auf 8
reference ['refrəns] Referenz, Empfehlung; jd., der eine Referenz erteilt 9: 2 (31)
refrigerator [rɪ'frɪdʒəreɪtə] Kühlschrank 8
refugee [refju'dʒiː] Flüchtling 7
region ['riːdʒən] Region 9: 4 (58/59)
regional ['riːdʒənl] regional 9: 4 (58/59)
registration [redʒɪ'streɪʃn]:
 1. Anmeldung; Zulassung, KFZ-Schein 8
 2. *Anwesenheitskontrolle und Ankündigung aktueller Ereignisse vor dem Unterricht* 5
registration number [redʒɪ'streɪʃn nʌmbə] Autokennzeichen 8
regular ['regjələ] regelmäßig; gewohnt, normal 9: 1 (12)
relationship [rɪ'leɪʃnʃɪp] Beziehung, Verhältnis 7 **be in a relationship with sb.** mit jm. eine Beziehung haben 7
relax [rɪ'læks] sich entspannen 7
relay (race) ['riːleɪ] Staffel(lauf) 8
reliable [rɪ'laɪəbl] verlässlich, zuverlässig 9: 4 (71)
relief [rɪ'liːf] Erleichterung; Linderung 8
religion [rɪ'lɪdʒən] Religion 8
religious [rɪ'lɪdʒəs] religiös 9: 4 (61)
reluctant [rɪ'lʌktənt] zurückhaltend, zögernd; widerwillig 8
remember [rɪ'membə]:
 1. daran denken, nicht vergessen 5
 remember to do sth. daran denken, etwas zu tun 5
 2. sich erinnern an 5
 remember doing sth. sich daran erinnern, etwas getan zu haben 5
remind sb. of sth. [rɪ'maɪnd] jn. an etwas erinnern 8

rent [rent]:
1. Miete 8
2. mieten; leihen 8
repair [rɪ'peə]:
1. Reparatur 8
2. reparieren 8
repeat [rɪ'piːt] wiederholen 6 **Repeat after me.** Sprich/Sprecht mir nach. 6
repellent [rɪ'pelənt] Schutzmittel 9: 1 (8/9)
replace (with) [rɪ'pleɪs] ersetzen (durch), austauschen (gegen) 8
reply (to) [rɪ'plaɪ]:
1. Antwort (auf) 9: 3 (51)
2. antworten (auf) 9: 3 (51)
report [rɪ'pɔːt]:
1. Bericht, Referat 6
2. report (on) berichten (über) 6
request [rɪ'kwest] Wunsch, Bitte; Anfrage 9: 3 (48)
require [rɪ'kwaɪə] erfordern, benötigen 9: 2 (31)
requirement [rɪ'kwaɪəmənt] Voraussetzung, Anforderung 9: 2 (31)
research [rɪ'sɜːtʃ] Forschung(en), Recherche(n) 6 **do research** recherchieren 6 **°His research was into robots.** Er erforschte Roboter.
reservation [rezə'veɪʃn]:
1. Reservierung, Buchung 9: 2 (31)
2. *infml auch* **rez** Reservat *(Gebiet)* 8
reserve [rɪ'zɜːv] reservieren 9: 2 (31)
reset [riː'set], **reset, reset** zurücksetzen; resetten 9: 3 (53)
respect [rɪ'spekt]:
1. Respekt 8
2. respektieren, achten 8
respectful [rɪ'spektfl] respektvoll 8
responsibility [rɪspɒnsə'bɪləti] Verantwortung; Zuständigkeit 8
responsible (for) [rɪ'spɒnsəbl] verantwortlich (für); verantwortungsbewusst 8
rest [rest]:
1. Ruhe, Pause, Erholung 9: 4 (67)
2. ruhen; sich (auf)stützen; sich ausruhen 9: 4 (67)
restaurant ['restrɒnt] Restaurant 5 **at a restaurant** in einem Restaurant 5
restroom ['restruːm] *(AE)* Toilette *(in öffentlichen Gebäuden)* 8
result [rɪ'zʌlt] Ergebnis 6 **as a result** folglich, demzufolge 6
résumé ['rezjumeɪ] *(AE)* Lebenslauf 8
return [rɪ'tɜːn]:
1. Rückkehr 9: 1 (13)
2. zurückkehren, zurückkommen 9: 1 (13)
reuse [riː'juːz] wiederverwenden 8
review [rɪ'vjuː]:
1. Besprechung, Rezension, Kritik 7
2. besprechen, rezensieren; überprüfen 7
revise [rɪ'vaɪz] *(Lernstoff)* wiederholen 7
revision [rɪ'vɪʒn] Wiederholung *(von Lernstoff)* 7
°rewrite [riː'raɪt], **rewrote, rewritten** neu schreiben, umschreiben
°rewritten [riː'rɪtn] *siehe* **rewrite**
°rewrote [riː'rəʊt] *siehe* **rewrite**
rez [rez] *siehe* **reservation**
rhetorical question [rɪtɒrɪkl 'kwestʃən] rhetorische Frage 9: 2 (37)
rhyme [raɪm]:
1. (sich) reimen 8
2. Reim 8
rhythm ['rɪðəm] Rhythmus 8
rice [raɪs] Reis 5
rich [rɪtʃ] reich 5
°rickshaw ['rɪkʃɔː] Rikscha
rid [rɪd]: **get rid of sth.** etwas loswerden 9: 1 (16)
ridden ['rɪdn] *siehe* **ride**
riddle ['rɪdl] Rätsel 9: 1 (18)
ride [raɪd], **rode, ridden** reiten 5 **ride a bike** mit dem Fahrrad fahren 5 **ride a horse** ein Pferd reiten 5
rider ['raɪdə] Reiter/in; Fahrer/in *(z. B. Fahrrad)* 8
rig [rɪg]: **oil rig** Ölbohrinsel 6
right [raɪt]:
1. richtig 5
be right Recht haben 6
2. Recht 7
a right to a fair trial ein Recht auf ein faires Gerichtsverfahren 8
civil rights *(pl)* Bürgerrechte 8
3. rechts; nach rechts 5
on the right rechts, auf der rechten Seite 5
4. right next to ... gleich/direkt neben ... 9: 2 (34)
ring [rɪŋ] Ring 6
ring [rɪŋ], **rang, rung** läuten, klingeln 7
°ringed [rɪŋd] geringelt; beringt
rink [rɪŋk]: **(skating) rink** Schlittschuhbahn 5
rise [raɪz], **rose, risen** sich erheben; (an)steigen 8
risen ['rɪzən] *siehe* **rise**
river ['rɪvə] Fluss 6 **on the river** am Fluss 8
roach [rəʊtʃ] *(AE, infml)* Kakerlak(e), (Küchen-)Schabe 8
road [rəʊd] Straße *(Straße in oder zwischen Orten)* 6
roast meat [rəʊst 'miːt] Braten 6
roasted [rəʊstɪd] gebraten, geröstet 6
robot ['rəʊbɒt] Roboter 8
rock [rɒk] Felsen 6
rode [rəʊd] *siehe* **ride**
rodeo ['rəʊdiəʊ] Rodeo 8
role [rəʊl] Rolle *(Film, Theater)* 9: 4 (62)
role model ['rəʊl mɒdl] Vorbild 8
°role-play ['rəʊl pleɪ]:
1. Rollenspiel
2. role-play sth. etwas in einem Rollenspiel darstellen
roll [rəʊl] rollen; (sich) verdrehen *(Augen)* 7 **roll your eyes** die Augen verdrehen 7
Roman ['rəʊmən] Römer/in; römisch 7
romantic [rəʊ'mæntɪk] romantisch 9: 4 (62)
roof [ruːf] Dach 8
room [ruːm], [rʊm] Raum, Zimmer 5
roommate ['ruːmmeɪt] Zimmergenosse/-genossin 7
root [ruːt] Wurzel 7
rose [rəʊz] *siehe* **rise**
round [raʊnd]:
1. rund 7
2. Runde 7
3. round ... um (... herum), in ... umher 7
turn round (sich) umdrehen 5
route [ruːt] Route, Weg 8
royal ['rɔɪəl] königlich 7
RSVP [ɑːr es viː 'pi] um Antwort wird gebeten 5
rub [rʌb] reiben, scheuern 8
rubber ['rʌbə] Radiergummi 5
rubbish ['rʌbɪʃ] (Haus-)Müll, Abfall 5
rucksack ['rʌksæk] *(BE)* Rucksack 6
rude [ruːd] unhöflich, frech 7
rug [rʌg] Teppich, Läufer 7
rule [ruːl]:
1. Herrschaft 9: 4 (58/59)
2. herrschen (über) 9: 4 (58/59)
rule [ruːl] Regel 6
ruler ['ruːlə]:
1. Lineal 5
2. Herrscher/in 9: 4 (58/59)
run [rʌn], **ran, run** rennen, laufen 5 **run after sb.** jm. nachlaufen 6 **°run sth.** etwas betreiben, leiten
rung [rʌŋ] *siehe* **ring**
rung [rʌŋ] Sprosse *(einer Leiter)* 9: 3 (50)

runner ['rʌnə] Läufer/in 9: 1 (20)
°rupee [ruː'piː] Rupie *(Währung in Indien)*

S

sacred ['seɪkrɪd] heilig 8
sad [sæd] traurig 5
saddle ['sædl]:
1. Sattel 8
2. satteln 8
sadness ['sædnəs] Traurigkeit 7
safe [seɪf] sicher *(gefahrlos)* 6
safety ['seɪfti] Sicherheit 8
said [sed] *siehe* **say** **it is said to be ...** man sagt, es sei ... 9: 4 (64)
sail [seɪl] segeln, *(mit dem Schiff)* fahren 5
Saint (= St) [seɪnt] Sankt (St) 7
salad ['sæləd] Salat *(als Gericht oder Beilage)* 5
salary ['sæləri] Gehalt 9: 4 (60)
sale [seɪl] Verkauf; Schlussverkauf *(mit Sonderangeboten)* 9: 3 (49)
for sale zu verkaufen 9: 3 (49)
salmon ['sæmən], *pl* **salmon** Lachs 8
salt [sɔːlt] Salz 6
salty ['sɔːlti] salzig 6
same [seɪm]: **the same** gleich; derselbe/dieselbe/dasselbe; dieselben 5 **just/all the same** trotzdem 9: 2 (34)
sand [sænd] Sand 6
sang [sæŋ] *siehe* **sing**
sat [sæt] *siehe* **sit**
satisfactory [sætɪs'fæktəri] zufriedenstellend 9: 2 (34)
Saturday ['sætədeɪ], ['sætədi] Samstag 5
sauce [sɔːs] Soße 5
sausage ['sɒsɪdʒ] (Brat-, Bock-)Würstchen, Wurst 6
save [seɪv]:
1. retten 6
2. sparen 6
saw [sɔː] *siehe* **see**
Saxon ['sæksn] Sachse/Sächsin; sächsisch 7
say [seɪ], **said, said** sagen 5 **Say hi to everyone.** Grüß/t alle. 7 **say sorry to sb.** sich bei jm. entschuldigen 5 **it says that ...** es (be-)sagt, dass ... 5
scalp [skælp] Kopfhaut 8
scam [skæm] Schwindel, Betrug 9: 2 (27)
scan (a text for) [skæn] (einen Text) überfliegen (nach), absuchen (nach) 7
scar [skɑː]:
1. Narbe 8
2. **scar sb.** bei jm. Narben hinterlassen 8
be scarred Narben haben 8
scared [skeəd] ängstlich, verängstigt 5 **be scared (of)** Angst haben (vor) 5
scarf [skɑːf], *pl* **scarves** Schal 7
scarves [skɑːvz] *Plural von* **scarf**
scary ['skeəri] unheimlich, beängstigend, gruselig 6
scene [siːn] Szene 7
schedule ['skedʒuːl]:
1. Stundenplan 6
2. Zeitplan 8
school [skuːl] Schule 5 **at school** in der Schule 5
school club [klʌb] AG *(in der Schule)* 5
schoolbag ['skuːlbæg] Schultasche 5
schoolroom ['skuːlruːm] Klassenraum, Schulzimmer 9: 2 (34)
schoolyard ['skuːljɑːd] *(AE)* Schulhof 9: 2 (35)
science ['saɪəns] Naturwissenschaft 5
scientist ['saɪəntɪst] (Natur-)Wissenschaftler/in 7
scooter ['skuːtə] (Motor-)Roller 5
score [skɔː]:
1. erzielen *(Punkt/Tor/Treffer)* 6
2. Spiel-/Punktestand; *(im Spiel/Sport erzielter)* Punkt 6
scrapbook ['skræpbʊk] Sammelalbum; Notizbuch 8
scrape [skreɪp] kratzen, schaben 7
scrapyard ['skræpjɑːd] Schrottplatz 9: 3 (50)
scream [skriːm]:
1. Schrei 8
2. schreien 8
screen [skriːn] Bildschirm 6
script [skrɪpt] Drehbuch 7
scroll (up/down) [skrəʊl] (hoch-/runter)scrollen 9: 3 (44)
scuba-diving ['skuːbə daɪvɪŋ] Sporttauchen 9: 1 (8/9)
sculpture ['skʌlptʃə] Skulptur 8
sea [siː] Meer, (die) See 5
sea level ['siː levl] Meeresspiegel 8
seafood ['siːfuːd] Meeresfrüchte 8
seal [siːl] Robbe, Seehund 8
search (for sth.) [sɜːtʃ]:
1. (etwas/nach etwas) suchen 8
2. Suche (nach etwas) 8
search engine ['sɜːtʃ endʒɪn] Suchmaschine 8
season ['siːzn] Jahreszeit; Saison 8
seat [siːt] (Sitz-)Platz 8 **take a seat** Platz nehmen 8
second ['sekənd] zweite(r, s) 5
second ['sekənd] Sekunde 9: 3 (51)
secondary school ['sekəndri skuːl] weiterführende Schule 9: 2 (26)
secondly ['sekəndli] zweitens 7
seconds *(pl)* ['sekəndz] Nachschlag 6
secret ['siːkrət]:
1. Geheimnis 7
2. geheim 7
in secret im Geheimen 7
°section ['sekʃn] Abschnitt
sector ['sektə] Sektor, Bereich 9: 2 (33)
secure [sɪ'kjuə]:
1. sicher, gesichert 9: 3 (51)
2. **secure sth.** (sich) etwas sichern; sicherstellen 9: 3 (51)
security [sɪ'kjʊərəti] Sicherheit 8
see [siː], **saw, seen** sehen 5 **See you tomorrow.** Bis morgen. 5
°seek shade [siːk], **sought, sought** Schatten (auf)suchen
seem (to be/do) [siːm] erscheinen; (zu sein / zu tun) scheinen 6
seen [siːn] *siehe* **see**
segregation [segrɪ'geɪʃn] Trennung *(nach Hautfarbe/Religion/Geschlecht)* 8
self-defence [self dɪ'fens] Selbstverteidigung 7
self-driving car [self draɪvɪŋ 'kɑː] selbstfahrendes Auto 8
self-employed [self ɪm'plɔɪd] selbstständig, freiberuflich 9: 2 (36)
sell [sel], **sold, sold** verkaufen 5
seller ['selə] Verkäufer/in 9: 4 (67)
send [send], **sent, sent** senden, schicken 5
sense [sens]:
1. Sinn 8
sense of smell Geruchssinn 8
sense of touch Tastsinn 8 **make sense** Sinn machen 8
2. Vernunft 9: 3 (48)
sensible ['sensəbl] vernünftig; praktisch, zweckmäßig 9: 3 (48)
sensible shoes vernünftige *(= bequeme, robuste)* Schuhe 9: 3 (48)
sensitive ['sensətɪv] einfühlsam, sensibel; heikel *(z. B. Thema)* 9: 4 (61)
sent [sent] *siehe* **send**
sentence ['sentəns] Satz 5
separate ['sepəreɪt] trennen 9: 1 (11)
separate ['seprət] getrennt, separat 9: 1 (11)

September [sep'tembə] September 5
series ['sɪəri:z], *pl* **series** Serie, Sendereihe 6
serious ['sɪəriəs] ernst 6
servant ['sɜ:vənt] Diener/in; Bedienstete/r 9: 4 (60)
service ['sɜ:vɪs] Service, Dienst 9: 2 (30)
set [set] Set, Garnitur 5 **tea set** Teeservice 5
set [set], **set, set** stellen, legen, setzen 7 **set off** aufbrechen *(sich auf den Weg machen)* 8 **set sth. (to)** etwas einstellen (auf) 9: 3 (49) **set sth. up** etwas einrichten, aufbauen 7 **set sth. up** etwas arrangieren 9: 2 (26) **set the table** den Tisch decken 7
setting ['setɪŋ] Schauplatz *(z. B. Film/Geschichte)* 7
settle ['setl] sich niederlassen, sich ansiedeln 7
settler ['setlə] Siedler/in 7
seven ['sevn] sieben 5
several ['sevrəl] mehrere, einige 7
sew [səʊ], **sewed, sewn** nähen 7
sewage ['su:ɪdʒ] Abwasser 9: 4 (64)
sewer ['su:ə] Abwasserkanal 9: 4 (60) **sewers** *(pl)* Kanalisation(ssystem) 9: 4 (60)
sewing machine ['səʊɪŋ məʃi:n] Nähmaschine 7
sewn [səʊn] *siehe* **sew**
sexuality [sekʃu'æləti] Sexualität 8
°**shade** [ʃeɪd] Schatten *(vor der Sonne geschützt)*
shadow ['ʃædəʊ] Schatten *(Umriss)* 8
°**shah** [ʃɑ:] Schah *(Herrscher)*
shake [ʃeɪk], **shook, shaken:**
1. schütteln 6
2. zittern 7
shaken ['ʃeɪkən] *siehe* **shake**
shallow ['ʃæləʊ] flach, seicht; oberflächlich 7
shame [ʃeɪm] Scham; Schande 8 **Shame on you!** Schäm dich! / Schämt euch! 8 **a shame** eine Schande; schade 8
shamrock ['ʃæmrɒk] Kleeblatt 7
share [ʃeə]:
1. (An-)Teil 9: 4 (71)
2. teilen 5
share a room (with ...) sich ein Zimmer teilen (mit ...) 5
shark [ʃɑ:k] Hai 7
sharpener ['ʃɑ:pnə] Spitzer 5
shave [ʃeɪv]:
1. (sich) rasieren 8
2. Rasur 8
she [ʃi:] sie *(weibliche Person)* 5
shelf [ʃelf], *pl* **shelves** Regal 5
shelter ['ʃeltə] (Obdachlosen-)Unterkunft; Schutzraum, Unterstand 8
shelves [ʃelvz] *Plural von* **shelf**
shine [ʃaɪn], [ʃɒn], **shone, shone** scheinen *(Sonne)*; leuchten, strahlen, glänzen 9: 4 (67)
ship [ʃɪp] Schiff 5
shirt [ʃɜ:t] Hemd 5
shock [ʃɒk]:
1. Schock 8
2. **shock sb.** jn. schockieren 8
shoe [ʃu:] Schuh 5 **in sb.'s shoes** an js. Stelle 7
shone [ʃɒn] *siehe* **shine**
shook [ʃʊk] *siehe* **shake**
shoot [ʃu:t], **shot, shot** (er)schießen 8
shooter ['ʃu:tə] Schütze/ Schützin 8
shooting ['ʃu:tɪŋ] Schießerei 8
shop [ʃɒp] Laden, Geschäft 5
shop assistant ['ʃɒp əsɪstənt] Verkäufer/in 5
shopping ['ʃɒpɪŋ] *(das)* Einkaufen 5 **go shopping** einkaufen gehen 5
shopping centre ['ʃɒpɪŋ sentə] Einkaufszentrum 5
shopping list ['ʃɒpɪŋ lɪst] Einkaufsliste 6
shore [ʃɔ:] Ufer; Küste 8
short [ʃɔ:t]:
1. kurz 5
2. klein *(Personen)* 6
short-term [ʃɔ:t 'tɜ:m] kurzfristig, Kurzzeit- 9: 1 (17)
shorten ['ʃɔ:tn] (ver)kürzen 9: 1 (15)
shorts *(pl)* [ʃɔ:ts] kurze Hose 5
shot [ʃɒt]:
1. *siehe* **shoot**
2. Schuss; Wurf *(Sport)* 8
3. Aufnahme, Foto; *(Film)* Einstellung 8
should [ʃʊd]: **we should ...** wir sollten ... 5
shoulder ['ʃəʊldə] Schulter 6
shout [ʃaʊt] rufen 5
shovel ['ʃʌvl] Schaufel 8
show [ʃəʊ], **showed, shown** zeigen 7
shower ['ʃaʊə] Dusche 5 **have a shower** (sich) duschen 5
shown [ʃəʊn] *siehe* **show**
shrug [ʃrʌg]:
1. Achselzucken 7
2. **shrug (your shoulders)** mit den Achseln/Schultern zucken 7
shut [ʃʌt], **shut, shut** schließen, verschließen 9: 3 (45) **shut sth. down** etwas schließen, stilllegen, abschalten 9: 3 (45)
shy [ʃaɪ] scheu, schüchtern 6
sick [sɪk] krank 6 **be sick** sich übergeben 6 **I feel sick.** Mir ist schlecht 6
side [saɪd] Seite *(z. B. Straßenseite)* 7
side dish ['saɪd dɪʃ] Beilage 6
sidewalk ['saɪdwɔ:k] *(AE)* Bürgersteig 6
sigh [saɪ]:
1. seufzen 9: 2 (35)
2. Seufzer 9: 2 (35)
sight [saɪt]:
1. Sehenswürdigkeit 6
2. Anblick, Bild 6
sightseeing ['saɪtsi:ɪŋ] Besichtigungen *(von Sehenswürdigkeiten)* 6
sign [saɪn] unterschreiben 9: 2 (31) **sign in** sich anmelden/eintragen 9: 3 (45) **sign out** sich abmelden/ austragen 9: 3 (45)
sign [saɪn] Schild, Zeichen 6
sign language ['saɪn læŋgwɪdʒ] Zeichensprache, Gebärdensprache 7
signature ['sɪgnətʃə] Unterschrift 7
significant [sɪg'nɪfɪkənt] deutlich, spürbar, erheblich, signifikant 9: 4 (71)
silence ['saɪləns]:
1. Stille; Schweigen 8
2. zum Schweigen bringen 8
silly ['sɪli] dumm, blöd; albern 7
silver ['sɪlvə] Silber 7
similar (to sb./sth.) ['sɪmələ] (jm./ einer Sache) ähnlich 7
simple ['sɪmpl] einfach 6
sin [sɪn] Sünde 9: 4 (64)
since [sɪns]:
1. seit 6
2. weil, da 8
since then [sɪns 'ðen] seitdem 7
sincerely [sɪn'sɪəli]: **Sincerely (yours)** *(AE)* Mit freundlichen Grüßen *(Briefschluss)* 8 **Yours sincerely** Mit freundlichen Grüßen *(Briefschluss)* 8
sing [sɪŋ], **sang, sung** singen 5
singer ['sɪŋə] Sänger/in 5
single ['sɪŋgl] Einzel-, einzelne(r, s) 7
single room [sɪŋgl 'ru:m] Einzelzimmer 7

sir [sɜː]: **Dear Sir or Madam** Sehr geehrte Damen und Herren 8
sister ['sɪstə] Schwester 5
sit [sɪt], **sat, sat:**
1. sitzen; sich setzen 5
sit down sich (hin)setzen 5 **sit up** sich aufsetzen, sich gerade hinsetzen 7
2. (herum)stehen/liegen 7
site [saɪt] *(kurz für)* Website; Stelle, Platz, Stätte 7
situation [sɪtʃu'eɪʃn] Situation 6
six [sɪks] sechs 5
size [saɪz] Größe 5 **What size do you take?** Welche Größe hast du? 5
skate [skeɪt] Skateboard fahren 7
skate park ['skeɪt pɑːk] Skatepark 7
skateboard ['skeɪtbɔːd]:
1. Skateboard 7
2. Skateboard fahren 7
skating ['skeɪtɪŋ] Schlittschuhlaufen; (Inline-)Skaten 5
skating rink ['skeɪtɪŋ rɪŋk] Schlittschuhbahn 5
ski [skiː] Skilaufen, Skifahren 5
skill [skɪl] Fähigkeit, Fertigkeit 7
skim a text [skɪm] einen Text überfliegen *(um den Inhalt grob zu erfassen)* 7
skin [skɪn] Haut; Schale *(z. B. Banane)* 8
skinny ['skɪni] mager, dürr; *(Kleidung)* eng anliegend 8
skirt [skɜːt] Rock 5
sky [skaɪ] Himmel 8
skyscraper ['skaɪskreɪpə] Wolkenkratzer 6
°slap on a hat [slæp] einen Hut aufsetzen
slave [sleɪv] Sklave, Sklavin 7
slavery ['sleɪvəri] Sklaverei 8
sleep [sliːp]:
1. Schlaf 6
go to sleep einschlafen; schlafen gehen 9: 3 (44)
2. **sleep, slept, slept** schlafen 5
sleeping bag ['sliːpɪŋ bæg] Schlafsack 8
sleepless ['sliːpləs] schlaflos 6
sleepy ['sliːpi] müde; verschlafen 9: 4 (67)
slept [slept] *siehe* **sleep**
°slid [slɪd] *siehe* **slide**
slide [slaɪd] Dia; Folie *(Präsentationssoftware)* 7
°slide [slaɪd], **slid, slid** schieben, gleiten (lassen) **slide on sunglasses** eine Sonnenbrille aufsetzen

slip [slɪp]:
1. (aus)rutschen 8
2. wegrutschen 9: 3 (51)
°3. **slip on clothes** Kleidung überziehen
°slop on sunscreen [slɒp] Sonnencreme auftragen
sloppy ['slɒpi] schlabberig; nachlässig, schludrig 7
slot [slɒt] Schlitz, Öffnung; (Karten-)Einzug 9: 2 (33)
sloth [sləʊθ] Faultier 9: 2 (27)
slow [sləʊ]:
1. langsam 5
2. **slow sb. down** jn. langsamer machen, aufhalten 9: 2 (34)
slow sth. down etwas langsamer machen, verlangsamen 9: 2 (34)
small [smɔːl] klein 5
smart [smɑːt]:
1. schick 5
2. intelligent, clever 8
smell [smel]:
1. riechen; schlecht riechen 5
2. Geruch; Gestank 6
smile [smaɪl]:
1. lächeln 5
2. *(ein/das)* Lächeln 5
snail [sneɪl] Schnecke 9: 1 (14)
snake [sneɪk] Schlange 7
snapshot ['snæpʃɒt] Schnappschuss 7
sneaker ['sniːkə] *(AE)* Sportschuh 8
snorkelling ['snɔːkəlɪŋ] Schnorcheln 9: 1 (8/9)
snow [snəʊ]:
1. Schnee 5
2. schneien 6
snowy ['snəʊi] schneebedeckt; verschneit 5
so [səʊ]:
1. so 6
so many so viele 6
2. also, daher 5
3. **so (that)** sodass 7
4. **So do I.** Ich auch. / Das tue ich auch. / Das gilt auch für mich. 9: 4 (64)
soak up [səʊk 'ʌp] aufsaugen, in sich aufnehmen 9: 1 (17)
soap [səʊp] Seife 6
soccer ['sɒkə] Fußball 6
social ['səʊʃl] sozial 7
social media *(pl)* [səʊʃl 'miːdiə] soziale Medien 7 **on social media** in den sozialen Medien 7
sock [sɒk] Socke 7
socket ['sɒkɪt] Steckdose, Anschluss(dose) 9: 3 (51)

soft [sɒft] weich; *(Stimme)* leise 7
in a soft voice mit leiser Stimme 7
software developer ['sɒftweə dɪveləpə] Softwareentwickler/in 9: 4 (61)
sold [səʊld] *siehe* **sell**
soldier ['səʊldʒə] Soldat/in 7
solution (to a problem) [sə'luːʃn] Lösung (eines Problems) 7
solve [sɒlv] lösen *(Rätsel, Problem)*, lüften *(Geheimnis)* 8
some [sʌm], [səm] einige, ein paar; etwas, ein wenig 5 **Would you like some tea/potatoes?** Möchtest du (etwas) Tee / (ein paar) Kartoffeln? 5
somebody ['sʌmbədi] jemand 6
someone ['sʌmwʌn] jemand 6
something ['sʌmθɪŋ] etwas 5
sometimes ['sʌmtaɪmz] manchmal 5
somewhere ['sʌmweə] irgendwo(hin) 6
son [sʌn] Sohn 7
song [sɒŋ] Lied 5
songwriter ['sɒŋraɪtə] Songwriter/in, Liedermacher/in 6
soon [suːn] bald 5 **as soon as** sobald; so bald wie 8
sore [sɔː]: **a sore throat** Halsschmerzen 6
sorry ['sɒri]: **Sorry. / I'm sorry.** Tut mir leid. / Entschuldigung. 5 **say sorry to sb.** sich bei jm. entschuldigen 5
sort (of) [sɔːt] Art (von) 9: 3 (45)
°sought [sɔːt] *siehe* **seek**
sound [saʊnd]:
1. Geräusch; Klang, Laut 6
2. Ton *(Fernseher, Radio)* 8
3. klingen 6
it sounds fun es klingt, als ob es Spaß macht 6
°sound file ['saʊnd faɪl] Tondatei
soundtrack ['saʊndtræk] Filmmusik; Tonspur 7
soup [suːp] Suppe 6
sour [saʊr] sauer 6
sour cream ['saʊr kriːm] saure Sahne 6
source [sɔːs] Quelle *(z. B. Website, Text)* 7
south [saʊθ] Süden; südlich; Süd- 6
south-east [saʊθ'iːst] Südosten, südöstlich 6
south-west [saʊθ'west] Südwesten, südwestlich 6
southbound ['saʊθbaʊnd] in Richtung Süden *(Zug, Bus)* 6

southern ['sʌðən] südlich, Süd- 7
space [speɪs] Raum, Fläche; Platz; Weltraum 8
spade [speɪd] Spaten, Schaufel 7
speak [spiːk], **spoke, spoken** sprechen 5 **speak out** sich äußern, seine Meinung äußern 9: 3 (45)
speaker ['spiːkə]:
1. Sprecher/in 7
2. Lautsprecher 8
special ['speʃl]:
1. besondere(r, s) 5
2. Sonderausgabe *(Magazin)*, Sondersendung *(Fernsehen)* 6
specific [spə'sɪfɪk] bestimmte(r, s), spezielle(r, s); genau, präzise 7
spectator [spek'teɪtə] Zuschauer/in 9: 1 (21)
sped [sped] *siehe* **speed**
speech [spiːtʃ] Rede, Ansprache; Sprache 8 **give a speech** eine Rede halten 8
speech bubble ['spiːtʃ bʌbl] Sprechblase 5
speed [spiːd]:
1. Geschwindigkeit 8
at a speed of ... mit einer Geschwindigkeit von ... 8
2. **speed, sped, sped** rasen, zu schnell fahren 8
speed climber ['spiːd klaɪmə] Speed-Kletterer/-in *(Geschwindigkeitskletterer/in)* 8
speed climbing ['spiːd klaɪmɪŋ] Speed(-Klettern) *(Geschwindigkeitsklettern)* 8
spell [spel] buchstabieren 5
spelling ['spelɪŋ] Schreibweise, Rechtschreibung 5
spend [spend], **spent, spent**:
1. ausgeben 5
spend 235 euros (on) 235 Euro ausgeben (für) 5
2. **spend time** Zeit verbringen 5
spent [spent] *siehe* **spend**
spice [spaɪs] Gewürz 6
spicy ['spaɪsi] würzig 6
spider ['spaɪdə] Spinne 5
spin [spɪn], **spun, spun** (sich) drehen 7
spirit ['spɪrɪt] Geist, Seele 8
spoke [spəʊk] *siehe* **speak**
°**spoke** [spəʊk] Speiche *(an einem Rad)*
spoken ['spəʊkən] *siehe* **speak**
sponsor ['spɒnsə]:
1. sponsern 7
2. Sponsor/in 7
spontaneous [spɒn'teɪniəs] spontan 9: 2 (29)
spoon [spuːn] Löffel 7
sport [spɔːt] Sport; Sportart 5 **do sport** Sport treiben 5 **play sport(s)** Sport treiben 7
sportsperson ['spɔːtspɜːsn], *pl* **sportspeople** Sportler/in 8
sporty ['spɔːti] sportlich 7
spread (sth.) [spred], **spread, spread** (etwas) verbreiten *(Virus, Krankheit)*; sich ausbreiten 7
spring [sprɪŋ]:
1. Frühling 8
°2. Quelle
spun [spʌn] *siehe* **spin**
square [skweə] Kästchen, Spielfeld; Platz *(in der Stadt)* 7 **km² = square kilometre(s)** Quadratkilometer 8
squint [skwɪnt] blinzeln, *(die Augen)* zusammenkneifen, spähen 9: 1 (17)
St = Saint [seɪnt] St = Sankt 7
stadium ['steɪdiəm] Stadion 6
staff [stɑːf] Personal, Belegschaft; Kollegium *(Schule)* 9: 2 (31)
staff manager [stɑːf 'mænɪdʒə] Personalchef/in 9: 2 (31)
stairs *(pl)* [steəz] Treppe; (Treppen-)Stufen 9: 4 (67)
stall [stɔːl] (Markt-)Stand, Bude 9: 4 (61)
stallholder ['stɔːlhəʊldə] Standinhaber/in 9: 4 (61)
stand [stænd], **stood, stood** stehen; sich (hin)stellen 6 **stand back (from)** zurücktreten (von) *(Schritte nach hinten machen)* 9: 3 (51) **stand up** aufstehen 5 **stand up (straight)** (gerade) stehen; sich (gerade) hinstellen 7
stand-alone ['stænd ələʊn] eigenständig; autark 8
star [stɑː] Stern 5
stare [steə]:
1. *(das)* Starren, starrer Blick 8
2. **stare (at)** (an)starren 8
start [stɑːt]:
1. Anfang, Start 7
2. beginnen, anfangen (mit) 5 **start a business** ein Geschäft aufmachen, einen Betrieb gründen/eröffnen 7
starting point ['stɑːtɪŋ pɔɪnt] Ausgangspunkt 7
starve [stɑːv] verhungern 7
state [steɪt]:
1. (Bundes-)Staat 6
2. Zustand 8
state of mind Gefühlslage, Geisteszustand 8
statement ['steɪtmənt] Aussage(satz) 9: 2 (30)
station ['steɪʃn]:
1. Bahnhof 5
2. **(radio/TV) station** (Radio-/Fernseh-)Sender 8
statistic [stə'tɪstɪk] statistische Tatsache/Größe 9: 2 (37)
statistics *(pl)* [stə'tɪstɪks] Statistik(en) 7
statue ['stætʃuː] Statue 7
status ['steɪtəs] Status 9: 3 (45)
stay [steɪ] bleiben; übernachten 5 **stay in touch (with)** in Verbindung/Kontakt bleiben (mit) 9: 3 (44)
steal [stiːl], **stole, stolen** stehlen, rauben 7
steer [stɪə] steuern, lenken 8
steering wheel ['stɪərɪŋ wiːl] Lenkrad, Steuer 8
step [step] Stufe; Schritt 5 **step by step** Schritt für Schritt 7
stepbrother ['stepbrʌðə] Stiefbruder 5
stepdad ['stepdæd] Stiefvater 5
stepfather ['stepfɑːðə] Stiefvater 5
stepmother ['stepmʌðə] Stiefmutter 5
stepmum ['stepmʌm] Stiefmutter 5
stepsister ['stepsɪstə] Stiefschwester 5
stereo ['steriəʊ] Stereo-; Stereoanlage 9: 3 (53)
stereotype ['steriətaɪp] Stereotyp, Klischee(vorstellung) 8
stereotypical [steriə'tɪpɪkl] stereotyp, klischeehaft 8
stew [stjuː] Eintopf(gericht) 7
stick [stɪk] Stock; Schläger *(Sport)* 7
still [stɪl]:
1. (immer) noch; trotzdem 6
2. still, ruhig 6
°3. **(film) still** Standbild *(Film)*
sting [stɪŋ]:
1. (Insekten-)Stich 9: 1 (14)
2. **sting, stung, stung** stechen *(Insekt)*; brennen 9: 1 (14)
stole [stəʊl] *siehe* **steal**
stolen ['stəʊlən] *siehe* **steal**
stomach ['stʌmək] Bauch; Magen 6
stomach ache ['stʌmək eɪk] Bauchschmerzen, Magenschmerzen 6
stone [stəʊn] Stein 6
stone circle [stəʊn 'sɜːkl] Steinkreis 6
stood [stʊd] *siehe* **stand**

stoop [stu:p] *(AE)* kleine Terrasse vor der Tür 8
stop [stɒp]:
1. (an)halten; stoppen; aufhören (mit) 5
stop sb. doing sth. jn. davon abhalten, etwas zu tun 7
2. Halt, Haltepunkt 6
bus stop Bushaltestelle 6
store [stɔ:] Geschäft 8
storm [stɔ:m] Sturm; Gewitter 5
stormy ['stɔ:mi] stürmisch 5
story ['stɔ:ri] Geschichte 5
storyteller ['stɔ:ri telə] (Geschichten-)Erzähler/in 9: 1 (12)
straight [streɪt]:
1. gerade; *(Haare)* glatt 6
2. heterosexuell 8
straight on [streɪt 'ɒn] geradeaus (weiter) 5
straightaway [streɪtə'weɪ] sofort 9: 4 (67)
strange [streɪndʒ] seltsam, sonderbar 6
stranger ['streɪndʒə] Fremde/r 7
strap [stræp] Gurt, Riemen 8
strategy ['strætədʒi] Strategie 7
strawberry ['strɔ:bəri] Erdbeere 5
stream [stri:m] streamen 9: 3 (53)
streaming service ['stri:mɪŋ sɜ:vɪs] Streamingdienst 9: 3 (53)
street [stri:t] Straße *(in Ortschaften)* 5
street sweeper ['tri:t swi:pə] Straßenfeger/in 9: 4 (60)
streetlight ['stri:t laɪt] Straßenlaterne 8
strength [streŋθ] Stärke, Kraft 9: 2 (30)
stress [stres]:
1. betonen 8
2. Betonung 8
strict [strɪkt] streng 5
strike [straɪk]:
1. Streik 9: 4 (71)
2. **strike, struck, struck** streiken; schlagen 9: 4 (71)
stripe [straɪp] Streifen 8
strong [strɒŋ] stark 6
struck [strʌk] *siehe* **strike**
structure ['strʌktʃə]:
1. strukturieren, aufbauen 7
2. Struktur 7
student ['stju:dnt] Schüler/in; Student/in 5
study ['stʌdi]:
1. studieren; lernen *(z. B. für Prüfungen)* 7
2. **study sth.** etwas untersuchen 9: 4 (71)
3. Untersuchung, Studie 9: 4 (71)

stuff [stʌf] *(infml)* Zeug, Kram 8
stung [stʌŋ] *siehe* **sting**
stupid ['stju:pɪd]:
1. dumm, blöd 5
2. *(infml, meist scherzhaft als Anrede)* Dummkopf 9: 2 (34)
style [staɪl]:
1. Stil; Art 7
2. *(Haare)* stylen; *(Kleidung)* schneiden 9: 4 (63)
subject ['sʌbdʒɪkt]:
1. (Schul-)Fach 5
2. Thema 6
subscribe to sth. [səb'skraɪb] etwas abonnieren 7
subscriber [səb'skraɪbə] Abonnent/in 7
subtitles *(pl)* ['sʌbtaɪtlz] Untertitel 8
subway ['sʌbweɪ] *(AE)* U-Bahn 8
succeed [sək'si:d] Erfolg haben 9: 2 (37) **succeed in doing sth.** es schaffen, etwas zu tun 9: 2 (37)
success [sək'ses] Erfolg 8
successful [sək'sesfl] erfolgreich 7
such (a) [sʌtʃ] so(lch) (ein/e) 8
such as ['sʌtʃ əz] wie (zum Beispiel) 8
suck [sʌk] saugen 9: 1 (14)
suddenly ['sʌdənli] plötzlich, auf einmal 6
suffer (from) ['sʌfə] leiden (an), erleiden 9: 1 (10)
suffering ['sʌfərɪŋ] *(das)* Leid, Leiden 9: 1 (10)
sugar ['ʃʊgə] Zucker 6
sugary ['ʃʊgəri] zuckrig, zuckerhaltig 6
suggest [sə'dʒest]:
1. vorschlagen 7
2. suggerieren 9: 3 (54)
suggestion [sə'dʒestʃən] Vorschlag 8
suicide ['su:ɪsaɪd] Selbstmord; Selbstmörder/in 8
suit [su:t]:
1. (Herren-)Anzug; (Damen-)Kostüm 7
2. **suit (sb.)** geeignet sein für, passen (zu); jm. stehen *(Frisur, Kleidung)* 7
suitable (for) ['su:təbl] geeignet, passend (für) 9: 2 (32)
sum sth. up [sʌm 'ʌp] etwas zusammenfassen 7 **To sum up, ...** Um (es) zusammenzufassen, ... / Zusammenfassend kann man sagen, ... 7
summer ['sʌmə] Sommer 5
summer camp ['sʌmə kæmp] Ferienlager *(im Sommer)* 6

sun [sʌn] Sonne 5
Sunday ['sʌndeɪ], ['sʌndi] Sonntag 5
sung [sʌŋ] *siehe* **sing**
sunglasses *(pl)* ['sʌnglɑ:sɪz] Sonnenbrille 6 **°slide on sunglasses** eine Sonnenbrille aufsetzen
sunny ['sʌni] sonnig 5
sunrise ['sʌnraɪz] Sonnenaufgang 9: 4 (70)
°sunscreen ['sʌnskri:n] Sonnenschutzcreme
sunset ['sʌnset] Sonnenuntergang 9: 4 (70)
°sunsmart ['sʌnsmɑ:t]: **Be sunsmart.** Schütze dich intelligent gegen die Sonne.
superhero ['su:pəhɪərəʊ], *pl* **superheroes** Superheld/in 7
superior (to sb./sth.) [su:'pɪəriə] (jm./einer Sache) überlegen; hervorragend 9: 2 (34)
supermarket ['su:pəmɑ:kɪt] Supermarkt 5
superpower ['su:pəpaʊə] Superkraft 7
superstrong [su:pə'strɒŋ] superstark 7
support [sə'pɔ:t]
1. unterstützen 6
2. Unterstützung 9: 1 (17)
supporter [sə'pɔ:tə] Anhänger/in, Fan 8
supposed [sə'pəʊzd]: **be supposed to be/do sth.** etwas sein sollen / etwas tun sollen 9: 2 (33)
sure [ʃʊə], [ʃɔ:] sicher *(ohne Zweifel)* 6 **make sure that ...** sicherstellen, dass ...; dafür sorgen, dass ... 7
surprise [sə'praɪz]:
1. überraschen 7
2. Überraschung 7
surprised [sə'praɪzd] überrascht 6
surprisingly [sə'praɪzɪŋli] überraschenderweise, überraschend *(Adv.)* 8
survey ['sɜ:veɪ] Umfrage 6 **do a survey** eine Umfrage durchführen 6
survival [sə'vaɪvl] Überleben 8
survive [sə'vaɪv] überleben 8
survivor [sə'vaɪvə] Überlebende/r 8
sushi ['su:ʃi] Sushi 5
suspicious (of) [sə'spɪʃəs] verdächtig; misstrauisch (gegenüber) 8
sustainability [səsteɪnə'bɪləti] Nachhaltigkeit 9: 2 (39)

sustainable [sə'steɪnəbl] nachhaltig, umweltverträglich; zukunftsfähig 8
swallow ['swɒləʊ] (ver)schlucken 8
swam [swæm] *siehe* **swim**
swamp [swɒmp] Sumpf 8
swap [swɒp] tauschen 5
sweat ['swet]:
1. Schweiß 8
2. schwitzen 8
sweep [swi:p], **swept, swept** fegen, kehren 9: 4 (60)
sweeper ['swi:pə] Straßenfeger/in 9: 4 (60)
sweet [swi:t] süß 7
sweets *(pl)* [swi:ts] Süßigkeiten 5
swept [swept] *siehe* **sweep**
swim [swɪm], **swam, swum** schwimmen 5
swimmer ['swɪmə] Schwimmer/in 9: 1 (18)
swimming costume ['swɪmɪŋ kɒstju:m] Badeanzug 6
swimming pool ['swɪmɪŋ pu:l] Schwimmbad 5
swimming trunks *(pl)* ['swɪmɪŋ trʌŋks] Badehose 6
swing [swɪŋ], **swung, swung** schwingen 9: 3 (51)
switch [swɪtʃ]:
1. Schalter 7
2. **switch sth. on/off** etwas einschalten / ausschalten 7
swum [swʌm] *siehe* **swim**
swung [swʌŋ] *siehe* **swing**
°Sydney funnel-web spider [sɪdni fʌnl web 'spaɪdə] Sydney-Trichternetzspinne
symbol (of) ['sɪmbl] Symbol (für) 7
synonym ['sɪnənɪm] Synonym *(Wort mit gleicher Bedeutung)* 8
system ['sɪstəm] System 8

T

table ['teɪbl]:
1. Tisch 5
2. Tabelle 6
table tennis ['teɪbl tenɪs] Tischtennis 5
tablet ['tæblət] Tablette, Pille 8
tail [teɪl] Schwanz 8
take [teɪk], **took, taken**:
1. dauern, *(Zeit)* brauchen, in Anspruch nehmen 5
2. (mit)nehmen; bringen 5 **take (a test / an exam)** (einen Test / eine Prüfung) machen 8 **take a break** Pause machen, abschalten 7 **take a photo** ein Foto machen 5 **take notes** sich Notizen machen 7 **take off** wegnehmen, aus dem Spiel nehmen 7 **take sb.'s blood pressure** bei jm. Blutdruck messen 8 **take sb.'s temperature** bei jm. Fieber messen 8 **take sth. off** etwas ausziehen, ablegen 6 **take sth. over** etwas übernehmen 9: 4 (61) **take your eyes off sth.** den Blick abwenden von etwas 8 **°take turns** sich abwechseln
take-off ['teɪk ɒf] Start *(Flugzeug)* 9: 3 (49)
takeaway ['teɪkəweɪ] Schnellrestaurant; Essen zum Mitnehmen 6
taken ['teɪkn] *siehe* **take**
tale [teɪl] Erzählung, Geschichte 7
talent ['tælənt] Talent 8
talented ['tæləntɪd] begabt, talentiert 8
talk [tɔ:k]:
1. Vortrag, Rede; Gespräch 5 **give a talk** einen Vortrag halten 5
2. **talk (to)** sprechen, reden (mit) 5
tall [tɔ:l] groß *(Person)*; hoch *(Gebäude)* 6
tap sth. [tæp] (leise) klopfen, tippen an etwas 7 **tap your fingers** mit den Fingern klopfen 7
target ['tɑ:gɪt] Ziel 9: 3 (54)
target audience [tɑ:gɪt 'ɔ:diəns] Zielgruppe, Zielpublikum 9: 3 (54)
target group ['tɑ:gɪt gru:p] Zielgruppe 9: 3 (54)
task [tɑ:sk] Aufgabe 5
Tasmanian devil [tæzmeɪniən 'devl] Beutelteufel *(Tierart)* 9: 1 (8/9)
taste [teɪst]:
1. Geschmack 6
2. schmecken; kosten, probieren 6
tasty ['teɪsti] schmackhaft, lecker 6
taught [tɔ:t] *siehe* **teach**
tax [tæks] *(die)* Steuer 9: 4 (62)
taxi ['tæksi] Taxi 6
tea [ti:] Tee 5
tea set ['ti: set] Teeservice 5
teabag ['ti:bæg] Teebeutel 9: 2 (28)
teach [ti:tʃ], **taught, taught** lehren, unterrichten 6 **teach sb. to do sth.** jm. beibringen, etwas zu tun 6
teacher ['ti:tʃə] Lehrer/in 5 **My dad is a teacher.** Mein Papa ist Lehrer (von Beruf). 5
teamwork ['ti:mwɜ:k] Teamwork, Zusammenarbeit 6
tear [tɪə] Träne 7
tear [teə], **tore, torn** reißen 8 **tear sth. up** etwas zerreißen 8
teaspoon ['ti:spu:n] Teelöffel 7
tech [tek] *(infml)* Technik 7
technique [tek'ni:k] Methode, Technik 9: 2 (24/25)
technology [tek'nɒlədʒi] Technik(unterricht); Technologie 5
teen [ti:n] Teenager 6
teeth [ti:θ] *Plural von* **tooth**
°telebook ['telibʊk] Telebuch *(Bildschirmbuch)*
television ['telɪvɪʒn] Fernsehen 9: 2 (33)
tell [tel], **told, told** sagen, erzählen, berichten 5 **tell about** erzählen von, berichten über 5 **tell sb. (not) to do sth.** jn. auffordern, etwas (nicht) zu tun; jm. sagen, dass er/sie etwas (nicht) tun soll 6
temperature ['temprətʃə] Temperatur; Fieber 6 **have a temperature** Fieber haben 6 **take sb.'s temperature** bei jm. Fieber messen 8
temple ['templ] Tempel 7
ten [ten] zehn 5
tennis court ['tenɪs kɔ:t] Tennisplatz 7
tent [tent] Zelt 6
terrible ['terəbl] schrecklich, fürchterlich 5
terrified ['terɪfaɪd]: **be terrified (of)** schreckliche Angst haben (vor) 8
terrify sb. ['terɪfaɪ] jm. schreckliche Angst einjagen 8
terrifying ['terɪfaɪɪŋ] Furcht erregend, erschreckend 8
°territory ['terətri] Gebiet, Territorium
terror ['terə] (panische) Angst 7
test [test] testen 6
test paper ['test peɪpə] Prüfungsarbeit 9: 2 (33)
testimony (to) ['testɪməni] (Zeugen-)Aussage; Beweis (für), Zeugnis 9: 1 (10)
text [tekst]:
1. **text (message)** SMS 5
2. **text sb.** jm. eine SMS schicken 7
textbook ['tekstbʊk] Schulbuch, Lehrbuch 9: 1 (16)
than [ðən]: **more than** mehr als 6
thank sb. [θæŋk] sich bei jm. bedanken 8
thank you ['θæŋk ju:] danke (schön) 5
thanks [θæŋks] danke (schön) 5

Thanksgiving Day [θæŋks'gɪvɪŋ deɪ] Erntedankfest 6
that [ðæt], [ðət]:
1. das (dort) 5
that night in jener Nacht 6
That's £2. Das macht 2 Pfund. 5
It's me that tells her ... und (ausgerechnet/nur) ich sage ihr... *(**me** betont)* 9: 3 (45)
2. dass 5
it says that ... es (be)sagt, dass ... 5 **so that** sodass 7
3. der, die, das *(Relativpronomen)* 7
sports that I do Sportarten, die ich mache 7
4. that bad so schlecht 9: 3 (54)
the [ðə] der, die, das 5
theatre ['θɪətə] Theater 5
their [ðeə] ihr/e *(Plural)* 5
theirs [ðeəz] ihrer, ihre, ihrs *(zu „they")* 6
them [ðem], [ðəm] sie, ihnen 5
themselves [ðəm'selvz] sie/sich selbst *(Plural)* 6
then [ðen]:
1. dann, danach 5
2. (back) then damals 9: 1 (11)
there [ðeə] da, dort; dahin, dorthin 5 **there are** es sind ... / es gibt ... 5
there's (= there is) es ist ... / es gibt ... 5
therefore ['ðeəfɔː] daher, deshalb 8
these [ðiːz] diese (hier) 5
they [ðeɪ]:
1. sie *(Plural)* 5
2. man 9: 4 (64)
They say ... Man sagt ... 9: 4 (64)
thick [θɪk] dick; dicht 8
thin [θɪn] dünn; schlank 8
thing [θɪŋ] Ding, Sache 5
think [θɪŋk], **thought, thought** denken, meinen, glauben 5 **think of** denken an 5 **What do they think of/about ...?** Was halten sie von ...? / Wie denken sie über ...? 7
third [θɜːd] dritte(r, s) 5 **one third** ein Drittel 7
Thirdly, ... ['θɜːdli] Drittens ... 7
thirties ['θɜːtiːz]: **the 30s / the thirties** die Dreißigerjahre 8
this [ðɪs]:
1. dies; diese(r, s) 5
this evening heute Abend 6
This is ... Dies ist ... / Das ist ... 5
2. this good so gut 9: 3 (54)
those [ðəʊz] die dort, jene (dort) 5
though [ðəʊ] obwohl 7 **even though** auch wenn, obwohl *(betont)* 9: 2 (27)
thought [θɔːt]:
1. *siehe* **think**
2. Gedanke 8
thousand ['θaʊznd] tausend 6
threat (to) ['θret] Drohung, Bedrohung, Gefahr (für) 8
threaten ['θretn] (be)drohen 8
three [θriː] drei 5
threw [θruː] *siehe* **throw**
thrilled [θrɪld] fasziniert, begeistert 9: 4 (66)
throat [θrəʊt] Hals 6 **a sore throat** Halsschmerzen 6
through [θruː] durch 6
throw [θrəʊ], **threw, thrown** werfen 7
thrown [θrəʊn] *siehe* **throw**
thunder ['θʌndə] Donner 7
Thursday ['θɜːzdeɪ], ['θɜːzdi] Donnerstag 5
tick [tɪk] Zecke 9: 1 (14)
ticket ['tɪkɪt]:
1. Eintrittskarte, Fahrkarte 5
child ticket Kinderfahrschein 6
2. Strafzettel 8
ticket gate ['tɪkɪt geɪt] Sperre *(zur Fahrkartenkontrolle)* 6
ticket office ['tɪkɪt ɒfɪs] Kartenschalter, Kartenverkaufsstelle 7
tidy ['taɪdi]:
1. ordentlich 5
2. aufräumen 5
tie [taɪ]:
1. Krawatte 5
2. binden, schnüren 7
tight [taɪt]:
1. fest, straff; streng 9: 3 (51)
2. knapp, eng (anliegend) *(Kleidung)* 8
tighten ['taɪtn] anziehen *(z. B. Schraube)*, straff ziehen; verschärfen *(z. B. Maßnahme)* 9: 3 (51)
time [taɪm]:
1. Zeit; Uhrzeit 5
at any time jederzeit 9: 2 (31)
have a good time Spaß haben, sich vergnügen 6 **on time** pünktlich 7 **What time is it?** Wie spät ist es? 5
2. Mal 6
timetable ['taɪmteɪbl]:
1. Stundenplan 5
2. Fahrplan, Zeitplan 5
tip [tɪp]:
1. Tipp 5
2. Trinkgeld 8
3. tip sb. jm. Trinkgeld geben 8
tired ['taɪəd] müde 5 **be tired of** die Nase voll haben von 9: 3 (44)
title ['taɪtl] Titel, Überschrift 8
to [tu], [tə]:
1. zu, nach 5
upload sth. to the internet etwas ins Internet (hoch)laden 7
2. bis 5
7 to 12 (von) 7 bis 12 5
3. vor *(Uhrzeiten)* 5
quarter to 7 viertel vor 7 5
4. (um) zu 5
how to do sth. wie man etwas macht 7 **I didn't know what to say.** Ich wusste nicht, was ich sagen sollte. 7 **time to go** Zeit, zu gehen 5
today [tə'deɪ] heute 5
toe [təʊ] Zehe 9: 4 (63)
toenail ['təʊneɪl] Zehennagel 9: 4 (63)
together [tə'geðə] zusammen 5
toilet ['tɔɪlət] Toilette 5
token ['təʊkən] Spielfigur; Chip (Wertmarke); (Geschenk-)Gutschein 7
told [təʊld] *siehe* **tell**
tomato [tə'mɑːtəʊ], *pl* **tomatoes** Tomate 5
tomorrow [tə'mɒrəʊ] morgen 5
See you tomorrow. Bis morgen. 5
tongue [tʌŋ] Zunge; Sprache 8
mother tongue Muttersprache 8
tonight [tə'naɪt] heute Nacht, heute Abend 9: 4 (66)
tonne [tʌn] Tonne *(= 1.000 kg)* 8
too [tuː] auch 5 **from Berlin too** auch aus Berlin 5
too expensive [tuː] zu teuer 6
took [tʊk] *siehe* **take**
tool [tuːl] Werkzeug; (Hilfs-)Mittel 9: 2 (30)
tooth [tuːθ], *pl* **teeth** Zahn 6
top [tɒp] Spitze, das obere Ende 6
the top ten tips die zehn besten Tipps 5
topic ['tɒpɪk] Thema 8
torch [tɔːtʃ] Taschenlampe 6
tore [tɔː] *siehe* **tear**
torn [tɔːn] *siehe* **tear**
tornado [tɔː'neɪdəʊ] Tornado 8
tortoise ['tɔːtəs] Schildkröte 8
total ['təʊtl]:
1. Gesamt-; total 7
2. Gesamtmenge, Gesamtzahl 7
touch [tʌtʃ]:
1. anfassen, berühren 7
2. Berührung 8
3. in touch with in Kontakt mit 9: 3 (44)
lose touch (with) den Kontakt verlieren (zu) 9: 3 (44) **get in touch (with)** (sich) in Verbindung setzen (mit), Kontakt aufnehmen

(zu) 9: 3 (44) **keep/stay in touch (with)** in Verbindung/Kontakt bleiben (mit) 9: 3 (44)
tour (of) [tʊə] Tour, Reise, Rundgang/Rundfahrt 5
tour guide ['tʊə gaɪd] Reiseleiter/in, Fremdenführer/in 9: 3 (50)
tourism ['tʊərɪzəm] Tourismus 9: 4 (73)
tournament ['tʊənəmənt] Turnier, Wettkampf 9: 1 (19)
toward(s) [tə'wɔːdz] nach, auf ... zu, in Richtung (von) 7
towel ['taʊəl] Handtuch 6
tower ['taʊə] Turm 5
town [taʊn] Stadt 5
toy [tɔɪ] Spielzeug 8
track [træk] Pfad, (Feld-)Weg 8
track sth. [træk] etwas (zurück-, nach)verfolgen, beobachten 8
trade [treɪd]:
1. Handel 7
2. handeln, Handel (be)treiben 7
trader ['treɪdə] Händler/in 9: 4 (60)
tradition [trə'dɪʃn] Tradition 7
traditional [trə'dɪʃənl] traditionell 6
traffic ['træfɪk] (Straßen-)Verkehr 8
train [treɪn] Zug, Eisenbahn 5
train sb. [treɪn] jn. trainieren; ausbilden 7
trainer ['treɪnə] Sportschuh 8
training ['treɪnɪŋ] Training; Ausbildung, Dressur 6
training course ['treɪnɪŋ kɔːs] Ausbildung(sgang) 9: 2 (24/25)
tram [træm] Straßenbahn 5
trampolining ['træmpəliːnɪŋ] Trampolinspringen/-turnen 5
transgender [trænz'dʒendə] Transgender 8
translate [træns'leɪt] übersetzen 9: 2 (36)
translation [træns'leɪʃn] Übersetzung 9: 2 (36)
transport [træn'spɔːt] transportieren, befördern 8
transport *(no pl)* ['trænspɔːt] Fortbewegungsmittel; Beförderung 5
trap [træp]:
1. Falle 8
2. einschließen, fangen *(mit einer Falle)* 8
be trapped gefangen sein, in der Falle sitzen 8
trash [træʃ] *(AE)* Abfall, Müll 7
travel ['trævl]:
1. reisen 5
2. *(das)* Reisen 8
traveller ['trævələ] Reisende/r 9: 4 (67)
travelling expenses *(pl)* ['trævəlɪŋ ɪkspensɪz] Reisekosten 9: 2 (24/25)
treasure ['treʒə] Schatz 5
treat [triːt] behandeln 8
treatment ['triːtmənt] Behandlung 8
tree [triː] Baum 5
tree bark ['triː bɑːk] Baumrinde 9: 1 (12)
trial ['traɪəl] (Gerichts-)Verfahren, Prozess 8 **a right to a fair trial** ein Recht auf ein faires Gerichtsverfahren 8 **be on trial for** vor Gericht stehen wegen 8
triangle ['traɪæŋgl] Dreieck 9: 4 (70)
tribal ['traɪbl] Stammes- 8
tribal elder [traɪbl 'eldə] Stammesälteste/r 8
tribe [traɪb] (Volks-)Stamm 7
trick [trɪk] List, Streich 7 **play a trick on sb.** jm. einen Streich spielen 7
trip [trɪp] Ausflug; Reise 5 **class trip** Klassenausflug 5 **school trip** Schulausflug 5
trip [trɪp] stolpern 8 **trip sb. up** jn. stolpern lassen; jm. ein Bein stellen 8
troll [trəʊl] Troll *(Provokateur/in in Online-Medien)* 8
trouble ['trʌbl] Ärger, Schwierigkeiten 5 **be in trouble** Ärger haben, in Schwierigkeiten sein 5
trousers *(pl)* ['traʊzəz] Hose 5
truck [trʌk] Last(kraft)wagen, LKW 7
true [truː] wahr, richtig 6 **come true** wahr werden 9: 3 (52)
truly ['truːli]: **Yours truly** *(AE)* Mit freundlichen Grüßen *(Briefschluss)* 8
trust [trʌst]:
1. vertrauen 6
2. *(das)* Vertrauen 6
truth [truːθ] Wahrheit 7
try [traɪ] versuchen, (aus)probieren 5 **try sth. on** anprobieren *(Kleidung)* 5 **try to do sth.** versuchen, etwas zu tun 5
Tube [tjuːb] *(infml)* Londoner U-Bahn 6
Tuesday ['tjuːzdeɪ], ['tjuːzdi] Dienstag 5
tunnel ['tʌnl] Tunnel 7
turkey ['tɜːki] Truthahn, Pute; Putenfleisch 6
turn [tɜːn]:
1. (sich) (um)drehen 7
turn (a)round (sich) umdrehen 5
turn (over) the page(s) umblättern *(Buch/Heft)* 9: 2 (33) **turn off** (sich) ausschalten 9: 3 (53) **turn on** (sich) einschalten 9: 3 (53)
turn sth. (over) etwas umdrehen 7 **turn sth. down** etwas leise(r) stellen, herunterregeln 7 **turn sth. on/off** etwas ein-/ausschalten 9: 2 (34) **turn your T-shirt inside out** dein T-Shirt auf links ziehen 7
2. **turn off** abbiegen 8
turn right/left (nach) rechts/links abbiegen 5
3. **turn to sth.** zu etwas werden 6
turn [tɜːn]: **It's your turn.** Du bist dran. / Du bist an der Reihe. 9: 1 (20) °**take turns** sich abwechseln
turtle ['tɜːtl] (Wasser-)Schildkröte 5
TV [tiː'viː] Fernseher 5
tweezers *(pl)* ['twiːzəz] Pinzette 9: 1 (14)
twelve [twelv] zwölf 5
twenty ['twenti] zwanzig 5
twice [twaɪs] zweimal 8
twin [twɪn]: **twin brother/sister** Zwillingsbruder/-schwester 7
twins *(pl)* Zwillinge 7
two [tuː] zwei 5
type (of) [taɪp] Art, Sorte 6
typical (of) ['tɪpɪkl] typisch (für) 7
tyre ['taɪə] Reifen 8

U

ugly ['ʌgli] hässlich 9: 2 (33)
UK [juː 'keɪ] das Vereinigte Königreich 5
umbrella [ʌm'brelə] (Regen-)Schirm 6
unarmed [ʌn'ɑːmd] unbewaffnet 8
uncle ['ʌŋkl] Onkel 5
unclear [ʌn'klɪə] unklar 7
under ['ʌndə] unter 5
underground ['ʌndəgraʊnd] U-Bahn 6
underline [ʌndə'laɪn] unterstreichen 8
understand [ʌndə'stænd], **understood, understood** verstehen 5
understanding [ʌndə'stændɪŋ] Verständnis 8
understood [ʌndə'stʊd] *siehe* **understand**
underwater [ʌndə'wɔːtə] unter Wasser, Unterwasser- 7

unemployed [ʌnɪm'plɔɪd] arbeitslos 8
unemployment [ʌnɪm'plɔɪmənt] Arbeitslosigkeit 9: 1 (11)
unequal [ʌn'iːkwəl] ungleich 9: 4 (58/59)
unfortunately [ʌn'fɔːtʃənətli] unglücklicherweise, leider 7
unfriendly [ʌn'frendli] unfreundlich 6
unhappy [ʌn'hæpi] unglücklich 6
unhealthy [ʌn'helθi] ungesund 6
uniform ['juːnɪfɔːm] Uniform 5
unit ['juːnɪt] Lektion, Kapitel *(Schulbuch)* 5
United Kingdom (= the UK) [junaɪtɪd 'kɪŋdəm] das Vereinigte Königreich 5
university [juːnɪ'vɜːsəti] Universität 5
unlikely [ʌn'laɪkli] unwahrscheinlich 7
unlock [ʌn'lɒk] aufschließen, entsperren 8
unpaid [ʌn'peɪd] unbezahlt 9: 2 (26)
unplug sth. [ʌn'plʌg] den Stecker von etwas herausziehen, etwas ausstöpseln 9: 3 (53)
unpopular (with) [ʌn'pɒpjələ] unbeliebt (bei) 6
unreal [ʌn'rɪəl] unwirklich, unrealistisch 8
unsafe [ʌn'seɪf] unsicher 6
unspecified [ʌn'spesɪfaɪd] nicht angegeben, keine Angabe *(Formular)* 7
unsure [ʌn'ʃʊə] unsicher 7
untidy [ʌn'taɪdi] unordentlich 6
until [ən'tɪl] bis *(zeitlich)* 6 **not … until** erst, wenn … 6
°untouchable [ʌn'tʌtʃəbl] unberührbar; unantastbar
°untouchables [ʌn'tʌtʃəblz] Unberührbare *(im alten indischen Kasten-System)*
unusual [ʌn'juːʒʊəl] ungewöhnlich 9: 2 (37)
up [ʌp] hinauf, hoch 5
upload [ʌp'ləʊd] hochladen 6
upset [ʌp'set]:
1. aufgebracht, verärgert 7
2. upset sb., upset, upset jn. aufregen, ärgern, erschüttern 7
upstairs [ʌp'steəz] (nach) oben *(die Treppe hoch)* 5
us [ʌs], [əs] uns 5
USA [juː es 'eɪ] USA (= die Vereinigten Staaten von Amerika) 5
use [juːz] benutzen, verwenden 5
use [juːs] Gebrauch, Verwendung 9: 1 (12)
used to ['juːst tə]:
1. they used to make … sie haben (früher) immer … gemacht 9: 1 (13)
2. be used to gewöhnt sein an 9: 2 (26)
get used to sich gewöhnen an 9: 2 (26)
useful ['juːsfl] nützlich, hilfreich 7
useless ['juːsləs] nutzlos 6
user ['juːzə] (Be-)Nutzer/in 9: 3 (44)
username [juːzəneɪm] Benutzername 7
usual ['juːʒuəl] üblich, gewöhnlich 6
usually ['juːʒuəli] normalerweise, meistens 5

V

vacation [və'keɪʃn] *(AE)* Urlaub, Ferien 6
vaccination [væksɪ'neɪʃn] (Schutz-)Impfung 9: 2 (27)
vacuum ['vækjuəm] Staub saugen 7
vacuum cleaner ['vækjuəm kliːnə] Staubsauger 7
value ['væljuː] Wert 8 **value for money** Preis-Leistungs-Verhältnis, Gegenwert 8 **values** *(pl)* Werte, Wertvorstellungen 8 **It's good value (for money).** Es ist preiswert / sein Geld wert. 8
veg [vedʒ], *pl* **veg** *(infml)* Gemüse 8
vegetables *(pl)* ['vedʒtəblz] Gemüse 5
vegetarian [vedʒə'teəriən] vegetarisch; Vegetarier/in 5
veggie ['vedʒi] *(infml)* vegetarisch; Vegetarier/in 8
vending machine ['vendɪŋ məʃiːn] Verkaufsautomat 8
venom ['venəm] Gift 9: 1 (14)
venomous ['venəməs] giftig 9: 1 (14)
venue ['venjuː] Veranstaltungsort, Veranstaltungsstätte 9: 1 (20)
version ['vɜːʃn] Version 9: 3 (44)
very ['veri] sehr 5
vet [vet] Tierarzt/-ärztin 6
vibrate [vaɪ'breɪt] vibrieren 8
victim ['vɪktɪm] Opfer 8
video game ['vɪdiəʊ geɪm] Videospiel 7
view [vjuː]:
1. anschauen 7
2. Aufruf *(eines Videos im Internet)* 7
3. (An-)Blick, (Aus-)Sicht 7
in my view meiner Ansicht nach 6 **point of view** Standpunkt, Meinung; Perspektive 9: 1 (18)
Viking ['vaɪkɪŋ] Wikinger/in 7
village ['vɪlɪdʒ] Dorf 5
villager ['vɪlɪdʒə] Dorfbewohner/in 9: 4 (61)
vinegar ['vɪnɪgə] Essig 9: 1 (14)
violence ['vaɪələns] Gewalt; Gewalttätigkeit 7
violent ['vaɪələnt] gewalttätig; gewaltsam 7
violin [vaɪə'lɪn] Geige, Violine 7
viral ['vaɪrəl] Virus-, viral 7 **go viral** sich *(im Internet)* rasend schnell verbreiten 7
virtual ['vɜːtʃʊəl] virtuell 8
visit ['vɪzɪt]:
1. besuchen 5
2. Besuch 7
visitor ['vɪzɪtə] Besucher/in; Gast 7
visual materials *(pl)* [vɪʒuəl mə'tɪəriəlz] visuelle Materialien/Hilfsmittel 8
visuals *(pl)* ['vɪʒuəlz] **(***kurz für:* **visual materials)** visuelle Materialien/Hilfsmittel 8
°vitamin ['vɪtəmɪn] Vitamin
vocab ['vəʊkæb] *siehe* **vocabulary**
vocabulary *infml auch* **vocab** [və'kæbjələri] Vokabeln; Vokabelverzeichnis; Wortschatz 7
voice [vɔɪs] Stimme 6 **in a loud voice** mit lauter Stimme 7
voice message ['vɔɪs mesɪdʒ] Sprachnachricht 7
voice-over ['vɔɪs əʊvə] Filmkommentar, Off-Stimme 8
volume ['vɒljuːm] Volumen, Menge 8
volunteer [vɒlən'tɪə]:
1. freiwillig/ehrenamtlich arbeiten *(unbezahlt)* 8
2. Freiwillige/r; ehrenamtliche/r Mitarbeiter/in 8
volunteer organisation [vɒləntɪər ɔːgənaɪ'zeɪʃn] Freiwilligenorganisation 6
vote [vəʊt]:
1. Abstimmung, Votum 7
have a vote (on) abstimmen (über) 7
2. vote (on) wählen; abstimmen (über) 7

W

wag [wæg] wedeln (mit) 8
wage [weɪdʒ], *oft auch:* **wages** *(pl)* Lohn 9: 4 (71)
wagon ['wægən] Planwagen, (Pferde-)Fuhrwerk 8
wait [weɪt]:
1. Wartezeit, *(das)* Warten 8
2. wait (for) warten (auf) 5
Wait a minute. Warte mal. / Einen Moment. 5
waiter ['weɪtə] Kellner 8
waitress ['weɪtrəs] Kellnerin 8
wake up [weɪk 'ʌp], **woke, woken** aufwachen 5 **wake sb. up** jn. (auf)wecken 8
wake-up time ['weɪk ʌp taɪm] Weckzeit 7
walk [wɔːk]:
1. wandern, (zu Fuß) gehen 5 **walk a dog** mit einem Hund spazieren gehen 9: 2 (24/25) **walk around** umhergehen 6
2. Spaziergang; Wanderung; Fußweg *(Weg zu Fuß)* 9: 2 (24/25) **go for a walk** einen Spaziergang machen 9: 2 (24/25) **take a dog for a walk** mit einem Hund spazieren gehen 9: 2 (24/25)
wall [wɔːl] Wand, Mauer 5
wallet ['wɒlɪt] Brieftasche; Portemonnaie 8
want [wɒnt] wollen 5 **want to do sth.** etwas tun wollen 5 **I didn't want them to know ....** Ich wollte nicht, dass sie ... wussten. 7
war [wɔː] Krieg 8
wardrobe ['wɔːdrəʊb] Kleiderschrank 5
warm [wɔːm] warm 5
warming ['wɔːmɪŋ] Erwärmung 8
warranty ['wɒrənti] Garantie, Gewährleistung 9: 3 (53)
warrior ['wɒriə] Krieger/in 9: 4 (60)
was [wɒz], [wəz]: **I/he/she/it was** *Vergangenheitsform von* **be** 5
wash [wɒʃ] (sich) waschen 6 **wash over sb.** jn. überkommen 8
washing ['wɒʃɪŋ] Wäsche 6
waste [weɪst]:
1. verschwenden 9: 2 (33)
2. Verschwendung 9: 2 (33)
3. Müll; Abfall; Fäkalien 9: 4 (60) **animal waste** tierische Fäkalien 9: 4 (60) **human waste** menschliche Fäkalien 9: 4 (60)
watch [wɒtʃ] *(sich etwas)* anschauen; beobachten 5 **watch TV** fernsehen 5
water ['wɔːtə] Wasser 5
waterfall ['wɔːtəfɔːl] Wasserfall 6
way [weɪ]:
1. Weg 7 **make your way (to/through)** sich auf den Weg (nach/durch) machen 8
2. Art und Weise 7 **by the way** übrigens 9: 4 (64) **(in) this way** so, auf diese Art 9: 2 (34) **in many ways** in mancher/vielerlei Hinsicht 9: 2 (34) **No way!** Auf keinen Fall! 6 **that way** so, auf jene Art 9: 2 (34)
way cooler [weɪ] *(infml)* viel cooler, weit(aus) cooler 9: 3 (44)
way of life [weɪ əv 'laɪf] Lebensweise 8
we [wiː] wir 5
weak [wiːk] schwach 7
weakness ['wiːknəs] Schwäche 8
weapon ['wepən] Waffe 7
wear [weə], **wore, worn** tragen, anhaben *(Kleidung)* 5
weather ['weðə] Wetter 5
web [web] Netz 5
webpage ['webpeɪdʒ] Webseite 7
wedding ['wedɪŋ] Hochzeit 6
wedding present ['wedɪŋ preznt] Hochzeitsgeschenk 6
Wednesday ['wenzdeɪ], ['wenzdi] Mittwoch 5
week [wiːk] Woche 5
weekday ['wiːkdeɪ] Werktag, Wochentag 7
weekend [wiːk'end] Wochenende 5 **at the weekend** am Wochenende 5
weigh [weɪ] wiegen 8
weight [weɪt] Gewicht 8
welcome ['welkʌm]:
1. Empfang; Willkommen 9: 2 (27) **Welcome to ...** Willkommen in/an ... 5 **get a warm/great welcome** herzlich begrüßt werden 9: 2 (27) **give sb. a warm/great welcome** jn. herzlich begrüßen 9: 2 (27)
2. welcome sb. (to) jn. begrüßen (in), jn. willkommen heißen (in) 9: 2 (27)
3. You're welcome. Bitte, gern geschehen. / Nichts zu danken. 5
welcoming ['welkəmɪŋ] (gast)freundlich 8
weld [weld] schweißen 8
welfare ['welfeə] Sozialhilfe; Wohlfahrt, Fürsorge; Wohl(ergehen) 9: 1 (11)
well [wel]:
1. gut *(Adv.)* 7
2. Well, ... Nun, .../ Also, .../ Na ja, ... 6
3. gesund 9: 2 (27) **get well** (wieder) gesund werden 9: 2 (27)
well [wel] Quelle, Brunnen 9: 4 (60)
well-known [wel 'nəʊn] bekannt 8
went [went] *siehe* **go**
were [wɜː], [wə]: **we/you/they were** *Vergangenheitsform von* **be** 5
west [west] Westen; westlich; West- 6
westbound ['westbaʊnd] in Richtung Westen *(Zug, Bus)* 6
western ['westən] westlich, West- 7
wet [wet] nass 6
wetsuit ['wetsuːt] Taucheranzug, Neoprenanzug 6
whale [weɪl] Wal 6
what [wɒt]:
1. was 5
2. welche(r, s) 5 **What about you?** Und du? / Was ist mit dir? 5 **What's your name?** Wie heißt du? 5 **What time is it?** Wie spät ist es? 5
whatever [wɒt'evə] was (auch) (immer) 9: 1 (16)
wheel [wiːl] Rad 6 **big wheel** Riesenrad 6
wheelchair ['wiːltʃeə] Rollstuhl 5
wheelchair accessible [wiːltʃeər ək'sesəbl] rollstuhlgerecht *(mit dem Rollstuhl zu erreichen)* 7
when [wen]:
1. als *(zeitlich)* 5
2. wann 5 **When's your birthday?** Wann hast du Geburtstag? 5
3. wenn *(zeitlich)* 5
where [weə] wo; wohin 5 **Where are you from?** Wo kommst du her? 5
whereas [weər'æz] während, wohingegen 9: 3 (54)
whether ['weðə] ob 9: 3 (48)
which [wɪtʃ]:
1. welche(r, s) 5
2. der, die, das; die *(Relativpronomen)* 7 **a film which has ...** ein Film, der ... hat 7
while [waɪl]:
1. während 6
2. a while eine Weile, einige Zeit 9: 1 (17)
whisper ['wɪspə]:
1. flüstern 9: 3 (47)

2. (das) Flüstern, Geflüster 9: 3 (47)
whistle ['wɪsl]:
1. pfeifen 8
2. Pfiff; (Triller-)Pfeife 8
white [waɪt] weiß 5
who [hu:]:
1. wer 5
2. wem; wen 6
3. der, die *(Relativpronomen, Person)* 7
a boy who … ein Junge, der … 7
whole [həʊl] ganze(r, s) 6
wholemeal ['həʊlmi:l] Vollkorn- 7
whose [hu:z]:
1. wessen 5
2. dessen, deren *(Relativpronomen)* 7
why [waɪ] warum 5 **Why not do …?** Warum sollte man … nicht tun? 9: 3 (54) **Why pay …?** Warum sollte man … bezahlen? 9: 3 (54)
Wi-Fi ['waɪ faɪ] WLAN, kabellose Datenübertragung 7
wide [waɪd]:
1. breit, weit; 9: 3 (51)
2. weit geöffnet *(Augen)* 9: 3 (51)
wife [waɪf], *pl* **wives** (Ehe-)Frau 8
wild [waɪld] wild 8
wilderness ['wɪldənəs] Wildnis 8
wildfire ['waɪldfaɪə] Flächenbrand 8
wildlife ['waɪldlaɪf] Tiere *(in freier Wildbahn)*, Tierwelt 8
will [wɪl]: **you'll (= you will) fall** du wirst fallen 6
win [wɪn], **won, won** gewinnen 6
wind [wɪnd] Wind 5
windmill ['wɪndmɪl] Windmühle, Windrad 9: 3 (50)
window ['wɪndəʊ] Fenster 5
windscreen ['wɪndskri:n] Windschutzscheibe *(Auto)* 8
windy ['wɪndi] windig 5
winner ['wɪnə] Gewinner/in, Sieger/in 6
winter ['wɪntə] Winter 5
°wire ['waɪə] Draht
wise [waɪz] weise 8
wish [wɪʃ]:
1. wünschen 5
2. Wunsch 5
Best wishes Viele Grüße *(Briefschluss)* 5 **make a wish** sich etwas wünschen 5
with [wɪð]:
1. mit 5
2. bei 5
with us bei uns 5
within [wɪ'ðɪn] innerhalb (von), in 9: 3 (51) **within walking distance** in fußläufiger Entfernung, fußläufig erreichbar 9: 3 (51)
without [wɪ'ðaʊt] ohne 6
wives [waɪvz] *Plural von* **wife**
woke up [wəʊk] *siehe* **wake up**
woken up ['wəʊkən] *siehe* **wake up**
wolf [wʊlf], *pl* **wolves** Wolf 8
wolves [wʊlvz] *Plural von* **wolf**
woman ['wʊmən], *pl* **women** Frau 5
women ['wɪmɪn] *Plural von* **woman**
won [wʌn] *siehe* **win**
wonder ['wʌndə] sich fragen 9: 4 (67)
wonderful ['wʌndəfl] wunderbar 9: 4 (63)
won't [wəʊnt]: **you won't need (= you will not need) …** du wirst … nicht brauchen 6
wood [wʊd] Holz; Wald 6
wooden ['wʊdn] Holz-, hölzern 9: 3 (51)
wool [wʊl] Wolle 7
word [wɜ:d] Wort 5
word building ['wɜ:d bɪldɪŋ] das Bilden von Wörtern 7
word web ['wɜ:d web] Wortnetz 5
wore [wɔ:] *siehe* **wear**
work [wɜ:k]:
1. Arbeit 5
at work bei der Arbeit, am Arbeitsplatz 5
2. arbeiten; funktionieren 5
work experience ['wɜ:k ɪkspɪəriəns] Arbeitserfahrung(en), Praxiserfahrung(en); Praktikum 9: 2 (24/25)
worker ['wɜ:kə] Arbeiter/in 6
working hours *(pl)* ['wɜ:kɪŋ aʊəz] Arbeitszeit(en) 9: 2 (31)
world [wɜ:ld] Welt 5 **the best place in the world** der beste Ort der Welt / auf der Welt 5
worn [wɔ:n] *siehe* **wear**
worried (about) ['wʌrid] beunruhigt, besorgt (wegen) 5
worry (about) ['wʌri] sich Sorgen machen (wegen, um) 6 **worry sb.** jn. beunruhigen 6
worse [wɜ:s] schlechter, schlimmer 6
worst [wɜ:st] der/die/das schlechteste, schlimmste; am schlechtesten, am schlimmsten 6
would [wʊd]: **Would you like …?** Möchtest du …? 5 **I'd (= I would) like …** Ich hätte gern … / Ich möchte … 5 **I'd (= I would) like to talk about …** Ich würde gern über … sprechen. 5
°wrestler ['reslə] Ringer/in
write [raɪt], **wrote, written** schreiben 5 **write sth. down** etwas aufschreiben 7 **write sth. out** etwas ausstellen, (ins Reine) schreiben 9: 2 (33)
writer ['raɪtə] Autor/in, Verfasser/in 6
writing ['raɪtɪŋ] Schrift 6
written ['rɪtn] *siehe* **write**
wrong [rɒŋ] falsch 5 **be wrong** Unrecht haben 6 **go wrong** schiefgehen 6 **What's wrong?** Was fehlt dir/Ihnen? *(beim Arzt)* 6
wrote [rəʊt] *siehe* **write**

Y

°yak [jæk] Jak *(wild lebendes, asiatisches Rind)*
yard [jɑ:d]:
1. Hof 8
2. *(AE)* Garten 8
year [jɪə] Jahr(gang) 5 **six-year-old** sechsjährig; Sechsjährige/r 8
yearn for sth. / to do sth. [jɜ:n] sich sehnen nach etwas / danach, etwas zu tun 8
yellow ['jeləʊ] gelb 5
yes [jes] ja 5
yesterday ['jestədeɪ] gestern 5
yet [jet]: **… yet?** … schon …? 6 **not … yet** noch nicht … 6
you [ju], [jə]:
1. du; dich; dir; ihr; euch; Sie; Ihnen 5
2. man 9: 4 (64)
young [jʌŋ] jung 6
your [jɔ:], [jə] dein/e; euer/eure; Ihr/e 5
yours [jɔ:z] deine, deiner, deins; eurer, eure, eures; Ihrer, Ihre, Ihres *(zu „you")* 6
yourself [jə'self] du/dir/dich (selbst) 6
yourselves [jɔ:'selvz], [jə'selvz] ihr/euch selbst 6
yum [jʌm] *(infml)* lecker 7

Z

zero ['zɪərəʊ] Null 5
zipper ['zɪpə] Reißverschluss 8
zone [zəʊn] Zone 6
zoo [zu:] Zoo 6

infinitive	simple past	past participle	
(to) **be**	I/he/she/it **was**; you/we/you/they **were**	**been**	sein
(to) **bear**	**bore**	**borne**	ertragen, aushalten; tragen
(to) **beat**	**beat**	**beaten**	schlagen, besiegen
(to) **become**	**became**	**become**	werden
(to) **begin**	**began**	**begun**	anfangen, beginnen
(to) **bite**	**bit**	**bitten**	beißen; stechen *(z. B. Insekten)*
(to) **bleed**	**bled**	**bled**	bluten
(to) **blow**	**blew** [uː]	**blown**	pusten, blasen; wehen
(to) **break** [eɪ]	**broke**	**broken**	brechen
(to) **bring**	**brought**	**brought**	bringen, mitbringen
(to) **build** [ɪ]	**built** [ɪ]	**built** [ɪ]	bauen
(to) **burn**	**burnt**	**burnt**	brennen, verbrennen
(to) **burst**	**burst**	**burst**	brechen, bersten, platzen
(to) **buy**	**bought**	**bought**	kaufen
(to) **catch**	**caught**	**caught**	(ein)fangen; erwischen
(to) **choose**	**chose**	**chosen**	wählen, auswählen
(to) **come**	**came**	**come**	kommen
(to) **cost**	**cost**	**cost**	kosten
(to) **cut**	**cut**	**cut**	schneiden; *(Rasen)* mähen
(to) **deal (with)**	**dealt**	**dealt**	sich kümmern (um); sich befassen (mit), behandeln *(z. B. Thema)*
(to) **do**	**did**	**done** [ʌ]	tun, machen
(to) **dig**	**dug**	**dug**	graben
(to) **draw**	**drew**	**drawn**	zeichnen
(to) **drink**	**drank**	**drunk**	trinken
(to) **drive** [aɪ]	**drove** [əʊ]	**driven** [ɪ]	fahren
(to) **eat** [iː]	**ate** [et, eɪt]	**eaten** [iː]	essen
(to) **fall**	**fell**	**fallen**	fallen
(to) **feed**	**fed**	**fed**	füttern
(to) **feel**	**felt**	**felt**	fühlen, sich fühlen
(to) **fight**	**fought**	**fought**	kämpfen, bekämpfen
(to) **find**	**found**	**found**	finden
(to) **fly**	**flew**	**flown**	fliegen
(to) **forget**	**forgot**	**forgotten**	vergessen
(to) **freeze**	**froze**	**frozen**	(ge)frieren; erstarren
(to) **get**	**got**	**got**	bekommen; (sich etw.) besorgen, holen
(to) **give** [ɪ]	**gave**	**given** [ɪ]	geben
(to) **go**	**went**	**gone**	gehen, fahren
(to) **grow**	**grew**	**grown**	anbauen; werden; wachsen
(to) **hang**	**hung** [ʌ]	**hung**	hängen
(to) **have**	**had**	**had**	haben
(to) **hear** [ɪə]	**heard** [ɜː]	**heard**	hören
(to) **hide**	**hid**	**hidden**	(sich) verstecken
(to) **hit**	**hit**	**hit**	treffen auf, schlagen, prallen, stoßen
(to) **hold**	**held**	**held**	halten
(to) **hurt**	**hurt**	**hurt**	verletzen; wehtun
(to) **keep**	**kept**	**kept**	(be)halten
(to) **kneel**	**knelt**	**knelt**	knien
(to) **know** [nəʊ]	**knew** [njuː]	**known** [nəʊn]	wissen; kennen
(to) **lead**	**led**	**led**	führen, leiten
(to) **leave**	**left**	**left**	lassen, zurücklassen, verlassen
(to) **lend**	**lent**	**lent**	(ver)leihen

infinitive	simple past	past participle	
(to) **let**	**let**	**let**	lassen
(to) **light**	**lit**	**lit**	anzünden
(to) **lose** [uː]	**lost**	**lost**	verlieren
(to) **make**	**made**	**made**	machen, herstellen
(to) **mean** [iː]	**meant** [e]	**meant** [e]	bedeuten; sagen wollen
(to) **meet**	**met**	**met**	treffen
(to) **pay**	**paid**	**paid**	(be)zahlen
(to) **put**	**put**	**put**	legen, stellen, stecken
(to) **read** [iː]	**read** [e]	**read** [e]	lesen
(to) **reset**	**reset**	**reset**	zurücksetzen; resetten
°(to) **rewrite**	**rewrote**	**rewritten**	neu schreiben, umschreiben
(to) **ride** [aɪ]	**rode**	**ridden** [ɪ]	reiten; *(Rad)* fahren
(to) **ring**	**rang**	**rung**	läuten, klingeln
(to) **rise**	**rose**	**risen**	(an)steigen; sich erheben
(to) **run**	**ran**	**run**	rennen, laufen
(to) **say**	**said** [sed]	**said** [sed]	sagen
(to) **see**	**saw**	**seen**	sehen
°(to) **seek**	**sought**	**sought**	suchen
(to) **sell**	**sold**	**sold**	verkaufen
(to) **send**	**sent**	**sent**	senden, schicken
(to) **set**	**set**	**set**	stellen, legen, setzen
(to) **sew**	**sewed**	**sewn**	nähen
(to) **shake**	**shook**	**shaken**	schütteln
(to) **shoot**	**shot**	**shot**	(er)schießen
(to) **show**	**showed**	**shown**	zeigen
(to) **shut**	**shut**	**shut**	(ver)schließen
(to) **sing**	**sang**	**sung**	singen
(to) **sit**	**sat**	**sat**	sitzen; sich setzen
(to) **sleep**	**slept**	**slept**	schlafen
°(to) **slide**	**slid**	**slid**	schieben, gleiten (lassen)
(to) **speak** [iː]	**spoke**	**spoken**	sprechen
(to) **speed**	**sped**	**sped**	rasen, zu schnell fahren
(to) **spend**	**spent**	**spent**	*(Geld)* ausgeben, *(Zeit)* verbringen
(to) **spin**	**spun**	**spun**	(sich) drehen
(to) **spread**	**spread**	**spread**	verbreiten, sich ausbreiten
(to) **stand**	**stood**	**stood**	stehen
(to) **steal**	**stole**	**stolen**	stehlen, rauben
°(to) **stick**	**stuck**	**stuck**	kleben
(to) **sting**	**stung**	**stung**	stechen *(Insekt)*; brennen
(to) **sweep**	**swept**	**swept**	fegen, kehren
(to) **swim**	**swam**	**swum**	schwimmen
(to) **swing**	**swung**	**swung**	schwingen
(to) **take**	**took**	**taken**	(mit)nehmen; bringen
(to) **teach** [iː]	**taught** [ɔː]	**taught** [ɔː]	lehren, unterrichten
(to) **tell**	**told**	**told**	sagen; erzählen, berichten
(to) **think**	**thought**	**thought**	denken, glauben, meinen
(to) **throw**	**threw**	**thrown**	werfen
(to) **understand**	**understood**	**understood**	verstehen
(to) **wake up**	**woke up**	**woken up**	aufwachen; (auf)wecken
(to) **wear** [eə]	**wore** [ɔː]	**worn** [ɔː]	tragen *(Kleidung)*
(to) **win**	**won** [ʌ]	**won** [ʌ]	gewinnen
(to) **write** [aɪ]	**wrote**	**written** [ɪ]	schreiben

°Mit diesem Kringel sind Wörter markiert, die nicht zum Lernwortschatz gehören.

First names (Vornamen)

Aamir [ə'mɪə]
Aisling ['æʃlɪŋ]
Albert ['ælbət]
Alexander [ælɪg'zɑːndə]
Alice ['ælɪs]
Alison ['ælɪsən]
Amar [ə'mɑː]
Andrew ['ændruː]
Anna ['ænə]
Archie ['ɑːtʃi]
Artem ['ɑːtəm]
Ashok [ʌ'ʃəʊk]
Ava ['ɑːvə]
Banda ['bændə]
Bashir [bə'ʃɪə]
Bella ['belə]
Bobby ['bɒbi]
Brady ['breɪdi]
Bruce [bruːs]
Bryan ['braɪən]
Carissa [kə'rɪsə]
Cooper ['kuːpə]
Corrie ['kɒri]
Dan [dæn]
Daniel ['dænjəl]
Dashiell ['dæʃiəl]
David ['deɪvɪd]
Davo ['deɪvəʊ]
Del [del]
Edwin ['edwɪn]
Eleanor ['elənə]
Elizabeth [i'lɪzəbəθ]
Emir [e'mɪə]
Evie ['iːvi]
Gavin ['gævɪn]
Geeta ['giːtʌ]
Geoffrey ['dʒefri]
Gilbert ['gɪlbət]
Godsten ['gɒdstən]
Gracy ['greɪsi]
Griffin ['grɪfɪn]
Guddu [gə'du]
Haarun ['hɑːruːn]
Hanita [hə'niːtə]
Hannah ['hænə]
Harry ['hæri]
Harvey ['hɑːvi]
Isaac ['aɪzək]
Isla ['aɪlə]
Jack [dʒæk]
Jahan [dʒə'hɑːn]
James [dʒeɪmz]
Jan [dʒæn]
Jawaharlal [dʒəvɑːhʌ'lʌl]
Jenny ['dʒeni]
Joel ['dʒəʊəl]
Jon [dʒɒn]
Kalino [kə'liːnəʊ]
Kallu [kə'lu]
Kate [keɪt]
Kevin ['kevɪn]
Kiruba ['kɪrʊbə]
Liz [lɪz]
Lou [luː]
Luke [luːk]
Marcos ['mɑːkɒs]
Margie [mɑːdʒi]
Marina [mə'riːnə]
Mike [maɪk]
Milo ['maɪləʊ]
Mumtaz [mʊm'tas]
Nadeem [nə'diːm]
Ned [ned]
Nic [nɪk]
Owen ['əʊɪn]
Parvati ['pɑːvəti]
Poppy ['pɒpi]
Robinson ['rɒbɪnsən]
Sam [sæm]
Sandhya ['sʌndjə]
Sanjay ['sændʒeɪ], ['sʌndʒeɪ]
Sara ['seərə]
Saroo [sə'ru]
Scott [skɒt]
Serenity [sə'renəti]
Sheena ['ʃiːnə]
Shekila ['ʃekɪlə]
Stevie ['stiːvi]
Teresa [tə'riːzə], [tə'reɪzə]
Tex [teks]
Tommy ['tɒmi]
Valerie ['væləri]
Violet ['vaɪələt]
Wesley ['wesli]
William ['wɪljəm]
Zendaya [zen'deɪə]

Family names/Surnames (Familiennamen)

Ali ['æli]
Asimov ['æsɪmɒv]
Bhatt [pʌt]
Brierley ['braɪəli]
Bryant ['braɪənt]
Celsius ['selsiəs]
Chen [tʃen]
Chopra ['tʃɒprə]
Clark [klɑːk]
Crusoe ['kruːsəʊ]
Dawson ['dɔːsn]
Defoe [di'fəʊ]
Fermer ['fɜːmə]
Gandhi ['gɑːndi]
Gupta ['gʊptə]
Harrison ['hærɪsən]
Henderson ['hendəsən]
Jackson ['dʒæksən]
Johnson ['dʒɒnsən]
Jones [dʒəʊnz]
Kamkwamba [kʌm'kwʌmbʌ]
Kelly ['keli]
Khan [kɑːn]
Knight ['naɪt]
Kumar [kʊ'mɑː]
Lee [liː]
Linnow ['lɪnəʊ]
Lopez ['ləʊpez]
Marika [mə'riːkə]
Mealer ['miːlə]
Nehru ['neəru]
Porter ['pɔːtə]
Potter ['pɒtə]
Rudd [rʌd]
Selkirk ['selkɜːk]
Singh [sɪŋ]
Smith [smɪθ]
Spooner ['spuːnə]
Thompson ['tɒmpsən]
Walker ['wɔːkə]
Woodhead ['wʊlhed]

Place names (Ortsnamen)

Agra ['ɑːg rə]
Alice Springs [ælɪs 'sprɪŋz]
Arnhem Land ['ɑːnəm lænd]
Assam [æ'sæm]
Bengal [ben'gɔːl]
Bengaluru ['beŋgəlʊru]
Bomaderry ['bɒmæderi]
Bombay [bɒm'beɪ]
Bondi Beach [bɒndaɪ 'biːtʃ]
Brighton ['braɪtn]
Burhanpur ['bʊrʌnpʊə]
Chandni Chowk [tʃʌndni 'tʃaʊk]
Chinatown ['tʃaɪnətaʊn]
Cootamundra [kuːtə'mʌndrə]
Daintree Rainforest [deɪntri 'reɪnfɒrɪst]
Darjeeling [dɑː'dʒiːlɪŋ]
Darwin ['dɑːwɪn]
Edmonton ['edməntən]
Framlingham ['fræmlɪŋəm]
Ganesh Talai [gæneɪʃ tə'laɪ]
Ganges ['gænʒiːz]
Great Barrier Reef [greɪt bæriə 'riːf]
Gujarat [gʊdʒə'rɑːt]
Hawa Mahal [hʌwʌ mə'hɑːl]
Hollywood ['hɒliwʊd]
Hong Kong [hɒŋ 'kɒŋ]
Hyderabad ['haɪdərəbæd]
Jaipur [dʒaɪ'pʊə], ['dʒeɪpʊə]
Khandwa ['kʌndwʌ]
Kolkata [kɒl'kʌtə]
Melbourne ['melbən], ['melbɔːn]
Mumbai [mʊm'baɪ]
Munich *(München)* ['mjuːnɪk]
Nairobi [naɪ'rəʊbi]
New Delhi [njuː 'deli]
New South Wales [njuː saʊθ 'weɪlz]
Northern Territory [nɔːðən 'terətri]
Plymouth ['plɪməθ]
Queensland ['kwiːnzlənd]
Rapid Creek [ræpɪd 'kriːk]
San Francisco [sæn frən'sɪskəʊ]
Silicon Valley [sɪlɪkən 'væli]
Sydney ['sɪdni]
Taj Mahal [tɑːdʒ mə'hɑːl]
Tasmania [tæz'meɪnɪə]
Uluru [ʊ'lʊəru], [uːlə'ru]
Victoria [vɪk'tɔːrɪə]
Wharfedale ['wɔːfdeɪl]
Wimbe ['wɪmbeɪ]
Yirrkala [jɪə'kɑːlə]
Yorkshire ['jɔːkʃə]

Other names (Andere Namen)

Ao [aʊ]
Assamese [æsə'miːz]
Bengali [ben'gɔːli]
Bollywood ['bɒliwʊd]
Brahmins ['brɑːmɪnz]
Chichewa [tʃɪ'tʃeɪwə]
Commonwealth ['kɒmənwelθ]
Dalits ['dʌlɪts]
Dangal [dʌŋ'gɑːl]
Diwali [dɪ'wɑːli]
Doggie Walkies ['dɒgi wɔːkiːz]
Eid al-Fitr [iːd ɔːl 'fɪtrə]
Gujarathi [gʊdʒə'rɑːti]
Holi ['həʊli]
Kannada ['kɑːnədə]
Kashmiri [kæʃ'mɪəri]
Khasi ['kʌsi]
Konkani ['kɒŋkəni]
Kshatriyas ['kʃætrɪəz]
Lagaan [lə'gɑːn]
Malayalam [mæleɪ'ɑːləm]
Manipuri [mʌnɪ'pʊəri]

Marathi [mə'rɑːti]
Marmite ['mɑːmaɪt]
masala [mə'sɑːlə]
metro ['metrəʊ]
Microsoft ['maɪkrəʊsɒft]
Mizo ['miːzəʊ]
Nelson ['nelsn]
Nepali [nɪ'pɔːli]
Nissi ['niːʃi]
Odia [ə'dɪə]
Punjabi [pʌn'dʒɑːbi]
Qutb Minar [kʊtʊb mɪ'nɑː]
Ramadan ['ræmədæn]
Shudras ['ʃʊdrəs]
Supersavers [supə'seɪvəz]
Tamil ['tæml]
Telugu ['teləgu]
Torres Strait Islander [tɒrɪs streɪt 'aɪləndə]
Vaishyas ['vʌɪsjəz]
Vegemite ['vedʒəmaɪt]
woomera ['wʊmərə]
Yolngu ['juːlŋʊ]

English sounds

[iː] gr**ee**n, h**e**, s**ea**
[ɑː] **a**sk, cl**a**ss, c**ar**, p**ar**k
[ɔː] **or**, b**a**ll, d**oor**, f**our**, m**or**ning
[uː] r**u**ler, bl**ue**, t**oo**, tw**o**, y**ou**
[ɜː] **ear**ly, h**er**, g**ir**l, w**or**k, T-sh**ir**t
[ɪ] **i**n, b**i**g, **e**xpens**i**ve
[e] y**e**s, b**e**d, ag**ai**n, br**ea**kfast
[æ] **a**nimal, **a**pple, bl**a**ck, c**a**t
[ʌ] m**u**m, b**u**s, c**o**lour
[ɒ] s**o**ng, **o**n, d**o**g, wh**a**t
[ʊ] b**oo**k, g**oo**d, p**u**llover
[ə] **a**gain, t**o**day, **a** sist**er**
[i] happ**y**, Turk**ey**, coff**ee**
[u] m**u**seum, y**ou**, t**o**
[eɪ] n**a**me, **eigh**t, pl**ay**, gr**ea**t
[aɪ] **I**, t**i**me, r**igh**t, m**y**
[ɔɪ] b**oy**, t**oi**let, n**oi**se
[əʊ] **o**ld, n**o**, b**oa**t, yell**ow**
[aʊ] n**ow**, h**ou**se
[eə] wh**ere**, h**air**, sh**are**, th**eir**
[ʊə] t**our**
[ɪə] h**ere**, th**ea**tre, z**e**ro
[b] **b**ike, ta**b**le, cra**b**
[p] **p**en, **p**o**p**ular, sho**p**
[d] **d**ay, win**d**ow, goo**d**
[t] **t**en, bu**tt**er, a**t**
[g] **g**o, a**g**ain, ba**g**
[k] **k**itchen, **c**ar, ba**ck**
[m] **m**an, re**m**e**m**ber, **m**u**m**
[n] **n**o, o**n**e, te**n**
[ŋ] wro**ng**, u**n**cle, tha**n**ks
[l] **l**ike, o**l**d, sma**ll**
[r] **r**uler, f**r**iend, so**rr**y
[w] **w**e, **wh**ere, **o**ne
[j] **y**es, **y**ou, **u**niform
[f] **f**amily, a**f**ter
[v] **v**ery, se**v**en, ha**ve**
[s] **s**ix, po**s**ter, ye**s**
[z] qui**z**, hi**s**, mu**s**ic, plea**se**
[ʃ] **sh**e, sta**ti**on, Engli**sh**
[ʒ] u**s**ually, trea**s**ure, gara**ge**
[tʃ] **ch**ild, tea**ch**er, wa**tch**
[dʒ] **j**ob, **G**erman, pro**j**ect, oran**ge**
[θ] **th**ing, **th**ree, ba**th**room, mon**th**
[ð] **th**e, fa**th**er, wi**th**
[h] **h**ouse, **wh**o, be**h**ind
[x] lo**ch**

The English alphabet

a	[eɪ]	**h**	[eɪtʃ]	**o**	[əʊ]	**v**	[viː]
b	[biː]	**i**	[aɪ]	**p**	[piː]	**w**	['dʌbljuː]
c	[siː]	**j**	[dʒeɪ]	**q**	[kjuː]	**x**	[eks]
d	[diː]	**k**	[keɪ]	**r**	[ɑː]	**y**	[waɪ]
e	[iː]	**l**	[el]	**s**	[es]	**z**	[zed]
f	[ef]	**m**	[em]	**t**	[tiː]		
g	[dʒiː]	**n**	[en]	**u**	[juː]		

Answers to YOUR CHECK

Unit 1 | p. 22

1 Check your vocabulary

a 8 points

1 kangaroo
2 camel
3 jellyfish
4 Tasmanian devil
5 crocodile
6 octopus
7 dingo
8 parrot

b 6 points

1 afternoon
2 Thank you!
3 barbecue
4 language
5 mosquitos
6 parents

c 6 points

1 c
2 d
3 a
4 e
5 f
6 b

2 Check your language

a 6 points

1 were living
2 arrived
3 died
4 had brought / brought
5 are fighting
6 present

b (example) 5 points

When I was a child ...

1 I used to eat less than today.
2 I used to play basketball every day.
3 I used to like playing with my brother.
4 I used to get up early on Sundays.
5 I didn't use to like vegetables.

3 Check your speaking 10 points

Child: Help!
You: What's happened?
Child: I've been stung by a jellyfish. The sting hurts!
You: I'll wash it out with vinegar.
Child: Do I need to go to hospital?
You: I don't know. Let's ask the lifeguard.

Child: Can you help me? I've been bitten by a tick.
You: Yes, I can see it, it's sucking your blood.
Child: Can you take it out?
You: Yes, I can. I have some tweezers.
Child: Is it out now?
You: Yes, it is.

4 Check your writing (example) 12 points

Hi Lou, At school I've just learned about the stolen generations in Australia. I didn't know that so many children from indigenous families were taken away from their homes and land to be brought up in white families. That's so terrible because these children and their parents suffered so much. And imagine how long did it take for the government to apologize? It took until 2008! The apology doesn't seem to have changed much; the government should definitely be doing more to fight discrimination of indigenous Australians. What do you think? What can be done to help? I send greetings from Germany!

Ex. 1–2: Für jede richtige Antwort bekommst du **einen Punkt**.
Ex. 3–4: Für jeden sprachlich und inhaltlich korrekten Satz oder jede korrekte Frage bekommst du **zwei Punkte**.
Zähle die Punkte zusammen.

53–45 points	44–27 points	26–0 points
☺ Very good!	OK, but you can do better. Which exercise wasn't easy for you? Practise and try again.	☹ You should practise more. Ask your teacher for help.

Unit 2 | p. 38

1 Check your vocabulary

a 6 points

1 set up
2 check out
3 set off
4 got along
5 give up
6 Carry on

b 6 points

1 received
2 contact
3 require
4 available
5 punctual
6 approximately

c 5 points

1 g
2 d
3 f
4 b
5 c

2 Check your language 5 points

Over the years, scientists (1) have made lots of human robots. In 2002 scientists (2) began to develop robots which look exactly like humans. Today we (3) are used to seeing these robots, but we still find them interesting because they look like us. Robots (4) have taken over a lot of jobs. Maybe in the future robots (5) will replace us completely.

3 Check your speaking 6 points

c **Alison:** The Park Cafe, Alison speaking.
g **Alex:** This is Alex Schumann. I'm contacting you to arrange an interview.
a **Alison:** Yes, hello Alex. Are you available on Monday at five o'clock?
f **Alex:** Yes, that's fine.
e **Alison:** Good, please come to the cafe.
d **Alex:** Thank you for your time. I look forward to meeting you next week.
b **Alison:** Thank you, goodbye.

4 Check your writing (example) 16 points

Institute for Applications: Looking for a full-time app designer
Our company is looking for an app designer to join our great team. We started as a small business and have recently grown into a bigger company because of the increasing number of requests we get. We help people design the app which they have invented and it is our aim to realize other people's ideas and plans. We would like you to work full-time with us.
You must have built at least one app. You should love programming, have a positive attitude, and enjoy working in a team. We would prefer it if you have work experience or at least have finished an apprenticeship as well.
Please send a written application with your CV to us – we will get in touch soon.

Ex. 1–2: Für jede richtige Antwort bekommst du **einen Punkt**.
Ex. 3–4: Für jeden sprachlich und inhaltlich korrekten Satz oder jede korrekte Frage bekommst du **zwei Punkte**.
Zähle die Punkte zusammen.

44-35 points	34–23 points	22–0 points
☺ Very good!	😐 OK, but you can do better. Which exercise wasn't easy for you? Practise and try again.	☹ You should practise more. Ask your teacher for help.

Unit 3 | p. 56

1 Check your vocabulary

a 5 points

1 account
2 following
3 get fed
4 jealous
5 subscription

b 6 points

1 log off
2 pop up
3 Switch off / Shut down
4 speak out
5 scrolling down
6 hacked into

2 Check your language

a 8 points

1 She said (that) she really liked me.
2 She said I was very kind.
3 She told Poppy that I cared about other people.
4 She asked Poppy if I had a girlfriend.
5 She asked her what my phone number was.
6 She asked Poppy to find out if I liked her.
7 She told Poppy to call me tomorrow.
8 She told Poppy not to tell me that she wants to know.

3 Check your speaking (example) 12 points

I like an advert which promotes the high-quality display of a mobile phone. The advert shows people dressed in different colours running around. This highlights how good the colours look on the phone. The scene is underlined with an entertaining song so that you feel good. I like the ad because it seems convincing. I would like it even more if the promoted product would be shown in the beginning as well, so that you knew right away what the ad was for.

4 Check your writing (example) 14 points

Hi Nick

I'm writing from my new phone – I love it. The screen is bigger than the one on my old phone, so now I can see everything easily. Compared to the other phones I looked at, it wasn't too expensive. I decided that I didn't need the best of the best. But this one still has some special features: I can use my voice to unlock the screen and it has a high-quality camera. That's great because I enjoy taking pictures so much. I can really recommend my new phone, if you need to buy a new one soon. It's not always about the highest price ...

See you tomorrow!

Ex. 1–2: Für jede richtige Antwort bekommst du **einen Punkt**.
Ex. 3–4: Für jeden sprachlich und inhaltlich korrekten Satz oder jede korrekte Frage bekommst du **zwei Punkte**.
Zähle die Punkte zusammen.

45–34 points	33–23 points	22–0 points
🙂 Very good!	😐 OK, but you can do better. Which exercise wasn't easy for you? Practise and try again.	☹ You should practise more. Ask your teacher for help.

Unit 4 | p. 72

1 Check your vocabulary

a 8 points

1 rupees
2 Hindus / Hindi
3 Cows
4 cricket
5 caste
6 illiterate
7 unemployment
8 positive discrimination

b 9 points

employ, employer, employee, employment
gold, golden
marry, marriage
pollute, pollution
produce, producer, product / production
religion, religious
share, share

c 6 points

1 You can have your hair cut.
2 You can have your car washed.
3 You can have your teeth checked / cleaned.
4 You can have sushi prepared.
5 You can have your photo taken.
6 You can have your phone repaired.

2 Check your language 8 points

1 was written
2 be filmed
3 been given
4 be learned
5 been chosen
6 was told
7 be sung
8 has been described

3 Check your speaking (example) 12 points

1 I prefer action films to musicals. – I agree. They are much more exciting.
2 I think it is more fun to do sport than to go to a festival. – I don't agree. It's so much fun to listen to music with all your friends instead of being exhausted from running.
3 I think it is better to eat vegetables than to eat meat. – So do I. It's much healthier.
4 I like both Indian and German food. – So do I. But I prefer Indian food because I like spicy food.
5 I prefer train journeys to plane journeys. – Me too. They are better for the environment.
6 I don't like tea or coffee. – Neither do I. I prefer hot chocolate.

4 Check your writing (example) 14 points

Dear Clara,
India is amazing because there are so many things to see. Today, we went on a trip in a hot air balloon to see the sunrise and the city Jaipur from above. That was my favourite thing to do so far – it was so exciting! The people are very nice to us everywhere we go, and they help us find our way. Yesterday a family gave us very useful information about famous sights, such as the Hawa Mahal which is the Palace of the Winds. And they laugh when we think their food is too spicy, but I like the food anyway. It's delicious and much better than the Indian food we are used to in Germany. I am looking forward to seeing you soon!

Ex. 1–2: Für jede richtige Antwort bekommst du **einen Punkt**.
Ex. 3–4: Für jeden sprachlich und inhaltlich korrekten Satz oder jede korrekte Frage bekommst du **zwei Punkte**.
Zähle die Punkte zusammen.

57–49 points	48–29 points	28–0 points
☺ Very good!	😐 OK, but you can do better. Which exercise wasn't easy for you? Practise and try again.	☹ You should practise more. Ask your teacher for help.

Quellenverzeichnis
Titelbild: Shutterstock.com / totajla

Illustrationen
Carlos Borrell Eiköter: Umschlaginnenseiten / vorn und hinten; S. 50 Karte; S. 58 Bild A Karte; S. 68; S. 70 Karte; S. 180 unten; **Petra Eberhard** / designcollective: S. 71: Handabdruck; S. 138 oben; **Jutta Melsheimer BILDBAD:** S. 17 alle; S. 33; S. 36; S. 46; S. 47 oben; S. 48; S. 51; S. 52; S. 70 oben Monsoons Icons; S. 82; S. 87 2. v. oben; S. 89; S. 90; S. 117.

Bilder
S. 8 Uluru: interfoto e.k. / David Wall, Dingo: Shutterstock.com / Arun Sankaragal, Hai: Shutterstock.com / Willyam Bradberry, Koala: Shutterstock.com / covenant, Papagei: Shutterstock.com / Wannakorn Yutthaard, Taucher: Shutterstock.com / Inspired By Maps, Känguru: Shutterstock.com / John Carnemolla, Australien-Karte: Shutterstock / Elisa Lara, Tasmanischer Teufel: Shutterstock.com / Jason Benz Bennee, Krokodil: Shutterstock.com / dangdumrong, Sydney: Shutterstock.com / Felix Bogren, Kamel: Shutterstock.com / Chris Ison, Bondi Beach: Shutterstock.com / Ray Hsiao; **S. 9** Be sunsmart! icons + Outback survival guide: The Royal Flying Doctor Service Australia, Beach safety icons „Pay attention to safety signs": stock.adobe.com / Bernd Leitner, unten „Get help here": Shutterstock.com / Atlaspix; **S. 10** oben: Shutterstock.com / Stanislav Fosenbauer, Mitte: mauritius images / alamy stock photo / doug steley, unten: mauritius images / alamy stock photo / Bill Bachman; **S. 11** Australien-Karte: Shutterstock.com / Filip Bjorkman, Mann / Frau-Icons: Shutterstock.com / AlexHliv; **S. 12** oben: mauritius images / alamy stock photo / Penny Tweedie, unten: mauritius images / alamy stock photo / Bill Bachman; **S. 13** oben: mauritius images/alamy stock photo / Penny Tweedie, unten: Shutterstock.com / ChameleonsEye; **S. 14** oben li.: Shutterstock.com / Ken Griffiths, oben re.: Shutterstock.com / SARAWUT KUNDEJ, unten li.: Shutterstock.com / almondd, unten re.: Shutterstock.com / Peter Waters; **S. 15** oben: Shutterstock.com / aslysun, unten: Shutterstock.com / Halfpoint; **S. 17** Coverfoto: mauritius images / Ryan Jorgensen; **S. 19** alle: Bruce Lee Played Badminton Too / Corrie Chen / interfilm Management Berlin GmbH; **S. 20**: dpa Picture-Alliance / Westend61; **S. 21** oben: stock.adobe.com / Danilo, unten: Shutterstock.com / Nicholas Rjabow; **S. 22:** mauritius images / alamy stock photo / Denis Moskvinov; **S. 23** oben: Shutterstock.com / simez78, Mitte: Shutterstock.com / pavalena, unten Hose u. Sonnenbrille: Shutterstock.com / iri.art, Rucksack: stock.adobe.com / macrovector, gefaltete Landkarte: Shutterstock.com / iri.art; **S. 24** alle: Rockfinch; **S. 26**: Shutterstock.com / michaeljung; **S. 27:** mauritius images / Minden Pictures; **S. 28** alle: Shutterstock.com / Barmaleeva; **S. 29** oben: Shutterstock.com / Kenneth Man, unten: stock.adobe.com / Africa Studio; **S. 32:** Shutterstock.com / Prostock-studio; **S. 34**: Shutterstock.com / Rawpixel.com; **S. 35:** Shutterstock.com / Phonlamai Photo; **S. 37**: Shutterstock.com / wavebreakmedia; **S. 38**: Shutterstock.com / Lia Koltyrina; **S. 39** oben: Shutterstock.com / Alexander Raths, unten: Shutterstock.com / Trueffelpix; **S. 40** oben: mauritius images / Mito Images; **S. 40** unten Feder: Shutterstock.com / tatishdesign; **S. 41:** Shutterstock.com / Illonajalll; **S. 42** Bildschirme (M): Shutterstock.com / kentoh, Bild 1–6 (M): iRony / Radheya Jegatheva / interfilm Berlin Management GmbH; **S. 43** Bild 7: Panther Media GmbH / Vichaya Kiatying-Angsulee, Bild 8: mauritius images / Pixtal, Bild 9: Shutterstock.com / Ollyy; **S. 44** Mädchen: imago images / Panthermedia; **S. 45:** Shutterstock.com / Rawpixel.com; **S. 47** unten: Shutterstock.com / Prostock-studio; **S. 49** oben: Shutterstock.com / Cineberg, unten: Shutterstock.com / Oleksiy Mark; **S. 50** unten Windmühle: Imago Stock & People GmbH / ZUMA Press; **S. 53** oben: Shutterstock.com / Andrey_Popov, Icson u. unten Mobiltelefon: Shutterstock.com / Andrey_Popov; **S. 54** oben: interfoto e.k. / Robert Harding / Amanda Hall, Bild A: imago images / Panthermedia, Bild B: stock.adobe.com / tanja_riedel; **S. 55:** Rockfinch; **S. 56** oben: Shutterstock.com / Darko Zeljkovic, unten: Shutterstock.com / G-Stock Studio; **S. 57:** Shutterstock.com / Rawpixel.com; **S. 58** Bild A Flagge: Shutterstock.com / T. Lesia, Bild A Geldscheine: Shutterstock.com / saisnaps, Bild B: dpa Picture-Alliance / OKAPIA / Peter Hertrampf / OKAPIA KG, Ge, Bild C: Shutterstock.com / ImagesofIndia, Bild D: mauritius images / alamy stock photo / Tim Gainey; Bild E: Shutterstock.com / Rawpixel.com, Bild F: mauritius images / United Archives / TopFoto; **S. 59** Bild G: Bridgeman Images / Mohandas Karamchand, Bild H: Shutterstock.com / Ashira Kuo, Bild I: Shutterstock.com / MOY YADEEN.S; **S. 60** A The street cleaner: mauritius images / alamy stock photo / Jake Norton, B: The scientist: Shutterstock.com / AshTproductions; **S. 61** C The technology GEO: Panther Media GmbH / Chris DeSilver, D The trader: Shutterstock.com / Dmitry Kalinovsky; **S. 62** oben: Shutterstock.com / OLESHKO GANNA, unten: dpa Picture-Alliance / ASSOCIATED PRESS; **S. 63:** Imago Stock & People GmbH / ZUMA Press / imago images; **S. 64:** mauritius images / Novarc Images; **S. 65:** Shutterstock.com / Photo Spirit; **S. 66** dpa Picture-Alliance / AP Phoe / AP Photo; **S. 67** li.: stock.adobe.com / IndiaPix, re.: mauritius images / alamy stock photo / MARK HICKEN; **S. 69** alle: Amar / PILGRIM FILMS PRODUCTION / interfilm Berlin Management GmbH; **S. 70** Palast: Shutterstock.com / RuthChoi, Girlanden: stock.adobe.com / MelissaMN, Heißluftballon: stock.adobe.com / Felix von Nida; **S. 71** Teeblätter: mauritius images / alamy stock photo / Ross McArthur; **S. 72** oben: Panther Media GmbH / Joerg Hackemann, unten: Shutterstock.com / Rawpixel.com; **S. 73** oben: StockFood / Asya Nurullina, unten: Panther Media GmbH / Sergio Monti; **S. 74** Bild 1: mauritius images / Maskot, Bild 2: Panther Media GmbH / TONO BALAGUER; **S. 75** oben li.: stock.adobe.com / fizkes, oben re.: mauritius images / alamy stock photo / Ivan Chiosea, unten li. Gemüse: Shutterstock.com / Sundra, Kelle: Shutterstock.com / Daria Ustiugova, unten re.: Shutterstock.com / SAM THOMAS A; **S. 76** oben: Bruce Lee Played Badminton Too / Corrie Chen / interfilm Management Berlin GmbH, unten The Donkey Charity Icon: Shutterstock.com / america365; **S. 77:** Shutterstock.com / VoodooDot; **S. 78:** Shutterstock.com / solarseven; **S. 79:** Shutterstock.com / Branislav Nenin; **S. 80:** interfoto e.k. / Danita Delimont / Chuck Haney; **S. 82:** Shutterstock.com/karelnoppe; **S. 86:** Shutterstock.com/SeventyFour; **S. 87** oben: Shutterstock.com / ChameleonsEye; **S. 87** Brot mit Vegemite: Shutterstock.com / PageSeven, unten: Bridgeman Images / Granger; **S. 88** oben: Shutterstock.com / Studio Romantic, unten: Imago Stock & People GmbH / Future Image; **S. 89** oben: imago / Panthermedia; **S. 90** oben: Imago Sportfotodienst GmbH / Xinhua unten: Amar / PILGRIM FILMS PRODUCTION / interfilm Berlin Management GmbH; **S. 91** Marathonläufer: Shutterstock.com / wavebreakmedia, Reiter: Shutterstock.com / Abramova Kseniya, Highlining: Shutterstock.com / Edu Silva 2ev, Motorsport: Shutterstock.com / Digital Storm, Weitsprung: Shutterstock.com / sportpoint, Schwimmbad: Shutterstock.com / sirtravelalot, Sportplätze: Shutterstock.com / animicsgo, Laufbahn: Shutterstock.com / Yuliyan Velchev, Tennisball u. Tennisschläger u. Federball u. Hockeyschläger: Shutterstock.com / Denis Pepin, Motorrad: Shutterstock.com / karlovserg, Baseballspiel: Shutterstock.com / wavebreakmedia, Pokal: Shutterstock.com / bioraven, Boxer u. Schiedsrichter: Shutterstock.com / Vladimir Sviracevic; **S. 92** 1. v. oben: mauritius images / Hero Images, 2. v. oben: Shutterstock.com / wavebreakmedia, 3. v. oben: Shutterstock.com / granata68, 4. v. oben: Shutterstock.com / Roman Kosolapov, 5. v. oben: Shutterstock.com / Daisy Daisy, 6. v. oben: Shutterstock.com / Monkey Business Images; **S. 93** media verbs: Shutterstock.com / Monthira, digital activities: Shutterstock.com / Pixel-Shot, social media: Shutterstock.com / Rawpixel.com, online issues: Shutterstock.com / MichaelJayBerlin, microphone: Shutterstock.com / Daiiji, Cover-

bild: Shutterstock.com / AlexLMX, battery: Shutterstock.com / shaineast, charger: Shutterstock.com / vitec, headphones: Shutterstock.com / Jes2u.photo, volume button: Shutterstock.com / yulia_lavrova, power cable: Shutterstock.com / Olga Popova, speaker: Shutterstock.com / arslaan, Mitte Geräte: Shutterstock.com / olegtoka, Tablet-Rahmen (M): Shutterstock.com / Andrey Mertsalov; **S. 94** oben: Shutterstock.com / Doremi, Mitte: imago images / Panthermedia, unten: Shutterstock.com / leolintang; **S. 95:** 1. v. oben: Shutterstock.com / Iryna Kalamurza, 2. v. oben: Shutterstock.com / sirtravelalot, 3. v. oben: Shutterstock.com / Elnur, 4. v. oben: Shutterstock.com / Dmitry Kalinovsky, 5. v. oben: stock.adobe.com / Africa Studio; **S. 96:** Shutterstock.com / Angela Jones; **S. 97** oben: Bridgeman Images / litho by Woodville, Richard Caton (1825–55), Mitte: Bridgeman Images / Peter Newark Pictures, unten: Bridgeman Images / Ned Kelly by English School (20th century); Private Collection © Look and Learn; **S. 98** oben: Shutterstock.com / carballo, unten: Shutterstock.com / mentatdgt; **S. 99:** Shutterstock.com / Rainer Lesniewski; **S. 100:** mauritius images / alamy stock photo / Jack Grieve; **S. 101** oben: Shutterstock.com, Mitte: Shutterstock.com / totajla, unten: dpa Picture-Alliance / REUTERS; **S. 102** oben: Shutterstock.com / WAYHOME studio, Mitte: Shutterstock.com / LightField Studios, unten: Shutterstock.com / leungchopan; **S. 103:** dpa Picture-Alliance / PA Wire / empics; **S. 104:** Bridgeman Images / Granger / George Cruikshank's etching for Charles Dickens', Oliver Twist, 1837–1838; **S. 105:** Bridgeman Images / Granger / Etching by George Cruikshank to the first edition, 1837–38; **S. 107:** ClipDealer GmbH / Monkey Business Images; **S. 108** Spiegel u. Bürste: stock.adobe.com / partyvector, Ball: Shutterstock.com / Barmaleeva, Bücher u. Notizblock u. Stifte: Shutterstock.com / sanumko, Spaten u. Schlafsack u. Lampe u. Seil u. Erste-Hilfe-Kasten u. Kessel u. Flasche u. Fernglas u. Beil u. Streichhölzer u. Hut u. Messer: Shutterstock.com / aliaksei kruhlenia, Robinson Crusoe Coverbild: Till Nachtmann; **S. 109:** Till Nachtmann; **S. 110** oben: Bridgeman Images / © Look and Learn English School, (19th century), Mitte li.: stock.adobe.com / marcorubino, Mitte re.: Bridgeman Images / Peter Phipp / Travelshots, unten: Imago Stock & People GmbH / Xinhua; **S. 111** oben: Shutterstock.com / imodraj, unten: Shutterstock.com / Slavenko; **S. 112:** Imago Stock & People GmbH / ZUMA Press; **S. 113:** dpa Picture-Alliance / AP Photo / Saurabh Das; **S. 126:** Shutterstock.com / LightField Studios; **S. 127:** © BBC; **S. 128:** stock.adobe.com / tonefotografia; **S. 132:** stock.adobe.com / Dan Race; **S. 133:** stock.adobe.com / franz12; **S. 134:** Shutterstock.com / Robert Kneschke; **S. 135:** Shutterstock.com / Monkey Business Images; **S. 139:** Shutterstock.com / fizkes; **S. 140:** Shutterstock.com / YanLev; **S. 141** oben li.: Shutterstock.com / hanss, oben re.: Shutterstock.com / SurfsUp, 2. v. oben li.: Shutterstock.com / MicroOne, 2. v. oben re.: Shutterstock.com / hanss, 3. v. oben li.: Shutterstock.com / Monika Hunackova, 3. v. oben re.: Shutterstock.com / hanss; **S. 142:** Shutterstock.com / Dean Drobot; **S. 143:** Shutterstock.com / wacpan; **S. 146** li.: Shutterstock.com / bajinda, re.: Shutterstock.com / ullrich; **S. 147** 1. v. oben: Shutterstock.com / Eric Isselee, 2. v. oben: Shutterstock.com / Anan Kaewkhammul, 3. v. oben: Shutterstock.com / kriangkrainetnangrong, 4. v. oben: Shutterstock.com / PhotocechCZ, 5. v. oben: Shutterstock.com / Sergiy Zavgorodny, 6. v. oben: Shutterstock.com / loreanto; **S. 148:** Shutterstock.com / Dmitriy NDM; **S. 149** oben: Shutterstock.com / everything possible, unten: Shutterstock.com / Moolkum; **S. 150** oben: Shutterstock.com / Stepan Bormotov, unten: Shutterstock.com / saraporn; **S. 151** 1. v. oben: Shutterstock.com / Ivaylo Ivanov, 2. v. oben: Shutterstock.com / nechaevkon, 3. v. oben: Shutterstock.com / Tarzhanova, 4. v. oben: Shutterstock.com / Yulia Davidovich; **S. 152:** Shutterstock.com / FooTToo; **S. 153:** Shutterstock.com / Steve Bower; **S. 155** oben: Shutterstock.com / nikiteev_konstantin, Mitte: Shutterstock.com / MAWart, unten: Shutterstock.com / Tetiana Yurchenko; **S. 156:** Shutterstock.com / Janossy Gergely; **S. 157:** Shutterstock.com / photomaster; **S. 158:** Shutterstock.com / Ascannio; **S. 159:** Shutterstock.com / Arthito; **S. 160** oben: Shutterstock.com / Yurchyks, unten: Shutterstock.com / schankz; **S. 161:** Shutterstock.com / Andrey_Popov; **S. 163:** Shutterstock.com / Svetlosila; **S. 165:** Shutterstock.com / Iurii Stepanov; **S. 166** oben li. u. re.: Shutterstock.com / Kilroy79, Mitte: Shutterstock.com / NosorogUA, unten: Shutterstock.com / Juice Flair; **S. 167** 1. v. oben: Shutterstock.com / symbiot, 2. v. oben: Shutterstock.com / vladm, 3. v. oben: Shutterstock.com / Karramba Production, 4. v. oben: Shutterstock.com / Magicleaf; **S. 168** oben: Shutterstock.com / Mauro Pezzotta, unten: Shutterstock.com / RTimages; **S. 169** oben: Shutterstock.com / creat OR76, unten: Shutterstock.com / ByEmo; **S. 170:** Shutterstock.com / Roman Samokhin; **S. 171:** Shutterstock.com / 06photo; **S. 172** oben: Shutterstock.com / Voyagerix, Mitte: Shutterstock.com / Vladimir Mulder, unten: Shutterstock.com / Inked Pixels; **S. 173** oben li.: Shutterstock.com / bajinda, oben re.: Shutterstock.com / ullrich, unten: Shutterstock.com / Sonyaudina; **S. 174** li.: Shutterstock.com / Viktoriia_P, re.: Shutterstock.com / Feng Yu; **S. 176:** Shutterstock.com / LORA MARCHENKO; **S. 177** oben: Shutterstock.com / CHAIWATPHOTOS, unten: Shutterstock.com / Jemastock; **S. 178** 1. v. oben: Shutterstock.com / OHishiapply, 2. v. oben: Shutterstock.com / MicroOne, 3. v. oben: Shutterstock.com / Butskykh Roman, 4. v. oben: Shutterstock.com / Artisticco, 5. v. oben: Shutterstock.com / Martial Red; **S. 179:** Shutterstock.com / Monkik; **S. 180** oben: Shutterstock.com / Valentina Proskurina).

Textquellen

◇ Texte mit diesem Zeichen wurden aus didaktischen Gründen gekürzt und/oder vereinfacht. Genaue Informationen stehen in diesem Quellenverzeichnis bei den betreffenden Texten.

S. 10 Nr. 3 Rudd, Kevin: *Apology to Australia's Indigenous peoples*, 13.02.2008. Commonwealth of Australia. Apology transcript: https://info.australia.gov.au/about-australia/our-country/our-people/apology-to-australias-indigenous-peoples (Zugriff 26.08.2020); **S. 11** Nr. 4: Stolen Generations Testimonies Foundation; **S. 11** (A): 2016: Australian Bureau of Statistics, 2016 Census of Aboriginal and Torres Strait Islander population, 2031: Australian Human Rights Commission, basierend auf: Australian National University, CAEPR Indigenous Population Project, 2011 Census Papers – Paper 14, Population Projections (2011), (B): Australian Bureau of Statistics, National Aboriginal and Torres Strait Islander Social Survey, 2014–15, (C): Australian Bureau of Statistics, Australian 2011 / 2016 Census of Population and Housing, (D): Australian Bureau of Statistics, Life Tables for Aboriginal and Torres Strait Islander Australians, 2015–2017; **S. 16–18:** David Fermer: *Coast to Coast*. Berlin, Cornelsen Verlag, 2016 ◇ Ausschnitt, gekürzt und leicht verändert; **S. 33–35:** Asimov, Isaac: *The Fun They Had*. In: The Best of Isaac Asimov. Ballantine Books, 1985, S. 174–177. Copyright © 1973 by Isaac Asimov, © Copyright 1973 by Sphere Asimov ◇ Ausschnitt, gekürzt und verändert; **S. 50–52:** Kamkwamba, William and Bryan Mealer. *The Boy Who Harnessed the Wind*. London: Puffin Books, 2016 ◇ Ausschnitt, gekürzt und verändert; **S. 66–67:** Brierley, Saroo. *Lion*. London: Penguin Random House UK, 2017, S. 25–30 ◇ Ausschnitt, gekürzt und verändert; **S. 100:** *Took the children away*: Mushroom Music Australia / Budde Music Publishing GmbH / Text: Archie Roach; **S. 103:** theguardian.com, 19.04.2019, Lyra McKee: Lyra McKee: *a letter to my 14-year-old self* (gekürzt) https://www.theguardian.com/commentisfree/2019/apr/19/lyra-mckee-letter-gay-journalism-northern-ireland (Zugriff 07.05.2020) Copyright Guardian News & Media Ltd 2020; **S. 104–105:** Charles Dickens: *Oliver Twist*; **S. 108–109:** Auszug aus: Daniel Defoe: *Robinson Crusoe*. Adapted by David Fermer. Cornelsen Verlag, 2019; **S. 111** Five famous quotes Nr. 1: Zitat aus: William Shakespeare: *Hamlet* (1603), Nr. 2:

Zitat aus: William Shakespeare: *Twelfth Night* (1601), Nr. 3: Zitat aus: William Shakespeare: *Romeo and Juliet* (1597), Nr. 4: Zitat aus: William Shakespeare: *As You Like It* (1623), Nr. 5: Zitat aus: William Shakespeare: *A Midsummer Night's Dream* (1596), Five good insults Nr. 1: Zitat aus: William Shakespeare: *Timon of Athens* (1623), Nr. 2: Zitat aus: William Shakespeare: *A Midsummer Night's Dream* (1596), Nr. 3: Zitat aus: William Shakespeare: *Much Ado About Nothing* (1600), Nr. 4: Zitat aus: William Shakespeare: *Troilus and Cressida* (1609), Nr. 5: Zitat aus: William Shakespeare: *Romeo and Juliet* (1597); S. 112–113: Brierley, Saroo. Lion. London: Penguin Random House UK, 2017, S. 172–175 ◈ Ausschnitt, gekürzt und verändert.